Luther: A Life

LUTHER

A Life

JOHN M. TODD

CROSSROAD · NEW YORK

To my three children

The Crossroad Publishing Company
575 Lexington Avenue, New York, NY 10022

Copyright © 1982 by John M. Todd

All rights reserved. No part of this book may be
reproduced, stored in a retrieval system, or transmitted,
in any form or by any means, electronic, mechanical,
photocopying, recording, or otherwise, without the
written permission of The Crossroad Publishing Company.

Printed in the United States of America

First published in Great Britain 1982
by Hamish Hamilton Ltd.

Library of Congress Cataloging in Publication Data

Todd, John Murray.
   Luther, a life.

   Bibliography: p. 379
   Includes index.
   1. Luther, Martin, 1483-1546.   2. Reformation—
Biography.   I. Title.
BR325.T59   284.1′092′4   [B]   82-5009
ISBN 0-8245-0479-8   AACR2

Contents

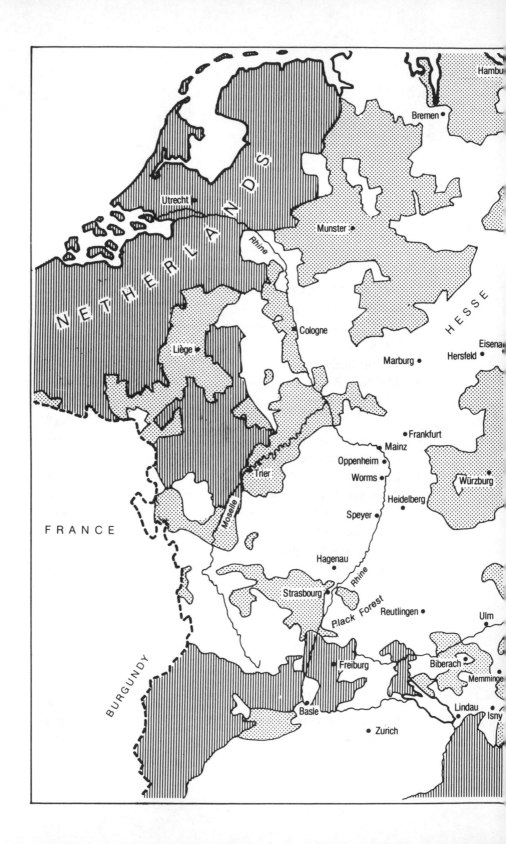

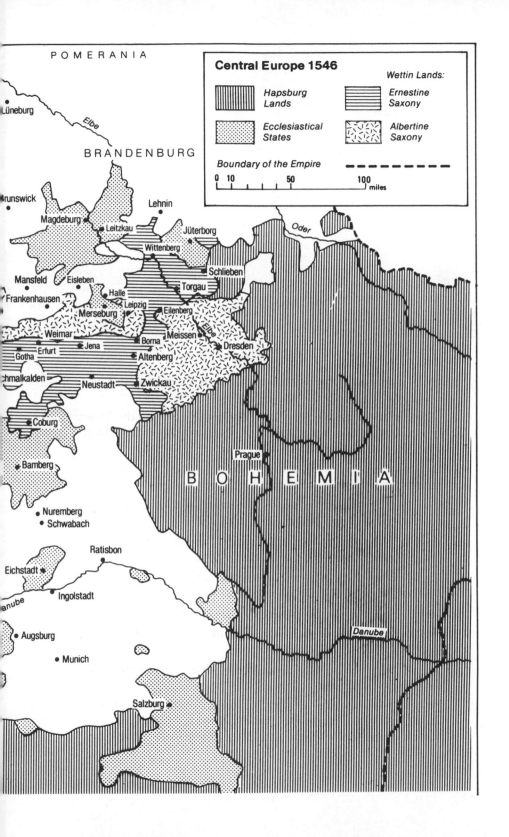

POMERANIA

Lüneburg

Elbe

BRANDENBURG

Brunswick

Lehnin

Magdeburg
Leitzkau

Jüterborg

Wittenberg

Oder

Mansfeld   Eisleben

Schlieben

Frankenhausen

Halle   Torgau

Weimar

Merseburg   Leipzig

Eilenberg

Jena   Meissen

Elbe

Erfurt   Borna   Dresden

Gotha

Altenberg

Schmalkalden   Neustadt   Zwickau

Coburg

Bamberg

Prague

Nuremberg
Schwabach

B O H E M I A

Ratisbon

Eichstadt

Danube   Ingolstadt

Augsburg

Munich

Danube

Salzburg

Central Europe 1546

Wettin Lands:

Hapsburg
Lands

Ernestine
Saxony

Ecclesiastical
States

Albertine
Saxony

Boundary of the Empire

0 10   50   100
                                miles

Illustrations

Acknowledgements

Thanks are due to many people for help in respect of a book which has taken five years to write. First to my publisher for being so patient. It is dangerous to make a contract with an author who is also a publisher; he tends to have a cavalier attitude when it comes to delivery dates. Over the years Hamish Hamilton's editors, first Raleigh Trevelyan and latterly Jane Everard, have been of great assistance in helping me to get the text into the right shape. Then with great pleasure, I must thank Professor George Yule of Aberdeen University who read my typescript and made many particular and a few general suggestions of great importance, and Professor Gordon Rupp who very kindly ran his critical eye over the proofs.

I give some account of sources in my Note at the end of the book. But I must mention here the great kindness of Fortress Press, Philadelphia, in allowing me to quote freely from many of the fifty-four volumes of their translation of *Luther's Works*. Their edition, together with all its numerous introductions and annotations, has been of inestimable value to me.

A special note of gratitude is due to my literary agent, Mark Hamilton of A. M. Heath and Co. Ltd, who has looked after me so well since the middle fifties, to the American publisher John McHale who first turned my mind to Luther, and to Boston College, America, who greatly daring allowed me to teach a Luther seminar for an invaluable semester in 1972. Finally, I must salute my family: my children who, so one daughter tells me, tolerated the writing of the book and provided some in-spiration, and my wife who has, in a manner of speaking, lived bravely with Luther for twenty years, after only a brief sojourn with John Wesley.

JOHN M. TODD

Introduction

Martin Luther was a professor at the Saxon University of Wittenberg. An Augustinian friar, Visitor of the group of friaries in the region, often preaching in the town church, at the age of thirty-two he was the successful local man. He had just published his first little book, a translation into German of the seven penitential psalms. Students flocked to his lectures, townsfolk flocked to his sermons. All were drawn by the flow of his quietly spoken but fiery words, full of intelligence and of feeling. The friars admired the persistence with which he kept the Rule. A solid career lay ahead, perhaps brilliant. But so far he had published no academic work, and seemed not specially to wish to do so. Wittenberg was a backwater, and no one had heard of him outside his circle.

Five years later, Luther was excommunicated and under the ban of the Empire, and people were reading his books and pamphlets all over Europe. Against all precedent he remained at his old posts with the support of colleagues, the populace and the local ruler. At the age of forty-one he married, settled with his wife in the old Friary which he had never left, and brought up his family there. He became an institution in Wittenberg, the most famous man and the originator of great changes in much of northern and central Europe.

Luther suffered from chronic and intense depression. During the years between his late twenties and early thirties he found a partial solution of the worst of it. Connected with the solution was a fresh grasp of the 'Myth' which underlay European culture and percolated all the operations of society. The realisation of this solution released a flow of writings and actions. Luther found himself pitted against the most powerful organisation in Europe, the Church. A member of it, like everyone else, he wanted to change it, to reform it. But the authorities would not have it. Normally they would have triumphed and Luther would have been burnt or permanently disgraced. But he voiced a message and a complaint which found an immediate and extraordinary response at every level of society, from that of the deepest spiritual experience to that of the most practical economic and political realities.

From the age of forty his story was that of a man of achievement. The prophet and priest had to turn politician and administrator. He had planned none of it, speaking only what he saw to be true. His is a story above all of success without really trying. It meant improvisation. From forty to sixty-two he did his best to continue to expound his message, to battle against the apparently irreformable old institution and to encourage new styles. And there was the battle against enemies within – the usual battles of a revolutionary against his supporters who want it done another way.

A major part of the phenomenon of Luther is the extraordinary corpus of writings, over one hundred volumes in the Weimar edition. In most big libraries, books by and about Luther occupy more shelf room than those concerned with any other human being except Jesus of Nazareth. He translated the Bible and set a style for the German language. He has something more than a minor place in the history of music. More than 2500 of his letters have survived. Together with the Table Talk they provide a lively picture of his life. But the heart of it all is religious and theological.

This religious content has boxed Luther off from a wide range of readers, not least because his friends and enemies in the subsequent centuries have made professional and technical capital out of his work. Religion, along with highlighted excerpts from the more ribald parts of the Table Talk, have tended to make a caricature of Luther, as though he might be some kind of a foul-mouthed Billy Graham. Certainly, it is not possible to avoid the technical content of his thought, any more than it is possible to understand the lives of Cromwell, Napoleon or Churchill without learning about military, naval and political matters; there has to be some theology. But in Luther it is lit with imagination, perception and humour. The power of the European Myth comes through. And Luther recognised his own penchant both for exaggeration and for somewhat earthly language, often caricaturing himself.

I use the general word 'myth' from time to time, rather than 'religion', to describe the basic assumptions which permeated the whole of society, because 'religion' can sometimes suggest something apart from the rest of life. But Christianity affected everything. The Myth was all. And 'myth' seemed a useful general term, because Christianity is indeed anchored firmly to a story. However, it is also clear at this point that the usefulness of 'myth' is limited. The essence of Christianity is that it claims to be a religion to end 'religions', a Myth to end all myths. It is based not just on one story among others, but on a story which its followers held to be a description of something that happened historically, not just true in a 'symbolical' sense. So it is a special Myth. Its uniqueness is sharply illustrated by the sign which it used, at first that of a cross, and then of a man dying crucified on the cross, sometimes transformed, reigning triumphant from it, sometimes shown dying an agonised death.

So when I use 'myth' I do so to indicate precisely the living and universal nature of religion, the sense in which 'Christianity', 'Gospel', 'Christ' or 'The New Testament' meant something unique, something different in kind from what they sometimes mean today, when these terms can conjure up a vision of the superannuated part of European culture. Already, in Luther's time Christianity was often decadent. But equally it was often vibrant. It was that vibrancy which gave power to Luther and his reforming colleagues. In any case it was all-embracing.

The 'story' was presented to everyone, including the people of Wittenberg, in the churches by the priests. Excerpts from 'the books', the Bible, were read out. Psalms, hymns and prayers were sung or read. The visual element was strong in a society in which many less than half the people could read or write. Wall paintings, painted windows, sculptures depicted particular stories and drew morals. The Church had the complete management of the Myth as the religious authority, run essentially by the Pope and the bishops. But life was univocal – all things were both secular and religious. There was a dual government of society by the State and the Church which were at the same time colleagues and competitors of one another in the exercise of power. They were assisted by the lawyers, the university men, the bankers, occasionally by organised representation from the rest of society, and by the military men. Behind it all was 'God' and his favour as preached and, more important, as dispensed by the Church.

The power which had come to the Church in this atmosphere of universal acceptance had led to massive economic involvement on the one hand and an 'adaptation' of the ideals of the Gospel on the other, an adaptation which also included residual superstition and paganism from pre-Christian times. The priests had begun to look and act rather like the very priests of the old Jewish Law or even of paganism which Jesus of Nazareth had, according to the story, come to displace for all time. And the story itself was severely misrepresented, so Luther, and then great numbers of his followers, concluded.

Biographies of 'great men' can be misleading in their selectivity. The history of any time must include a record of the lives of the millions of ordinary people. In the twentieth century, study of local archives, agricultural history, industrial archaeology, sociology and many other disciplines has sometimes given a quite different emphasis, even a totally new meaning to the small number of public events which used to occupy the history books, political events, wars, the lives of 'great' men and women. History is not the story of an élite. In some sense the 'great' men and women of history were only the 'enablers' of what would certainly have occurred in some form. And this certainly includes the Reformation. Yet the fact remains that they did set their own personal seal on events, and on institutions which then survived for centuries. As persons, and makers of events and institutions they remain perennially fascinating.

Not many people have read the story of Luther outside the ranks of theologians and historians. Yet he changed the face of Europe as radically as Napoleon. And while Cromwell put English history into a new gear, Luther ushered in a whole new way of life in Europe which had been struggling to birth for a century and more. Both Cromwell and Luther are difficult in that not only were they convinced of divine commission, but expressed that conviction. In Luther's case this has tended to make him seem some kind of fanatic. One cannot evade the truth lying at the heart of such a suspicion; and he is sometimes touched with what may be called the psychopathology of genius. Yet, in many ways he was an ordinary man. The portrait at forty-two shows a notably human face. The letters and Table Talk reveal a man with ordinary family problems, a normal concern with sex, expressed with that half innocent openness so typically German. He had, too, a typical German attitude to those in authority, realistic and conscientious.

I have tried to give a picture of this man of gigantic accomplishment, a man, however, who was rather less than the hero and rather more than the mere villain of some older biographies. I attempted a previous picture in *Martin Luther, a Biographical Study*, written primarily for specialists in history and theology. One paragraph and the Appendix on Indulgences are reproduced in this book. The present study is an attempt to present the man more fully. Theology is indeed the inner stuff of the revolution he worked. But I start from the man, and in particular from his letters.

CHAPTER ONE

Young Luther

Mansfeld, where Martin Luther was brought up, was a small country town, with a population of a little over 3000. Its walls were stout and ancient, with four corner towers. Outside and on a hill top was the great castle of the Counts of Anhalt. Altogether the place provided a sense of security, implying a certain doubt about security outside the walls of town or castle. The townsfolk at Mansfeld as elsewhere felt superior to the countryfolk who lived outside on the farms and came to Mansfeld to sell their produce and buy what they needed. In a sense everyone was 'rural' – almost everyone had a fair smattering of knowledge about crops and cattle and country matters. But, inside the walls, the burghers thought highly of themselves, all the more so since they themselves were subservient to the princes of Church and State. The town community, although lacking modern police, and subject finally to the will of the local ruler, was able to regulate its own economic and political affairs. Within it the Church operated as a separate privileged corporation. A sizeable slice of local affairs was in its affluent, authoritarian, often corrupt but also quite often sincere and able hands.

Mansfeld had at its centre the Church of St George, and near to it the town school, to which Martin went at the age of seven. He had been born not at Mansfeld, but at Eisleben, late at night, and was baptised the next day, 11 November, St Martin's Day, 1483. It was the following year that Margaret and Hans Luder (as they usually spelt it) moved with the baby to Mansfeld and settled there for good.

.The town was set in a variegated landscape of forest and field. Copper mining occupied as many people as the farms. The copper was sold to travelling merchants, Mansfeld being on the route from Nuremberg to Hamburg – Hamburg and the sea which hardly anyone in this inland area had ever seen. Martin's grandfather was a farmer, but the farm went to a younger son. His father had taken up mining, at first working for someone else, before he gradually built up his own business. Before Martin was eight, his father, along with a partner, had a lease of a foundry, having borrowed capital from a merchant – he was a shareholder in one of the small firms engaged in mining. He was a success. 'Big Hans', as he was called, was elected in 1491 to be one of the 'Four', representatives of the citizens, who sat on the town council – 'Big Hans', to distinguish him from his brother 'Little Hans', who was frequently in the courts for brawling and use of a knife when his temper was roused. Hans Luther's identity as a respected senior citizen is attested by the inclusion of his name in a list of citizens requesting the local bishop for a special Indulgence to be attached to the local church in 1497. By 1511 he was part owner of not less than six mines and two foundries.

In the last years of their lives, Martin's parents were painted by Cranach the Elder. The paintings show the rough, determined, resigned faces of hard-working small proprietors. Big Hans was tough, shrewd, earthy, sometimes drinking a little too much beer; but, said Martin, this brightened the family atmosphere. His father was 'by nature a jovial companion, always ready for fun and games!' His mother Margaret (*née* Lindemann) has a suffering look about her, and seems to have had the strong traditional piety of the age. Her sharp eyes are the same as the famous glinting eyes of her son, which Cranach often portrayed – he lived in Wittenberg and came to the painting of Luther's parents from a very close friendship with Martin of over ten years.

If there was a convivial atmosphere most of the time, it was within the context of hard physical facts. Birth and death were frequent events. Plague, bubonic and other, was a regular visitor. There was a new child in the family most years; perhaps half or more died. Nobody could remember how many there had been. Eight were living when Martin was twenty-two. He was the eldest. Discipline within the family as in society at large was equally rough and ready. There was a lot of beating which Luther continued to resent for the rest of his life. He remembered the severity of both his mother who beat him for stealing a nut, drawing blood, and of his father who laid into him so hard on one occasion that it took the father some time to get Luther (so he said) to stop holding a grudge against him. 'My parents kept me under very strict discipline, even to the point of making me timid.' But these strongly felt statements in the 'Table Talk' are immediately followed by: 'they meant it heartily well.' This quite lengthy passage is full both of tension and of understanding: 'It's a bad thing if children and pupils lose their spirit on account of their parents and teacher.' It is clear that Luther thought his parents, combined with his schoolmasters, managed to cow him. 'They weren't able to keep a right balance between indulgence and punishment. One must punish in such a way that the rod is accompanied by the apple.' This passage also contains a classic piece of hindsight: 'By such strict discipline they finally forced me into the monastery.' He is speaking, at the age of fifty-two, about an event in his early twenties. In fact, he entered the monastery in direct opposition to his father's wishes. What he sees, however, looking back, is a young man, so fearful of all the demands of life and religion that he thought the best thing to do was to retire from it to a monastery. The argument suited the general religious polemic of the later Luther. But there was insight here, as well as hindsight. Luther had a sense of inferiority, and believed its origins to lie in the sometimes over-strict home régime. It may also have postponed the flowering of Luther's energies and abilities, heightening them when they did burst forth with an almost pathological force.

Luther's relationship with his father in adult life was important, and involved great tension between the two of them. Big Hans was a forceful character and, although law abiding, a man with the same drive that got his brother into trouble with the peace-keeping authorities, and later his son into collision with some of the establishment structure of society. During Martin's childhood his father must have dominated at home, as he dominated also at work. Luther was frightened of him at times. Later he was grateful as he realised that his father's success had enabled him to go to school.

Luther recalled that his mother used to go out, like many others, to gather the firewood for the house from the surrounding forests. Later in life Luther, with his wife, engaged in a good deal of gardening and small farming, and drew on the early experience, of his parents, his grandfather, and of his uncle who had inherited the old family farm.

In spite of regular visitations by the plague, and the threats to health and safety from both disease and, in the countryside, occasional robbers, there was an emphatic though provisional economic and social stability. No foreign troops had threatened the town or district for many years, no recruiting sergeant threatened to take away the young men of the district; though occasionally disbanded mercenaries, or followers of the few remaining knights, were a danger. And it was only a few hundred years since a finally settled civilisation had arisen. Everyone carried weapons. It was a special proviso of university examination boards that such weapons were not to be carried into the examinations. Violence lay thin below the surface. University authorities sometimes stood in danger of assassination for failing to pass a candidate.

There was a long-established system of rights and proprietorship; it was a society which was a large step on from subsistence economy, through trade, banking and regular communications. This stability needed to be called provisional because of the bitter resentment of property and monopoly rights felt from time to time by apprentices, journeymen, the generally less privileged, and by the peasants throughout the countryside. The stability was anchored to religion and its highly structured expression of the Christian 'Myth'. Ritual observance and inner devotion gave a strong motivation to numerous norms at all points of behaviour. But partly blanketing this motivation was a universal resentment of the privileges, economic and legal, of the very numerous clergy.

Though solemn and serious in background, religion provided more occasions for jollification than the opposite. 'Holy days', which were holidays, were numerous, commonly the celebration of the life and achievement of a saint. The annual cycle of seasons, roughly attuned to the life of Jesus, with its main stages at Advent, Christmas, Lent, Easter, the Ascension and Whitsun, were again more joyful than sombre. A hint of the atmosphere survives in the continued celebration of carnival in Europe today, particularly the festive goings-on in the older German towns during the enormously long carnival season from St Martin's Day (11 November) till Shrove Tuesday in February.

The reverse side was sombre. There was a final reckoning to come, a 'last judgement'. The 'four last things', death, judgement, heaven or hell, were commonly depicted on the frescoed walls, or sculptured stone in the church. Even the crucifix came, so Luther says, to have for him a threatening appearance – the suffering Christ, arms at full stretch, seeming to hang over him, demanding more than he could ever give. Keyed in with this was something of hysteria and violence to be seen not only in movements like those of the flagellants who whipped themselves in public, and of the craze for relics of every kind, but in the art of the time too. In Dürer's famous pictures of *Melancholy* and of *The Knight, Death and the Devil*, and even more in Grünewald's pictures of the crucifixion there is a kind of desperation. In trying to reach a truly actual depiction of the horror of the subject, the painters imparted a sense of despair, or expectation of terror, which became a common psychological coin.

Along with this dark side of religion went the widespread 'superstition', belief in the work of evil spirits, witches and the like. Luther's father spoke of the injuries he had seen on a miner's body, made by an evil spirit. His mother believed one of her children to have been killed by a witch. Luther believed that a lake in Prussia was haunted by evil spirits, and certainly attributed many troublesome events, including his own ill health, to preternatural influence. Partly it was simple lack of knowledge of how thunder and lightning work and a hundred other mechanisms of the natural world; partly it was response to the mystery of life itself, the human potential for malice and for love, a mystery which still calls for answers beyond those easily formulated by the human sciences.

'Superstition' is hardly a satisfactory description of the sense of 'something else' and the half-instinctive 'pagan' activities which went with it. Sound hypotheses can be advanced for various experiences of telepathy, sense of terror, and of healing, and of other things which come under the umbrella of extrasensory perception. Religious activity and phenomena are not adequately identified as merely subjective or merely functions of other systems, biological, psychological and sociological. Understood in their own right, they comprehend everything, the whole of a person's experience. Instead of there being no room left for religion, it could be that today there is only a little room left for superstition. Many phenomena previously thought of as part of a world of superstition may be seen to have a genuine religious validity; or the phenomena themselves may be seen after all to be systematic parts of the mechanics of new models of the cosmos.

If such a position is to be acceptable some definition of the 'genuinely religious' is needed. Two components stand out: dependence and freedom. 1. Man is genuinely free, he can take decisions which are not predictable. Most notably he is a 'moral' being. In his relations with other people, he can act from the dictates of his own conscience; at its highest the relationship of love can be elevated to a degree of complete service and good will which seems to transcend the space-time continuum. 2. The sense of this extra dimension is that which leads to a recognition by man of his final dependence on something which must also, in some sense, be the organising principle of the whole cosmos. These two are the characteristics of the genuinely religious. Their presence, and their absence, enabled Luther's parents and Martin himself to feel a sense of rightness and of satisfaction in their religious life, and equally distress and revulsion at its exploitation and corruption.

Hans found that he had a very promising boy, one who could do honour to the family and to the town. Rather than apprentice him in his own business, or some other, he decided to send Martin to school. At primary schools the Trivium, the threefold discipline of grammar, logic and rhetoric was taught. Often, perhaps, the students got little further than grammar. But they also did some music, at any rate in the form of the songs which all schoolchildren sang frequently in the street. In the case of older children away from home this was a means to begging at least a part of their daily bread. All teaching was in Latin and began with the standard religious prayers, the Pater Noster ('Our Father'), the creed, and the Ten Commandments. There was a standard grammar text book, an old classic work by Aelius Donatus. Latin was the language of all educated people. German was forbidden in school to older boys, even in the playground, and most rigidly in the classroom. People who had been to school in the end found it easier to use Latin than

German for many professional purposes. Shorthand notes of meetings often used a combination of Latin and German, and the combination became very common in popular writing and songs.

Martin found his schoolmasters at Mansfeld to be no less strict than his parents, according to many comments: 'Ah, what a time we had on Fridays, with the *lupus* and on Thursdays with the parsings from Donatus.' The *lupus* (wolf) was the Latin name for the senior pupil who acted as prefect and reported any misdemeanours such as speaking German. Donatus's grammar seems to have given trouble even to Martin Luther, but probably he was remembering some of the less gifted pupils and their miseries when he said of these parsing sessions: 'These tests were nothing short of torture. Whatever the method that is used, it ought to pay attention to the difference in aptitudes and teach in such a way that all children are treated with equal love.'

In 1496 Martin, now twelve, was sent away to school, to the great commercial and cathedral town of Magdeburg, forty miles down the Elbe on the way to Hamburg, the famous trading port. The journey itself was undertaken by Martin in company with the son of one of his father's business associates at Mansfeld. This was Hans Reinecke, a little older than Martin; the two of them were to remain friendly for the rest of their lives.

Magdeburg, the first sizeable town he had seen, was a revelation to Martin. Instead of one main paved street, there was a medley of surfaced streets, churches, buildings of all kinds, and all the noise of a busy urban and commercial environment to be found in a town with a population of 12,000. He was on his own for the first time, and in a quite new dimension. He had the fun of going round with a group of other schoolchildren singing from house to house – the traditional way of earning something to help defray living costs. They were at the cathedral school. Some of the teachers were from the house of the Brethren of the Common Life, recently established in Magdeburg. This was an Order founded in the Netherlands in the previous century, intended to provide a way of dedicating one's life, with the traditional vows of poverty, chastity and obedience but without becoming a priest. The idea was to devote oneself to work for the good of society, often to teaching. The brothers preferred a quiet, contemplative kind of piety to the more demonstrative

kind of liturgy. From this they got the popular name of
Nüllbrüder, which is how Luther referred to them later in life.
They probably contributed their quota of serious and devoted,
one might reasonably say authentic, religion to Luther's make-
up.

There is only one other reference in Luther's writings to his
year at Magdeburg. This was to his seeing an old man, a Franciscan friar, carrying a bag of bread which he had begged. He
looked very ascetic and exhausted to the boy's eyes, 'the picture
of death, mere skin and bones'. Martin was overcome with
wonderment and a secret wish to emulate him, when he was told
that this wizened old man was not in fact so very old, and was no
less than one of the Dukes of Anhalt who had left his affluent
circle and devoted himself to the strict life of a friar.

The impact of such a sight on Martin was part of his
awakening to the greatest single driving force in church and
society. The 'religious orders' were single sex communities of
monks or friars, and of nuns. These 'religious' took the three
vows: to own nothing personally, to be obedient to the head of
their community, and to live a celibate life. 'Monk' was generally
used for members of the older orders using the Rule of St
Benedict (sixth century AD) who remained in the same monastery
for life and were broadly 'contemplatives'. Friar was used for the
modern orders of men who were committed to working in
society, and to 'passing on the fruits of contemplation', and
were frequently moved from one friary to another.

The early monks in Europe had practised a subsistence
economy. They had been so successful at it that they quickly
became rich and the abbeys were the greatest landowners after
the monarchs themselves. The strict rule enabled them to work
more effectively than any other group in society. The sheer
efficiency of people keeping a strict rule and living without
family ties was such that the religious orders had become not
only a spiritual ideal but a kingpin of society. Add to these con-
siderations the current theological theory that 'the religious life'
was a way of perfection and offered greater prospects for salvation than other ways of life, and it is not difficult to see how the
monks, the friars and the nuns became so ubiquitous. And given
the resultant wide ranging power, it is not difficult to see how

devastatingly corruption was able to seep into the communities at every level, and in every way.

For the following ten years the power of the ideal reverberated in Martin's mind. The habits were to be seen daily in the street, and inside them all conditions of men and women, but always some whose devotion and holiness impressed him.

Next year Martin was moved to another school; this was at Eisenach, as far away again from his home but in the opposite direction. The Luthers had relations there, including the man elected mayor the year of Martin's arrival. This was Heinrich Lindemann, brother of Luther's mother. At Eisenach Luther continued with the normal curriculum, and in a setting which appealed strongly to his artistic sense. In later times he often referred to his love of the 'good old town of Eisenach'. With a population of only 2000, set on the edge of the Thuringian forest, it was picturesque as it still is. Above it towered the hill on which was the great castle of the Wartburg. Already so old that it was no longer in regular use by the local Wettin princes, the castle was for military and special occasions, for hunting parties and security, and would sometimes be used to house an un-expected guest who wished not to be seen in the town. As such it was to play an important part in Luther's own life. In the thirteenth century it had been the residence of the Landgrave of Thuringia, and in the time of the Landgrave Hermann the Minnesingers and the epic poets, and notably Walter von Vogelweide, came to it. In the nineteenth century it became a central inspiring symbol for a number of Wagner's operas. Musical life was strong in all German towns and in their schools, specially so at Eisenach.

Martin imbibed the traditional culture and kept his place in a severe social hierarchy, shuttling between various respectable and well-set-up families, the Schalbes and the Cottas for whom he did baby sitting, and accompanied Heinrich Schalbe's son to school. The Schalbes supported a charitable foundation, the Collegium Schalbe, a small alms house community. The town was full of churches and the ringing of bells. Martin went to Vespers on Sunday evenings and acquired a great love of the *Magnificat*, and a lifelong devotion to Mary the Mother of Jesus, which was not lessened in later years by new ecclesiastical styles.

Again there was singing in the streets and the memory of an angry voice shouting as the boys ran away from a door thrown open, only to return when it was clear that the voice was offering them some sausage. Commerce, which had dominated the streets of Mansfeld and Magdeburg, was swamped at Eisenach by cloisters and schools. When in a polemical rather than a romantic mood, Luther later referred to it as a 'nest of priests'; they were one in ten of the population.

Martin's great-aunt Margarete and her husband Conrad Hutter befriended the boy. Hutter was sacristan of the church of St Nicholas. Ten years later Martin included him in an invitation to the first Mass he would celebrate as a priest, in a letter written to the rector of another church at Eisenach, the Rev. Johann Braun, a Franciscan friar with whom Luther kept up a friendship for many years. In a postscript to this same letter Luther tentatively suggested that the Schalbes would be very welcome, but feared he was being presumptuous even to suggest it on account of their superior social status.

A story retailed by Dr Matthäus Ratzeberger, Luther's medical doctor at Wittenberg in later years, about the headmaster of Luther's school at Eisenach, Johann Trebonius, tells of the customs to be found there. This master on entering the classroom would take off his scholar's beret and bow to his students; his assistant masters were instructed to act likewise. His reason was that 'God may intend many of them for burgomasters, chancellors, scholars or rulers'. This solid German self-respect went along with great care for discipline and convention and for the detail of the school work. The other side of it was an arrogance, and a carelessness about justice, which led to revolts among the poorest, and a certain self-indulgence. It was an affluent culture, rather decadent and unimaginative.

We get a useful echo of what Martin's schooldays were like from sermons and letters of twenty years later. When he was forty-six, Luther published a 'Sermon on Sending Children to School', encouraging parents to send their children to school.

God wishes to make beggars into Lords . . . Look about you at the courts of all the kings and princes, at the cities and the parishes . . . There you will find lawyers, doctors, counsellors, writers, preachers, who for the most part were poor and who have certainly all attended school, and who by means of the pen have risen to where they are lords. Do not look down on the fellows who come to your door saying 'Bread for the love of God', and singing for a morsel of bread . . . I too was such a collector of crumbs, begging from door to door, especially in my beloved city of Eisenach – though afterwards my dear father lovingly and faithfully kept me at the University of Erfurt, by his sweat and labour helping me to get where I am. Nevertheless, I was once a collector of crumbs, and I have got where I am through the writer's pen.

From this time comes Luther's love of German proverbs and of Aesop's fables, and his ability with language. The gruelling mandarin world of grammar and syntax, at the same time sophisticated and effete, involving the memorising of long catalogues of types of expression, turned out to be a tool he could use to enormous effect. He understood how these two disciplines are at the service of rhetoric, or 'communication'; the sole purpose of language was to get across what one wanted to say. Meanwhile, however, rhetoric had its rules which had to be learnt by the schoolboy, now looking beyond the school to university.

Schooldays came to an end. Martin had fulfilled the early promise and was clearly university material. In the previous one hundred and fifty years, tertiary education had grown apace in German-speaking lands. For Luther's father there were two universities to choose from within sixty miles of home. Leipzig was nearer but the less attractive of the two. Erfurt had a number of points in its favour, most notably that it was only thirty miles from Eisenach. Luther's schoolmasters had sent many other pupils on to Erfurt University, and there was a regular exchange of information between the school at Eisenach and Erfurt. One of the lecturers at Erfurt, Johann Trutvetter, a future chancellor of the University, was a native of Eisenach. In the heart of Saxony, Erfurt was, like Eisenach, both a beautiful and a prestigious place, with something of the same traditional atmosphere about it. But Erfurt was on a far bigger scale, ten times the size, set on another attractive site surrounded by vineyards, forest and farmland. Martin's move there was part of a natural progression through the best of the Saxon educational structure.

Erfurt University had a history of a hundred and fifty years, going well back behind the date of its first official registration in 1392. It was thus one of the older of the fifteen universities founded in central Europe in the fourteenth and fifteenth centuries. Together they witnessed to the prosperity and the intellectual vigour of the region, as great in its way as that of Renaissance Italy, and far greater than that of England where no university had been founded subsequent to the thirteenth-century foundations of Oxford and Cambridge, though Scotland could boast three universities founded in more recent times. The presence of the university had attracted houses of monks, friars, and nuns to the city, and by the time Martin arrived there were many, including communities of most of the best known orders – the Benedictines, Augustinians, Carthusians, Dominicans, Franciscans and Servites. Their various habits were to be seen daily in the streets, though in the case of the Carthusians only one or two lay brothers ever went outside the monastic walls. It was another veritable 'priests' nest'; indeed its local nickname was 'Little Rome'.

The population was over 20,000. Economically the town depended much on the marketing of woad, the famous dye grown in the surrounding district, used for dyeing textiles and marketed to merchants who travelled through Erfurt to pick it up. The town itself was an ecclesiastical town, part of the property of the archbishopric of Mainz. This complicated its financial operations and tended to keep business away. The surrounding country was under the jurisdiction of the competing secular authority, the Ernestine branch of the Saxon House of Wettin. Dues had to be paid as boundaries were crossed. Inside Erfurt, too many authorities were taking their tax cut, and too much cash ended up, as interest on loans, in the hands of the bankers. There was chronic unrest, often breaking out in the form of angry protests by those at the bottom of the economic ladder. The contrast between their condition and that of the wealthy burghers and the over-numerous and sometimes very well-fed priests who often had little to do, was provocative. Preachers had been known to remind people that if a man was starving it was not a sin for him to steal. Outside the town walls

lay a few pitiful shanty-type suburbs. Typhus was endemic and
the plague a regular visitor; it had an open invitation in these
slums.

The wealthy Augustinian house was busy building new halls
for library and refectory and also a lecture hall beside their great
Gothic church, already a landmark in the town on their
property which formed an island in the busy streets – the Order
was wealthy, as a result of numerous bequests in the past
century. There were many other fine buildings, including the
Cathedral of Mary the Virgin, and the magnificent Church of St
Severus right beside it. Both stood, and still stand, on an
eminence with a beautifully modulated flight of steps up to
them. Higher up again behind them was the episcopal palace
and the ancient Benedictine abbey, whose history took one back
hundreds of years into Erfurt's past; later, Napoleon would use
it for stables, and today the German Democratic Republic uses it
as a warehouse. Such architecture influenced the lives of those
who lived in Erfurt. They were conscious of privilege. The
buildings played their part in enhancing grand occasions such as
the visit in October 1502 of the papal legate, the Cardinal
Archbishop of Gurk, when there were great processions, with
banners and litanies and hymns throughout the town.

When Martin arrived, he was not seeing Erfurt for the first
time, since the city was directly on the route from Eisenach to
Mansfeld. He had been used to do the three- or four-day
journey on foot while at school. Erfurt was not so different from
Magdeburg in being an important and sizeable city. But it had
an air of ecclesiastical authority and of learning which impressed Luther. He was proud to belong to the University. He
took his place with ease in the traditional religious set-up,
within the structure of church occasions, Masses for the dead,
Masses for all sorts of guilds and fraternities, veneration of
relics, plans for pilgrimages.

Luther was never easily impressed by criticism of existing conventions or authority, though he must certainly have heard such
criticism. His father and uncles occasionally let drop an oath
about the behaviour of the clergy. Even at pious Eisenach, the
schoolboys were not ignorant of the wheeling and dealing for
ecclesiastical promotion. Many priests had no job save that of
offering Mass daily. Enquiring minds asked what was the use of

these pensioners and whether they might not have contributed a little more to the well-being of society. People in various parts of Europe had been asking this and similar questions for much more than a century. Numerous official synods and pro- grammes had been drawn up to curb the abuses of money- raising through Indulgences, and a wide variety of corrupt prac- tices. But this very fact provided an effective inoculation against any really revolutionary movement. Everyone criticised the abuses and the clergy all the time. The strongest critics were often themselves members of the clerical class. Every reform programme got bogged down in a chorus of assent to it, and in the lack of will power to surmount the enormous difficulties inherent in any attempt to tamper with the finances and the Canon Law which immediately became involved.

The picture was also confusing because there was a widespread seam of strict observance. At Erfurt the priory of the Augustinians was one of a group entitled 'observant' on account of fairly recent commitment to a stricter régime than had pre- viously been customary. The friars there followed a rule of con- siderable asceticism. The standard fasts, every Friday, and during other long periods of time including Lent, allowed for only one meal taken late in the day. Indulged in strictly, these fasts could and sometimes did undermine health. But at other times they ate and drank massively. The allowance of beer and wine on the numerous feast days saw them red faced as they left the table, Luther observed later.

At Erfurt certainly both sides of the coin were in full view, from the sometimes strict life of the observant Augustinians and the stricter life of the Carthusians, to the interference in daily affairs of the representatives of the Archbishop of Mainz. The Archbishop died in 1505, and in order to save the expenses involved in electing and then in providing for a new archbishop the seat was left vacant for eight years. It was then filled in an election of extraordinary irregularity. Twenty-three-year-old Prince Albrecht Hohenzollern of Brandenburg, who was already Archbishop of Magdeburg and administrator of the diocese of Halberstadt, was elected in addition to his existing benefices. He had been under age for Magdeburg according to Canon Law, and he was still under age for Mainz. He had had to pay a great fine to Rome in order to get approval of the former;

a further great fine was payable again for approval of the latter: a fine of 21,000 ducats for the appointment, and one of 10,000 ducats for wrongly accumulating ecclesiastical offices. This money was lent to him by the banking house of Fugger. It was to be repaid from cash collected by means of the preaching of an Indulgence which would encourage the faithful to do the good work of subscribing to church funds. Half of the proceeds would go to the building of St Peter's Basilica in Rome (the present building) and half to the Fuggers, as the Archbishop's repayment. That was ten years ahead; but this was the normal atmosphere of ecclesiastical affairs which had aroused intense criticism and resentment for many years. It was not only that every baptism, every marriage, every possible occasion involved some contribution. Reformers inside the Church were continually defeated by the problems involved in trying to see how both to maintain the Church in existence and to rid it of the incubus of this obviously corrupting structure.

The student Martin Luther came humbly into this complex world of the great Saxon university town of Erfurt. The University register of May 1501 shows that *Martinus Ludher ex Mansfeldt* was entered as a student in the faculty of arts. He was numbered thirty-eight out of 300 or so newcomers. He had a long oath to take in Latin, swearing by God and the gospels to obey the rector and the statutes, to refrain from creating disturbances in the University and in the town, to look to the University courts not to the town courts if he was in trouble, and to leave the University if commanded to do so. Universities were indeed part of that threefold magisterium of social authorities which operated throughout Europe, church, state and university.

Luther is listed among those who were able to support themselves. Big Hans had made the advance payment of twenty groschen, and had put enough money in Martin's pocket to enable him to live as a student. Nearly all students were members of a particular college or Bursa, as it was called, and Martin was almost certainly in St George's. It was a stone building and had the nickname 'beer-bag' among the students. There was some kind of initiation ceremony of an unofficial student kind permitted by authority and defended by Luther many years later as a necessary bit of 'experience'. But discipline in general was strict. Each Bursa had its college chapel and a

lecture hall. The students slept in dormitories with a young
lecturer close by under the same roof. The day began and ended
with a service in chapel. During meals the Bible and other
suitable books were read aloud. Dress had to be dignified.
Special permission was required for exit after dark. There was
no street lighting in Erfurt, and the carrying of lanterns was essential at night if numerous small brooks were to be avoided.
The lantern count was used as a check to know who was absent.

When Luther was in a polemical mood in later years, he
would say that the city was 'a bawdy house and a beer house'. It
was normal for such a city to have a tolerated brothel, a
Frauenhaus, and Erfurt was no exception, although married men
were forbidden to visit it. Sometimes it was engagingly called the
Muhmenhaus, the Aunties' House. After a great fire in 1472 the
city council took responsibility for rebuilding it. Erotic and
religious interest went side by side. Society was both permissive
and conventional. Perhaps a cliché may be valid – the reaction
from self-indulgence found an outlet in pilgrimages and formal
religious gestures of all kinds, sometimes hysterical. As contemporary painting shows, from burgher to worker, from student to
professor, from priest to bishop the town atmosphere was
reassuring in its closeness and humanity. But in many European
towns there was tension near the surface, and this was certainly
so in Erfurt as in London: tension between the underdog and
the authorities and the wealthy generally, tension between the
whole populace and the clergy. Faced with such tension
throughout his life, Luther had a lively sense of the importance
of established authority as long as it was not blatantly tyrannical
or unjust. When he came to live in Erfurt he was in a mood to
reverence those who ran the University and the town, and to
range himself on their side in any dispute.

In later years Luther remembered the seamy side of things,
but he also remembered the impressive nature of the University
and the satisfactory nature of participating in it, regretting the
disappearance of much of the great tradition. He looked back
with some yearning to the day of graduation for those taking
their degrees of Master: 'What majesty and splendour there was
when one received his master's degree. They brought torches to
him and presented them. I think that no earthly joy could be
compared with it.'

The first degree, the BA, could be taken in a minimum of eighteen months and Martin took it in just that time. It was fairly grinding work. To start with, the course was a completion of study he had already been doing in language, the complicated structure of logic and grammar. Bracketed with them was rhetoric. There was also the beginning of natural philosophy, and some study of nature largely as categorised by Aristotle. Aristotle also supplied the essential basis for the logical studies; the first text book on logic had been written by Luther's own lecturer Trutvetter, who was also Rector of the University. There was much memory work. But the essential work was in the true academic tradition, in the sense that students were forbidden to take verbatim notes and had to digest the material and re-present it at regular disputations, first daily in the college, and then at weekly public debates in the University's faculty hall. Luther soon became adept in propounding a hundred or so arguments for a thesis.

Once a year on 24 August there was a grand 'free for all' in the University lasting the whole day, when any proposition from the liberal arts could be put forward. Facetiousness was tempting and was not always avoided, even though forbidden. Luther recalled one of the jokes which related to the conventional posture usually given to statues of St Dominic and St Francis respectively: 'Query: why is Dominic represented with threatening fingers, but Francis is always depicted with out-stretched hands? Answer: Dominic is saying "Oh, Francis, what naughty fellows you have in your order", and Francis is replying "What can I do about it?"'

Luther got through the exam, placed thirtieth out of a total of fifty-seven. Two-thirds of the students had already fallen away, as usual. Luther was a slow developer and was only to rise almost to the top in the finals. This first degree was taken by him in the autumn of 1502. It involved a promise under oath that he had studied the books set, and that he would lecture in the faculty of philosophy at the end of his course.

Study of the *quadrivium*, for the Master's degree, now began, and the student was set on a serious career. The *quadrivium* was something like a preliminary, but academically serious study of all that was known. The four headings were music, astronomy, arithmetic and geometry; and there were other studies which lay

outside those formally required. In this latter area Martin found
time to become closely acquainted with a selection of classical
authors, long sequences of whose work he had off by heart, due
to his remarkable gift of memory. Throughout his life he could
quote easily from Vergil, Plautus, Ovid and Livy; and he read at
this time also Juvenal, Horace and Terence.

Martin's artistic side developed, and he became an expert
musician. He was known among his comrades as an excellent
lute player, and one who enjoyed singing. He had a chance to
practise his music when lying up after an accident. When
journeying cross country a short sword was carried, and Martin
had one with him on his occasional walks home to Mansfeld. On
one of these occasions, near the end of the return journey, after
resting before the last mile or two, he cut himself severely with
his sword through some carelessness. He lost a great quantity of
blood both then and again during the following night when the
wound which a doctor had bound broke open again. Luther
remembered the occasion as one of some panic when he prayed
to Mary the Mother of Jesus for help, and then of a time of convalescence when he was able to indulge his love of music.

Martin enjoyed university life, but attracted little attention
apart from being recognised as a most promising student. To
judge by his capacity for typically German buffoonery on
occasion in later life and his ability to drink deeply, he must have
been in these respects a normal student. The University turned
out to be an almost perfect preparation for the life he was to
lead. Erfurt gave him the entrée into the cultural life of
Germany, and indeed of sixteenth-century Europe. He met
there many of the people who would become close friends or
remain acquaintances for the rest of his life, and many of whom
would play some part in the unfolding drama which was to be
set in motion by himself. A fellow student who was also destined
to join the same Order, was Johann Lang. Another who would
eventually become the chaplain, librarian and right-hand man
in religious matters of the Saxon Elector, Frederick, at
Wittenberg was Spalt. Another again was the poet Johann Jäger
from Hesse who liked to change his name to the Latinised
Crotus Rubeanus, to signify his allegiance to the humanist
movement.

Scholars who liked to call themselves humanists found in

Erfurt one of their perennial meeting places; it was not the principal centre of the humanist movement, but the leaders visited it regularly. The Italian Renaissance was becoming naturalised in northern Europe. Saxon humanists had been visiting Italy for some decades. These men had glimpsed the idea that beyond all the philosophical and theological systems lay the study of man and the study of the means he used to express himself. As humanists they tended to distance themselves intellectually from the somewhat claustrophobic curricula of the largely clericalised German lecture halls, just as they had already distanced themselves geographically by their Italian trips.

The movement had its roots in the new and serious attention to classical texts. The philologist Lorenzo Valla (d. 1457) was the inspirer of many who began to realise how important it was to assure themselves of the accuracy of the texts they were studying, and of the real meaning intended by their authors. They learnt Hebrew and Greek to study the original texts of the Bible. Great scholars were already at work in this way, Ximenes in Spain and Erasmus in northern Europe. One of the superficial but important symbols of this distancing was the renaming by scholars of themselves with Latinised versions of their names – Hausschein (Houselight) becomes Oecolampadius, and Schwarzerd (Blackheath) becomes Melancthon. For a few months about 1516, Luther began to call himself Eleutherius (Freeman) but soon reverted to his Saxon identity.

German humanism developed a nature of its own. In 1500 appeared a new student edition of Tacitus' *Germania* published by the humanist poet Celtis who accompanied it with a poem *Germania Generalis*. Enthusiasm began to be generated for the native culture, and renaissance patriotism burgeoned in verse and prose. In 1495, Celtis had done a Latin description of the origins and customs of the model town of Nuremberg. This Saxon humanism was taken up enthusiastically by Ulrich von Hutten, the knight poet and anti-clerical. The Latin of these men became the Latin of Cicero and Ovid and Plautus, rather than of St Bernard.

Conrad Mudt, calling himself Mutianus was one of the leading German humanists and visited Erfurt regularly from his base in Gotha. He had been in Italy for a whole decade and professed a detached and a patronising attitude to the Church's

rites, while drawing a fat salary as a Canon. In 1515, just when
Luther himself would be starting his really serious criticism of
the current syllabus, Mutianus was also voicing criticism, but
from the superior position of a literary man, rather than a
theologian. He was influenced by Erasmus, whose criticism of
the whole theological scene had been widely disseminated for
the previous seven years in *In Praise of Folly*, a *jeu d'ésprit*, written
for Thomas More, being in fact a play on his name in its original
Latin title *Encomium Moriae* – a piece begun as Erasmus was
journeying happily across Europe in 1509 to a reunion he was
greatly looking forward to after a stay in Italy, where neither the
food nor the hours at which it was eaten pleased him. Mutianus
wrote to a friend: 'Today the apes of theology occupy the whole
university, teaching their students the figures of Donatus, a most
unintelligible thing; the figures of Parvulus, pure nonsense;
mere exercises in complexities, the silliest stuff.' Such criticisms
were already abroad when Martin was a student.

These superior literary men formed a kind of snobbish club.
With their new classical names, and their insights into history
and literature, their attitudes stretched all the way from a lam-
pooning of the gullible piety of the masses to a more
philosophical agnosticism or a mysticism, which stood apart
from ecclesiastical authority.

The humanists were criticising virtually the entire range of
existing educational norms at the university, hardly bothering
to distinguish any more between the various schools whose pro-
tagonists, however, were in a substantial majority and still took
their own differences very seriously. The dominant group at
Erfurt, as at most other universities, was that of the narrow
logicians of the day, followers of the philosopher William of
Occam. This was known as the modernist movement, and its
philosophy was that of nominalism: philosophical argument
was no more than a descriptive tool, the words were just names,
and pointed no further. Philosophy was to stick to its world, and
theology would keep to its territory of revealed truth, grasped
not by the reason but by faith. Other groups were the Scotists
using the works of the philosopher Duns Scotus, championed by
the Franciscans; the Thomists using the texts of Thomas
Aquinas, championed by the Dominicans – Aquinas had
worked philosophy and religion into a great single *Summa*,

transposing Aristotle into the context of Christian theology under the influence of Augustine and Bernard, in which *fides quaerens intellectum*, faith seeking understanding, was integrated organically with philosophy; finally there was also a *via antiqua*, the ancient way, which was centred on Plato, but was also used to describe the Thomists.

The cross currents and interrelationships were numerous. At Erfurt the Occamists gave Martin a confidence in logical processes and the use of argument and dialectic which never left him, however much he thundered against it as a way to religious faith. He often said that, philosophically, he remained of the 'modernist' persuasion. The humanist movement in its turn gave him a confidence in human culture, a love of the classics and a connatural feeling for language, for beauty in the form of words, and for words in their natural setting of everyday language that eventually flowered in the German Bible, a whole language coming both to birth and to a first apotheosis – a miracle of the sixteenth century to set beside the achievement of Shakespeare in England at the end of the century.

Luther's own thought was to develop out beyond all these various influences. Yet he remained the product of a sixteenth-century university. All his life the influences could still be traced, and could be confusing in their complexity. Like other innovators he was deeply marked by the influences of his formative intellectual years, and made use, sometimes in very unexpected ways, of the theories which first excited him, even though he had essentially outgrown them. Luther would come to echo the modernists that philosophy was indeed in no sense the handmaid of theology, not because of the merely intellectual inappropriateness of this as he saw it, but because the whole world of man, all the world of philosophy was thrown entirely into the deepest of shadows under the sign of sin when a man had become bound by the Word of God. In spite of this Aristotle remained a permanent influence. Luther, the graduating student, soaked up his texts, so that, though he would fulminate later against the habit of using this 'pagan' for an understanding of religion, he would himself retain Aristotle's *Poetics* and the *Organon* in his proposed educational system of 1521 (*An Den Christlichen Adel*). The poetry of Vergil was becoming an important part of his life, as well as music and the love of ceremony.

At the final examination for the MA, twenty-one-year-old Luther came second out of the mere seventeen pupils who had survived. The graduation ceremony was in February 1505. He swore the oath not to receive the Master's degree at any other university. He was invested with his Master's brown beret and his ring. And he duly gave the usual address and provided a feast as all new Masters had to do. These were great and glorious moments for him, symbolised for the rest of his life by the torches, having about them an atmosphere of almost unearthly joy.

CHAPTER TWO

The New Brother

One characteristic has still to be added to the picture of the young graduate at Erfurt. Martin suffered from depression. The first time there is some hint of this is a reference to a mood in the period after his finals, a time of anti-climax when, having attained one's goal, there seems to be nothing so well defined left. It seemed to be so for Luther, and other things conspired to depress him. A close friend had died. And there was a month before his post-graduate course started. The course itself excited little enthusiasm in Luther's mind. The future indicated to him by his tutors and his father was study of the Law. Hans Luther looked to his son to become a successful man in the local community, a good lawyer, well married. Perhaps even service to the Elector, or the Emperor, might be envisaged.

Conventional society was closing in. But Martin's discontent was not just a matter of the perennial discomforture of the young man viewing society with a jaundiced eye, realising with dismay the actual limits of the options available to him. There was something deeper seated. Sensitive, fond of music, rather afraid of his father, and of all authorities, religiously inclined, very intelligent, unfulfilled emotionally, perhaps no more than half awakened sexually – some of the characteristics of the pedigree western intellectual seemed to be emerging. However, these characteristics went along with the vigour of the Saxon peasant stock, the blunt and realistic honesty of a man who faces the facts and acts on them. It was a strange and explosive mixture, this capacity for appraisal, judgement, action, together with great nervousness, an almost neurotic dimension to the capacity for effective action.

Just now a pall of uncertainty, and a sense of inadequacy and apathy inappropriate to, but not untypical of, gifted young men, hung over him. In Luther's case it was a built-in physical and psychological syndrome, already beginning to be entrenched in a series of experiences. Physically there were the symptoms which became so marked later on in his life, sweating, constipation and general nervousness. Constipation became so much trouble that later the letters often have a reference. At thirty-seven he would complain in a letter to a friend: '. . . Defecation is so hard that I am forced to press with all my strength, even to the point of sweating, and the longer I delay the worse it gets.' Psychologically, he could get very merry but also very sad. Later in life he would say of melancholy: 'Those who are troubled with melancholy ought to be very careful not to be alone . . .' and again 'Watch out for melancholy . . . it is so destructive to one's health.' It was certainly the voice of experience speaking. At that time, aged fifty, he had taken the measure of the affliction, and had even used the attacks to enhance his theology; it was almost his most familiar experience. But in his twenty-second year he was only just beginning to wonder what was hitting him when he was suddenly overwhelmed with this sadness and heartless misery. It was undoubtedly the dreaded modern plague, depression.

The medievals knew about it and had also identified and categorised it, in their own terminology, as deadly. Despair, the abandonment of hope, was the ultimate theological category for it. The depressive is precisely in the grip of despair. The medievals saw it as a sin, indeed the final sin. The argument was simple, hardly needing to be made explicit. Life came from God; to despair of a good outcome for that life was then a kind of blasphemy. On the surface the argument looks brutal to the twentieth-century clinician, because the depressive, it seems, cannot help himself. Nevertheless, as theory, the judgement is logical – the abandonment of hope, despair, is the final 'sin' whether or not the subject is really responsible for it. Dante reflected society's assessment conversely in his famous motto set over the gates of hell: 'Abandon all hope ye who enter here.'

The way to this despair was the emotion of sadness, *tristia*. Luther, in his later years, warned severely against indulging in this emotion. Even *accedie*, boredom, apathy, dry indifference, was known as a deadly danger on the way down the slope. Melancholia was a growing obsession in the fourteenth and fifteenth centuries, symbolised by its apothesosis in Burton's sixteenth-century English text, *The Anatomy of Melancholy*. The sophisticated Spanish court was a long way from Saxony, but the knight of the mournful countenance, Don Quixote, one can imagine in some kind of Thuringian* transposition. Throughout Europe the cathedrals offered opportunity for sculptors to provoke somewhat hollow laughter with their skin and bone effigies of 'death', set beside or over the memorial of a deceased prelate represented in all his earthly glory. Here the melancholy is laughed off the stage. But it was always ready to creep back with the musician's lute, and the verses of a poet, or with the sheer horror of the mortality rate. At the first arrival of the Black Death, forty per cent of the population died.

Martin's depressions were not so severe as to immobilise him, but they provided an important dimension for what followed. Graduation over, after a visit home, he settled in again, bought his law books, including the great *Corpus Juris*, the book of Canon Law, and registered for the course. It was May 1505. Martin had allowed things to take their course till now, and still did so. But at the back of his mind for years had been burgeoning an ideal – aim for the highest. There was only one highest in that world, in terms of ideas, and that was to become a monk or friar, to be a 'religious', someone utterly dedicated to God. It was a safe way, too. We do not know and probably it was largely unconscious, but it would have been like him to have smouldering in the back of his mind the attraction of this life. Probably it had been given no formal voice. Something was needed to fan the flame, and set it blazing. In this case a moment of terror did the trick. Lightning.

Martin was perhaps already in some state of disarray by late June. He had undertaken one of his walks home to Mansfeld. There was a five days' break at this time running from the Feast of SS Peter and Paul on 28 June to The Feast of the Visitation of the Blessed Virgin on 2 July. Martin was not much more than half a mile from the gates of Erfurt, in the afternoon of 2 July, returning to be ready for work the next day. He was at a little place called Stotternheim. Thunder clouds had built up, and suddenly the lightning flashed, a bolt striking right beside

* Thuringia is the geographical area of wooded hills and valleys roughly including Eisenach and Weimar down to Coburg.

Martin who was knocked to the ground, though unhurt. In terror he shouted out: 'Beloved St Anne! I will become a monk.' St Anne was the patron saint of miners; Martin had heard prayers to her throughout his childhood perhaps more than to any other saint. He turned instinctively to her when in real trouble. The unconscious had spoken, in the language of current religious coin. In later years he described himself at the moment when the lightning struck as 'walled around with the terror and horror of sudden death'; judgement loomed.

Back in Erfurt, Martin told his friends what had happened. Was he bound? Must he keep a vow, unpremeditated, spoken under such stress and with no witnesses? Most said no. A few said yes. His friend Crotus Rubeanus said, fourteen years later, that Luther's final affirmative decision was a surprise, even a disappointment to his friends. Luther himself spoke of it as a sudden decision. But the historian has to add that, psychologically, it could not have been entirely unexpected. The decision gave Martin his first major act of independence. It was a way out and a way forward, and one which would be approved by religious authority. It would also solve any emerging emotional and sexual troubles. Any such incipient involvement or expectation had to be firmly abandoned. Above all Martin was taking his own life in hand, swiftly.

Within a fortnight he was having his last party, and saying goodbye to his fellow students, before going the next morning to the great gates of the Augustinian Friary which he had walked past so often as a student. No time had been lost. The Prior and the Novice Master needed a few days to consider the young man's application to be admitted. Martin had himself to cancel his registration for the law course, sell his books, and settle his affairs. Of the books, Vergil and Plautus alone he took with him.

It was a classic picture, one of the best of the final small batch of graduates at one of the best universities deciding to opt for the most demanding sector of the local religious life. (The Carthusians indeed led a stricter life, but they were in fact hermits, never leaving the monastery, and in another category; vocations to their way of life were rare.) The Augustinians regarded the application from the successful young graduate as very satisfactory, part of the proper order of things. Martin himself was overawed at the thought of the tradition to which he was binding himself, in a friary lately reformed under its own volition. The Order of Augustinian Eremites, to give them their full name, had the best reputation in Erfurt; and there would be every likelihood of further university work to come.

Yet somewhere at the very heart of all this reputation and status lay a contradiction of the original drive of the religious order. No one fully understood the contradiction. Spreading like an unobserved dry rot it would lead to the widespread and spectacular collapse of much of this way of life in less than two decades' time. There were scandals of course; and even the very way the friars sometimes maintained themselves, by collecting cash gifts from the faithful when preaching, and encouraging them to gain an Indulgence (see Appendix) had for a long time been criticised. But there was something more fundamental.

The virtues of the 'religious' life – poverty, chastity and obedience – were the formal signs of the special life of prayer and dedication, but they had somehow ceased to be its *raison d'être*. Like so many others, the Augustinian cloister had in fact taken on a life of its own as a social and economic unit in a society devoted to the maintenance of the policy and economy of the Church with all its complicated and expensive structures. Status, social and economic, had come to play the overriding part; the virtues had come, in a way, to be a function, even a decoration, of this important social unit. Instead of being primarily the special calling of a few, the religious life had become the profession of many. Theology had become, to a great extent, a vast rationalisation of this state of affairs.

To walk out into the streets of Erfurt in the Augustinian habit was to command respect. But there were those with resentments in society at large, some poor and ill-paid, who regarded all those committed full time to the Church as part of a well-heeled world into which they were not admitted. Critics from their own class were numerous enough for the clergy officials to be alert and ready with measures against those who seemed to threaten the structure with their criticisms. In a society still largely univocal, there was a feeling of something threateningly revolutionary about stinging criticisms from their own class. Neither side often thought in exactly such terms. In good faith the one attacked the established theories because they did not seem to tie in with the Gospel of Jesus Christ the 'revelation' of the New Testament. In good faith the other defended them as part of the Church's guaranteed sacred interpretation of that revelation. But what made it all so tense was that these matters would quickly escalate into matters of life and death. The Church's decision that a man was a 'heretic' led to his being handed over to the 'secular arm' of society, the political authority; heresy equalled treason. Burning was the normal retribution. Lollards were being tried and burnt quite frequently in England. A group of Catholic priests, members of the Church's Dominican Order, had been declared to be heretics and burnt in Germany, within living memory. Only a few decades previously the famous preacher Savanorola, also a priest member of the Dominicans, had been burnt for heresy in the great piazza at Florence. All this added a hardness and an edge to theology and its practice; it became a political tool.

Inside the monastery and in the university the rules had become very strict, with detailed regulations about how far junior lecturers might go in doing anything more than expound a text as distinct from adding their own comments and glosses. Their lectures were regularly monitored by senior men. Canon Law ruled – with all the force of the received religion behind it, the certainty that through this law in a manner spoke the voice of God. Official theology had come to be a Freudian superego, the law-giver. Luther's father-obsession was strongly tickled, his attraction to the system was all the stronger.

A religious community sharpens the personal characteristics of its individual members. Shut up together for life this company of men or of women breeds definition. It has rules, and conventions. The community does not have that mixed biological and psychological drive which commonly holds a family together. If the religious community is to prosper, it has to keep the Rule; even the conventions as distinct from the Rule are important and cannot be continually overlooked without danger of disruption. Since the purpose of the community is to release its members from the problems inherent in possessions, in sexual and family life, and in the detailed and general ordering of one's own life, so to be able to serve God through the prayer and work of the community, then the sense of importance attached to every item of its life can become unbearable, or totally glorious. In practice, day by day, it is simply a hard grind, and often remains so throughout life. The rewards are considerable, streaming out along the psychological and spiritual to the social and practical. Substantial and speedy achievement is possible for such a community, and the sense of unity in spiritual purpose is thrilling. Failure is equally dispiriting, and the disunity and disagreement behind it disconcerting. Martin reacted to all this with his usual intensity. His ultra-sensitive antennae were dangerously fascinated by an atmosphere which seemed to offer both a total solution, complete security, and at the same time a sense of dynamic spiritual energy. The generic religious dimension was intensified: within a context of emphatic dependence were opportunities for initiatives springing from an inner spiritual freedom.

Martin was received as a 'postulant', and lived for a few weeks in the guest house, still to be seen just inside the great gates. During this period of preliminary vetting by the community, he wore his own clothes, but took full part in the church services in the fine Gothic church, and the daily life along with the other novices. Meanwhile, he had sent a message home about his great decision. His father was mad with rage when he heard what Martin had done. Later in life Luther recalled that his father had 'cut me off from all further paternal grace'. Big Hans saw all his plans destroyed at a single blow. All that investment, the expense and careful planning of sixteen years of primary, secondary and tertiary schooling, was about to be handed over to the priests. But the rage was then, shortly after, cancelled out. The plague was sweeping across Thuringia. Several university lecturers and students died in Erfurt. At Mansfeld two of Martin's brothers died. Friends told Hans Luther that this was divine retribution: he relented sufficiently so as not absolutely to oppose Martin's formal entry into the Augustinian Order.

Within the walls Martin found peace. The days and nights went by with a regularity and a rhythm to which his body and mind quickly responded. Regular sleep; regular meals, few indeed yet adequate; the rhythm of the services in church, study, the meals in common, sleep in common – such rhythm was a great restorer. And, over all, a great silence for much of the time. There was no anxiety. He did what he was told to do.

After a few weeks as a postulant it was seen by the Novice Master that Martin was behaving as he should, and could be

admitted formally to the novitiate. This was done at the first of
three serious initiation-type ceremonies, to be spread over the
next two years. In this first the postulant was 'clothed'. His
secular clothes were formally removed and the new novice was
clothed in the habit of the Order within which he intended to
live for the next year in the hope that at the end of that time, he
would be admitted fully and allowed to take vows, which would
bind him for the rest of his life.

Brother Martin lay prostrate before the altar, arms stretched
out in the form of a cross in the great church, while the Prior
recited: 'Lord Jesus Christ our leader and our strength, Thou
has set aside this servant of Thine by the fire of holy humility
from the rest of mankind. We humbly pray that this will also
separate him from carnal intercourse and from the community
of earthly deeds through the sanctity shed from heaven upon
him and that Thou wilt bestow on him grace to remain Thine.'
This was but one of numerous prayers, exhortations and
warnings – the latter included a list of all the unpleasant things
which the novice must expect, the restricted diet, the cold, the
rising to recite the Office in church while it was still dark, the
shame of having to go begging in the streets. The ceremony had
a strong psychological resonance. The habit provided a new,
ready-made identity, and at the same time both an ideal and an
ever-present reminder of rules and other people to be obeyed.
The new identity was further rubbed home in the form of a
haircut, the tonsure, a physical initiation.

Brother Martin now moved into the Friary proper. With the
other monks he slept in the large upstairs dormitory, ate in the
refectory, listening to suitable reading at the same time; and had
his stall in the church for the services which were patterned
across the day and some of the night. These services were centred
on the recitation of the sacred poetry of the Jews, the 150 Psalms,
which the early Jewish Christians had continued to recite when
they became followers of Jesus, and which had become the
staple Christian prayer. Martin had these Psalms off by heart
within a year or two. And it was the Psalms which would be the
chosen subject of his very first lectures in the university – when
he was twenty-nine. Meanwhile, the impressionable young
brother of twenty-one was feeding on the rich diet of the Bible,
both in choir and his cell. He had a copy for his own use with a

red cover to it, as he recalled in later years. In it he found the great myths of the creation, the fall, the flood, the escape from Egypt, the promised land, the twelve tribes, the exile, the prophets, all full of semitic poetry and wisdom, and great human stories, followed by the incomparable religious texts of the New Testament – 'He who would save his life must lose it'. All his life he had heard readings, short excerpts, in the regular church services, but now he read right through the Bible, and then began to study it seriously. By the time he came to lecture he had by heart long sections from all over the text, and was able to quote with extraordinary facility. It is a commonplace that memories were incomparably more efficient and enabled people to recall large quantities of written material in the days when the mind was not bombarded all day long with verbal sights and sound. But Luther had a special gift in this direction over and above the widespread facility. The Bible came to be his most familiar and most loved text. His reading of the Latin classics had given him an appetite for well-shaped language, and the Bible came to be for him, not just words but The Word.

Brother Martin was totally at the service of religion, a neophyte, new born. His depressions had retreated for the time being. 'I experienced in myself and in many others how quiet Satan is in the first years of monastic life,' Luther would tell his friends in later years. Apart from anything else, the sheer novelty of the life made a great impact. Within a few months the hardships were beginning to bite as the winter came on and there was heating nowhere except in one room where the brethren could go to warm up if the cold became too intense; and with Advent at the beginning of December the meals fell to one a day with only some dry bread and wine in the evening. But this was all grist to his mill. He read the *Lives of the Fathers* and wondered at the austerities of the desert hermits: 'I used to imagine such a saint, who would live in the desert, and abstain from food and drink and live on a few vegetables and roots and cold water.' His Novice Master was a father in God to him and enabled him quite easily to adapt himself to the life, 'a fine old man' and a 'true Christian' as Luther referred to him later. The community spent between four and five hours a day in church. The time that was over from this and other monastic exercises, Brother Martin spent in memorising the Rule and other such texts, studying the Augustinian tradition, and doing some chores about the house, including cleaning the latrines. Then there was begging in the town with a sack on one's back.

Silence was obligatory for most of the day, and a series of signs were used to substitute for the ordinary business of life, asking for the butter at table or enquiring what the time was. There were set times of recreation when conversation was normal. The atmosphere in the house was influenced by Father Johann von Staupitz, Head of the Saxon-Thuringian province of the Order, and author of the new statutes for the thirty reformed or 'observant' friaries. He was a man of insight who tried to keep a high standard of observance without going to extremes. He had the knack of understanding others, and of enabling an authentic religious dimension to flower within the dangerous ambience of the social and political authoritarianism which continually threatened to destroy it. At this time, he was often away in Wittenberg where he had recently co-operated with Elector Frederick in founding a new university; its philosophical and theological sector was largely in the hands of the Augustinians who had had a house in the town for many years. But as provincial Superior of the Order, Staupitz called in at Erfurt from time to time, trying to keep the numerous tensions at a low pitch. From the first he was excited about the arrival of the brilliant young graduate from the university, with a suggestion of some special charisma about him.

Another friar of outstanding importance in the Friary during Martin's first year was Johann Jeuser von Paltz, head of theological studies in the house for the last twenty years, also a professor of theology in the University. Like Martin, he had come to the cloister from the University. He was a man of high spiritual and theological reputation, who went on preaching tours, which combined encouragement of piety among the faithful with financial service to the monastery since Indulgences were the principal reward that he offered the listeners. In 1502 he had a set of his sermons printed under the title 'The Mine of Heaven'. It proved a valuable mine for the Friary, which was able to complete the rebuilding of their library with the income. The library would itself further contribute to the theological and spiritual standards of the Friary. The sermons would help the numerous people who heard them to keep on the right path in this world and to save their souls in the next. The widespread criticism of Indulgences he thought of as the perverse ravings of ill-instructed fools.

The twelve months went by, and before the end of the summer in 1506 Brother Martin was recommended by the Novice Master for full profession of vows. The second initiation ceremony was held, again before the altar in the church, and even more solemn moments. Holding a lighted candle in his hand, Luther said aloud in front of the whole community: 'I, Brother Martin, do make profession and promise obedience to Almighty God, to Mary the Sacred Virgin, and to you, the prior of this cloister as representative of the general head of the order of Eremites of the holy bishop, St Augustine, and his rightful successors, to live until death without worldly possessions and in chastity according to the rule of St Augustine.' He received the reply, 'Keep this Rule, and I promise you eternal life.' The next stretch of time led up to the crown of his new life, ordination to the priesthood. During this year, Martin's inner tensions began to tangle with the tensions in the community, and a worrying sadness took over from time to time, while great inner joy was also experienced by him. The momentum of life within the conventional structure carried him forward on its flowing tide.

CHAPTER THREE

The New Priest

In the early evenings the friars chanted Vespers in the great church, leaning back on the misericords in the choir stalls; as each psalm came to an end they stood up and bowed in praise of the trinitarian God, 'Glory be to the Father, the Son and the Holy Spirit – through all ages of ages; *per omnia saecula saeculorum.*' There was a sense of timelessness further enhanced on Sundays when the Psalms were sung in one or other of the eight plain chant modes. Towards the end came the *Magnificat* (the song Luke put into the mouth of Mary, the mother of Jesus, in his version of the Gospel), with its inspiring poetry, *Magnificat anima mea Dominum*, 'My soul doth magnify the Lord . . . He that is mighty hath done great things for me: and holy is his name . . . He hath scattered the proud in the imagination of their hearts . . . He hath put down the mighty from their seat and hath exalted the humble and meek . . . He hath filled the hungry with good things and the rich he hath sent empty away.' Brother Martin's spirit soared and remained high as the friars processed out of the church to the refectory, along the other side of the cloister garth, for supper.

Later, before bed, came the final choir office, Compline, completion, with its brief and beautiful little 'anthem' to Mary at the end; it changed with the seasons, but for much of the year, from late May till December it was the *Salve Regina*, 'Hail, Holy Queen'. And so to the communal dormitory under the roof, hot in the middle of summer, cold in winter, but at all times providing the security of the common life.

Early in the morning, before first light during most of the year, the friars went with lanterns or candles into the church for the first office of the day, Matins, a lengthy text, followed by Lauds, an office of praise and rejoicing. Then the friars who

were priests would disperse to individual altars to say their own
daily Mass, those who were not away preaching in another town
or village, or who were not required for some public Mass in
Erfurt. The day went on with shaking up the mattresses, other
duties and more offices, eventually a meal. In Brother Martin's
mind the poetry of the Psalms jostled with Vergil's Georgics and
other classical Latin texts. Already he was becoming sharply
aware of the crucial semitic dimension of the Psalms, wanting to
study the Old Testament text in its original Hebrew. Again when
the text of the New Testament itself was intoned, in readings
from the New Testament, from John, from Paul and other
writers, he began to sense the bite of the original and more intellectual Greek, standing behind the fourth-century Latin text
of Jerome's translation (the Vulgate), Latin which was now part
of Luther's natural and normal way of expressing himself.

The seasons changed: the short but hot summer, with its
sultry days, the vines ripening on the lower hillsides along with
nuts and other fruits, the haymaking and cattle fattening in the
valleys, fields of corn for bread and beer, and all around the
great rolling forests. In Erfurt itself there was a sense of civilisation over-ripe, with the tenseness which goes with too many
people knowing too much about the unresolved problems, an
increasing number of intellectuals opting out into the
burgeoning renaissance of human studies, the arts; others
moving as ever into the law, or into banking and commerce.
And everywhere were the priests to forgive the sinfulness of it all,
and make amends with their frequent sacrifices in church.
Finally, back behind it all was a sense of 'the other', for many not
much more than a fear of what they deserved, for others a deep
yearning for the spiritual life. And soon Brother Martin would
himself have the burden of all this on his own priestly shoulders.

Monastic communities were divided into the educated and
the uneducated. The latter, lay brothers, did most of the menial
tasks, assisted by the novices; in a big community like that of the
Augustinian house, these tasks might include such things as
brewing beer – the Erfurt cloister was substantial, and
sometimes they would be putting on a meal for as many as two
hundred. The educated members of the community were
priests, or aspiring priests; normally they were ordained within
two or three years of joining. When the major reforms of the

Catholic Church eventually came, late in the century, they included new regulations for a six-year preparation of men for the priesthood; in Luther's time preparation was brief. Brother Martin studied an exposition of the Mass by Gabriel Biel – a well-written book, intellectual and inspiring; the author had died only twelve years previously. Apart from that, major emphasis was laid on learning the precise detail of the actions of the priest when celebrating Mass, as well as on memorising the text. Then there was some training for preaching, and later for hearing confessions. But the Mass was the heart of a priest's life. In a few months' time Martin would be saying Mass at twenty-three years old, still so close to his contemporaries, and yet now so definitely different.

The rite of Mass arose sometime in the first years after the death of Jesus of Nazareth in Israel. It was intended as a re-enactment of the supper which Jesus had with his disciples on the night before he was crucified, a supper in the context of the annual Jewish Passover. The New Testament has several descriptions of it, and records that Jesus told his disciples to do again what he then did. Almost certainly the earliest description of the 'Last Supper', as it came to be known, is that which reads as follows: 'The Lord Jesus, on the night of his arrest, took some bread, and, after giving thanks to God, broke it and said: "This is my body which is for you; do this in remembrance of me." In the same way he took the cup after supper and said: "This cup is the new covenant in my blood. Whenever you drink it, do this in remembrance of me."' The followers of Jesus, soon to be called Christians (after 'Christ', meaning the Anointed, a name given, early on, to Jesus), began to meet together in the earliest days, to celebrate this remembrance, which they called also thanksgiving, eucharist. And from early days they set men aside to conduct the rite. They spoke of it as a sacrament and believed Jesus, crucified, risen and ascended to his Father in heaven, to be especially present in the bread and wine, which they consumed. Gradually the assemblies became more formalised. At their best these ritual meetings seem to have become great liturgical occasions, a public expression of the generically religious experience, the sense both of ultimate dependence and of spiritual freedom. At their worst they became very like the pagan rituals which the Bible text holds not to be pleasing to God or appropriate to men, occasions for offering sacrifices in order to bribe God and buy off his anger. Even at their worst there was something authentic about them, some recognition of man's dependence on 'something else', something genuinely exciting and inspiring. But there was a grave tension between the mechanical, indeed financial approach to the divine, and authentic religion – a tension already sensed by Martin.

The best theologians were aware of the danger that ordinary folk would treat the Mass as the equivalent of a pagan sacrifice, and all the more so on account of the use made of Indulgences. It all looked like a routine, and like magic. Their explanations of the Mass often tended to sound only like super-magic. Biel taught a mysticism which said that the soul of a worthy participant was changed into the body of Christ through a most intimate union, when he or she consumed the consecrated bread (only priests took the wine as well). Three centuries earlier the western love of definition had led scholars to say that the bread and wine used at Mass were changed during the rite in a way they defined as 'transubstantiation'. The Mass itself was a sacrificial prayer which could be applied to those for whom it was specially celebrated, even if not present. It was, however, specially for those who were present – at this point, Biel added: 'I mean those who really participate, not those loafing around [*circumgirantium*].' Biel is not entirely happy, as a theologian, with 'transubstantiation' as a description of what happens to the bread and wine though he entirely accepted it, and often waxed lyrical about the Mass: 'What super-excellent glory of the priest to hold and dispense his God, distributing Him to others.' Looking back on these months of study in later years, Luther commented, 'My heart would bleed when I read Biel's text.'

One thing Biel emphasised, like all expositors of the Mass, was the need for purity of heart in the priest, in him who dispensed this sacrament of the divine life. And this took him straight to the question that theologians had discussed for more than a thousand years, about the extent to which man could do something about purifying himself, and about whether he could do anything good without God's help. 'Grace', *gratia*, was the word used for the help God gave, the divine life in each Christian. This grace, available through baptism and the other sacraments, was it not available in any way to those who had not been baptised through no fault of their own? How did grace work? Was it necessary even before man could take any steps towards the good, even for preparing the heart for full grace to take root there? Logically and psychologically they felt they must allow for an initiative in man's self, for what they came to call '*facere quod in se est*', to do what one could. (Some have labelled this as semi-Pelagianism – Pelagius was the fifth-century British heretic of free will.) So Biel reached the point where he could say that absolute love of God for God's sake, or above everything, even though a tough assignment, is within reach of natural man; grace is not the root but the fruit of the preparatory good works which a Christian can do by himself.

This measuring up to God was already an anxiety to Martin. He wondered how he could be fit to perform the priestly acts. His depressive side began to express itself theologically; how could he ever succeed in living up to the Christian ideals? Sex seems not to have been a major problem, at first anyway, in these moral worries. 'In the monastery I felt little sexual desire. I had nocturnal pollutions in answer to nature,' he said in later years. It was 'not women, but really knotty problems' that worried him. Even after the emptying of the friaries, Luther did not, like many others, marry within months. Conscious sexual drives were not dominant. In the first two years it was rather a growing concern about his relationship with God, a feeling that he was always doing something wrong, was never as good as he ought to be, a failure to love God. It was common among dedicated monks and friars. Canon Law provided for numerous Big Brothers. Law and love provided a special tension in the Mass itself.

The first Mass was an ordeal. Although his brethren would be entirely sympathetic, Luther knew they would all be watching out for slips; and any mistake at Mass was a serious sin. The enormous importance attached to the precise fulfilment of a very large number of rubrics about how the text should be read and what gestures should be made, threatened one. There were sharp contradictions here. The priesthood was concerned with people's 'souls', and nothing could be of a higher or more wonderful stature than the priest. At the same time all the emphasis, in the day-to-day life, was put on the detail of how to earn merit, how to do right all the things which Canon Law said needed to be done, including the sacred ritual to be meticulously observed. As yet, however, for Martin the tension remained largely unformulated at any theological level. Worry about achievement was dominant.

First came the ordination itself. On 3 April Brother Martin ascended the steps out of Erfurt's central *Platz* up to the recently built great late Gothic Cathedral of St Mary, next to its older sister church of St Severus. It was another occasion like that of the clothing and of the vows. Martin was prostrate again before the altar. The local Bishop, Johann Bonemilch von Lasphe, put the symbolic stole, a long thin scarf, and the chasuble, the vestment, on him and said, 'Receive the power of consecrating and sacrificing for the living and the dead.' Back in the Friary the brethren congratulated him, and there was a little celebration.

Now he had to start serious preparation for his first Mass in a few weeks' time. Martin was half glad and half disconcerted to hear that his father was going to make a special occasion of this event and ride over to Erfurt with some friends. A date had to be found which would suit him, as well as the Friary. Sunday, 2 May, was decided on.

Martin wanted his friends and patrons to be there – one had remained strongly supporting him and specially close since the Eisenach days, Father Johann Braun of the Franciscan house there. Martin wrote and invited him. The letter is the earliest surviving example of Luther's words. Though not of outstanding importance, it introduces the *ipsissima verba* for the first time; one can see what sort of an impact the young man makes on paper. It was a rather florid sort of letter, in the obsequious style considered right to be adopted by a junior to a senior with, however, a certain personal and affectionate character to it, typical of Luther. Written in Latin it was addressed: 'To the pious and venerable Johann Braun, a priest of Christ and Mary, Superior at Eisenach, my dearest friend in Christ.' The text then starts:

Greetings in Christ Jesus, our Lord. I would be afraid, kindest Sir, to disturb your loving self with my burdensome letters and wishes, if I did not know (on the basis of your gracious heart, so generously inclined towards me) of the sincere friendship I have experienced in so many ways and favours.

So I do not hesitate to write this letter to you, trusting that in the closeness of our mutual friendship you will listen, and that it might find you easily approachable.

God, who is glorious and holy in all his works, has deigned to exalt me magnificently – a miserable and totally unworthy sinner – by calling me into his supreme ministry solely on the basis of his bounteous mercy. Therefore I have to fulfil completely the office entrusted to me so that I may be acceptable (as much as dust can be acceptable to God) to such great splendour of divine goodness.

Though not so far removed from the language, for instance, of the fifteenth-century *Of the Imitation of Christ*, there was a certain vehemence about the language which was a presage of things to come: 'According to the decision of the fathers here, it is settled that I should start, with the help of God's grace, on the fourth Sunday following Easter, which we call *Cantate*. This is the day appointed for my first Mass before God, because it is convenient to my father. To this then, kind friend, I invite you humbly, perhaps even boldly.' But it was not really so bold, because Father Braun had evidently always seen in Luther someone he would like to help and had entertained Martin quite recently, when the latter was on a visit for the Friars to Eisenach:

I do this certainly not because I consider myself in a position . . . to request you to inconvenience yourself with the trouble of such a journey to visit me, a poor and humble man; but I do so because I experienced your good will and your obvious kindness toward me when I visited you the other day, and in great abundance on many other occasions.

Therefore, dearest Father, Sir and Friar (the first title is due to your age and office, the second due to your merits, the third due to your Order), please honour me with your presence if time and your clerical or domestic duties permit, and support me with your valuable presence and prayers, that my sacrifice may be acceptable to God . . . Perhaps you will bring along my relation Conrad, who was once sacristan at St Nicholas' Church, and anyone you may wish as a travelling companion, so long as he has freed himself from domestic obligations and will enjoy coming.

Luther was always keen about domestic duties, and the social order generally – these had to be satisfied before an outing was to be undertaken. Finally, there is a brief paragraph about Father Braun's sleeping and boarding arrangements for the visit. It would be appropriate for him to stay not in the noisy guest house but in an unoccupied cell in the friary.

> Finally I urge you to come right into the monastery to stay with us this little while (I am not afraid that you will settle down here!) and not look for quarters elsewhere. You will have to become a *cellarius*, that is an inhabitant of a monastic cell.
> Farewell in Christ Jesus, our Lord.
> Written at our cloister in Erfurt on 22 April, the year of our Lord, 1507.

Then Martin suddenly remembers the Schalbes. Until then, apparently, it had not occurred to him that these superior people might like to come; but of course they might hear about the event from Father Braun, so he added after the signature a further note which speaks volumes about the social stratification in little Eisenach:

> I do not dare to importune or burden those excellent people of the Schalbe Foundation, who certainly have done so much for me. I am sure that it would not befit their social position and prestige to be invited to such an unimportant and humble affair, or to be bothered by the wishes of a monk who is now dead to the world. In addition I am uncertain and somewhat dubious whether an invitation would please or annoy them. Therefore I have decided to be silent; but if there should be an opportunity, I wish you would express my gratitude to them. Farewell.

The messages went off, and above all arrangements were made for Martin's father's party to come. Big Hans was bringing a cash gift of about £200, and coming with twenty friends on horseback. Martin toiled away at the rite, the gestures and the text; and kept up his prayers, and tried ever to be in that good disposition in which a monk or friar is supposed to be.

Martin's nervousness did not abate as the day drew nearer. The day of the first Mass shared some of the tensions of a wedding, being the intensely public celebration of something which in some ways was a matter that made one wish to withdraw from the public eye. The new priest wanted to keep himself very collected in his mind, detached, 'recollected' as the jargon goes in church circles. Yet it was impossibly difficult to keep out the 'distractions' of the world. Friends and relations and all Martin's brethren would be present for the first public liturgy that he would conduct. There would be torches, again. Possibly his mother would be present for him to bless after the Mass, and she would kiss his newly appointed hands.

The day itself proved to be, if not exactly a disaster, a day which Luther could not remember without quaking, and he often returned to the topic in later years. The 'Table Talk' has a number of references to it. Taken down by different hands and differing in detail, they witness to two things which remained burnt into Martin's mind.

First was the celebration of the Mass itself. He made no mistakes. But his state of spiritual and theological seriousness triggered off a moment of paralysis and horror. It occurred at the beginning of the 'Canon' of the Mass, the long central prayer, which recalls the 'Last Supper' and includes the consecration of the bread and the wine. Martin was standing at the high altar, and began the prayer: *'Te igitur, clementissime Pater . . .* Therefore, oh most merciful Father.' Suddenly, he was overtaken in a flash by an instant identity crisis. How dare he, how could he actually speak to God? The whole thing was unthinkable. He felt obliterated in the face of the assumption that he was to address God. For a moment he made as if to leave the altar, and said something to the Prior who was standing by him, to assist him at his first Mass, as was the custom, precisely in case the new celebrant experienced any difficulty. The Prior smiled and turned him back to his task. In a moment it was over. From the body of the church, nothing strange would have been noticed – the celebrant with his back to the congregation had to move about from time to time in any case. Martin returned to the text and continued the Mass, sweating and shaken, but safely couched again in the routine.

Writing in later years, Luther said of this moment: 'At these words I was utterly stupefied and terror-struck. I thought to myself, "With what tongue shall I address such Majesty . . . Who am I that I should lift up my eyes . . . ? At his nod the earth trembles . . . And shall I, a miserable pygmy, say I want this, I ask for that? For I am dust and ashes and I am speaking to the living, eternal and true God"!' The interesting thing is that the prayer, like almost every Christian liturgical prayer, does not in fact presume to address God directly. God is always addressed through his 'Son', Jesus. The prayer in question goes: 'Therefore oh most merciful Father, through Jesus Christ thy Son our Lord we come to thee . . .', and Luther had known this for some time, probably many years. But, Jesus tended to be thought of as 'God' rather than 'man'; and Luther's mind was already tending towards a crisis; the paralysing four Latin words with which the prayer began had their effect regardless of what the rational mind knew would follow them; the moment of horror ensued. If linked to a psychosis about authority through his father, it would have been all the stronger and the more unbearable – the words addressed God precisely as 'Father'.

Luther's existential psychosis about addressing God had a respectable pedigree. The Jews had always refused to address Him directly – they had a name for him, Jehovah, Yahweh, or 'the Lord'. God himself was the unnameable, the unmentionable, the one before whom one must veil one's face. Here was Luther putting it to the test, psychologically, and nearly succumbing. His anguished internal cry, only marginally visible externally, was the first note of a theme which he was to orchestrate vastly in later years. The revolution he started was precisely about the matter of how man is to manage his relationship with that which men call God.

The Mass over, there followed the relaxation of the Rule usual on such occasions, with a celebratory meal in the Guest House, Father Braun and Martin's other friends in attendance. But dominating the scene were the burghers of Mansfeld. They felt they could enjoy themselves now that the purpose of the visit had been fulfilled and they had witnessed the first Mass of Hans Luder's son – Hans Luder who had further justified his visit with a substantial gift to the monastery. But now the second crucial event of this crucial day occurred. The whole business of his son's vocation still rankled in Hans Luther's mind. Martin had acted against his wishes, and resentment still glowed. Excited by the Prior's best wine and beer, he ragged Martin when the conversation turned to his decision to become a friar and priest, the thunderstorm, the vow. 'Ha, so long as it wasn't all some illusion of the devil,' he said, with typical German badinage of the rather crude kind. Martin tried to explain, but his father was more than half serious and in no mood to be answered back: 'Haven't you heard the commandment "Thou shalt honour thy Father and Mother"?' This produced silence in the room, for a moment. Luther's glands were working and his whole person was deeply embarrassed and upset, to judge by the frequency with which he returned to the event later in life. His father was suggesting on the basis of those authoritative Ten Commandments of the Old Testament that he should never have become a monk at all.

The day came to an end and Martin, chastened, could fall back into his place in the community as the junior priest. He was told to resume his University studies. It was, in its way, a comforting feeling, to be back at the beginning again of a lengthy journey, this time through the post-graduate stages. Father Martin was already earmarked as a future teacher. Study, especially study of the Bible, was a pleasure to him: 'At first, in the monastery, I devoured the Bible.' His theology tutor in the Friary, Father Nathin (Father Paltz had moved to be Prior in a Rhineland friary after a disagreement with his brethren at Erfurt), had known Biel and been one of his pupils.

Luther's path was well marked out. First he would study for the Baccalaureus Biblicus, a five-year course which was often shortened in the case of good students from Religious Orders. This degree qualified a man to lecture on the Bible – at the moment Father Luther could lecture only in philosophy, on the strength of his Master's degree, though he had not been called on to do so. After the biblical degree came another, two-year course leading to the crown of the Theology programme; by this final degree a man was designated Sententiarius, qualified to lecture on the Sentences of Peter Lombard, the key theology text in all theology schools, a great compilation of texts made in the twelfth century, and very widely commentated since then. After that there remained only a Doctorate in Theology, something which a man might or might not hope to obtain later in life.

After ordination, the young priest soon found celebration of Mass to be a rewarding experience. The worry about getting the

rubrics perfectly right gradually resolved itself into the pleasure
of achieving a satisfactory celebration of the rite. Luther took
great delight in making the rite as nearly as possible adequate to
that which it signified. Sometimes this would be out in the town,
or in one of the villages, and Martin felt he was playing his part
in the divine economy. 'I was a great archpapist and a really
valiant knight of the Mass' in those days, so he said later. Social
status went hand in hand with spiritual and pastoral duty. From
the day of this ordination, in spite of accusations of failure to
honour him, Luther's father addressed his son no longer in the
familiar second person singular, but with respect in the second
person plural. He was 'Father Martin' now.

The university programme, supplemented by a theology programme in the cloister itself (often the same teacher), was heavy.
When attendance in choir had to be missed on account of a
lecture, the office missed had to be made up by a private recital
later. The days were full. Martin's deepening response to the
round of psalm and prayer, to the study of how man was
meant to live, set his emotions ever more stingingly alight,
sometimes affirmatively, often negatively. His tendency to
depression led him to despair of ever being able to measure up
to the set standard, of ever being able to love God. Christ's arms
outstretched seemed to promise a threat rather than an
embrace. In later days he said he often imagined Christ sitting in
judgement on him at the Last Day. He took up the common
practice of prayer to Mary to hold back the arm of her Son, justly
threatening. He had a round of twenty-one saints to whom he
prayed, three at each Mass, for the seven days of the week. 'The
communion of saints', which in one sense was understood as a
sign of present glory, a realisation here and now of a share in the
glory of God and his saints in 'the last times', became a kind of
last hope, a rescue operation. As the despair mounted, Martin
saw it as a terrible temptation of the devil. What from a clinical
point of view was an attack of acute depression, to him was
indeed an attack, but an attack of the devil, an almost physical
attack on the inner citadel of his soul. '*Anfechtung*' was the word
Luther came to use for this which was at the same time an
'attack' and a 'temptation', and something which, at last, he
declared to be the only way to find out what theology was really
about. Only after an experience of this kind does one fully un-

derstand one's need, fully grasp man's essential destitution
when acting on his own.

Martin took to going to confession frequently. From now on
for the next six or eight years his disquiet grew and grew, until
he found an answer which at the same time satisfied his intellect
and gave him some sense of relief in a wider sense. At times
the disquiet became extreme, bordering on some kind of
breakdown. In 1518, he wrote of what he had felt not many years
before. He was explaining what he took to be the pain of
someone, after death, suffering in 'purgatory' before admission
to heaven, and then went on, quite clearly referring to himself:

> I myself 'knew a man' [he quotes from St Paul's famous
> description of himself being taken up in ecstasy which begins
> 'I knew a man'] who claimed that he had often suffered these
> punishments in fact, over a brief period of time. Yet they were
> so great and so much like hell that no tongue could
> adequately express them, no pen could describe them, and
> one who had not himself experienced them could not believe
> them. And so great were they that, if they had been sustained
> or had lasted for half an hour, even for one tenth of an hour,
> he would have ceased to exist completely and all of his bones
> would have been reduced to ashes. At such a time God seems
> terribly angry, and with him the whole creation.

The passage leads on to a description of a kind of mystical
suffering with Christ: '. . . All that remains is the stark naked
desire for help and a terrible groaning, but it does not know
where to turn for help . . . In this instance the person is stretched
out with Christ so that all his bones may be counted, and every
corner of the soul is filled with the greatest bitterness, dread,
trembling and sorrow of a kind that is everlasting.' Allowing for
all the natural forcefulness of Luther's style and for the
customary emphasis of contemporary language, this remains a
witness to a psychological experience of a devastating kind.

A case could be made for saying that Luther became hysterical
at times. One of his greatest detractors, later in the century,
mounted a case of this kind. Cochlaeus records that he was told
by one of Luther's brethren that on one occasion he shouted out
in choir, 'It's not I, it's not I' when the passage was being read
from the gospel which describes the cure of the deaf mute, and

that he fell over in a swoon. Not too much credence can be put on this; at the same time the supposed event is something that one can imagine happening to Luther in his early days as friar. But to make this a prime symbol of a portrait of an hysteric or someone mentally unreliable, is not possible. Martin was to make and keep friends of a notably able kind. Promotion was to come quickly, and frequently, both in responsibility within the Order and within the University. He was not 'unbalanced'. Yet already it is clear that Martin had something unusual about him. His own writings witness to this. Later in life he would relish the memory of a remark to him from someone finally out of patience with his endless complaints about God's anger. 'You are a fool! God is not angry with you. You are angry with God.' And in retailing this, Pastor Luther commented, 'That was very well said, although it was before the light of the gospel.' Although this was said from within the Church of the old days, he recognised it as true and something which had helped him, a distraught young man on his way, with its down-to-earth humour and insight into his temperament, aggressive and depressive.

The Psalms with their frequent agonising calls of man to God became a favourite source of expression. Later in life, when Luther was composing words and music for Saxon hymns from the Latin Psalms, the first one he did was 'Out of the depths I have cried to Thee oh Lord . . .', a Psalm used in the old Roman liturgy for requiems, and used, in Luther's Saxon version, at his own funeral. With its words of sombre suffering it always appealed to Luther: 'If you take note of our sin, Lord; Lord who can survive? . . . From the morning watch even to the night let Israel hope in the Lord.'

But Luther's troubles were not such as to strike his superiors as markedly different from those of other dedicated young religious with their scruples, their enthusiasm for study, and their surfeit of energy. On the contrary his application to study and his observance of the Rule were noted; and he had developed a satisfactory speaking voice, in conformity with the specific requirements of clear enunciation. It was just these things which led to an unexpected change in his life.

CHAPTER FOUR

Wittenberg

Even on a wet day in winter Erfurt had something rather fine about it. Even though the brooks were overflowing on to the streets, and the sewage was stinking in the gutters, there was something to celebrate. The two great churches on the little hill, and behind them, higher again, the centuries-old Benedictine abbey on the Petersburg dominated the town. The University, with its ancient traditions, was seldom without some public event. The students were all around with their energy, their disputations, their singing and their beer drinking. Even when the Archbishop of Mainz's officials were at their most tiresome in demanding taxes, and the day workers at their most aggressive in resenting the situation, still there was something to be proud of, something with which to identify, a long tradition symbolised by the many fine buildings. And out in the near countryside there was a burgeoning peasant life.

Wittenberg offered less. Set beside a sluggish stretch of the Elbe in flat country, often the outlook in this small market town of little more than 2000 inhabitants was simply dull. And the town itself as a result of its flat site had the reputation of being even smellier than most towns. However, small and at first sight unprepossessing as it was, the town had a history of hundreds of years and something to bring the visitors to it. Furthermore, when the Elector Frederick succeeded in 1486 to the title of Ruler (and Imperial Elector) of this Ernestine portion of the Wettin lands, in Saxony, he set about raising its reputation with great determination. He wanted to show that he could produce something to rival Leipzig in the other Albertine part of the Wettin lands ruled first by his uncle and then from 1500 by his cousin Duke George. He started with disadvantages. Wittenberg was a frontier town between the German and the Slav peoples.

The Slavs, known here as the Wends, were the successors of the invading barbarians from many centuries previously, and were now there farming on the east side of the Elbe – and a surviving Wend community still holds together in twentieth-century East Germany. There was a general impression that Wittenberg was out on a limb. Its internal arrangements were much the same as those for Mansfeld and Eisenach, towns of about the same size. Citizens were responsible for keeping the streets clean and were fined if they failed. But paving was confined to the one long main street and one or two short stretches off it. However, it did have the privilege of marketing salt to the rest of the region. And it did have an incomparable collection of relics, to revere which many pilgrims came from afar. Frederick started on this.

He went to the Holy Land and picked up a great quantity more. He got the Pope to issue a letter encouraging ecclesiastical authorities, bishops, abbots and others to hand over relics to his safe-keeping. By the early years of the sixteenth century he was able to have a vast illustrated catalogue drawn up showing 5005 items, including pieces of the bodies of the 'Holy Innocents' (babies murdered by King Herod as described in the New Testament), a thorn from the crown of thorns worn by Jesus before his crucifixion, milk from the Blessed Virgin Mary the mother of Jesus, teeth from various saints, and so on. It seems people wanted to believe in these things and had a passion for the 'very thing itself', even though these were often enough ridiculed by intellectuals, who, however, themselves could not resist the sheer curiosity aroused. Valuable Indulgences were attached to pious reverencing of these relics. And all was good for business. The brewing of beer was a major part of the economy of Wittenberg, and from time to time an important part of it must have been drunk by visitors. The new Elector built a good bridge over the Elbe to make the final approach to the town more easy.

Father Martin perhaps knew little more, or perhaps even less, than all this about Wittenberg when he was suddenly told, to his astonishment, that he had been appointed to go to the little Augustinian Friary at Wittenberg. The purpose was that he should lecture in philosophy at the University. For a new university had been the very ambitious second part of the Elector's plan virtually to refound Wittenberg. In the last years of the

fifteenth century he began talks with the Augustinians about
founding a university there. Elector Frederick would himself
provide the buildings if the Augustinians would provide the
core of professors. They agreed to do this and to increase their
community in Wittenberg, eventually arranging that Father
Staupitz, a member of a noble Saxon family and thus suited to
working with the Elector, should be invited to come over from
their Munich house and take on the chair of Bible Study.
Frederick set about building the University lecture halls and
provided money both for new buildings for the friars and for his
own property at the other end of the main street, the Castle (for
his occasional visits from his permanent residence at Torgau)
and the Castle Church, together with a worthy building where
the relics could be kept and displayed.

All was agreed, and after the normal negotiations with the
Emperor Maximilian, a charter was granted which founded the
University of Wittenberg, its patrons to be St Augustine and the
Blessed Virgin. This was in 1502, and the University now had the
right to grant degrees. Its graduates would have the right to
teach in all other universities throughout the Christian world.
The building began. Straw roofed wooden houses down the
main street began to give way to stone and brick. The town
Council played its part by providing the desks and benches
required. Doors of temporary lecture halls were opened; pro-
spectuses sent out. The first rush of students came, either those
rejected by other universities, or residents not far away, or those
attracted by a new foundation where the teaching was not so
rigid. The Elector and Staupitz went out of their way to organise
a modern university. There were lectures in Greek from the
start. The modernist school of Occamites was not to dominate;
representatives of other schools were there, notably Andreas
Bodenstein, known as Karlstadt a follower of Aquinas, and later
Scotus. There were the usual Medical and Law Schools; the
latter with young Christoph Scheurl as its Dean, was housed in
the castle buildings which also had the University library within
its walls. As the buildings went up painters were invited to
decorate the interiors. Albrecht Dürer was there for a few
months; Cranach, later to be a leading citizen and a close friend
of Luther's, was already in residence and at work on the castle
rooms when Father Martin arrived in the autumn of 1508.

It had been a big shock to Luther when the news of the appointment was first given to him at Erfurt. He had conflicting emotions – fear, excitement, pride, and pleasure at the challenge as the outline of the job began to emerge. He would have to continue with his own studies in theology, while lecturing to the students in philosophy. And clearly he would be someone much more important in the little community at Wittenberg than he had been, a mere post-graduate student, in the great friary at Erfurt. On arriving at Wittenberg he found it still in the hands of the builders. The friars were still in the little chapel they had had for numberless years, holding only about twenty people. But there was bustle and promise in the air everywhere. Luther was one of a batch of seven friars recruited from various friaries to improve the performance at Wittenberg.

As the weeks went by, it became clear that Father Staupitz was wanting the brilliant young priest to hasten on with his studies so that he could begin to lecture eventually in Staupitz's own discipline. Some six years previously, Father Staupitz had been elected Superior of the whole big group of Reformed or Observant Friaries. He was not able to carry out properly the duties involved at the same time as lecturing regularly at Wittenberg. Luther's sudden appointment, it began to be clear, was related to this fact. He had shown himself to be exactly the kind of man Staupitz favoured. He had not gone along with the more sophisticated humanists, or followers of *bonae litterae* as they referred to themselves. On the other hand, his penetrating and lively mind had been in evidence from the days of his Master's degree before he entered the Augustinians. He was meticulous in his monastic observance and always specially loyal to Church authority. The sometimes overwrought expression on his face might mean that what he needed was more demanding work, and more responsibility. The Rector of the new University already knew Martin well; Staupitz had persuaded Dr Trutvetter, a reliable man who had had enough, after twenty-five years, of the difficulties always generated in such a complex ancient foundation as Erfurt was, to come over to teach at Wittenberg. Soon after his arrival he had been elected Rector.

When Father Luther arrived, the first flush of enthusiasm for the new University was well over, and the hard business of making it work had begun. In 1502 between 600 and 700 students had matriculated. In most subsequent years the new students numbered between one and two hundred, though in 1508 dropping to only sixty-eight. Large numbers fell by the way each year in all universities, but there were not less than 500 students in Wittenberg. The little place was swamped by them. Luther found himself with too much to do and began the habit of overwork that ruined his health in later life. He was determined to keep up his own studies, as well as doing the lectures required, on Aristotle's Nichomachean Ethics and keeping up strict monastic observance; and theology continued to excite him. The hard work and the excitement both come through in a letter to Father Braun. He wrote it in March 1511, and had to apologise that only now was he telling his old patron and friend that he had left Erfurt and was now in Wittenberg, alas teaching philosophy, though he so much preferred theology: 'The study is tough, especially in philosophy which from the beginning I would gladly have exchanged for theology. I mean that theology which searches out the nut from the shell, the grain from the husk, the marrow from the bone.' This letter also gives a strong hint of Luther's growing, aggressive, antipathy to philosophy, a merely human way of trying to understand the Christian message as distinguished from theology which gets to the heart of the matter through an assent to Christ, through faith. 'But God is God; man often, no rather always, fails in his judgement. This is where God comes in, who rules us in sweetness and for all time.'

The young lecturer was beginning to express himself confidently. The Wittenberg University authorities in that month of March told him he could qualify for the Baccalaureus Biblicum. The only difficulty was that he was still formally a member of the Erfurt community and they would have to pay the degree fees. This took some time to be done; there was resentment at his somewhat precipitate promotion. But worse was to come from that point of view. Father Luther began to work for his final theological degree as Sententiarius, and to lecture on the Bible. In the autumn, the Wittenberg authorities suddenly gave him permission to apply for the degree, several years ahead of the normal schedule at Erfurt. Staupitz was anxious that Father Luther should be able to take over his work at Wittenberg. But the realisation of his hopes were to be postponed.

Only a year had gone by when, in this autumn of 1509, the summons came from Erfurt that Father Martin should return to his mother community. He was required for teaching in the cloister. Now that he was well qualified and had continued to work so hard, they were glad to be able to use his services. However, on his return, the University authorities were understandably cool about the young man who had left Erfurt only thirteen months previously, with no theology degree, and came back not only with his Bible 'Baca', but with his application already well advanced for the final degree of Sententiarius; they refused to proceed with it. In fact they were out of order, and were obliged in the end to proceed with granting a degree already inaugurated by Wittenberg. However, some kind of contretemps occurred at the ceremony itself.

Early on in the proceedings for the formal recognition of Father Luther as Sententiarius, Father Nathin, the Augustinian theologian, came forward and started to read from a large sheet all the requirements to be filled by a candidate, evidently implying that he was doubtful whether Luther had fulfilled them all. Furthermore, Luther was apparently not asked to take the usual oath nor to take higher degrees (and this could only be the Doctorate) at no other university. But Father Nathin represented only one, authoritarian, element of the Erfurt establishment. The ceremony was duly completed. Luther entered into his theology teaching with enormous zest, and the evidence can be seen today in the margins of several vast tomes he used in his cell. They were designed and printed to leave room for interlinear gloss, and for long comment in the margin. One lecturer would inherit the markings of a previous lecturer and treasure them and still find plenty of room for his own comment. Father Luther's careful handwriting, small and precise, gives both his own personal thoughts and the notes he made to remind him what he wanted to say in his lectures when he had the great tome in front of him on a lectern, and the young men, not so very much younger than he, looking up expectantly from the benches. The writer of any such notes was also aware of himself as author of words which his successors would read; in Luther's case these notes have been reprinted and are now pored over by twentieth-century theologians, as part of the Weimar edition of *Luther's Collected Works*.

The books concerned were Augustine's on *The Trinity*, on God as threefold, and on *The City of God*, written in the early years of the fifth century when the city of man, notably Rome, was looking to be shaky, texts still of great interest to historians and theologians in the twentieth century. And, primarily, there was Lombard's Collection of *Sentences* in four volumes. The young lecturer's words show that from these early days Luther began to prefer the dynamic and personal, even biographical, approach to theology, rather than an intellectual structure, and 'summas', based essentially on a philosophical outlook, reaching back to Aristotle for their assumptions. He quickly began to feel that a philosophical approach was even a betrayal of the message of the New Testament. Aristotle earned in these margins the title 'rancid philosopher', and was often designated 'pagan' with some special force, and a betrayer too of the Augustinian tradition of his own Order. Life, far from being a settled planned matter, was a *fluxus*, a flow of events, and in those events, man met his God. At that point Luther found it easy to be what he was, an orthodox Catholic, and to point the way to the normal medieval pieties.

In a number of ways Luther's approach was a return to an older style, dating back to a time before Ockham and indeed before Thomas Aquinas, who was primarily responsible for the systematisation that made such wide use of Aristotle – although when it came to theology Aquinas also treated the non-systematic and much more personal Augustine as a – often the – primary authority after the New Testament. Luther's style of theology was deeply attuned to Augustine's; 'Beautiful, beautiful,' he wrote in the margin of Augustine's text. He preferred to do without the support of philosophy when it came to theology; here, ironically, he linked directly if superficially with his modernist nominalist teachers, who always insisted that philosophy and theology were entirely distinct disciplines and that theology was coherent within itself, based on revelation. At the deeper level, however, Luther's approach was entirely new and distinct, for his dynamic theology was in effect flowing back to cover the whole of life. So when he came to analyse the psychology of a Christian he did not like to speak in terms of the 'habit' (an Aristotelean and Thomist category) of charity, inspired by the Holy Spirit, but preferred to speak directly of the

Holy Spirit of God, working in man, immediately, not mediately. This may seem complex. But it is fundamental to any understanding of what was going on in the young don's mind. He was trying to present in intellectual fashion, in a style appropriate to the high discipline of the schools, a description of theology which was dynamic, 'divine' and, in the end, one strictly 'indescribable' on account of its nature as the working of the 'holy spirit'. As yet he was only struggling towards it. And he was tremendously conscious of the censors, and of his own wish to be strictly loyal to the Church which he understood as itself the infallible oracle. So after he had propounded in these notes, partly for his own private guidance, and partly as actual lecture material, the idea of charity being not a 'habit' but directly the 'Holy Spirit', he added: 'unless perhaps there be a decision of the Church in favour of the opposite view'. Although his own view chimed with Lombard and traditional piety, yet perhaps (he thought) the nominalists had persuaded authority to accept their categorical analysis as correct and he did not know about it. But in fact Father Luther was on safe ground. There was no such formal definition.

Many commentators have read the notes Luther wrote in these years when he was an unknown, reliable, respected young lecturer at Erfurt and tried to discern the seeds of the future reformer. The thing which really stands out is that he disliked the abstract statement, and preferred to see life as a flux, rather than as a status. From Augustine's *De Vera Religione* he dug out a reference to prime matter, which enabled him to propound a dynamic theory of the nature of all things. We live moment by moment, in a continuum, in God's presence. The second thing is the intense personal and vibrant piety; *coram deo*, in God's presence, is the note continually restruck in this unorganised array of themes, ideas and comments.

As Luther worked away, the streets of Erfurt were ceasing to be so safe. The tensions were beginning to burst into action. In 1510 the journeymen went into open revolt against the low level of their rewards, and chose the administration of the city as their target. There was rioting in the streets outside the Cloister and the University, and a local civil war broke out of a serious nature. The town was being ruined by excessive taxation, and it reflected on everybody in it. At first the students and the Cloister

were on the side of the journeymen. But eventually the mayor
was taken prisoner and beheaded, and the Augustinians took his
four-year-old son into protective custody, as a hostage in case of
the situation worsening with reprisals to be taken by the family
of the murdered man. Meanwhile, a fire started by the rioters
had burnt down some of the University buildings, including the
Old College and the Library. Eventually the revolt was put
down. No reforms were made. It was a scenario to be repeated
more widely in fifteen years' time. The friars played an important part in trying to hold a just balance between the claims of
the ill-paid and the requirements of law and order. Such trouble
had occurred before; the younger members of the community
were not involved, and went on with their daily life largely undisturbed by Erfurt's 'mad year', as it was called.

By the autumn of 1510, twenty-seven-year-old Luther was
getting into his stride. He had taught philosophy for a year at
Wittenberg, theology for a year at Erfurt. As Sententiarius he
was among the youngest in Germany. The margins of the text
books witness to a mind intensely involved with its material.
Every question was thought through afresh. In some cases this
would lead only to acceptance of the conventional line. But on
many issues there was in any case a pluralist approach: he was
free to follow any of a number of options and take the open-
ended discussion forward. The question of 'freedom' drew him.
Today, the question is posited in the context of inherited and
acquired influences, and of social psychology, asking how free
we are to take decisions, showing that we are free only within a
maybe very small area of inherited genetic data and acquired
social and psychological habits. Luther was interested rather in
the quality of free human activity, the moral category. His notes
show him moving away from Biel's (and many others') complicated scheme which, while saving God's prerogative, main-
tains that the 'natural' man has a chance of doing something
worthwhile by 'doing what is in him', back to an idea that God's
'prevenient Grace' is always available and always necessary for a
life worthy of man and God. But only to the man who believes.
Faith is the key, faith bracketed with the other two virtues,
traditionally named as 'theological', those of hope and love, the
latter also in a further sense under-girding faith. It requires a
personal act, an assent, already being solicited from within him,

for a man to reach to his spiritual destiny, to live as a godly man. There is a divinity beckoning within man's own life, promising a new freedom.

Luther's studies were becoming more exciting than ever, because he had time to start Greek, the original language of the Christian source texts and was dabbling in Hebrew the language of the Old Testament, getting to know at least the alphabet, and a few words, from Reuchlin's *Rudiments* which he already possessed. More importantly, from his long hours of recitation of the Psalms and from his growing intimate knowledge of the Old Testament, he was getting an intuitive grasp of the Hebrew mind and its language. He had a Greek dictionary, and was convinced that there was no way to penetrate the meaning of the Christian texts except by mastering the original language. In 1509 the French scholar Faber Stapulensis, or Lefèvre, had published his version of the Psalms in no fewer than five different Latin versions. Luther possibly had that in his cell already, certainly a year or two later. But already he was learning to make sharp distinctions between one humanist scholar and another. He was moved to fierce expostulations against an Alsatian priest, Jakob Wimpfeling, who had written a *Little Book on Purity* attacking the worldliness and self-indulgence of clergy, both those in the monasteries and the ordinary massing priests, and had specially attacked the Augustinians for accepting the well-known Sermon to the Eremites as written by St Augustine himself. It was normal to attack one's adversary with real animus. But there was already a special penchant for abuse in Martin. His notes say of Wimpfeling that he was an 'aged and distracted scarecrow', a 'chattering bleater and critic of the fame of the Augustinians', and had better 'recall his reason' and put some spectacles on his 'mole's eyes'. Sixteenth-century readers, used to this kind of colourful swordplay, took it as a matter of course, looking to the heart of the argument, awarding only a mark or two for any particularly appropriate and telling invective. The young Sententiarius wanted to display his ability to his close and valued humanist friends.

Luther's reputation and his career were growing. But his depressions were also growing. His obligations were no longer sufficient to distract him. At Wittenberg, Staupitz had been there to help, at least some of the time, and his advice must have tied

in with Luther's own attraction to an earlier spirituality. In the
annotations is a significant quote from St Bernard that in the
Christian life to stand still is to go backwards, the Christian must
always be moving forward. And the repeated emphasis on
humility, while traditional and genuine, has a special note of
dissatisfaction with himself. In the end, however, none of this
touched the depressions, the attacks, the temptations to despair
and the conviction of guilt. But then, again, out of the blue came
another distraction to put off the day of reckoning.

Luther was sent, under obedience, on a journey to Rome as
the companion of an older brother friar, on business to the
Procurator of the Augustinian Order. Friars always travelled in
twos for company and protection. His superiors thought of this
journey as an ideal opportunity to give more breadth to the
mind of this so promising but rather precocious theologian,
promoted too young by hasty Wittenberg.

The business of the journey was essentially an attempt to
prevent twenty-five other Saxon Augustinian friaries from
joining the group of Reformed Augustinians to which Erfurt
belonged. A great deal of heat had been generated when
Staupitz had got Rome to issue a Bull putting this juncture into
effect. And it was not in fact envisaged that a community could
be allowed to appeal against such a Bull, once issued; there had
been plenty of discussion in the preceding years. But Erfurt went
ahead anyhow. Whether Martin thought Erfurt was right in not
wanting the risk of having the reform diluted by this big new
influx of undesirables, we do not know. Excitement was all that
remained in Martin's memory in later years, the excitement of
going to the centre of Christendom, the place of the first
martyrs, and the place where special spiritual gifts could be obtained. And then there was the journey itself.

The lush north Italian countryside and the bare Alps
remained imprinted on his mind. At first he was very impressed
by the Italians as rather better at many of life's tasks than the
Germans – they seemed to get drunk less often and less obviously, they cut their clothes better, they were more polite, and
their hospitals were more efficient, cleaner and more obviously
Christian. The warmer climate and the large grapes and
pomegranates topped the picture off. From religious house to
religious house, walking twenty miles or more a day, they

covered the thousand miles or so within two months. At last in sight of Rome, Luther prostrated himself on the ground. 'Blessed art thou, Rome, Holy Rome.' Once in the city, however, lodged at the Augustinian house near the Piazza del Popolo, half an hour's walk from the Vatican, it was another story. Luther was not the first German and certainly not the last to be shocked by the city. If he had found a lot to admire in the Italian way of life, there was plenty to criticise in the Christian life-style here: casual priests, wheeling and dealing for preferment on a scale which beggared the German scene, prostitutes, a general lack of seriousness. It was only in later years that the negative aspects came to have real significance in Luther's mind. For the moment, while they impressed him, it was all discounted against Rome's great status, the Indulgences to be gained by visiting the basilicas, the sheer fact of being at the heart of Christendom, and the usual Christian tourist reaction of the time – he admired the Pantheon, its size and its symbolism, once the place of the classical gods, now a Christian church. But of Bramante, of the new building and painting and what we now call Renaissance art and architecture, nothing really impressed him.

In all his later writings in which the visit to Rome is sometimes referred to either directly or indirectly, no reference is made by Luther to the purpose of the visit. It was the responsibility of the senior brother. The records of the Augustinian Order show that the request to be allowed to appeal to the Pope against the Bull amalgamating other Saxon friaries to Erfurt and the other reformed communities, was not allowed by the Procurator General of the Order. So after what was in fact a month of wet and cold weather in Rome, when the city was certainly at its least inviting as far as climate goes, the two priests started the trek home.

Back in Erfurt, the travellers delivered their disappointing message of refusal. In the best tradition of those with everything to gain and nothing to lose by fighting, if necessary against the rules, for what they want, the friaries of Erfurt and the six other communities who had joined together to send the deputation immediately sent another two friars off to Rome, with a further objection and request. Tensions and tempers were high in the Friary at Erfurt. As the office was recited, minds revolved with angry thoughts, and determination still to resist the threatened incursion. Other minds wondered whether this was fair on their much loved Provincial Superior, Father Staupitz. Others again looked at Canon Law, or at their obligations to be humble and concluded that it was neither just nor right to resist the Bull of amalgamation any further. The latter were few, but Father Martin Luther and Father Johann Lang remained determined in their assertion of this position. The result was difficult for Martin as a still very young member of the Order. Cut off for several months from his lecture course, which was now being given by someone else, he was already in less of a central position, an ex-member of a deputation that had failed in its object, and now in a small minority on a matter of policy. Staupitz solved the difficulty very easily, and for him satisfactorily. Father Luther was soon back in Wittenberg, on the teaching staff at the Friary and at the University. Luther's move back to Wittenberg in the summer or early autumn of 1511 turned out to be both final and crucial for the whole of his future life.

Staupitz is sometimes thought of as somewhat gentle and almost easy-going; and his portrait shows a friendly face. But he had a streak of sharp determination in him. He had a further shock in store for Martin, though not quite immediately. Luther returned to the usual round of study and lecture, office and Mass and monastic rule, in the University and in the Cloister at Wittenberg. The buildings were coming on now. The libraries were improving. The movement of thought was that of a young university. About to become Dean of the Faculty of Theology in 1512, and Archdeacon of the castle church was Andreas Karlstadt, who had been promoted to the Doctorate in 1510, the year after Martin had returned to Erfurt. A year went by. In the autumn of 1512 the Order held a meeting at Cologne, to elect priors and sub-priors among other things. Father Staupitz took Father Luther in his party, and in later years Luther remembered the wine they had. When the Wittenberg Friary elections came up, the vote for sub-prior was for Luther. It was a vote of confidence in the young man and a genuine step up. Shortly after their return to Wittenberg, came the real shock.

After the main meal each day the friars would walk up and down outside in good weather, or they would gather in the calefactory, the only warm room in bad weather, taking their conventional 'recreation'. It was pleasant, to pass the time of day, to take a little rest, to hear the latest news about Cranach's painting at the castle, or the international political news, what Emperor Maximilian was doing, or even the new young King of England, or the latest church gossip. One such midday, Father Staupitz was sitting outside silently under the pear tree. At last he made Father Martin sit down and said to him that he was to arrange to take a Doctorate. Martin nearly fainted. At twenty-eight? That was something for a man of forty or more. At Erfurt they were nearer fifty. And how could he possibly add the work entailed to all his other tasks, now that he was sub-prior? 'It will kill me.' 'Ah well,' said Staupitz, 'the Lord has need of people in heaven, and if it kills you *tant pis, tant mieux*. He has great need of assistants up there.' He found it quite easy to deal with Father Luther's slightly hysterical reaction. Admittedly the suggestion was a challenge. Though Staupitz had also got Karlstadt a Wittenberg doctorate early in life, and young Father Wenceslaus Link in 1511, it was unusual for a man to aim at a doctorate so early, and after such a short and narrow experience, unless destined for high position.

The conversation with Staupitz stuck in Martin's mind for the rest of his life. Bracketed with the honour of the doctorate and the requirement to lecture on the Bible, went a requirement to preach to his brethren, his own brother friars, some twice his age, and more.

Martin soon recovered his balance. Staupitz had asked him. In the *fluxus* of life one must respond to what God sent through one's neighbour and above all through one's superior. Arrangements were set on foot. And in no time Father Luther was penning the inevitable letter of invitation to Erfurt. He knew how irritated some of them must have been by this further pro-motion. There was no point in going through a lot of apologies, and talk of humility. And by now he had in any case learnt to cut down a little on the circumlocutions. The letter, dated 22 September 1512, was addressed to: 'The reverend, venerable and godly fathers, to the Prior, the Master, and the seniors of the monastery of the Order of the Eremites of Bishop St Augustine in Erfurt, my fathers, honoured in the Lord.' Then came the word 'Jesus' set down on a new line in the middle of the page, a medieval pious custom, and one that has in fact survived into the twentieth century among some Christians but mostly among monks and nuns.

> Greeting in the Lord. Reverend, venerable and beloved fathers: Attention! St Luke's day is approaching. On that day in obedience to the fathers and the Reverend Father Vicar, I shall be solemnly graduated as a Doctor of Theology. I assume that you, my fathers, are already very well aware of this due to a letter from our Reverend Father Prior here at Wittenberg. I omit all self-accusations, and do not mention unworthiness, lest I seem to seek honour and praise by means of humility. God knows, and my conscience also knows, to what extent I am worthy and grateful for such a bestowal of glory and honour.

He asked for their prayers and to 'honour me with your presence, if it can be managed, and to take part in this my solemn "parade" (I am honest) for the sake of decorum and the honour of the Order, and especially of our district'. He continued with a carefully worded section, saying he would not 'presume to bother you with the inconveniences and expenses involved in such a journey, had the Most Reverend Father Vicar not ordered it'. He was clearly worried lest the tension between Erfurt and himself might come out in public: '. . . It would seem shameful, disgraceful and even scandalous that I should ascend to such dignity without you in Erfurt knowing of it, or being invited to it.'

On 4 October, Luther swore the usual oath of fidelity to the University and the Church of Rome. This event set everything in motion, giving the candidate the 'licence'. But a large fee was now due. The Elector came to the rescue of the Cloister and its inmates in such a matter. But the cash itself had to be handed over to the University authorities; and first had to be collected from the Elector's agent. Luther went himself to Leipzig to collect it. His receipt can still be seen: 'I, Martin, brother of the monastic order at Wittenberg, do acknowledge with this my hand on behalf of the Prior at Wittenberg that I have received from the Honourable Degenhart Pfeffinger and Johann Doltzer, chamberlains of my gracious Lord, fifty guldens, Sunday after St Francis' Day, 9 October 1512.' On 18 October was the ceremony itself, the solemn presentation of the Doctor's ring,

which Luther ever after wore and regarded as giving him a brief
that he was obliged to fulfil. There were debates after Vespers on
the evening before, and then the next morning the ceremony
itself up in All Saints, the castle church, with further oaths to
obey the dean and faculty and the Church, and then the presentation of the symbolical open Bible and the shut Bible, and the
silver ring. Then there was a sermon from the new doctor, and
after that a Disputation. Martin's two 'seconds' at this were his
Prior, Dr Wenceslaus Link, and Nikolaus Grünberg, parish
priest of Wittenberg. There were the usual medieval fringe
events, with a fool taking off the principal. Martin enjoyed it, in
spite of the sweating and the fearful anxiety of it all. He had
made it to the top quicker than anyone had ever heard of. Now
he must teach, and preach, and express what he had so far been
able only to set down in the margins of his text books, or give to
his students, or express informally to his brethren, who were not
always either interested or in agreement, though never less than
aware of his gifts. Father Luther already had many friends, and
had already been Sub-Prior for a year. Now he was Professor of
the Bible at the University. It meant much work, but many opportunities.

CHAPTER FIVE

The Reverend Don, 1512–16

There was unrest in the air at Wittenberg. It had not led to anything like the open revolt at Erfurt; the new university, financially underwritten by the Elector, brought a definite increase in prosperity to almost everyone in the town. But the Wittenbergers shared in the same sense of unease to be found everywhere. The Myth by which they lived was only half understood, only a quarter truly known. Even those who could read had not read more than a small part of the full story as it was found in the New Testament. Martin Luther himself had only handled a Bible for the first time when he entered the Friary. The castle church at Wittenberg had sixty-four priests attached to it, to celebrate the daily Requiem Masses, intended to ensure the everlasting salvation of those who had died, funded by the dead or their relatives. They stood as a kind of protective barrier between people and the power centres of society. Even in their own parish church, with sermons in German, for many people religion had the sense of the frightening 'unknown' of the old pagan myths. At Mass there was communion, but they only went to communion a few times a year, some only at Easter; and then they took only the consecrated bread.

In the past fifty years as many as eighteen separate editions of German translations of the complete Bible had been circulating, neither forbidden nor approved by Church authority, in some cases printed without a printer's name for fear of ecclesiastical reprisals. They were expensive and were not seen often, outside of universities and the houses of priests and wealthy laymen. But excerpts were common enough, the Seven Penitential Psalms, or the story of Tobias, St John's Gospel, the Book of Revelation. Travelling merchants often brought printed matter with them for sale, usually decorated with woodcuts. Sometimes they were chronicles, histories of the world, poems, romances, but the majority were religious, booklets about Saints, or on the Art of Dying, instructing one how not to despair when faced by the tally of a lifetime's sinning; one should remember the repentant sinners in the Bible. Despair was the one unforgivable final sin which might damn a person.

In church the gospel passages gave hope and reassurance: 'Come to me all you who are burdened and I will give you rest . . . My yoke is light'; 'I was thirsty and you gave me drink . . . In so far as you did this to one of the least of these my brothers you did it to me . . . Come, you whom my Father has blessed, take for your heritage the kingdom prepared for you since the foundation of the world'. But to be sure of being in this category, and not among those who heard 'Depart from me, with your curse upon you . . .', one had to be a well-paid-up member of the Elect; and there were many ways of improving one's position. Indulgences was one way, Requiem Masses another. And yet somehow these did not tie in quite harmoniously with the gospel at all points: 'He who would save his life, must lose it' – the glorious insouciance of the gospel: 'Seek ye first the kingdom of God and all these things shall be added unto you . . .'

Meanwhile, life went on, woven through with the threads of all the delights of life, the glory of love and its sexual expression, the celebration of food and drink, song and dance, sometimes to make a divine harmony of family life, blessed by a mutual charity, welcoming alike suffering and happiness on the journey to heaven. But too often the anomalies came to the fore. And the artists seemed to delight in them – terrible pictures of the devil stoking his fires with the bodies of the damned, tempted for all eternity and never satisfied by the things on which they had made themselves happy, and unhappy, in life; likewise the delineation of the crucifixion of the man-God, Jesus looking out from a realistic scene of terrible torture. The resurrection seemed to play a secondary part, or had only the function of indicating the terrors of the Last Judgement. But then again the sky would clear and they would be dancing in the streets on Easter Day, or on the feast of the Birthday of St John the Baptist, midsummer's day. It was the usual complex human picture. But

the feeling was of some instability, some underground disturbance. There was spare capacity in terms of time, energy, ability
in many people's lives. The printing presses were beginning to
provide opportunities for using it.

Luther was no more than dimly and subjectively aware of
these giant stirrings. He had never known anything else but a
society both stable and yet somehow dissatisfied. Information
from afar about the old Emperor Maximilian, 'the last of the
knights' as he was sometimes called; about the anti-clericalism
which stretched right across Europe, and of the attempts in
London by the young King Henry VIII to keep it under control;
about the pseudo-Council of Pisa, called by King Louis XII of
France, denounced by the warlike Pope Julius II, was of little
significance to him. Even the world of international biblical
scholarship only began to impinge forcefully on his world about
1514. He had more than enough to cope with in Wittenberg.
And the pressure kept building up through the years for himself
to understand, to grasp more fully, to embrace more totally that
which lay at the centre of all things, Jesus Christ, the incarnate
Son of God, who could be found again, multiform, through His
words, in the sacraments of the church, and deep in one's own
heart – and yet somehow just there was where He disappeared,
chased away by the fear of damnation, the knowledge of one's
utter failure. Depression, indeed utter despair would set in, the
terrible *Anfechtung*, which brought him alone in his cell into
absolute negation. In the end, that which he would work out in
his own inner citadel was to become the heart of his lectures and
his sermons, and that which would bring students and populace
flocking to hear him. From his suddenly grateful and relaxed
heart would pour forth a fierce stream of witness, advice,
theology, powered by the sheer intellectual validity of the
witness, and finally by its religious authenticity and coherence.
This was the achievement of the six years between 1512 and 1518.
They were also the years of a general consolidation of his life, of
further promotion, and then of the beginning of fame.

In the winter of 1512, The Reverend Doctor Martin Luther,
twenty-nine years old, Sub-Prior of the Friary at Wittenberg,
Professor of Bible in the University, had to start preparation for
his professorial lectures which would begin the following year.
He had also to start preaching to his brethren. Something like a

settled existence was at last beginning. After a year at Wittenberg, instead of being moved elsewhere, as he had been, roughly at the end of each year for the last four years, Luther had been allowed to stay. The months passed swiftly. He was a success as sub-prior, and had begun lecturing in the University at 6 a.m., twice a week on the Psalms. Early in 1515, his lecture course on The Psalms was at last drawing to a close, and another was scheduled to follow it. And now came substantial promotion within his Order. He was appointed Vicar Provincial, with responsibilities for the administrative and spiritual oversight of eleven communities across Saxony and Thuringia, including his own mother house at Erfurt. He had to make regular visits of inspection, and intervene whenever there was trouble. It was a vote of confidence from his brethren, confidence both in his practical judgement and in his high spiritual standards. It was a new burden of considerable substance.

The appointment had been made at a meeting of the Augustinians at Gotha which opened on 29 April 1515. Fr Luther preached at the gathering and gave his brethren a forceful harangue about that prime sin of the cloister, backbiting and slander. In a stream of crapulous analogies, breaking into German, he let the Fathers have it in no uncertain terms, which they apparently approved. 'The detractor, like a dog, digs up and eats a man's rotting and wormy corpse . . . He lives in manure . . . sets about plastering anyone who is clean . . . indeed uses the stuff for food.' The humanist Canon Mudt, who lived at Gotha, enquired from Johann Lang about the identity of this 'sharp preacher', and was delighted with the text Lang sent to him. Martin was thoroughly in his stride now as far as preaching went, because in the previous year he had begun to preach to the populace at the parish church of St Mary in Wittenberg, three or four minutes' walk from the Cloister. At first he had been asked to stand in when the regular preacher was ill; he was so much liked that the City Council invited him to be the regular assistant.

In the parish church, as in the University lecture halls and the Friary study rooms, the ascetic face, the evident sincerity, the sometimes almost frightening intensity of his quiet though easily audible voice, his glinting eyes, and his ability to speak to the condition of those he was addressing, won people to him. In the church he spoke in German, and enjoyed the Saxon idiom, often quoting from an Aesop fable, or from some well-known saying; always there was the quality of speaking to people's own needs, seeing into their deepest felt concerns. In an early sermon he put the high ideals before them from a text of the New Testament, quoting the words of Jesus: 'Whatever you wish that men would do to you, do so to them.' Luther commented: 'It is possible that one may think to himself: Would it be sufficient if I wish the other person well in my heart, especially if I have been injured and offended by him?' and he goes on with other excuses which people make to themselves for not going all the way in charity and answers them forthrightly, telling them the gospel means what it says. On the matter of property, he said: 'All the goods we have are from God and they are not given to us to retain and abuse, but rather to dispense.' He drew a picture from daily life: 'When a pig is slaughtered or taken hold of and other pigs see this, we see that the other pigs set up a clamour and grunting as if in compassion. Chickens and geese and all wild animals do the same thing . . . Only man, who after all is rational, does not spring to the aid of his suffering neighbour in time of need and has no pity on him.'

These sermons were a popularisation of Latin sermons he gave to the brethren in the cloister chapel and, more distantly, of the Latin lecture commentaries and expositions he gave in the University halls – though there too he would occasionally add some German phrase or word to give a particular emphasis or shade of meaning. Luther was bilingual, as many were. The use of German was no concession or mere trimming; it was a wish to use the more expressive and experienced vocabulary of the native language. He tended to turn to it when in need of vituperative words: pig-theologians or sow-theologians was a favourite description of conventional teachers who just repeated the same old lectures, snoring and grunting.

These years were a time of the deepening of friendships which remained for life. When he came back to Wittenberg Fr Martin already had a normal range of acquaintances and friends. But during these six years in Wittenberg he began to put down roots and to get specially close to colleagues and friends in the cloister and the town. Most notable was Georg Spalt, an old student acquaintance from the Erfurt days. Spalatin, as he was always called, had been ordained priest, an ordinary massing priest not a religious; he became University Librarian and Counsellor to the Elector in the year that Luther gained his doctorate. Originally he had been appointed to educate the Elector's son, Prince John Frederick, and resided at court at Torgau, about twenty miles up the river. After the appointment as University Librarian, with a good budget from the Elector, he was often at Wittenberg, working with the assistance from Manutius in Gotha who put him in touch with the great Aldus in Venice, to build up the library. He became Martin's most frequent correspondent, most reliable friend, and the crucial go-between with the Elector. Already by 1513, Spalatin was finding Luther the one really important man in the University and had begun to consult him about the University on Frederick's behalf. In that year Spalatin wrote that Dr Martin was 'an excellent man and scholar, whose judgement I value very highly' and even said, the following year, that he would like to 'become wholly his'. The confidence was reciprocated. Even when Spalatin was in Wittenberg at the castle, Luther could not always wait to see him but would dispatch a messenger up the road with a letter. The earliest chance survival of a letter from Luther in his own hand-writing was one to Spalatin in 1514, and the tone of the letter shows that Fr Martin was enjoying his life. It was about a matter of great interest and concern to all the intelligentsia in the Church in Germany during the previous year or two, the Reuchlin Affair.

Reuchlin, the great Hebrew scholar (Luther had studied his Grammar for some years) had recently led a campaign against the burning of valuable Hebrew manuscripts and against a regular anti-semitic programme of the Dominican friars at Cologne, in the name of what they saw to be doctrinal orthodoxy. The affair was destined to produce a famous book in 1515, the *Book of Obscure Men*, a satire representing the Cologne theologians as dry as dust academics, 'scholastics', busied about the most ludicrous subjects and discussing their own foolish and decadent lives. In 1514 the matter was still in its early stages. Luther's letter conveys the atmosphere, half chatty, half serious in this matter of deep concern to University men. It is addressed: 'To the most learned and highly esteemed priest in Christ, Georg Spalatin, my dearest friend. Greetings . . .' The usual

'Jesus' does not appear at the head of the letter – Luther sometimes omitted it in these relatively casual personal missives. Luther indulges in some classical punning about the asininity of a Cologne priest, Ortwin who had written a poem against Reuchlin: 'In corresponding with you, I could laugh at many details if it were not that one should rather weep over than laugh at such great depravity.' But he found comfort in the fact that the case had gone to Rome, where justice was sure to be done. 'Since Rome has the most learned people among the cardinals, Reuchlin's case will at least be considered more favourably than those jealous people of Cologne – those beginners in grammar! – would ever allow.' Fr Luther was still the provincial cleric with little idea of the human factors that could dominate procedures of the most elevated, as well as of the most humble bodies.

Two years later there was a rushed note sent up the street to the library by hand in great haste:

> To my friend George Spalatin, servant of God. Jesus. Greetings. I seek a service, dearest Spalatin, . . . Please loan me a copy of St Jerome's letters for an hour, or at least (indeed I would like this even better) copy for me as quickly as you can what the saint has written about St Bartholomew the Apostle in the little book *On Famous People*. I need it before noon, as I shall then be preaching to the people . . . Farewell, excellent Brother. From our Little monastery. Friar Martin Luther Augustinian.

That was August 1516. Three weeks later a similar missive was sent. A travelling book merchant had enquired through Spalatin whether he could have something to sell from Luther's pen: 'To the most learned George Spalatin, a priest of Christ, whom I venerate in the Lord. Jesus. Greetings. When I finally returned yesterday late in the day I found your letter, best Spalatin. Please answer Martin Mercator in my behalf that he cannot expect to have my lecture notes on The Psalms.' Luther explains that the Liberal Arts Faculty wanted the lectures to be printed by 'our printer', the University Press, and that in any case Luther will have to supervise it. This was a reference to printer Johan Grünenberg who had been in Wittenberg for some years now. 'This would please me too – if they must be published at all – primarily because they would then be printed in a rough type face. I am not impressed with publications printed in elegant type by famous printers. Usually they are trifles, worthy only of the eraser. Farewell. Written in haste from the monastery, at noon, the day after the Nativity, 1516. Friar Martin Luder, Augustinian.'

The 'Nativity' was the Feast of the Nativity of the Blessed Virgin Mary, 8 September. For a few years Fr Martin used the form 'Luder' occasionally, perhaps some kind of identity sign for him, tying him into his Saxon roots. The reference to his preference for the local printer seems to be in the same vein. He was continuing to emphasise that he was no humanist, no mere follower of *bonae litterae*. While valuing highly the scholarship of humanists, he detested the snobbish aesthetic posturing of some of them. However, within a year or two he would be complaining about the inefficiency, the sheer inaccuracy of Grünenberg, and resorting to various more modern printers.

The note of haste in the last two letters is something which began with Luther's appointment as District Vicar and virtually never again disappeared. From then on, he always had more to do than he could manage. The following month he wrote to his old friend Fr Johann Lang, who had recently been elected Prior of the Friary at Erfurt. The letter is long but extracts suggest, together with those from the two letters to Spalatin, something of the atmosphere of Luther's life as Vicar and Professor of Bible. He was writing to his old friend of the Erfurt days, with whom he had formed the pro-Staupitz minority in 1511. Now the tables were turned; they were both in positions of authority:

To the venerable Father Johann Lang, Bachelor of Theology, Prior of the Augustinians at Erfurt, my friend. Jesus. Greetings, I nearly need two copyists or secretaries. All day long I do almost nothing else than write letters; so I am sometimes unaware of whether I am forever repeating myself, but you will see. I am a preacher at the monastery, I am a reader during mealtimes, I am invited daily to preach in the city church, I have to supervise the studies of the novices, I am a vicar (and that means I am eleven times prior), I am caretaker of the fishpond at Leitzkau, I represent the people of Herzberg at the court in Torgau, I lecture on Paul, and I am assembling a commentary on the Psalms . . . I hardly have any uninterrupted time to say the 'Hours' and celebrate Mass. Beside all this there are my own struggles with the flesh, the world, and the devil. See what a lazy man I am!

Then there is a paragraph serious but sardonic, about the placing of various friars who seem to have been welcome at neither friary: 'How do you think I can house your *Sardanapales* and *Sybarites*? If you have trained them poorly then you must put up with those poorly trained people. I have enough useless friars around here – if anyone is useless to a suffering soul . . . I have become convinced that those who are no good at all are more useful than the most useful ones; therefore for the time being, keep them.' Luther manages to fend off the possible arrival of more drones at the little Wittenberg Friary – and ironically implies it will be a spiritual benefit to Lang to keep them. He says he is just starting to lecture on St Paul's lecture to the Galatians, but 'I fear the plague may not allow the course to continue. . . . Today a son of a craftsman (a neighbour living across from us) was buried; yesterday he was still healthy . . . The plague attacks quite cruelly and suddenly.' Should he leave Wittenberg? Should he disperse the friars? 'It would not be proper for me to leave until the Reverend Father orders me for the second time to leave.'

Beneath the voluble busy exterior, enormous concerns were working away in Martin's spirit. And his fellow friars knew something of what his life was costing him. On more than one occasion he took his duties so seriously, getting very badly behind with the recitation of the Office – not just a day, but weeks – that he decided to shut himself up in his cell and read the required texts over and over until he got to the end of the complete tally. So strongly did he feel the obligation imposed by Canon Law – and indeed it was an obligation felt equally strongly by many Roman Catholic priests until very recently – that he could not hold himself excused for any reason. The consecrated man felt he could not face his superiors or his God if he had not fulfilled the rules, which seemed to flow so ineluctably from the Church and its Canon Law.

Both Luther's own writings and those of others record that he made himself ill, shutting himself up with neither food nor drink, to complete the Office until it was done; one account said he was finally insensible. Luther himself, possibly exaggerating, but undoubtedly remembering a frightening experience, wrote in 1533:

> When I was a monk I was unwilling to omit any of the prayers, but when I was busy with public lecturing and writing I often accumulated my appointed prayers for a whole week, or even two or three weeks. Then I would take a Saturday off, or shut myself in for as long as three days without food or drink, until I had said the prescribed prayers. This made my head split, and as a consequence I couldn't close my eyes for five nights, lay deathly ill and went out of my senses. Soon after I had recovered and tried again to read, my head went round and round.

And it was in this period that Fr Luther had the terrible experience quoted earlier, when he felt totally annihilated. The attacks, the acute depressions, became even more acute, while the times of fulfilment also grew greater. The excitement and penetration of his lecture and sermon texts fed on these tensions and on the beginnings of light at the end of Luther's personal tunnel. He recommended the emerging solution to a fellow friar in a letter of advice, written in April 1516. 'To the godly and sincere Friar Georg Spenlein, Augustinian Eremite in the monastery at Memmingen, my dear friend in the Lord . . . I should like to know whether your soul, tired of its own righteousness, is learning to be revived by and to trust in the righteousness of Christ.' There follow five paragraphs of his new understanding of what eventually became the fully fledged doctrine of justification by faith alone. The essential elements are here in this letter – that man can gain nothing by actions intended to earn him merit. On the contrary it is only by abandoning all hope of achievement by oneself or others, throwing oneself entirely into the hands of God, and recognising oneself as a sinner like other sinners, that hope can be found. It permits a profoundly realistic and apparently cynical view of life: 'Why, then, do you imagine that you are among friends?' On the contrary, 'The rule of Christ is in the midst of His enemies, as the Psalm puts it.' There is a strong personal attachment to Jesus on the Cross – the *theologia crucis*. But it is active and communitarian: 'You will find peace only in Him and only when you

despair of yourself and your own works . . . just as He has
received you, so He has made your sins His own and has made
His righteousness yours . . . Receive your untaught and until
now misled brothers, patiently help them, make their sins yours,
and, if you have any goodness, let it be theirs.' He quotes Paul:
'Receive one another as Christ also received you to the glory of
God' and 'Have this mind among yourselves, which you have in
Christ Jesus, who, though he was in the form of God . . .
emptied himself'. Luther says he, too, was once one of those
who try 'to do good of themselves in order that they might stand
before God clothed in their own virtues and merits . . . I am still
fighting against the error without having conquered it as yet.'

In the lectures between 1512 and 1518, the growth of the
transformed doctrine can be traced. It is already partially there
half way through the first lectures on his beloved Psalms.
Sometime in this period there was a moment, or moments of
sudden insight, marking a definitive stage in the growth of this
new understanding. Luther referred to this insight as coming to
him in 'the tower room'. The precise room has never been certainly identified. At one time it was thought to be the lavatory, to
the delight of some and the dismay of others. But the matter
remains open. At any rate it was a sudden clinching of the
emerging solution of his emotional worries and intellectual
problems. There was a prolonged process going on for several
years before the final insight came.

The inner terror of Martin's life first came to a head over the
matter of confession. The 'sacrament of penance' was part of the
range of formal procedures which revolved round the Christian
religion. Men sinned – they failed whether in their relations with
each other, or with themselves; when the failure had an element
of deliberation in it, it was in some sense an attack on the
Church, on society and on the inner life of grace in a person.
Reconciliation and some righting of the wrong were needed.
The Church evolved a system by which a person confessed his
sins, expressed his sorrow and determination to do better, and
was then formally absolved by a priest. Not only lay people, but
priests, bishops and the Pope himself were human beings and
required this 'sacrament' like anyone else. Martin's trouble was
that, though he found the system made some sense, and believed

in it intellectually, it nevertheless did not seem to work. He would confess his sins, be absolved by a priest and within moments he was grumbling against God again in his thoughts, and despairing. He took Staupitz into his confidence. He simply could not get away from his obsession with his vision of the angry God, Christ looming over him, the hopelessness of the whole human situation.

Staupitz was not taken by surprise. He had often come across what seemed to him to be the scruples of young idealists who had been determined to do everything perfectly and then worried at their failure. It had been his own experience too. It was just to try to take his mind off all this that he had put the brilliant young man to getting a doctorate and preaching and giving the senior Bible lectures. He was ready for Martin and told him kindly and with authority that he must abandon the idea of God as judge and look to the 'man' who is called Christ, on the cross, contemplate Him and His wounds. He let Martin into his own secret: 'I, too, once confessed daily and daily resolved to be devout and remain devout. But every day I utterly failed. Then I decided that I could deceive God no longer; I could not have done it anyhow.' Instead he spoke of waiting on God, waiting 'for an opportune hour that God may come to me with his grace'. It was a vast relief to Martin to know that someone else, and Staupitz of all people, had had the same experience and emerged from it intact.

The next step in Staupitz's attempt to provide therapy for the young priest was again important. Repentance, he said in his simple, old-fashioned way, begins with the love of God. The subtle and sophisticated Biel had said it begins with the love of self, an intellectual cliché that left Martin struggling with the idea of trying to improve himself. Staupitz turned Luther's mind away from himself with his simple words about the love of God. A man may gaze at a highly formalised icon and gradually see through it to the world of spiritual truth which it symbolises; the 'love of God' can act as an iconic form of words able to be understood actively or passively; the genitive can be understood in either the ablative or the dative sense. Luther told Staupitz in a letter a few years later, how the simple formula that repentance begins with the love of God suddenly opened his mind:

These words stuck in me like some sharp and mighty arrow and I began from that time onward to look up what the Scriptures teach about penitence. And then, what a game began. The words came up to me on every side jostling one another and smiling in agreement so that, where before there was hardly any word in the whole of Scripture more bitter to me than *penitentia* (which I sought to feign in the presence of God – *coram Deo* – and tried to express with a fictitious and forced love), now nothing sounds sweeter or more gracious to me than *penitentia*. For thus the precepts of God become sweet to us when we understand them, not only by reading books, but in the wounds of the most sweet Saviour.

Luther continued in the same letter to show how this understanding linked in with the new understanding of the original Greek word of the gospel text, translated wrongly in the Vulgate Latin by Jerome as 'Do Penance', but correctly by Erasmus as 'change your heart'. Luther explained how he saw so well that the Greek word *metanoiete* could not possibly have meant what it conjured up to the sixteenth-century reader; the priest and the penitent. On the contrary, it meant that joyful movement of the heart which goes along with faith, forgiveness and God's love for man.

Whatever may be the correct psychological analysis of Luther's condition, it would not be too much to say that Staupitz saved him from a complete nervous breakdown. It is also true that he enabled him, through the work he gave him, to find his way to an intellectual formulation of the theology that was being hammered out in his mind. All his life Luther recognised the sovereign part Staupitz played in his life: 'If Dr Staupitz had not helped me out . . . I should have been swallowed up in hell'; 'I cannot forget or be ungrateful, for it was through you that the light of the Gospel began first to shine out of the darkness of my heart'; 'He was my very first father in this teaching, and bore me in Christ.'

The worst of the terror was exorcised, and Luther was pointed towards solutions, but the fundamental psychological tensions and the spiritual struggle were not brought to an end, nor the theological problems solved. Luther was relieved of his own terrible guilt. But though it was now of less importance, he was still failing to gain that merit towards which so much of the Church's official procedures seemed to be directed. Spiritual therapies could not bridge the gap which yawned between what the Bible text seemed to say and the implications of much of the received teaching and procedures of the Church. Staupitz himself eventually confessed that he was beaten. After he had applied all the cures he knew, and had in fact brought much relief to Luther, the patient continued to belly-ache. 'I do not understand you,' said Staupitz. 'Then,' Luther wrote later, 'I thought I was the only one who had ever experienced these "spiritual temptations" and I felt like a dead man.' In Luther were pinpointed, in one man experiencing them in the isolated intimacy of his own self-reflection, things which he found it impossible to share. He was like a dead man. His unique 'death' would eventually enable him to propound a unique solution, with exceptional force. Luther was thrown back on his own resources. If Staupitz who had helped him so much could go no further with him, then he was truly alone and had somehow to fight the battle out on his own. He returned to the Bible, to his anguish, to St Augustine, and to Christ – sufficiently relaxed by the reassurances of Staupitz not to be totally inhibited by the impasse of the man/God relationship, and finding some comfort in the Cross, in the crucified.

The eventual theological outcome was described by Luther in the last year of his life in 1545, in a Preface which he wrote at the request of Spalatin for an edition of his collected Latin works. The Introduction was primarily a piece of autobiography; early on he begged the reader to 'be mindful of the fact that I was once a monk and a most enthusiastic papist . . . I pursued the matter with all seriousness, as one, who in dread of the last day, nevertheless from the depth of my heart wanted to be saved'. Then, towards the end of the Preface he turned to the heart of the matter and the famous text from the Letter to the Romans on which he had been lecturing 1515–16:

Though I lived as a monk without reproach, I felt that I was a sinner before God with an extremely disturbed conscience. I could not believe that he was placated by my satisfaction. I did not love, indeed I hated the righteous God who punishes sinners, and secretly. At last, by the mercy of God, meditating day and night, I turned to the context of the following words: 'In it (the Gospel) the righteousness of God is revealed, as it is written, "He who through faith is righteous shall live."' There I began to understand the righteousness of God is that by which the righteous live through a gift of God, namely by faith. And this is the meaning: The righteousness of God which is revealed by the gospel, is a passive righteousness with which the merciful God justifies us by faith, as it is written, "He who through faith is righteous shall live." Here I felt that I was altogether born again and had entered paradise itself through open gates. There a totally other face of the entire Scripture showed itself to me. So then I ran through the Scriptures from memory. I found analogies in other phrases as: the work of God, that is, what God does in us; the power of God, with which he makes us strong; the wisdom of God, with which he makes us wise; the strength of God, the salvation of God, the glory of God.

And I extolled my sweetest word with a love as great as the hatred with which I had before hated the word "righteousness of God". So that place in Paul was for me truly the gate to paradise. Later I read Augustine's *The Spirit and the Letter*, where contrary to expectation I found that he, too, interpreted God's righteousness in a similar way, as the righteousness with which God clothes us when he justifies us. Although at that time this was said imperfectly and he did not explain all things concerning imputation clearly, it nevertheless was pleasing that God's righteousness with which we are justified was taught. Armed more fully with these thoughts, I began, for a second time, to interpret the Psalter.

It was a second and definitive breakthrough, a confirmation of the first psychological breakthrough when the 'Lawgiver', the dreadful super-ego had been exorcised. It was something more than a matter of being able now to sit loosely to Canon Law, to the Church's rules. Indeed, Luther continued to live with great care and integrity the life that he had avowed himself to. What it meant was that 'everything was all right', that when he failed in some way, the failure no longer meant that he was destroyed. Jesus saved him, Faith justified. To use the words of the New

Testament, his 'faith made him whole'. A change of this sort cannot destroy habits of mind, temperament, emotional tendencies, genetic and acquired behavioural patterns. The terrible depressions still came; the devil still laughed at him. But now he could find a way out, and eventually laugh back at the devil.

Semper peccator, semper justus. Man was always a sinner, but always justified – if he only turned to Christ. It was the way of *sola fides*, faith alone, which he found through *Scriptura sola*, only through the words of Scripture, and not through Canon Law or conventions. *Sola gratia*, grace alone, and not any action of man's part, enabled him to be a Christian, and to do the good works which flowed freely and strongly from a faithful Christian. This now provided the substance, the heart, of all Luther's lecturing and preaching. It provided a solution to the problem of free will and grace which had bothered theologians for centuries. It was a profoundly simple solution, and at first no one saw heresy or unorthodoxy in it. Gradually it was recognised as a transformation of current teaching.

Luther had worked out the solution in his lectures on the Letter to the Romans. His notes and commentary for the lectures show the vivid mixture of personal experience of an almost mystical kind, and the sharply intellectual solution to the theological problems. In his use of the single Latin word 'nudus', bare, is summed up what he was saying. Man can hope in God alone [*Deus nudus*]. 'He who depends on the true God has put aside all tangible things and lives by naked hope [*nuda spe vivit*].' Hope stands beside Faith and Love in the man whom God can now never desert. All fear was banished in the certainty of grace. No longer was it a matter of an assent to certain doctrines, but a simple personal act of surrender, a total trust in God known in the Word, his Son, Jesus of Nazareth.

This summary of the conclusions to which Luther gradually came, and which can be seen evolving throughout the long texts of his early lectures in the University on the Psalms, the Letter to the Romans, the Galatians, the Hebrews (1515–18) is only a summary. Luther never systematised in the abstract sense. He read the texts of the Bible, he stood before the 'Word' of God, increasingly admiring and revering it all his life, ever wishing to hear more clearly what it had to say. Thus the method he had learnt, and the great intellectual expertise he would at times deploy, was always at the service of expounding a prophecy or a teaching, whose inner meaning he was trying to penetrate. Of the images he turned to most frequently, one was the image of Jesus as the Good Samaritan in the famous New Testament parable, in which a wounded man left beside the road was ignored by representatives of the Establishment while only a despised foreigner stopped to tend him, took him to an inn and paid for his care. Jesus, said Luther, was the kind foreigner, 'the Good Samaritan' and the Church was the inn. Then again he often turned his mind and the hearts of his listeners to the yearning phrase of Jesus looking across at Jerusalem on the hill, and saying, 'Oh, how I have longed to gather thee, as a hen gathers the chicks under its wings.' He loved this domestic scene of the mother hen and her chicks. It was completely familiar. It was scriptural. 'The hen is the saviour under whose covering wings the chicks may gather together and be protected.' Here was the gentle, poetic, affirmative side of a mind which when rejecting the systems that had nearly destroyed it, and still seemed to threaten him and all men, turned to vituperation extreme. The reverse side of ultra-sensitivity was anger. Anger always lurked among his emotions. It had been expressed in those early marginal denunciations of Aristotle; it had been used against intellectual enemies, and against the spiritual backsliders denounced in the sermon that had perhaps helped to bring him promotion to Vicar Provincial at Gotha. Now, with his own base secure, Martin's critical mind turned increasingly outwards, and beyond the bounds of his immediate academic and religious world, and it would get more angry and more combative.

CHAPTER SIX

First Encounters, 1516

Staupitz had been right. Wittenberg was the making of Martin. It produced many different Luthers: the Religious Superior, the theology lecturer, the popular preacher, the spiritual guide, the University man, and Luther the man, universal friend and acquaintance and, soon now, author. In Wittenberg all his gifts gelled together into a mix which fitted what he was given to do. While his own inner life churned away, sometimes to his own utter misery, it commonly enhanced, rather than otherwise, all his numerous activities. Sometimes his exaggerated self-denigration or his compensating impetuosity could be a disadvantage, but it often proved attractive. Then he had good judgement about men, in an almost instinctive way; and along with it went rapid action and an intense sincerity born of the inner struggles.

Luther the District Vicar had to write and depose a Prior, and tell the Community to elect a new one, in a letter addressed to the Fathers and the Prior jointly at Neustadt/Oral (25 September 1516). It was not an easy thing to do. But Luther had attained a good measure of *savoir faire* by watching others at it. The opening paragraph is one of embarrassment. The community, he says, is not of one mind, or one heart or one soul, and this wretched way of living is partly the fault of the community and partly Luther's own fault (in the sense of negligence); the latter can hardly have been true since Luther had been District Vicar for such a short time. However, it was a prudent thing to say and undoubtedly Luther felt responsibility for the state of affairs. He expressed the sense of spiritual failure which was becoming his diagnosis of the human condition: 'We do not weep aloud to the Lord . . . nor pray that he make our way straight in his sight and lead us in his righteousness [a

quotation from the Psalms]. He errs, he errs, who presumes to
guide himself by his own wisdom – not to speak of guiding
others.' He makes it clear that he is not just waving a big stick –
and then asks, 'What now? Life without peace is dangerous
because it is life without Christ, and it is death rather than life.'

He soon came to the point and put the matter clearly and
finally: 'I order you, Friar Michael Dressel, to resign from your
office and surrender the seal. By the same authority I release you
from the office of prior . . . I do not want you to complain that I
have judged you without a hearing, or that I have not accepted
your defence . . . You have done as much as you had grace to do
. . .' But 'it is not enough that a man be good and pious by
himself. Peace and harmony with those around him are also
necessary.' He went on with explicit directions about the new
election, begging the friars not to go in for an, apparently
common, foolish approach to such matters by trying to elect a
friar not in fact eligible.

The word 'peace' in the letter is a key word. It was becoming
an obsessive theme in Martin's mind. The words of the Old
Testament prophet Jeremiah were forever echoing there:
'"Peace! Peace!" they say, but there is no peace' – they occur in
a long lyrical denunciatory section of semitic poetry. The word
for peace is Shalom, not just the absence of conflict, but the
blessed harmony of those who lived by God's Law, perhaps the
peace of the coming age of the Messiah. Luther seldom does
more than quote a word or two, but the Bible was his daily
reading and he knew long sections by heart simply from
frequent reading. The highly significant context from which
Luther took his thoughts about peace runs:

> For thus says Yahweh Sabaoth
> 'Be warned, Jerusalem,
> lest I should turn away from you,
> and reduce you to a desert,
> a land without people'.
> Yahweh Sabaoth says this:
> 'Glean, glean, as a vine is gleaned,
> what is left of Israel;
> like a grape-picker pass your hand again
> over the branches'.
> . . . . . .

Plainly the word of Yahweh is for them something
contemptible,
they have no taste for it.
But I am full of the wrath of Yahweh,
I am weary of holding it in.
Then pour it on the children in the streets,
and where young men gather, too.
All shall be taken: husband and wife,
the greybeard and the man weighed down with years.
. . . . . .
For all, least no less than greatest,
all are out for dishonest gain;
prophet no less than priest,
all practise fraud.
They dress my people's wound
without concern: "Peace! Peace!" they say,
but there is no peace.
They should be ashamed of their abominable deeds.
But not they! They feel no shame,
They have forgotten how to blush
And so as others fall, they too shall fall;
and they shall be thrown down when I come to
deal with them
– says Yahweh.

In his earlier letter to Michael Dressel, Luther had said to
him, in a vein similar to that of his words quoted to Friar
Spenlein: 'God . . . has placed his peace in the middle of no
peace, that is in the middle of trial' and the man who is disturbed
by nothing is not a man who has real peace (Shalom), he has only
the 'peace of the world'. On the other hand, the man who has
true peace is the man 'whom all men and all things harass and
who yet bears it quietly with joy'. Instead of saying 'Peace,
peace', where there is no peace, he says rather 'Cross, cross' and
there is no cross – for as soon as you say joyfully: 'Blessed cross,
there is no tree like you', the cross ceases to be a cross. 'Seek
peace and you will find it, but seek only to bear trials with joy as if
they were holy relics.' 'Relics' was another word Luther built up
into a whole metaphorical usage of his own. Veneration of relics
(especially of the 'True Cross' – supposedly pieces of the cross of

Jesus's crucifixion found in Israel) became suspect to him and objects of criticism by him as mere substitutes for true religion; Luther began to speak of personal 'crosses' as things to be welcomed like veritably 'true' relics.

Another letter from Luther the District Vicar earlier the same year was to his old friend Lang, just after the latter's appointment as Superior at Erfurt. Luther had been there on an official visitation and on his return to Wittenberg wrote to Lang about the Guest House. It was being used too much as a convenient hotel. Luther suggested that Lang might keep a tally of exactly how much was eaten and drunk there each day.

People were beginning to respond to Fr Luther's insights. The friars, the students, the townspeople, listened to his sermons and came to his lectures. People began asking for copies of his lectures and addresses. Printers and merchants were always on the look-out for authors who would provide them with a product they could market. They liked pious material best; they could market it not only to the numerous laity who could read, but also to the less snobbish members of the clerical and academic world. More scholarly material obviously was limited to university circles, but there were funds, public and private, to make sure of an adequate sale. Luther was able to provide the printer-publishers with both kinds of material. In the winter and spring, 1516–17 he brought out his first publication in each sphere.

His beloved Psalms provided the material for his more popular book. It was a translation, in the vigorous and accurate German he was beginning to enjoy writing, of the Seven Penitential Psalms, together with a commentary. It pleased him greatly. He sent a copy to his old mentor Staupitz, but thought it best not to send copies off to his humanist friends, who would find this an old-fashioned kind of thing to publish. A German humanist, if he must produce something in his own language, ought to look to native literary traditions. Spalatin complained that no copy had been sent to him, and Luther replied: 'The fact is, I do not want you to have them. They have not been published for refined minds but for the roughest sort.' Such thrice-chewed food was not for the humanist palate. And he had to write in similar vein to his friend Christoph Scheurl, once the Dean of Law at Wittenberg and now a leading humanist at Nuremberg, to whom Staupitz had shown the book. 'They were not put out for the Nurembergers, that is for highly sensitive and sharp-nosed souls, but for rough Saxons, the sort you know, the sort for whom Christian scholarship can never be chewed small enough.'

Martin had put something of himself into these Psalms, as he did into everything he wrote. In his Preface, he spoke of reliance on the great Reuchlin in his attempt to render the Hebrew truthfully. He was thinking much about the world into which Jesus came. In his lectures on the Letter to the Hebrews he called the Jews, 'the very Sacrament, that is, the kind Father's beloved children in Christ'. Publishing this Jewish poetry, used by Christians as prayer now for nearly fifteen hundred years, gave him both great literary pleasure and the enormous reassurance that the people to whom he preached in St Mary's Church in Wittenberg wanted it. An English translation uses many 'Saxon' (rather than 'Latin') words and gives some idea of the flavour of Luther's translation:

> For my days pass away like smoke
> and my bones burn like a furnace
> My heart is smitten like grass and withered;
> I forget to eat my bread . . .
> For I eat ashes like bread,
> and mingle my tears with my drink,
> because of thy indignation and anger;
> for thou hast taken me up and thrown me away.
> My days are like an evening shadow;
> I wither away like grass.
> But thou O Lord art enthroned for ever;
> Thy name endures to all generations.
> Thou wilt arise and have pity on Zion;
> it is the time to favour her.
>
> (from *Psalm* 102)

This came out in the spring of 1517. Into it had gone something of Luther's new theological assurance but also of a new spirituality which was to be seen in his other 'first' book, in the more scholarly sphere. Although scholarly, it was also in German, not Latin. In the autumn of 1516 he had come across the intellectual element in that seam of medieval culture usually

called 'Rhineland mysticism'. He read Tauler (d. 1361), a
member of the Order of Dominican Friars, and another book in
the same tradition called *A German Theology*. From their teaching
on the Cross, on *Verlassenheit* (abandonment of all things for
God) and *Gelassenheit* (a word indicating the result of abandonment of self to God, that is serenity or sometimes resignation),
he hammered out part of his theology of the Cross and
strengthened further his sense of inner commitment. In an
excited letter to Spalatin (on this occasion he was considered
highly suitable for a discussion of the text), dated 14 December
1516, Luther wrote: 'If reading a pure and solid theology, which
is available in German and is of a quality closest to that of the
Fathers, might please you, then get yourself the sermons of
Johann Tauler, the Dominican . . . I have seen no theological
work in Latin or German that is more sound and more in
harmony with the gospel than this . . . Taste it and see how sweet
the Lord is, [a quotation from the Psalms] after you have first
tried and realised how bitter is whatever we are'. The enclosure
was in fact the anonymous treatise *A German Theology*, which
Luther thought to be by Tauler and had just had printed in
Wittenberg, and to which he had contributed an Introduction.
It was his first printed text, offered for sale by a printer-
publisher, to the general public. These two German
publications were significant coming from a man for whom
Latin was the normal means of communication when it came to
the written word.

In the University at Wittenberg by the autumn of 1516, Luther
had become the unacknowledged leader of what amounted to a
campaign to change syllabus. The students had been voting with
their feet. Hardly any of them attended the lectures on Aristotle;
they were to be found in the biggest numbers in the lecture
hall of the Bible man. Dr Luther, however, was not as yet seen by
his colleagues as any kind of unique phenomenon, but simply as
part of the *avant garde*, one of the followers of Erasmus, Reuchlin
and others who, throughout the European universities, were
demanding new syllabuses in line with the 'new learning'.
Johann Lang, in a letter to Spalatin in March 1516 (shortly
before he was appointed to Erfurt) referring to the large
numbers of students who were dropping out of the courses on
scholastic philosophy and theology, and explaining the rebirth

of biblical studies (he used the Renaissance-type word *reviviscere*) and the new strong interest in *antiquae scriptores*, identified the phenomenon by pointing to the international influence of Reuchlin and Erasmus, 'men of great erudition and integrity'. That same month, Erasmus had published the epoch-making new version of the New Testament based on Greek manuscripts. It was printed in Greek, but also in Latin, translated for the benefit of the majority who could not read Greek; many ecclesiastics considered it almost sacrilegious to read the Bible in any version except that of Jerome's fifth-century Latin Vulgate.

On 7 September 1516, Luther gave the final lecture in his course on the Letter to the Romans. He had time now to devote to one of the most able of the students who had gathered around him, Bartholomaeus Bernhardi, a mature student, graduate of Erfurt, only four years younger than Luther. He was about to proceed later in the month to the Degree of Sententiarius. For his thesis he had taken Fr Luther's great central theme from *Romans* on the uselessness of the powers and will of man without grace. It was an exciting occasion for the young professor. He had been getting support for his idea, but by no means all the faculty had been won over and that included Archdeacon Karlstadt, DD, previously and now once again Dean of Theology. The latter was just back from an eighteen-month absence in Italy, collecting some humanist scalps, notably (notoriously easily won) Doctorates of Canon and Civil Law in Siena and some lovely Italian clothes. He allowed Fr Luther to preside at the Disputation, but made his disagreement with the thesis abundantly clear. Karlstadt had been the light of theology at Wittenberg from the earliest days and had had works published there as early as 1507 and 1508, marking out the University's first claims to a reputation. He was shocked to find this young candidate for Sententiarius being encouraged to question the scholastic method. But, once convinced of something, Luther took little account of opposition however much it upset him, and his student was given full rein to present Luther's ideas.

The date of this Disputation, 25 September, is also the date of the letter deposing Prior Michael Dressel. It was the end of the following month that Luther wrote to Johann Lang about his need of two secretaries. The small friary was beginning to fill up

with those who wanted to come and hear Luther. And he himself
already had too much to do. He was thinking about the texts of
his two books in German to be published in the coming seven
months. He was reading with a raging excitement Erasmus's
Novum Instrumentum, with its new text of the New Testament,
while preparing for his next lecture course on the Letter to the
Galatians, due to start at the end of October; and he was preparing sermons to be preached in St Mary's.

In this latter sphere he was more and more worried by the Indulgences which the parishioners were for ever running after, a
passion which reached its height each year on 1 November, All
Saints Day, when they repaired to the Elector's Museum to see
and venerate the relics, the bones, the holy wood and the rest,
and gain an Indulgence, paying for the privilege as they went in.
On 31 October, Fr Martin preached in Wittenberg on the need
for that true repentance, which does not try to evade punishment by buying an Indulgence, but on the contrary welcomes it.
He followed this in subsequent weeks with a series of sermons
warning against the abuse of prayer to the saints, and held up
many practices to ridicule – 'I am astonished that St
Bartholomew is not pictured in yellow trousers and spurs'. All
this brought a query from Spalatin as to whether Martin was not
falling into the Hussite heresy. Martin replied truthfully that he
was preaching only against abuse, not the practices themselves;
he encouraged people to pray to the saints not just for material
things, but for spiritual goods. Not much more than normal
stock-in-trade of university intellectuals, this exchange,
however, did signal the first note of alarm from a friend at the
direction of Luther's thought.

It was a matter of doctrine which had roused the query, what
might today be called ideology. Spalatin, at court, was more
conscious than Luther of lines beyond which it was advisable not
to stray: Spalatin had not worried about Luther's denunciations
of corruption in the Church, occurring in his university lectures
for more than a year now, so common were these throughout
Europe. Though the Office of the Church was sublime, it was
filled with corrupt officials, Luther had said. Pope and prelates
were arraigned for enriching themselves on the income from Indulgences, and seducing Christians from the true worship of
God; they branded people as heretics merely for opposing the

purely temporal rights of the Church. That had been in the lecture hall, not the parish church. Not long after Spalatin's enquiry, however, Luther returned to the attack in sermons in the parish church. On 24 February, at St Mary's, he said: 'People learn to fear and run away from the penalty of sins, but not the sins themselves . . . Indulgences are rightly so called, for to indulge means to permit . . . Not through Indulgences, but through gentleness and lowliness, says he [Jesus], is rest for your souls found . . . Oh the dangers of our times! Oh, you snoring priests! Oh, darkness deeper than Egyptian! How secure we are in the midst of the worst of all our evils!' Many people had attacked Indulgences, and although some had been labelled heretics, many had not. Luther was thought of only as a young man fighting for desirable reforms.

The Elector remained remarkably unmoved by the explosions from the pulpit in the parish church, even though they were implicitly an attack on his income and his great museum of relics. At the moment, in Luther's sermons, it was only a matter of emphasis; the principle of Indulgences was not attacked, only its obtrusion, and the greater importance given to it than to the life of faith through the Bible and the sacraments. But the sermons must have given the Elector some pause. Two years previously, he had had difficulty in raising the cash for rebuilding the bridge over the Elbe at Torgau; it was done by means of a local Indulgence allowing people to be dispensed from fasting during Lent – they called it the 'Butter Tax'. He had had to beg the Bishop to tell his priests to emphasise the fact that the faithful must buy the Indulgence if they wished to avail themselves of the privilege of not fasting.

Reform was the great cliché of the last hundred years. The Pope had a Council of the Church sitting at this very time, the Fifth Lateran Council, dedicated to that purpose. It had opened in 1512 with the glorious announcement that Reform had at last arrived, and a claim that the apocalyptic Third stage of Time, of Joachim, was in sight – an announcement by Giles Viterbo, Superior General of the Augustinians, Luther's own Order. *Emendatio* was the Fabian-like word used. Espousal of reform was not in itself at all a ground for suspicion of heresy. On the other hand, as in every totalitarian polity, everyone and every action was implicitly under suspicion all the time. And the moment espousal of reform became strongly linked with criticism of doctrine, and particularly of practice linked with doctrine, and very particularly if it had financial implications, it was time to beware. Only Spalatin had noticed the possible congruence.

Luther himself was entirely unaware where his thought might take him. He and his colleagues in cloister and university were Christians, loyal members of the Church, living in the ancient framework of the Christian religion, the Mass, and Divine Office; sacrament, priest and Canon Law. Elsewhere in Europe, sometimes in considerable numbers, deviants were to be found, Waldensians, Hussites, Lollards, sometimes much harassed, sometimes relatively free; then, in Bohemia, not so far away in the land of the Czechs a whole church was in permanent schism from Rome.

Luther sometimes preached against the Hussites; heresy should always be opposed. The life of the Friary, University and town experienced only a generalised sense of unease, the endemic irritation with ecclesiastical authority, common to so much of Europe. But this was always increasing. Everywhere it was liable to flare into crisis. In this year, 1516, tension in London reached extremes after the death in prison of a merchant tailor, Hunne, who had had a disagreement with the clergy about mortuary fees, was arrested by the Bishop of London, accused of heresy, and died, inexplicably, in prison. In Germany itself, among the more affluent, the growing sense of national identity was beginning to express itself in a new and stronger resentment against Rome. Aleander, the papal nuncio, reported perceptively to his Curial superior in Rome that the whole of Germany was only waiting for a leader to enable it to rise in revolt against Rome. But Wittenberg went on its way, as yet largely undisturbed except by the bubonic plague which was raging just now; two hundred students left Wittenberg temporarily late in 1516 for their homes, or to stay elsewhere for a while till the plague should move on. Johann Lang suggested to Luther that he ought to go as well. In his letter of 26 October, Luther wrote: 'You . . . advise me to escape. Where should I go to? I hope the world will not fall to pieces when Friar Martin tumbles down. Of course I shall disperse the friars across the whole countryside if the plague increases. My place is here, due to obedience.'

In that busy October of 1516, Luther was preparing his lectures on Galatians. He had before him the perfect text to enable him to grapple with the consequences in Church life of his ideas about faith. This text concerns the relation between an inherited legal structure and a new community spirit, between Law and Love, between divine threats and divine approval. The first Christians, as Jews, continued to live by the old Judaic Law, the Torah, including circumcision of all males. But was the message of Jesus for Jews only, or for all men, asked Paul? Clearly it was intended for all men; clearly it was a teaching of love in a kind of freedom; new, non-Jewish Christians need not follow the Law and be circumcised. So the Jewish Christians who wished to insist on circumcision were wrong. This was not a worry about the physical or sexual nature of circumcision. In fact, Paul played up the physical side, contrasting the ritual circumcision with the beatings he had had: 'The marks on *my* body are those of Jesus.' The point was simply that 'Christians are told by the Spirit to look to faith . . . whether you are circumcised or not makes no matter'. But Paul reckoned that 'everyone who accepts circumcision is obliged to keep the whole Law' – 'When Christ freed us he meant us to remain free'.

Luther found himself applying this by analogy to the legalism of the Church authorities on the one hand, with its Canon Law and its theological rationale for Indulgences, and, on the other, to the free life of faith as proclaimed by Paul. The Christian life was not the keeping of a Law, leading to a series of minute obligations, 'works' to obtain 'grace', but rather a service to one another, and a waiting on the Spirit, faithful to the simplicities and demands, normally beyond human capacity, of humility and love. This was the gospel of freedom in Christ, said Luther, as preached by John (the Gospel and Epistles of St John in the New Testament) and by Paul.

The theme of Romans had spoken to Luther's inner condition. The theme of Galatians spoke perfectly to his already burning sense of the evil involved in Christians treating their observances as the core of their religion. Later in his life he called this text his 'Katie von Bora', his favourite, after the name of his wife. Students jotted down their notes of what Luther was saying, interlineally on the great pages. Echoes of Tauler and of that passive sense of man in God's world can be caught in one such note: 'To know God – or rather to be known by God' – 'All our works are rather our sufferings and the works of God'. The text, to be published three years later, showed Luther reaching up to substantial heights of conviction and intellectual achievement:

> For the life of the Christian is not of himself, but of Christ living in him . . . it is to be noted that it is true that Christ is not exactly 'formed' in anybody 'personaliter', and thus the gloss is correct which says that faith in Christ or the knowledge of Christ should be taken here for Christ' . . . but beware most carefully lest this be taken as a kind of speculative knowledge, with which Christ is known as a kind of object . . . for this is dead knowledge and even the demons have this . . . but it is to be taken practically, as life, essence and experience of the example and image of Christ, that Christ may be no longer an object of our knowledge but rather we are the object of his knowledge'.

Luther was using the new text of Erasmus and finding it invaluable. But not so with Erasmus's commentary. It was superficial and missed the point, so Luther thought, sadly typical of the world of humanistic culture. He wrote to Spalatin: 'What disturbs me about Erasmus, the most learned man . . . in explaining Paul he understands the righteousness which originates in "works" or in the "law" or "our own righteousness" as referring to ceremonial observances.' In a sense, this was correct, but Erasmus had missed the point that behind the observances was the Law which led to them, underestimating the real importance of the Law. Paul was contrasting the Law with Freedom in Christ. The Law was not just a matter of observances; it comprised, for instance, the Ten Commandments and a whole range of connected morals and conventions, necessary for human society, appropriate indeed for human nature, but which man in his weakness was in fact never able to obey fully. 'Thou shalt not commit adultery. Thou shalt not kill . . .' – so often they were broken, so often, when kept, they were broken in the heart, and when kept were the cause of hypocritical spiritual pride. All that was swept away by the life in Christ, where grace enabled a man to be fully human, and often to live up to this standard, and, when he failed, to be quickly reconciled in Christ who bears men's sins. Such was Paul's dynamic theology, and Erasmus had failed, so Luther judged, to understand on the one hand the relative dignity and goodness of the Law, on its own merits, and on the other the fact that in any case to keep it was useless, and indeed largely impossible for most men without Christ: 'Fulfilment without faith in Christ, even if it creates men like Fabricius, Regulus and others (heroes of Roman history) who are wholly irreproachable in the sight of men – no more resembles righteousness than sorb apples resemble figs.'

Luther asked Spalatin to pass on his criticism to Erasmus, since he knew him. Luther did not want to tangle personally with the great scholar, seventeen years his senior, and the best known literary man in Europe; only this very year (1516), Erasmus the famous author of *Enchiridion Militis Christiani* (*Manual of the Christian Knight*, 1503) had published in addition to the Greek New Testament his edition of Jerome, and an original work commissioned for the likely future emperor, sixteen-year-old Charles Habsburg of Castile and the Netherlands, grandson of Emperor Maximilian, *Institutio Principis Christiani* (*The Education of a Christian Prince*), a plea for international peace and the encouragement of learning. But Luther wanted to alert Erasmus to the proper understanding of New Testament theology. He said the French scholar Stapulensis was also guilty – although 'a man otherwise spiritual and most sound', he 'lacks spiritual understanding in interpreting divine Scripture; yet he definitely shows so much of it in the conduct of his own life and the encouragement of others. You could call me rash for bringing such famous men under the whip of Aristarch.' However, 'I do this out of concern for theology and the salvation of the brethren.' It was this letter that ended: 'In great haste, from a corner in our monastery, 19 October 1516. Friar Martin Luder, Augustinian.'

Here Fr Martin sounded for the first time a note which will be increasingly repeated, 'from a corner in our monastery'. The Latin word is *angulum*. Luther had a real feeling of inferiority – he was after all only the son of the mine owner from Mansfeld, a

young Saxon in the reformed Augustinians. 'Our little
monastery' was another oft-repeated identification. There was
always a balancing phrase, often a reference to the fact that he
was a Doctor of Theology, and had a duty. On this occasion, he
emphasised: 'I do this out of concern for theology and the salvation of the brethren.' A man of the people, an intellectual, a man
of pastoral care, a man of determination and an ability to ignore
the fear which sent the adrenalin racing through his body so
often, was becoming someone to be reckoned with. 'Why then
do you imagine you are among friends?' he had asked the young
friar in April. He had taken the measure of life. It would always
be a battle. Friends were only human. He felt he would be
happier if he might be allowed to stay quiet in his little *angulum*,
in the Friary. But his demon would not let him. He kept seeing
gaps in everyone's case – and everyone tended to come under the
whip of his tongue, already bitter. Somewhere deep in Luther
was burning resentment. Fed by the early sense of guilt, it was
always ready to surface in angry demonstration against the in-
adequacies around him. As yet, however, he was restrained. This
was a confidential letter to Spalatin, not for the public.

Through the winter, daily life brought its unrelenting
sequences of demands on Luther. A letter from Luther to
Spalatin on 14 December provides a profile. There had been
postal difficulties: 'You were right to be worried and to tell me to
forward my mail via the Wittenberg carrier if I want to send
something to you or to Hirschfeld' – Hirschfeld was one of the
Elector's Councillors. Snow was threatening, it was cold,
Luther's habit was in need of attention and the Cloister was
short of money: 'Thank the Sovereign on my behalf for so
generously providing me with cloth . . . better quality perhaps
than is fitting for a monk's cowl were it not a sovereign's gift.'
Then there was a piece of relic business to report on. The Elector
had for a long time had his eye on the relics of the 'Eleven
Thousand Virgins' – allegedly driven from Britain in the fifth
century, and led by a chieftain's daughter Ursula to the
Netherlands, where they were killed by Huns. These relics were
in St Ursula's Convent in Cologne, and Frederick had asked
Staupitz to try to obtain them for him and the Wittenberg
Museum. Luther had the task of reporting: 'The Reverend
Father Vicar has succeeded in getting permission from the

Archbishop of Cologne to obtain the relics for the Sovereign',
but 'the Mother Superior of St Ursula's took refuge behind a
papal prohibition . . . Although a copy of the papal permission
to you to obtain the relics was shown to her, so far she has
refused to surrender them on the grounds that the copy was not
attested and sealed.' Luther asked that the Elector should either
send a properly authorised document or desist. He was acting
scrupulously as the agent of his Superior, Fr Staupitz, and made
no comment on the transaction, which was certainly a great
bore, and distasteful to him.

Then Luther turned to a remark from Spalatin's previous
letter to the effect that the Elector often referred to him, Luther,
with great respect. Luther replied, a little laboriously, and with
some embarrassment, that it is better to praise God than man.
However, he sent back a message of gratitude, though again
qualified with 'the praise of men is always vain', a pious remark
that had an energy about it rather beyond mere 'piety'. Then
Spalatin had been asking his advice about translating some
writings into German. Again the comment is laboured: 'This is
beyond my competence. Who am I to judge?' However,
Spalatin was to go ahead, by all means, if it was God's will. But
he must not expect many people would thank him for his pains.

On the intellectual front, Luther continued to be concerned
and worried about the formal presence of Aristotelean studies as
the principal basis for the University syllabus in philosophy,
with its further strong influence on theology; he began a serious
study of the question. On 8 February 1517, he sent his old
teacher, the one time Rector of Wittenberg University, now back
at Erfurt, Jodocus Trutvetter, a letter 'filled with serious
questions regarding logic, philosophy and theology . . . against
the hopeless studies which characterise our age'. Such is the
description Luther gives of it to Johann Lang in a covering letter
in which he asks Lang to pass on his letter to Trutvetter.

Luther had good arguments with which to make his case. But,
in addition behind them he put a strong emotional drive and
presented the arguments in words that were sharp even in an age
of strong speaking: 'What will they not believe who have taken
for granted everything which Aristotle, this chief of all
charlatans, insinuates and imposes on others, things which are
so absurd that not even a donkey or a stone could remain silent

about them!' The emotion was partly frustration at the sight of young men caught up in futile studies: 'Part of my cross, indeed its heaviest portion, is that I have to see friars born with the highest gifts for fine studies spending their lives and wasting their energies in such play-acting . . . All my files are filled with material against these books which I consider absolutely useless. Everyone else could see that too, if only they would not be bound by that everlasting law of silence.'

Three weeks later, Luther's mind was still full of his worries about Erasmus, running along the same lines as those in his letters to Spalatin a few months earlier. In a letter to Lang he said he was glad to see that Erasmus constantly yet learnedly exposed and condemned 'monks and priests, snoring in their deep rooted ignorance', but found him superficial; 'human things weigh with him more than divine'. The communication, however, was confidential: 'I definitely wish to keep this opinion a secret so that I do not strengthen the conspiracy of Erasmus's enemies. Perhaps the Lord will give him, in his own good time, a true understanding.' Luther's confidences to Lang and Spalatin were not betrayed, but letters easily went astray, were in fact frequently quoted, even put into print without reference to the writer. Luther regarded himself, rightly, as not of great importance and so could not see any harm in writing the letter. But his fierce avowals carried with them a certain measure of naïveté, as though the letter might have been written by someone out of touch with affairs. Possibly the idea entered Luther's own head. On this occasion, he ended the letter with a reference to the official title of his Order as one of eremites or hermits: 'From our hermitage in Wittenberg, 1 March 1517, Friar Martin Luther Augustinian Vicar.' At this time Luther ceased to use the form 'Luder', and from now on normally used 'Luther'.

Luther's work as Superior called regularly for special measures. In March he had to send a tiresome friar, Gabriel Zwilling, over to Lang at Erfurt in need of discipline. Another letter to Lang, in May, was brief, written only because there was a friar travelling from Wittenberg to Erfurt – 'I thought this father should not leave without a letter and greetings.' But the truth was that Luther was on top form again. His views were more and more being underwritten by the rest of the University and he wanted to tell Lang about it: 'No one can expect to have any students if he does not want to teach this theology, that is, lecture on the Bible or on Augustine . . . Aristotle is gradually falling from his throne.'

The clinching factor was that Dean Karlstadt had done an about-turn. Stung by the criticisms of the traditional course made by Luther and his pupil the previous autumn, he had been up to Leipzig in the winter and bought a complete set of St Augustine's works, since it was primarily on St Augustine that the case against the traditional theology had been made. All his life Karlstadt was a great 'student'. He finally found Luther's arguments convincing. He felt indeed that Luther's case needed his support, amazed to discover how cogent it was. A year later, in his rather pompous, rhetorical way he wrote that he had been quite overcome at this time: *obstupui, obmutui, succensui* – stupefied, silenced, excited, in turns. Karlstadt drew up 151 Theses of his own, opposing medieval theology and championing Augustinian theology, which in a general way was what Luther had been propounding. He presented these 151 Theses at the University in April. Luther, delighted, sent a copy to Christoph Scheurl in Nuremberg with whom he was having an intense correspondence: 'Not the paradoxes of Cicero, but of our own Karlstadt, nay rather, of Augustine . . . Blessed be God who once again bids the light shine out of darkness.' Scheurl, who had been Dean of Law in the early days at Wittenberg, had written to Luther in January formally requesting his friendship on the basis of their common admiration for Staupitz. (In Nuremberg a conversazione group had been founded, the *Sodalitas Staupitziana*.) It was one of a number of important contacts for Luther and was sealed towards the end of the summer, when Scheurl was visiting the Elector as an official envoy from Nuremberg. Luther invited Spalatin to a party and hoped he would bring Scheurl with him: 'See to it that you also get some wine for us, because as you know you will come from the castle to the monastery and not from the monastery to the castle . . . if his honour Counsellor Christoph is with you, please let him come along.'

Luther was becoming one of the leading men in the University now. It was time for a formal attack on the traditional syllabus.

CHAPTER SEVEN

Crisis

The Elector Frederick had been ruling Ernestine Saxony for thirty years. He was able to look at some substantial achievements. Government itself was more efficient. More money was coming into the fisc. An important matter here was that he confined permission for the preaching of Indulgences to those sponsored locally; he would not grant permission for papal Indulgences issued from Rome to be preached in his lands. Money did not flow out. He was able to achieve a substantial surplus in the balance of payments in and out of his territory. From this he undertook public works, roads, bridges, buildings, among which, and most notable, were the University and new buildings at the castle at Wittenberg.

The University had become his favourite project. Frederick had been right to get Staupitz in. He in his turn had attracted some brilliant people. Some had moved on, like Christoph Scheurl and Albrecht Dürer. Others had stayed, like Karlstadt; and a brilliant young painter, Lucas Cranach had stayed in his service to adorn the interior of the castle. Wittenberg was becoming an outpost of the whole *avant garde* movement. Frederick had also chosen well in his 'chaplain and librarian', Spalt, who kept him informed of all the details of what was going on at Wittenberg. For two years now he had been bringing his sovereign news about a brilliant young friar, Dr Martin Luther. Frederick's policy was to keep himself away from direct personal contact with events, but to have a very efficient information service, and a few chosen servants, to bring him news not only of everything going on in his own lands, but everywhere in Europe. On the international scene, the Emperor Maximilian was getting iller and older and would die sometime. Elector Frederick, his Deputy, though old, might succeed him.

Meanwhile, he continued with energy and care to govern his domains in Saxony and Thuringia.

He had no reason for any particular concern about a papal Indulgence being preached in 1517 in the Brandenburg territory to the north. As usual he had declined to invite the preachers into his domain. It was the Indulgence, previously referred to, which the young pluralist Archbishop of Mainz had promoted – half of all the money collected was going to his bankers, the Fugger, to whom he owed a very substantial sum on account of the fines paid by them to Rome on his behalf for his election to the Archbishopric, and for his pluralism (see p. 14). This arrangement was known or suspected by Frederick but was not public knowledge. The people knew, doubtless, that the preacher, Father Tetzel, OP, and his assistant, could draw their expenses from what was collected – they had to live after all, but assumed that the rest went towards the object for which they were told it was being collected, the erection of the great new Basilica of St Peter in Rome. In any case that was not really their concern. In return for their cash they got their Letter of Indulgence which assured them of relief from punishment after death for sins committed, for which they had repented and been to Confession. The Letter of Indulgence could alternatively be attributed to their deceased friends or relations, whom they feared might still be suffering in purgatory. When Fr Tetzel came to the town of Jüterborg in the bordering territory he was within eighteen miles of Wittenberg. Many Wittenbergers felt it was worth the walk or the ride to attend his session. They would hear the sermons, frightening and then consoling. They would see the banners, get their script, and receive solid assurance from this confidently conducted occasion.

> As soon as the coin in coffer rings
> So the soul to heaven springs

went the little jingle. And Tetzel thundered forth: 'How many mortal sins are committed in a day, how many in a week, how many in a year, how many in a whole lifetime? They are all but infinite and they have to undergo an infinite penalty in the flaming punishment of purgatory . . . yet in virtue of these confessional letters, you shall be able to gain, once in a life, full pardon of the penalties . . .' So ran one of his sample sermons.

No reputable theologian could really defend the idea that a
sincere Christian frequently committed numerous mortal sins,
but a burden of personal guilt lay heavily in the sermons of the
day, and people looked for an assurance, not just of absolution,
but of release from the punishment that they feared they had in-
curred.

Although the attendance of Wittenbergers was sufficient to
irritate Luther greatly, the relatively small loss of cash did not
make Frederick think that he should take any action. On the
argument about Indulgences as such, he had an open mind.
They were for ever being denounced – Luther was only the last in
a long line of denouncers. But Indulgences did seem to encourage devotion, and at the same time brought in so much
money both to the civil and to the ecclesiastical governments
that it was to be wondered how else such sums of money could
be found. His own magnificent collection of relics with its
attached Indulgence was one of the successes of his reign. But
Frederick did not silence the critics. Such things ought not to be
abused. He wanted his university to love the truth, both intellectually and religiously. So when Spalatin told him of the plans
that were afoot for reform of the University studies, he was not
displeased. And he was proud to have in his land a university
that might some day rival the great University of Leipzig in the
lands of his Cousin, Duke George, Albertine Saxony.

Through the months of 1517, Luther pondered on the paper
he was drawing up about University studies, and its Aristotelean
basis. He had also begun to lecture on the Letter to the Hebrews.
His lecturing style was still changing. He was moving further
away from the complicated conventional method, with its
fourfold approach to the meaning of the text. He was moving
gradually to a style that strikes a single prophetic note, a distinc-
tively personal style, which he also shared with some of the other
greatest commentators. This approach can lead to sheer
banality. But with the great men it works. Augustine was a
model. Luther could afford to break out in these lectures in this
way, his own psychological and spiritual crisis enriching the
tone: 'Oh, it is a great thing to be a Christian man, and have a
hidden life, hidden not in some cell, like the hermits, or even in
the human heart, which is an unsearchable abyss, but in the invisible God himself, and thus to live in the things of the world,

but to feed on him who never appears except in the one vehicle of the hearing of the Word.' The religious dimensions of dependence and freedom had a personal stamp on them.

This was far removed from the dry theology of the logical 'Moderns'. However, Luther was happy to use the clear and logical approach when he wished to show how unsuited the Modernist style was to an interpretation of the Gospel to religion as distinct from philosophy. He shared his working paper with a student, conveniently in need of a thesis for his next examination. On 4 September 1517, Franz Günther, graduate of Erfurt and now proceeding to the Biblical Baccalaureate, defended, in the presence of Dr Luther, now himself Dean of the Faculty of Theology, theses entitled: *Disputation against Scholastic Theology.* In assisting with the preparation of these Theses, Luther got the bit between his teeth. Aristotle, whom he had disliked for so long, he was able at last to denounce in a full-scale attack, along with modern writers, including his own one-time beloved Biel whose book on the Mass had so inspired him. The Theses thunder out: 'No syllogistic form is valid when applied to divine terms. This in opposition to the Cardinal [D'Ailly]'; 'It is not true that God can accept man without his justifying grace. This in opposition to Ockham'; 'It is dangerous to say that the law commands that an act of obeying the commandment be done in the grace of God. This in opposition to the Cardinal and Gabriel'; and so they go on, all ninety-seven of them. 'Briefly, the whole of Aristotle is to theology as darkness is to light. This in opposition to the scholastics.' Underlying the text was an impassioned certainty and a religious fire that must have begun to stir those who heard it with a little fear or a little excitement, if, like Spalatin, they had not already begun to wonder where it was all leading.

The University problems were proving entirely tractable. Spalatin was in favour of the changes. The Elector was pleased with the good intake of students being achieved, and was placing no opposition in the way of the formation of a new policy which was generally accepted now that Karlstadt had come round to it, and a formal set of Theses on the subject had been successfully defended. Luther was glad for his students and for his fellow dons and friars. But his worries about the ordinary people, the congregation at St Mary's, were increasing; it was quite another

matter to try to change their programme. Luther had regrouped
the emphases in theology so that the institutional played a much
smaller part than the communitarian and the personal. He
found more difficulty in preaching this in church than expounding it in the lecture hall. His congregation were caught up in a
tissue of observances, of which while he did not absolutely dis-
approve, and which though in theory they were an acceptable
expression of a deeply personal and communal faith, in practice
seemed to be used more like insurance policies for the life after
death. One of these observances, the Mass, he was himself
deeply committed to, since it was rooted in the New Testament
text; it was abuse of it that he opposed. But other devotional
practices, and most notably the obtaining of Indulgences,
seemed to have nothing, in principle, to do with the gospel.
Every week in choir (or reciting to himself in his cell), Luther
came on the verse in the Psalms – 'I want no holocausts but the
sacrifice of a broken heart.' The repentant heart was what he had
asked for in his sermons for the last year. The Indulgence sellers
traded on people's sense of guilt and offered them spurious ways
of dissipating it. It is true, he thought, they helped to reassure
nervous souls. Perhaps they were better than nothing; to some
extent maybe they encouraged people to turn away from evil
doing. But they were second or third best, and a whole dimension away from that 'repentance', that 'change of heart' which
the gospel asked for. They encouraged a kind of bogus
dependence which outlawed the very freedom it should have
promoted.

It was second nature to Luther to begin to write down his
thoughts, so he started on a Treatise on Indulgences which led in
turn to a new set of Theses for debate. Yet another file took its
place on his desk, cluttered with reports from the Augustinian
friaries, sermons, Wittenberg Friary matters, University reform
plans, letters from the humanist wing in Nuremberg, and much
else. He set the propositions down in short, dense, dialectical
sentences, sometimes theological, sometimes practical, sometimes hortatory.

The opening words ring out sharply:

When our Lord and Master Jesus Christ said, 'Repent', he
willed the entire life of believers to be one of repentance.

This word cannot be understood as referring to the sacrament of penance, that is, confession and satisfaction, as administered by the clergy.

Yet it does not mean solely inner repentance; such inner repentance is worthless unless it produces various outward mortifications of the flesh.

This was dialectic with a practical edge. The Theses roll ineluctably on, powered by a fundamentally spiritual but also practical understanding of man, an understanding which Luther had learnt in the first place from his parents, his schools and University and his fellow friars; and in preaching which he shared with many other preachers and most notably his 'father-in-God', Fr Staupitz. Most of the Theses are single sentences like the first three above.

After a series of distinctions, and theologically unexceptionable expositions of the limitations of Indulgences, put, however, in the same dialectical and somewhat provocative form, Luther moves into a more affirmative and prophetic tone:

'Christians are to be taught . . .', *Christiani docendi*, rings out nine times. He has gone beyond argumentation – although in fact the Thesis form makes it clear that these demanding sentences are still intended as something to be debated. 'Christians are to be taught that the Pope does not intend that the buying of Indulgences should in any way be compared with works of mercy. Christians are to be taught that he who gives to the poor or lends to the needy does a better deed than he who buys Indulgences. Christians are to be taught . . .' They must support their families and not squander money on Indulgences, and the Pope should wish to sell the basilica of St Peter so that he can give alms to many of those whose money is wheedled out of them by Indulgence sellers – to build the Pope's basilica.

Then the Theses become very spirited and specific: 'To say that the cross emblazoned with the papal coat of arms, and set up by the Indulgence preachers, is equal in worth to the cross of Christ, is blasphemy.' The Theses wind up with Luther's favourite finale from the prophet Jeremiah: 'Away then with all those prophets who say to the people of Christ, "Peace, peace", and there is no peace. Blessed be all those prophets who say to the people of Christ, "Cross, Cross", and then there is no cross.

Christians should be exhorted to be diligent in following Christ, their head, through penalties, death and hell; and thus be confident of entering into heaven through many tribulations rather than through the false security of peace.'

Luther was not the first to be aroused by the anomaly of Indulgences. It was precisely the preaching of an Indulgence in Bohemia, in 1412 (an Indulgence issued by the pseudo-Pope John XXIII to raise money for a war he was fighting against Naples), that had encouraged Reverend Father John Hus to believe he must persevere in his reform movement. In a Swiss valley in 1517 another Catholic priest was agonising about the pilgrimages, relics and Indulgences which brought so much business and so much worldliness and apparent abuse of the Gospel, to the Benedictine monastery of Einsiedeln where he ministered. That was Ulrich Zwingli – who knew nothing of young Dr Luther. For more than a hundred years, European literature had been full of irony and sarcasm at the expense of the easy money ecclesiastic. Chaucer's 'Pardoner', whose relics turned out to be chicken bones, pre-dated Luther by nearly a hundred and fifty years. In early fourteenth-century Montaillou in south-west France, Indulgences had been thought of as a racket.

To try to tackle Indulgences was to start to tamper with the whole ecclesiastical economic structure, held together by financial, political and psychological ties. It needed some courage and some naïveté to set about cutting them: courage because to cut some of them was defined, ultimately, as treason; naïveté because many people had attempted the job before and had failed. In this circumstance, not to know too much about the whole interlocking scene was a help. Today's historian knows more about it than anyone living at the time; Luther in particular was working from a very limited standpoint. He did not see himself as another Hus, another Savonarola, even less as a prophet come to turn the whole Church upside down. He was simply trying, out at Wittenberg, to get to the root of Christian theology and then to live by it, and encourage others to do so. While he was often very nervous, he seemed to be largely devoid of that paralysing fear which sometimes attacks people once they see the full dimensions of what they are attempting to change. Not fear, but anger was the emotion that attacked him when he was shown the Instruction being distributed to the preachers (Fr Tetzel, notably) of the new Indulgence being offered in Jüter-borg about twenty miles away, over the border in Albertine Saxony. Its authoritarian way of dealing out spiritual riches was the last straw; the phrases were all well known to Luther, but their formulation for the sub-commissioners of the Indulgence, in this *Instructio Summaria* seemed to him to reach a height of spiritual presumption and contradiction of the New Testament that he could stomach no longer: subscribers would receive plenary and perfect remission of all their sins; they would be relieved of all the pains of purgatory; Indulgences obtained on behalf of those who had died did not require confession of one's sins as Indulgences for oneself did. It was all presented with the absolute assurance that man could dispose of the goods of God, and that man's authority reached into the ultimate domains of the Almighty. Conditions were attached indeed, that the In-dulgence seeker should go to Confession. But this was no way to handle spiritual responsibilities.

The man immediately responsible locally was young Albrecht, the Archbishop of Mainz. It flashed into Luther's mind that the time had come when he should write a formal protest to him; and he would have his new Treatise on In-dulgences and the set of Theses copied out, and send them too. They had been growing on his desk during the last two months. It was 'Indulgence time' again, with All Saints Day coming up; on 1 November a dozen or more priests would be hearing con-fessions in the castle church. It was on 31 October that Luther sent a letter to the Archbishop. It was a typically 'Lutheran' letter, starting with an exaggerated self-abasement but even-tually reaching what was practically a studied denunciation of him.

> To the Most Reverend Father in Christ, the Most illustrious Lord, your Honour Albrecht, archbishop of the churches of Magdeburg and Mainz, primate, margrave of Brandenburg, etc., my lord and shepherd in Christ, esteemed in respect and love
>
> ### Jesus
>
> Grace and mercy from God, and my complete devotion Most Reverend Father in Christ, Most Illustrious Sovereign:

Forgive me that I, the least of all men, have the temerity to
consider writing to Your Highness. The lord Jesus is my
witness that I have long hesitated doing this . . .

The letter contained in discursive prose form the heart of
what was in the Theses, and what was at greater length and far
more moderately in the Treatise. Luther played the conventional line that of course the Archbishop himself did not know
what was being done in his name. 'Under your most distinguished name, papal Indulgences are offered all across the
land for the construction of St Peter's.' He starts in immediately
on the theological abuse: 'The poor people believe that when
they have bought Indulgence Letters they are then assured of
their salvation.' After elaborating on the detail of this, Luther
burst forth in a manner hardly consonant with the opening self-
abasement: 'Oh great God! The souls committed to your care,
excellent Father, are thus directed to death. For all these souls
you have the heaviest and a constantly increasing responsibility
. . . No man can be assured of his salvation by an episcopal
function.'

Luther then came to what really concerned him, the failure of
the Church to present the Gospel and this led him to warn the
Bishop with some severity of his own spiritual predicament: 'The
first and only duty of the bishops, however, is to see that the
people learn the Gospel and love of Christ. For on no occasion
has Christ ordered that Indulgences should be preached, but he
forcefully commanded the Gospel to be preached. What a
horror, what a danger for a bishop to permit the loud noise of
Indulgences among his people while the Gospel is silenced.' The
words 'Gospel is silenced' was a reference to the prohibition put
on all other sermons when an Indulgence was being preached,
in order to encourage maximum participation in it.

Then Luther refers to the *Instruction* which had so outraged
him: 'Published under your Highness's name, . . . certainly
without your full awareness and consent . . . What can I do,
excellent Bishop and Most Illustrious Sovereign? I can only beg
you, Most Reverend Father, through the Lord Jesus Christ, to
deign to give this matter your fatherly attention and totally
withdraw that little brief and command the preachers of Indulgences to preach in another way.' The letter virtually

becomes a threat at this point. Something must be allowed for a convention of a considerably greater freedom of speech between subjects and sovereigns, within a formal structure of great obeisance, than one would expect today. And it is to be remembered that Luther was in fact the Archbishop's senior by a decade. Even so, the phrases must surprise. The writer has leapt from his *angulum*, and is behaving as the Old Testament prophets behaved when denouncing the evils of their times, though here in the quiet and clear, practical sentences of western man: 'If this is not done, someone may rise, and, by means of publications, silence those preachers and refute the little book. This would be the greatest disgrace for your Most Illustrious Highness. I certainly shudder at this possibility, yet I am afraid it will happen if things are not quickly remedied.'

This was an accurate forecast of what was to happen apart from the 'disgrace' (if political or ecclesiastical disgrace was meant) of the Archbishop. Luther had no specific plan to be himself the one destined to fulfil the prophecy. But, like the papal nuncio Aleander, he understood the widespread disillusion and could imagine the events which had inevitably to follow. And he had a sharp eye for practicalities; it was the pamphlets, the *Flugschriften*, the 'flying writings' that would play the crucial role.

> I beg Your Most Illustrious Grace to accept the faithful service of my humble self in a princely and episcopal – that is in the most kind – way, just as I am rendering it with a most honest heart, and in absolute loyalty to you, Most Reverend Father. For I too am a part of your flock. May the Lord Jesus protect you, Most Reverend Father, forever. Amen.
>
> *From Wittenberg, 31 October 1517.* Were it agreeable to you, Most Reverend Father, you could examine my disputation theses, so that you may see how dubious is this belief concerning Indulgences, which these preachers propagate as if it was the surest thing in the whole world. Your unworthy son, Martin Luther, Augustinian, called Doctor of Theology.

Like the young Henry VIII, Albrecht considered himself a sincere Christian, with a sense of responsibility for his people, and above all he was proud of his intellectual ability, of his acquaintance with the followers of good letters, very pleased to think that he knew Erasmus. He would be polite, considerate, circumspect. He had been brought up at court. Diplomacy was all – in a world of which, however, the distinctive thing was that he ruled it. He had not previously received anything like the missive which reached him in November from the University professor at Wittenberg, just coming up to his thirty-fourth year. He soon saw that it needed attention on various levels: pastoral (which covered financial), theological (which included legal) and disciplinary. Luther had asked for action to be taken about the inflated claims of the Indulgence preachers. That was easily attended to, and it certainly needed to be done for financial reasons – the last thing Albrecht wanted was for the preachers to provoke a reaction which would reduce his takings and upset his arrangements with the Fugger and the Roman Curia. The matter was referred for pastoral attention to the Council of those North German churches which came under the Archbishop's jurisdiction, and to the local Bishop of Brandenburg. Then the letter and theses were sent to the University of Mainz for the theologians and lawyers (most dangerous of combinations) to look at – these questions of theology were not Albrecht's forte. Finally the important disciplinary matter: that was easily settled, upwards to Rome; the method was to send the letter, treatise and theses to Rome and request an inhibitory process, to send also Luther's previous scholastic theology theses and mention 'new doctrines'. The matter was soon off the Archbishop's desk. The 'impudent monk', as the documents call him, was quickly dealt with. Little more happened. The University reported it was a matter for the Pope. The Council which looked after Albrecht's various diocesan responsibilities sat tight, wishing not to offend other rulers, or anyone.

Luther had himself already sent a second copy of the Theses to his own local Bishop, Dr Schulz of Brandenburg. He delayed some days before showing one to anyone else, saying later that he wanted to avoid all possibility of involving the Elector in responsibility for his criticisms of the young Archbishop, whose elder brother in Brandenburg was another of the imperial electors.*

Seven days after dispatching the letters to Mainz and Brandenburg, Luther was in a depressed state. The inevitable

---

* Probably Luther did not nail the Theses on the door of the castle church.

silence was irking him, and three small things all connected with the Elector were also irritating him. He sent a note to Frederick marked 'Personal', and with the minimum of formal address. Luther's thanks of a year previously for cloth for a new cowl had been premature; he tells the Elector he is still waiting for it; the Saxon treasurer Pfeffinger is 'very good at spinning a mighty good yarn; but these do not produce good cloth'. The second matter is that the Elector was apparently annoyed with Staupitz over something and Luther feels bound to try to put matters right: 'I plead on his behalf . . . that Your Grace continue to favour and be loyal to him . . . just as Your Grace has undoubtedly experienced his loyalty many times.' Luther has not finished with the Elector but moves on to give advice about taxes – not to increase them; and he has the humour which might be thought impertinent to suggest that this gratuitous advice 'may earn my courtly cowl'. It was a further tax on drink that the Elector was planning. 'Even the last taxation has reduced your Grace's reputation.' The letter is soon ended, signed 'Your Grace's dedicated priest, Doctor Martin Luder at Wittenberg', after a further apology and a suggestion that maybe 'even great wisdom' might sometimes need to 'be guided by the lesser'. The Saxon vernacular form 'Luder' went appropriately with this personal note in German.

Frederick, swarthy, pragmatic, of vast experience, known as 'the Wise', was practically unflappable, and knew all about young dons liable to get themselves involved in politics. His reaction to the letter was covered in the usual silence.

Meanwhile, at the University on 11 November, Luther sent a copy of the new Theses to his closest friend, Johann Lang, still Prior at Erfurt. He also gave copies to friends at the Priory and University. But no formal steps were taken to set up a place and time for a formal defence of the Theses; instead of that, Luther added a note at the beginning, saying that the Theses were to be 'publicly discussed', inviting anyone who liked to do so to send him their views. Reactions from his friends were immediate and strong, favourable and unfavourable.

The Prior and Sub-Prior of the Friary were worried that Luther would bring some disgrace on the Order. Dr Schurf of the University Law Faculty was equally worried when Luther visited him at his home at Kemburg eight miles from

Wittenberg; he warned Luther that he had better not attack the
Pope. They all seemed to realise that the Theses had hit the nail
on the head, decisively. Canon Ulrich von Dinstedt at the castle
church sent a copy to Christoph Scheurl at Nuremberg – Luther
had deliberately avoided sending copies to him, or to Spalatin at
court since he was not out for publicity. When Spalatin protested at not having received a copy, Luther wrote to him saying
that he did not want the Elector to see the Theses until those
whom Luther had criticised had received copies. On receiving
his copy, Scheurl acted immediately and got the Theses printed
and translated into German. Within weeks, copies were flying
about Europe; compliments began to reach Luther from a wide
constituency. Albrecht Dürer, resident in Nuremberg, sent
Luther a set of prints of woodcuts, as thanks for expressing what
everyone wanted said. One of the printers added numbers to the
Theses and from then on they became the famous '95 Theses of
Martin Luther'.

From Nuremberg, on 5 January, Scheurl acknowledged the
Theses to Canon von Dinstedt: 'I am most grateful to have
received Martin's theses. Friends here have translated them and
we think highly of them.' Three days later he wrote to an
Augustinian friar in Eisleben: 'I am gradually ensuring for Dr
M. Luther the friendship of illustrious men. Pirkheimer, A.
Tucher and Wenzeslaus are amazed and delighted with his
Theses. C. Nutzel translated them into German, and I sent them
on to Augsburg and Ingolstadt.' By this time editions were also
appearing in Magdeburg, Leipzig and Basle. In the latter town
was Erasmus's printer Froben, who began collecting Luther's
texts with a view to an edition of his writings. Erasmus sent Sir
Thomas More a copy of the theses on 5 March. On the same day,
Luther sent a letter to Christoph Scheurl who had written complaining that Luther had not seen fit to send him a copy direct;
with his letter, Scheurl sent copies of the Theses reprinted in
Latin and German. Luther replied:

> You are surprised that I did not send them to you. But I did
> not want to circulate them widely. I only intended to submit
> them to a few close friends for discussion, and if they disap-
> proved of the Theses, to suppress them. I wanted to publish
> them, only if they met with approval. But now they are being

printed and spread everywhere far beyond my expectation, a result that I regret. It is not that I am against telling the people the truth, in fact that is all that I want, but this is not the proper way to instruct the people. For I have doubts about some of the Theses, and others I would have put much differently and more cogently, and some I would have omitted, had I known what was to come. Still, the spread of my Theses shows what people everywhere really think of Indulgences, although they conceal their thoughts 'out of fear of the Jews.' Therefore, I had to write out proofs for my Theses, but I do not yet have permission to publish these.

'For fear of the Jews' was a phrase from the New Testament, describing the fear which the first followers of Jesus had for the Jewish authorities. Luther was categorising the Church authorities as equivalent to the chief priests and heads of the Jewish groups who persecuted the first Christians; the rest of the Church, he suggested, priests and people, was afraid to face the truth for fear of the higher authorities. The 'proofs' to which he refers was a large seventy-thousand-word document he had worked on through January and early February, when he realised that the Theses had gone abroad and would need some more thorough, and carefully and quietly argued defence than was contained within their own sharp and sometimes paradoxical sentences.

The reaction of the preacher Fr Tetzel, a friar priest of the Dominican Order, to the Theses, which were in his hands before the turn of the year, was to turn the whole thing into a legal dogfight; he took the battle into the enemy's country and denounced the author to Rome. At the Dominican Friary at Frankfort-am-Oder on 15 January, counter-theses drawn up by Dr Konrad Koch (or Wimpina as he was sometimes called) were defended by Fr Tetzel and a formal denunciation of Luther as a heretic was sent off to the powerful Cardinal protector of the Dominicans, Thomas de Vio, better known as Cajetan. Tetzel boasted that Luther would be in the flames within three weeks. The counter-theses upset Luther more than anything had done previously. In an argument which was becoming public, he was being offered a virtually magical doctrine, a sort of *droit de papauté* extending autocratically into life after death, and all of it

backed with the threat of public violence, the violence of death
by fire. His own *Explanations* were the more necessary and soon
his desk was littered with page after page of Latin.

The argument was careful, assured, and impeccably laid out
to keep it within orthodox bounds. It was prefaced by a statement insisting on his loyalty to Rome and making the common
and theologically proper distinction between, on the one hand,
Scripture and its interpretation in canonical statements from
Rome and, on the other, the opinions, however venerable, of
Aquinas and other Fathers of the Church. But while it was not
doctrinally incorrect to do it, he continued dangerously to
flaunt his independent attitude in regard to the papacy: 'It
makes no difference to me what pleases or displeases the Pope.
He is a human being like the rest of us.' It was only when the
Pope spoke in accordance with the Canons and with a General
Council that he was to be listened to as the Pope. This was a
commonly received opinion; six years later Sir Thomas More
was advising Henry VIII not to defend the papacy as though it
was of divine origin, when Henry wrote his reply to Luther, the
reply which earned him the papal title 'Defender of the Faith'
still used by English sovereigns. Finally, Luther makes all clear,
summing up in masterly fashion at the end of the *Explanations*
what was in so many minds throughout Europe: there must be a
Reformation, and please God it should come from a general
consensus: 'The Church needs a reformation which is not the
work of one man, namely the Pope, nor of many men, namely
the cardinals [such as the recent 5th Lateran Council], . . . but
the work of the whole world, indeed . . . the work of God alone.
However, only God who has created time knows the time for
this reformation' – the sense of history *sub specie aeternatitatis*
breaks in. These remarks are part of the comment on Theses 89
and 90. After that, he had said all he had to say. Leaving Theses
92, 93, 94 and 95 with their famous finale from Jeremiah, un-
commented, Luther packed the whole thing up and sent it to his
Bishop at Brandenburg. It was about the middle of February.

Meanwhile, Luther's correspondence with Spalatin shows life
going on much as before, with University reforms proceeding
and much thought devoted to the proper basis for understanding the Christian Gospel. The Indulgence controversy did not
occupy Luther's mind to the exclusion of other things – it was

not mentioned in a letter to Spalatin of 18 January. Luther was worried by both the enthusiasm for, and the opposition to, the Theses, but he had experienced these things before and had found his own view eventually triumphing. The theological business of explaining his Theses was really less important than the underlying truth, concern for which still occupied the exchanges with his dear friend and confidant, the key man, standing outside University and Religious Order; and, as yet, Luther was still really reluctant to believe that the academic Theses, enigmatic, and dialectical, could stir opinion widely.

It was rewarding to sit down and write to his friend in his accustomed fashion: 'To my honest friend Georg Spalatin, truly a disciple of Christ and a brother. Jesus. Greetings, excellent Spalatin: You have previously asked me questions that were within my power – or at least my temerity – to answer.' Spalatin had asked about the best way of studying Scripture. Before replying to that, Luther had to clear his mind once again of the extreme embarrassment of disagreeing with Erasmus, but at the same time not to underplay the disagreement; he still thinks Erasmus thoroughly misguided, if superior to most people: 'In the face of all who either passionately hate or lazily neglect good learning . . . I always give Erasmus the highest praise and defend him as much as I can; I am very careful not to air my disagreements with him less by chance I too would confirm such people in their hatred of him. Yet, if I have to speak as a theologian rather than as a philologian, there are many things in Erasmus which seem to me to be completely incongruous with a knowledge of Christ.' But that is confidential, Luther added in another five sentences. Then he comes to his own reply to Spalatin's question:

> It is absolutely certain that one cannot enter into the meaning of Scripture by study or innate intelligence. Therefore your first task is to begin with prayer. You must ask that the Lord in his great mercy grant you a true understanding of his words . . . You must therefore completely despair of your own diligence and intelligence and rely solely on the infusion of the spirit. Believe me, for I have had experience in this matter.

Erasmus would no doubt have agreed that Scripture had to be approached with prayer and humility. Yet the difference lay here

– and Luther made it the very heart of his approach: 'prayer' and 'humility' become a matter of self-despair, part of a complete existential complex, an early version perhaps of the special German *Angst*. For Erasmus, 'prayer' and 'humility' would be understood as though said in limpid classical Latin, the only proper approach to Scripture indeed, but not the crucial key to it, and certainly not voiced with Luther's succession of superlatives.

Luther continued his instructions: having 'achieved this despairing humility, read the Bible in order from beginning to end, so that first you get the simple story in your mind'. At this point, one should remember that the Bible contains little less than two million words, and that 'simple story' is a magnificent understatement of a description of the enormously varied history, poetry, law, prophecy and counsel. The advice rolls on with a reading list, a work of Karlstadt's being strongly recommended. Then Luther is smitten with embarrassment again – 'Forgive my temerity that in such a difficult subject I dare set forth my ideas over and above those of such famous men.' Finally there was a word of obviously genuine sorrow that Erasmus was engaged in a quarrel with the scholar Lefèvre d'Etaples, with the usual complicated mixture of judgements: 'Erasmus is certainly by far the superior of the two, and he is a great master of language. However, he is also more violent, though he makes great effort to preserve friendship.' Luther had not yet begun to display to the public in writing the extreme violence and anger of his own spirit. So far, his sermons of denunciation were only common form, whereas in his *In Praise of Folly* (1511) Erasmus had given public vent to a violent sarcasm, which some people had found offensive, denouncing the warlike Pope Julius II and referring in his correspondence to 'the monopoly of the Roman High Priest'.

In February, after getting to the end of his *Explanations*, destined to be published later in the year, his first full-length work to be put into print, Luther was discussing Greek vocabulary in a letter to Lang, and was also in correspondence with Wolfgang Capito, a rising young priest in Basle working part-time for Froben, looking forward to reading the *Utopia* of More and Erasmus's reply to Lefèvre. Then he received a query from Spalatin who was getting increasingly worried, asking for a further briefing on the development of theology at the University. Karlstadt received a similar letter from Spalatin, and referred Spalatin to two forthcoming books, one by Karlstadt himself, another his editing of an Augustine text; and he took the opportunity to suggest that the Elector might manage a contribution of thirty florins for the cost of paper for the books he was about to produce. Luther's reply, providing further theological detail, showed that he realised the seriousness with which he might have to take the controversy – subvention he never requested. He regretted the rumour that the Theses had been written under incitement from the Elector, as a political act, a shot against the Archbishop of Mainz. For the first time the possibility of canonical action was hinted at – Luther said he was willing to appear at a juridical investigation. However, a few days later, on 22 February, a further letter to Spalatin started with only a few words about the Theses, explaining that what Luther really regretted was not that his enemies were 'speaking badly of me or that they stamp the Elector as the author of my Theses', but that hostility might be created 'between our great rulers'. The rest of the letter concerned Luther's further representations to Trutvetter whom he was still trying to convert – the University reforms were still the things that really mattered. Luther signed the letter 'Eleutherius', the Greek version of his name which he had been using for a few months. He had come to feel accepted within the whole humanist circle and signified his sense of solidarity in this way. However, it was not long before he reverted permanently to plain 'Luther'. His own special identity was being hammered out in the exchanges of these months, exchanges of an increasing intensity, on an increasing variety of levels.

Waiting for a reply from the Bishop of Brandenburg, to his request to be allowed to publish his substantial *Explanations*, Luther was overcome with frustration. All around him people were agitating pro and contra his Theses, which he had in any case only intended as exploratory and as a weapon to try to force the Archbishop of Mainz to tame the preachers of Indulgences. In the middle of the growing controversy it was intolerable to remain silent. Luther wrote out in German what he called a Sermon on Indulgence and Grace, a straightforward account for ordinary people of his own opinions. This meant taking a

further step into the open – his personal view was that Indulgences were simply permitted for the sake of imperfect
Christians; as far as he was concerned, 'no one should buy Indulgences'. And he did not believe that they could free souls
from purgatory. If people accused him of heresy, well, 'I pay
little attention to that kind of chatter, for no one does that but a
few blockheads who never smelled the Bible or read a word of
Christian doctrine'. He sent the text down to Grünenberg in the
printing shop, who sold copies to the travelling merchants.
Luther was using the public press for the first time to speak
directly, in German, to everyone interested; and that was almost
everyone. This brought the Bishop swiftly into play. Luther felt
things had begun to move at last when, early in March, the
Abbot of Lehnin, a Benedictine abbey in the Diocese, was announced at the Friary. He had come to see Fr Martin on behalf
of the Bishop. The message he brought was a polite request from
the Bishop not to publish anything more on the topic for the
moment, and for the moment not to publish the *Explanations*
either. The Abbot assured him that the Bishop was sympathetic
to Luther's concerns, but did not want to inflame public opinion
any further. He would be in touch again. This was much better
than the total silence from the Archbishop of Mainz.

Life went on as before, the lectures on the Letter to the
Hebrews, work with Karlstadt and others on plans for the
syllabus reform, and sermons in the parish church. Two
sermons from mid-Lent, the time of preparation for Easter,
have survived, and give an idea of the Luther whom the
Wittenbergers encountered, a man like them, sincere and to the
point. His words were rooted in the words of the New
Testament:

> You well know, dear friends, that I understand little about
> preaching, and so shall preach a foolish sermon; for I am a
> fool and thank God for it . . . Let every man, if he has a
> blessing or gift from God, learn to divest himself of it, shun it,
> give it up . . . Your attitude should be like that of Christ, who
> did not exalt himself and utterly lowered himself, and took on
> the form of a servant . . . Christ pays no attention to the dis-
> tinctions we make, for he bestows children and honour upon

an old unattractive woman just as readily as upon a beautiful woman.

There is here a first suggestion of the Lutheran twinkle in the eye, which later became such a typical part of his down-to-earth spirituality.

As the sermon went on, like so many Lutheran texts, it became more biting. It was acceptable, he said, to venerate relics, 'to encase the bones of saints in silver', yet 'it is the inward relic we must seek . . . for what Jesus sends to his devout children is not the wood, stone or clothing which he touched but rather the suffering, the cross'. Then, suddenly, he broke out against the bishops: 'They are unwilling to accept their "relic" of "suffering" when they get criticised! They flee from this relic. If you speak plainly to them they would rather tear the whole place down than give in; they start the game of excommunication and the banning letters begin to fly about like bats. They say it is their duty to defend the patrimony of Christ and St Peter. Oh, you poor Christ, Oh, you wretched Peter! If you have no inheritance but wood and stone and silver and gold, you are of all people the most needy.'

This was sharp criticism for a public sermon in a parish church. Luther drove his point home with quotations from the great Old Testament prophet, Isaiah:

> What house could you build me,
> What place could you make for my rest?
> All of this was made by my hand
> and all of this is mine – it is Yahweh who speaks.
> But my eyes are drawn to the man
> of humble and contrite spirit,
> who trembles at my word

Such speaking was no less provocative in Luther's own day than it was in a previous millennium, some hundreds of years before the time of Jesus. The congregation left the Church uplifted. Outside in their market place they came on a messenger, with leaflets. He had a great bag full of Tetzel's reply to Fr Martin's famous Theses. The students began to rag and jostle him. Eventually there was something near to a riot. The man was

pushed and pulled about and all his 800 copies of Tetzel's sheets
were thrown on to a fire. Luther, all undemanding, had become
the man of the hour, the students' man and the man of the
people of the little town.

Two days later, Luther was preaching again, on his favourite
theme that the saints were also ordinary men, sinners. At the end
of the transcript are the words: 'Luther was annoyed because the
students burnt Tetzel's theses in the market place.' He wanted to
calm things down, and had not yet grasped the extent to which
religion and politics were totally mixed in, the one with the
other. If he preached a radical Christian sermon, his listeners
would apply it crudely. Political polarisation was inevitable.
Within a couple of weeks the Elector himself would have to show
his hand to some extent. Unknown to Luther himself, other
wheels were turning. As early as February, Viterbo, Superior
General of the Augustinians, had received a memorandum from
the Pope requesting him to quieten a bumptious friar in
Wittenberg before he created too much trouble. Staupitz was informed, and was writing to Luther about it, realising that some
kind of crisis in the matter must come at the forthcoming
chapter meeting of the Reformed Group of Augustinians due to
be held at Heidelberg, at the end of April. Fr Luther would have
to be present as a Provincial Superior in Saxony. Meanwhile,
Luther worked away at the University reforms and sent Lang a
triumphant letter on 21 March; the University curriculum
reform was to receive formal consideration at the Elector's
Council. He said that people were advising him not to go to
Heidelberg in case of attack en route; however, he was determined to go.

A famous theologian, Dr Johann Eck, had thought to
promote himself by giving his local Bishop at Eichstädt an
account of the worst that could be said against Luther and his
Theses. A trouble-maker got hold of the document and sent it to
Luther who was deeply shocked, since he and Johann were supposedly vowed in friendship. In a letter to a friend at Zwickau,
Luther wrote about Eck's text in desperate apocalyptic mood:
'The book . . . is nothing less than the malice and envy of a
maniac . . . Rejoice, Brother, rejoice, and be not terrified by
these whirling leaves . . . The more they rage the more cause I
give them . . .'

Staupitz wrote and told Luther of the bad impression his Theses had been making on high authority, sticking quietly to the facts in his usual way. In his reply on 31 March, Luther said he had simply been following Staupitz's own teaching and that of Tauler and the other authorities Staupitz knew. He said he should be allowed to express his own opinion about doctrines not settled, just as scholastics were allowed to disagree among each other. Meanwhile, Staupitz had had a warning from the Elector to make sure Luther had adequate security at Heidelberg. With tempers rising high, there could be attempts to abduct him or worse. And at this point the Elector himself had to make adequate arrangements for Luther's personal safety on his journey to Heidelberg. He gave Fr Martin a 'safe conduct' letter, which turned out to be something more than that. It was an introduction to political and ecclesiastical authority en route and at Heidelberg. The Elector was positively proud of his young Professor.

Luther finished his Lectures on the Letter to the Hebrews before leaving for Heidelberg. The surviving text ends a little before the end of the book. The author of the Letter was expounding the faith of an Old Testament figure, Moses; it was on account of his faith that Moses fled to Midian. Luther's ending words go: 'He chose the wisdom or rather the foolishness of the Cross . . . he was repudiated by the very brethren on account of whom he despised all these things . . . and so he was forced to flee unto Midian.'

Luther always lived at a high pitch, his inner struggles visible to onlookers in his eyes, and audible in his words. Now, with a single companion, he set out on the long walk to Heidelberg, knowing that while he had an excellent recommendation from his political master, the Elector Frederick, and knowing that he had the perhaps dangerous support of many students and many *avant garde* university men, the big Church authorities, though for the most part silent, were possibly planning to silence him. Still no reply had come from the Archbishop. Staupitz hinted at displeasure in the highest places.

CHAPTER EIGHT

Demands from Rome

There had been little time for deeply depressive agonising in the months since November of 1517; and there had been a good deal for Luther to be pleased with. Apart from progress with university reform, many people had reacted not only favourably but with enthusiasm to his Theses on Indulgences. But there were worries about this. The Theses had not been written for general consumption, and the support they had received tended to have something superficial about it – whether it was the arrogance of the humanists, or the prejudiced anti-clericalism of all who enjoyed any attack on the clergy. Added to this was the fact that Church authority seemed to be unwilling to respond to Luther's protest. For weeks there was merely silence. This was followed by rumours, increasingly strong, that the letter to the Archbishop and the criticism of Tetzel were being treated as matters for discipline at Rome. However, these things did not bother Luther as much as the thought that the Theses might be misrepresenting his case, particularly to the general public. Yet there was the warming fact of encouraging signs locally. The Elector and his chaplain, Luther's close friend, were taking a positive attitude. And his own local bishop, though forbidding publication of his long *Explanations*, had implied that perhaps they should be published eventually, treating with Luther through an eminent local abbot.

Luther left Wittenberg on foot in the second week in April on the 250-mile journey to the Rhineland, for the Augustinian Chapter meeting at the ancient university town of Heidelberg, due to open at the end of the month. Depressives have their 'up' periods, and the visit to Heidelberg led Luther into something like euphoria; the trip went well from the moment Luther and his friar companion, Leonard Beyer, he of the Theses, crossed the bridge out of Wittenberg into the springtime countryside. Five weeks later, Luther was bubbling over with happiness about it. As soon as he was back in his cell and had attended to immediate business, he sat down and wrote to Spalatin: 'At last my Spalatin, by the grace of Christ I have returned to our hearth [*penates*],' – Luther was writing on the Tuesday after the Saturday of his return – 'I who left on foot, returned on wheels.' He had come back as a minor hero, with a vehicle specially lent from a neighbouring friary, and the detail was to be relished: 'My superiors made me ride almost up to Würzburg with the delegation from Nuremberg. From there I travelled with the Erfurt delegation, and from Erfurt on, with the party from Eisleben; and they finally brought me, both at their own expense and with their horses, to Wittenberg.' Furthermore, security had been no worry after all: 'I certainly have been quite safe during the whole trip.' And his health had been better: 'Food and drink agreed wonderfully with me, so much so that several people think I look less strained and have put on some weight.' The whole thing had been a succession of minor, sometimes major, triumphs.

Their first port of call out of Wittenberg had been at the village of Judenbach, where they were well entertained by Pfeffinger, Frederick's Chancellor of the Exchequer – Luther had by now received that cloth, so long promised for a new habit. A careful route and stopping places had been planned to provide the minimum of danger of attack or kidnap. They continued on down through the lovely Thuringian valleys, and then over the hill to Coburg and on to Würzburg, where Frederick's letters gave Luther the entrée to the episcopal palace and lavish entertainment from Prince Bishop Lorenz in the Marienberg Castle above the city. On his arrival, Luther heard that the Erfurt party were still in the city, and from here on Luther and Beyer were able to ride in the Erfurt wagon instead of walking. Once he had arrived at Heidelberg, instead of possible reprimands there was nothing but good to report. The young local ruler, Count Palatinate Pfalzgraf Wolfgang, was a graduate of Wittenberg and was happy to ask Luther, along with the Observants' Superior, Father Staupitz, and Luther's old friend the Erfurt Prior, Johann Lang, to a grand meal: 'We enjoyed ourselves in pleasant and delightful conversation while we dined and wined. We viewed all the treasures of the castle chapel, and saw the armoury, and just about every precious object with which his truly royal and extraordinary famous castle sparkles.' The Count's old tutor was present and gave Luther further ground to flush with pleasure: 'Master James could not praise highly enough the letter our sovereign had written on my behalf; in his Necker dialect, he said "By God, you have excellent Credentials!" I was given every possible courtesy.'

Staupitz had decided to back his protégé. He gave Luther the podium and invited him to give the lead lecture, to preside at the defence of a set of theses, propounded by Luther and defended by his companion. They were not on the controversial Indulgence issue, but on the fundamental underlying theology of sin, grace and justification. It all went well: 'The doctors willingly allowed my disputation and debated with me in such a fair way that they have my highest esteem.' The next sentence was a reference to the domination of the schools by philosophy: 'Theology seemed to be some strange thing to them; nevertheless they debated keenly and with finesse.' One of the opposition speakers received not support but laughter from the meeting by saying: 'If the peasants were to hear you, they would certainly stone you to death.' There was opposition from the elderly nominalists from Erfurt: 'My theology is like twice deadly cabbage to the Erfurters.' But that was to be expected. Luther's theology of the cross went beyond the intellect to the heart and to the spirit: 'The man who deserves to be called a theologian is not the one who seeks to understand the invisible things of God through the things that are made but the one who understands that the visible things of God are seen through suffering and the cross.'

It was an open occasion, and among the local citizens and graduates who came in to hear the disputation was a young Dominican priest, destined to become Regius Professor of Divinity in the University of Cambridge thirty-one years later. Fr Martin Bucer, OP, wrote a letter to a friend a few days after the meeting, to tell him about Luther and give him an idea of the magnetism of the friar's presence. Something of this was caught in the earliest engraving of him by Cranach (two years later), showing Father Luther in his white habit. The mixture of intellect, spirituality and emotion in a body still thin, and visibly sculpted by asceticism came across to young Martin Bucer.

Luther's quiet voice, sharp eyes, intense conviction and his powerful arguments were overwhelming – or to others deeply offensive. Bucer wrote to his friend: 'His sweetness in answering is remarkable, his patience in listening is incomparable . . . his answers, so brief, so wise, and drawn from the Holy Scriptures, easily made admirers of everyone who heard him.' He was not saying that Luther had it all his own way. 'Our best men argued against him as hard as they could. However, they were unable to make him budge an inch from his propositions.' The contrast struck Bucer very forcibly, between the conventional language of the schools and what Luther was putting across. Here was something quite new and yet apparently difficult to defeat in argument. 'He had got so far away from the bonds of the sophists and the trifling of Aristotle, is so devoted to the Bible and so suspicious of antiquated theologians of our schools . . . that he appears to be diametrically opposed to our teachers.' What was exciting him as much as what Luther was actually saying, was that it was challenging all the old assumptions, and that it was being said with great intellectual confidence and conviction, backed evidently by deep emotion.

The day after the great debate, Bucer managed to have a meal with Luther: 'I had a close and friendly discussion with the man alone; it was a supper rich with doctrine rather than fancy food.' Bucer, like everyone else, related Luther to Erasmus, as taking Erasmus to a logical conclusion – evidently Luther kept his disagreements secret. 'He agrees with Erasmus in all things, but with this difference in his favour – that where Erasmus only insinuates, he teaches openly.' Bucer had not grasped that this difference in temperament was already part of a much more far-reaching difference in attitude to the Christian Gospel. Luther's was a more deeply subjective commitment which led to a more impassioned and practical policy.

Luther learnt at Heidelberg from Staupitz that attempts had been made to turn the occasion into one at which he would be silenced. A quiet word from his Superior in Germany, with a reference to the wishes of the Order's Superior General in Rome, and to criticism at the papal court, would, it had been thought, do the trick. Instead, Staupitz had treated Luther and his theology simply as theologians were used to treating professors with theological initiatives – these things were a matter

for debate and argument, doubtless of the expression of strong
and even very strong opinions about them, but still for the
moment a matter for debate. The Indulgence matter was left
aside – everyone agreed with Luther's attitude and with many of
his propositions on this topic in any case. But no one wanted to
debate it because of the sheer danger associated with debating
matters which involved the authority of the Pope. However, the
whole matter of the way Church authority carried on was
irritating Luther more and more. It was not just that he felt it all
to be unseemly or even scandalous in the way that Erasmus and
so many people of all classes did; he certainly felt that. But he
was more deeply scandalised and hurt in his own inner being;
his own nature was in some sort under attack. He had acted on
his own conscience in the deepest interest of the Gospel and of
the Church, and in tune, as he understood it, with the theology
of St Paul and St John. Yet it was beginning to seem that Church
authority had no interest in these things, or in himself as a
member of the Church.

One matter on the agenda at Heidelberg was the post of local
provincial superior, which Luther held. He had completed his
three-year stint, and it was an obvious choice to replace him with
the man whose name had often been coupled with his, the Erfurt
Prior, Johann Lang. And it suited Staupitz to have Luther out of
the official local job for the moment. In any case, Luther was
overburdened. Although not the president of the University, he
had become in effect the man principally responsible for the
reorganisation of the syllabus and the new appointments. So
Johann Lang was voted in to take over the office of local
superior of the group of Saxon friaries.

Back in Wittenberg, Luther was due to preach in the parish
church. His mind was still agonising over the matter of the
exercise of authority, and in particular the matter of the 'Ban' on
the sacraments so often exercised by Church authorities when
they wanted an overdue debt paying – bans 'flying about like
bats', as he had said in March – and in general the whole
business of excommunication. Heidelberg had encouraged
him. Whenever he grappled with a topic, the opposition seemed
to melt away. So up into the pulpit he went and began the kind
of classic but easily intelligible exposition he was so good at:
'The Latin word *communio* means "fellowship", and this is what

scholars call the holy sacrament. Its opposite is the word "excommunication", which means "exclusion" from this fellowship.' He pointed out that at the deepest level the ban cannot reach into a man's deepest relation with God, quoting St Paul: 'Who shall separate us from the love of God. . . ? I am sure that neither death, nor life, nor angels, nor height, nor power, nor anything else on earth.' The ban was about their visible fellowship in the Church, an essential element in Christian life. Luther expounded the orthodox view which he accepted. There had to be a structured community and discipline; the origins of the organised Church could be found in some of Christ's own words.

This was all impeccably orthodox. But Luther soon got on to what so affronted him, and what had been an annoyance in the Church for centuries: misuse of ecclesiastical disciplines. He said they had to put up with it – unjust excommunication had to be borne like a sickness. Unfortunately, it seemed that, more often than not – and here he began to express the biting criticism and anger inside him – authority was put into the hands of the Pilates, Herods, Annases and Caiaphases of this world. But these authorities should realise, he said, as he got into his stride, that they stood in greater spiritual danger than the people they excommunicated. They used it to get a debt paid, when the debt 'is so small that correspondence and costs amount to more than the sum concerned'. While real sinners, especially if they were the great of this earth, 'big Johns', were not touched, in spite of being fornicators, slanderers, usurers and the like. An unjust ban should be endured but its importance exploded, just the way you could pop a pig's bladder filled with peas for rattling. Another vernacular reference came fast on the heels of that one: as soon as they picked up the spoon, they smashed the bowl – bringing the whole Church into disrepute by wielding their petty powers.

Thus were the more or less inadequate, casual or corrupt officers of the European Myth exposed as functionaries of a social machine, rather than servants of men in their religious affairs. Luther knew the sermon was provocative, but was already becoming convinced that he must speak out. The force of his own inner storm was driving him on to say what others held back from. The atmosphere was becoming tense. Luther had only been back from Heidelberg two days and he was already attacking authority again. People wondered how long authority would hold back from touching him.

There were continuous exchanges with his old friends and masters in the Augustinian Order. At Heidelberg, Luther had failed to convince the old men from Erfurt; particularly saddening was the opposition of Fr Trutvetter, whom Luther loved and held in esteem, though he spoke sharply about him sometimes in letters to Spalatin. Luther tried and failed to convince Trutvetter on his way back through Erfurt. Back at Wittenberg he wrote a long, warm letter to his old Master, saying that nearly all the principal teachers at Wittenberg agreed with him, and even the prelates, when hearing the new theology,

> feel that someone is speaking to them of Christ and the Gospel. Allow me to share their judgment until the question is resolved by the Church . . . I pray daily to my Lord that the pure study of the Bible and the Fathers shall be restored to honour. You don't consider me a logician, and perhaps I am not; but I fear no man's logic in defending this position . . . Doesn't it disturb you that Christ's unfortunate people are tormented and fooled by indulgences? . . . If you can still tolerate the advice of him who was your most obedient and devoted disciple, I would say this; it was from you that I first learned to trust only the canonical books . . . I am ready to endure and to accept all your criticisms. However severe they are, they will appear very gentle to me.

There were deep ties both personal and communal with the old man, and Luther hated to be out of harmony with his one-time mentor.

At Heidelberg, Luther had heard some detail of what was being said against him at Rome. On his return to Wittenberg he decided to send his *Explanations* to the Pope. Into it he had put all his theological expertise. This text would show the Pope what was the real purpose of the 95 Theses. With it he sent a letter to the Pope himself, written with all the frankness, openness, intellectual integrity and respect for authority of which Luther was capable. He had it all ready by the end of May. 'Most Holy Father . . . my reputation has been seriously maligned before you and your counsellors, as if I had undertaken to diminish the authority and power of the keys which belong to the sovereign pontiff. I am accused of being a heretic, an impostor and a traitor, which leaves me overwhelmed with astonishment and horror . . .' Luther then described the preaching and Indulgence traffic in Saxony and said it stirred opposition, 'malicious talk was much in evidence around their booths', and only the threat of the stake prevented people speaking openly. 'It was then that I became incensed with zeal for Christ, as it seemed to me (or, if you prefer, by a juvenile enthusiasm).' He wrote to prelates about the matter, and 'I published my theses, inviting learned men and them alone to discuss them with me . . . By a miracle which astounded me more than anyone, these theses were spread through almost the entire world', even though, being academic theses, the text was dense and summary. So, he had written the *Resolutions*, and as a precaution was now 'putting them under the protection of your name'. He reminded the Pope that his University and the local ruler, Elector Frederick, approved. However, 'I offer myself with all that I am and possess. Make me live or die, say yes or no, approve or blame according to your pleasure. I recognise in your voice the voice of Christ who reigns in you and speaks through your voice. If I have deserved death, I will not refuse to die. "The earth is the Lord's and the fullness thereafter." May he be blessed for ever and ever, amen, and keep you unto him eternally, Amen.' However calmly he started, there was always a great emotional outburst before the end.

The Roman authorities were used to the kind of 'fanaticism' displayed in the somewhat desperate last sentences. For years they had been using Canon Law, and the traditional legal norms, essentially inherited from the Roman Empire, to deal with visionaries, mystics and prophets of all kinds. Such people had to obey the Curial authority, acting on behalf of the Pope, or indeed the Pope himself.

Fr Martin knew something of this attitude, but he had not met it at first hand before. He knew there were corrupt and politically minded ambitious men everywhere as his sermon on the Ban, and many previous sermons, had made clear. He knew that Canon Law was paramount. But he thought that among the corrupt were some men, and at the moment among them the Pope, who accepted the New Testament norms as the norms for the regulation of their lives.

The *Resolutions* and the letter to the Pope he sent off to his immediate superior, his only one great Master, Fr Staupitz, with the request to forward it on to Rome. And to Staupitz he wrote a covering letter, which provided for his Master's benefit a potted religious autobiography showing how he had got where he was, a disarming *exposé*, which also involved Staupitz himself, including the sequence about the love of God and metanoia. Then he told how the 'new war trumpets of Indulgences and the bugles of pardon started to sound, even to blast' around in the district, using all the old arguments of threat and fear. Luther felt he had to protest: 'This is the reason, Reverend Father, why I now, unfortunately, step out into public view. I have always loved privacy and would much prefer to watch the splendid performance of the gifted people of our age.' As to the threats, 'I have no other answer . . . than the word of Reuchlin, "He who is poor has nothing to fear; he has nothing to lose." I have no property and desire none . . . There is only one thing left: my poor worn body, which is exhausted by constant hardships. If they take this away by a trap or by force (in order to serve God), then they will deprive me of perhaps only two or three hours of life . . . My dearest Father, the Lord Jesus keep you unto eternity.'

Luther's 'worn out body', however, was to last another twenty-eight years, though he was undoubtedly tired, and often on the edge of exhaustion. And now he had reached a situation where he was pouring out many thousand written words a day in letters and statements, much of it for publication. In a short time, he would be producing material which amounted to a publication a fortnight for the rest of his life. And he realised well that the ultimate price might easily be exacted from him by the authorities of Church and State.

Luther secured the whole package, a substantial parcel with the 70,000-word *Explanations* in it, and sent it off by messenger to Staupitz who was by now at Augsburg in southern Germany, where he had come for the Imperial Diet which Emperor Maximilian was about to open. Though worried, Luther was still fairly confident of a satisfactory outcome. His enemies were trying to bring him down, but so far his case had been given a good hearing whenever there was someone willing to listen to it; and the opposition seemed to melt away or remain ineffective.

Meanwhile, among the people making their way laboriously across Europe to the Imperial town of Augsburg was the Superior General of the Dominicans, Tetzel's Order, the famous theologian Cardinal de Vio or Cajetan. He was one of the minority of theologians who were ultra-papalist and regarded the papacy as a divine, rather than human and merely historical, institution. The Pope had made Cajetan his Legate to the Emperor's assembly. But the Germans were not content with an Italian Legate and demanded a second German Legate, and Cardinal Matthaeus Lang of Gurk was named in addition – the same thing happened to Legate Campeggio in England and Cardinal Wolsey also became a legate there. Various official obstructions were made as Cajetan moved from Italian lands to German, but eventually he reached Augsburg late in the summer. His arrival was ceremonial. On a white horse draped with Roman purple, the Cardinal processed through the stone gates of the little German town, making for the Fugger House, the mansion of the international bankers where the principal dignitaries attending the Diet were lodging and where the meetings would also take place. The Cardinal brought gifts with him; a great sword of honour for the Emperor; the announcement of a Cardinal's hat for young Albrecht the Archbishop of Mainz, still in his middle twenties and the pluralist whose debts to Rome and the Fugger had made the recent Indulgence of particular importance; and finally the 'Golden Rose of Virtue', a scented golden artefact, a kind of degenerate Nobel Peace Prize. It might be usefully presented with 'strings', to the Elector of Saxony, Frederick the Wise, *Reichsvikar*, number two to the Emperor, and a man of great importance on all matters, specially because he so seldom uttered and appeared to be less easily bought than most rulers, possibly not for hire at all. The Italian party surveyed their chambers and requested satin linings for Cardinal de Vio's room, consciously exerting their sense of superiority in the rather barbarian surroundings north of the Alps.

The major item on Cajetan's agenda (as on Campeggio's in England) was the Turks. The Pope was worried about the threat to Christendom, with the Holy Land not only lost but the Turks far into Europe now, not far from Vienna. Indeed, the Pope would have liked to lead a new crusade himself. In a sermon in the Cathedral soon after his arrival, Cajetan presented the Diet with the need to defeat the infidel finally.

That meant only one thing to his German listeners: more taxes. The answer came very swiftly, in a meeting at the Diet; Rome was already taking far too much money, unjustly and dishonestly, out of Germany. The Bishop of Liège listed the complaints, the oft repeated *Gravamina* of the German nation. 'These sons of Nimrod grab cloisters, abbeys, prebends, canonaries and parish churches, and they leave these churches without pastors, the people without shepherds. Annates and Indulgences increase. In cases before the ecclesiastical courts, the Roman Church smiles on both sides for a little palm grease. German money, in violation of nature, flies over the Alps. The pastors given to us are shepherds only in name. They care for nothing, but fleece and batten on the sins of the people. Endowed Masses are neglected, the pious founders cry for vengeance. Let the Holy Pope Leo stop these abuses.' It was nearly as virulent as Luther himself – only it did not enquire into the doctrine behind it all, the dangerous world of ideology and ultimate commitment.

Cajetan had to stall, particularly because power politics had landed another and more serious matter on his plate. The Emperor was attempting to buy the votes of the Electors for the imperial election which must follow his death. Only fifty-nine, he was clearly sickening. His one wish was to ensure that his grandson, Charles Habsburg, already ruler of most of Spain and of Burgundy and the Netherlands, should succeed him. It was the one thing the Roman Curia and with him the Pope did not wish to happen; it would put half Europe into the hands of a single man and pose real threat to the political power of the Holy See, and of the Italian families so often associated with it. On 8 September, Cajetan wrote to the Pope that there was no alternative to shelving the Crusade plan. And, meanwhile, time was being taken on another matter, which had occupied a small place in the Cardinal's files on leaving Rome, but which was becoming a material factor in the diplomatic manoeuvres relating to the future imperial election.

This was the matter of an Augustinian friar at Wittenberg who had been following the well-worn path of denunciation of Indulgences, but had taken the matter beyond them to theology and papal power. As an exceptionally able theologian and a man of intellectual integrity, Cajetan had read the Theses of Dr Martin Luther and agreed with many of them. But the Pope's authority should not be impugned, and the friar should respect previous papal statements which had established Indulgences as a permitted pastoral and financial instrument. The matter was perhaps not too difficult to deal with. The visit to Augsburg would afford opportunity to speak both with the man's ecclesiastical superior, Fr Staupitz, and with his civil ruler. However, on arrival in Germany he found that the local Principal Superior had not in fact taken the steps which had been asked for, at the recent Chapter meeting of the Order in Heidelberg. And messages were coming from Rome requesting sharper action, including denunciation of Luther and a call to him to attend an examination in Rome. Following the arrival in August of this denunciation, the Emperor heard of the matter and his advisers suggested it could be used as a way of keeping the Holy See in good will towards him. He wrote to Rome requesting firm measures against the 'heretic' from Saxony. The Roman authorities were predictably pleased and sent a fresh command to Cajetan, formally denouncing Luther as a heretic and requesting Cajetan summarily to arrest him, with letters to the Emperor and Elector Frederick to assist the process. But a few days later, in the second week in September, the whole operation was being slowed down, qualified, and even put into reverse. The need of the Papacy to make close friends with Luther's own ruler, Elector Frederick, in the matter of future imperial election came to override all other matters. Frederick had expressed his opposition to the election of Charles Habsburg as Emperor. Everything must be done to support and encourage Frederick. And he became the Papacy's own first choice, their candidate for Emperor. If Frederick was reluctant to have Luther arrested, then the Luther affair must be played down.

Giovanni de Medici, Pope Leo X, had treated the Luther affair as an administrative nuisance, something for the theologians and canon lawyers, when the first missive from the

Archbishop of Mainz had arrived at the beginning of the year. Intelligent, deeply concerned for his famous Florentine family, both suave and genial, Pope Leo was destined for high office from the moment of his birth. Short-sighted and commonly using a gold monocle, but very fond of hunting and often able to give the *coup de grâce* to some (fairly) wild beast held by the huntsmen, monocle in one hand, sword in the other, he used to get through business at a kind of morning levée in his private rooms, leaving the rest of the day free for the hunt, the banquet, family affairs, and all the glorious social life.

Further papers kept coming to the Pope about the affair in Wittenberg, including formal complaints from the Indulgence Commissioner, Fr Tetzel, OP, who was able to enlist Cardinal Cajetan. The failure to achieve anything at Heidelberg, and the failure to quieten Tetzel with a Doctorate of Theology presented to him by the University of Frankfort-am-Oder, founded in 1506 was irritating. The curial Office decided it was necessary to teach the bumptious young Saxon a lesson and raise a formal charge of suspicion of disseminating heresy. The auditor of the Sacred Palace drew up a summons requiring Fr Martin Luther to come to a personal hearing in Rome and requested the commissioner of the Palace, seventy-year-old Sylvester Prierias (the only man in the Curia to vote against Reuchlin), to draw up a text about the theological points. He did it, boasting it took him but three days to deal with the 95 Theses of Dr Martin Luther.

Sylvester Prierias left aside almost entirely the substance of the 95 Theses, concentrating instead on the authority of the Pope and on personal abuse of Luther. His description of papal authority would be disowned by Catholics today and was scorned by most serious theologians in the sixteenth century. But in the power battles which had been raging for some centuries, the contentions were common enough: 'The Church's authority is greater than the authority of Scripture . . . the decretals of the Roman Church have to be added to Scripture . . . in the New Law the Pope's judgment is the oracle of God.' The abuse was puerile. Luther was a 'leper and a loathsome fellow . . . a false libeller and calumniator . . . a dog and the son of a bitch, born to snap and bite at the sky with his canine mouth . . . with a brain of brass and a nose of iron.' This was as rich as anything Luther had yet said in a sermon, and far sharper than anything he had written as yet in the public press. Coming in an official papal text, it had a particularly degrading quality about it. Copies went off to Cajetan and Luther.

Polarisation was almost inevitable from now on. Luther had sited the crux of his case in theology. Christian truth was its own authority, found in Scripture, the preaching Church and in the theology which arose from it. The papacy sited the crux in authority itself; theology was a tool, and Scripture a quarry of quotations to back up the decisions of a divinely backed organisation. The mantle of the Roman Emperors, absolute and not to be challenged, still lay ambivalently across the shoulders of the Pope, and indeed was to rest there in some sort for several centuries more. Luther accepted papal authority, but assumed that it was a service to the Church of a kind which would necessarily underwrite, or at least permit, clearly expounded doctrine stemming from scripture.

In the end, any theology worthy of the name would need to work out some accommodation between the structures of the Church, on the one hand, with its monarchical papal authority, its traditions and practice, and, on the other, Scripture, the written record of the life, death and resurrection of Jesus Christ, together with the records of the life and teachings of the group of His first followers. In the twentieth century this process of accommodation has proceeded, and has involved further questions on the one hand about 'God', and on the other about the religious and spiritual traditions of cultures other than the European. But for the moment, encounter was inevitable.

Accommodation was to become the policy of a few in the sixteenth century with little influence at their disposal, Erasmus the first among them. Meanwhile, a battle for power was going on at many levels, not only between the individual prophetic Christian and Church officials but between Rome and Saxony, between papacy and Emperor, between clerics and laity, educated and uneducated; between humanists and spirituals; between conservatives and radicals; and the perennial struggle between the owners of wealth and the illiterate poorest members of society. The lines of each contest did not coincide exactly with those of any other. But when the prophetic Christian's case was voiced by the Saxon Augustinian friar, its tones obliterated for the moment many other lines and drew powerfully to itself the laity, the anti-clericals among the priests, all nationally minded Germans, the humanists, the spirituals, the poor and the ordinary people who heard him preach – in fact the great majority of the population.

In Wittenberg, as the year ran on, the mosquitoes multiplying alongside the slow moving Elbe, and Wittenberg smelling in the summer warmth, Luther's daily life did not change greatly. He continued to feed on the great texts of scripture and on the Psalms as they were chanted in the choir, first one side then the other, when he was able to find time to attend rather than reciting them privately late at night in his room. Mass, choir, preaching in town and cloister, lecturing, planning university developments, teaching the best students – and the continued development of the affair of his Theses; it was a perpetual round with too little time for sleep.

Karlstadt continued to be a support, sometimes however overdoing it. He produced 405 Theses defending Luther, jumping in to attack Johann Eck just as Christoph Scheurl was organising a détente between Eck and Luther, following on a very sharp reply of Luther's against Eck's contention that man could please God by his own unaided actions. This glorification of man's will was, Luther had said sarcastically, true indeed. The will was indeed master in its own house, just as a brothel mistress is mistress in the brothel, one of a string of abusive Lutheran epithets. Both academics were, however, prepared now to retire, but Karlstadt tiresomely maintained the feud for the honour of Wittenberg University and Martin Luther. Tetzel had published a reply to Martin's 'Sermon on Indulgences', harping on papal authority and largely ignoring the substantial issue.

Luther's fame was spreading. Johann Lang took him on a visit to Dresden, in Albertine Saxony, where Duke George, cousin of Frederick the Elector, wanted to hear Luther preach and was shocked when he did so, on 25 July. After the banquet Luther got into an argument with an old Erfurt man, Hieronymus Emser. Dominicans, loitering outside, jotted down some of the angry words, shouted apparently on the other side of the door, joined these with some sharp sentences from the Sermon on the Ban and published the resulting concoction. When Luther hurried back to Wittenberg to prepare for the arrival of the new, and first Professor of Greek, late in August, Spalatin wrote to him that the concocted pamphlet was circulating and doing him harm. So Luther got Grünenburg to print the correct text of his Sermon on the Ban. From this time on it was difficult for Luther to control publication of his works, particularly of sermons which were taken down. Agricola, a student admirer, published Luther's 'Our Father' at this time without permission.

The bombshell came on 7 August. Sylvester Prierias's text arrived – and Luther laughed. Was this the best they could do? He was soon boasting of writing the reply to such stuff not in three days, but one. Then the horror began to grow. He had been summoned to Rome, and they were threatening his life. That did not matter too much – he had surrendered that a long time ago and had been working harder than was sensible for some years. The horror was that these men in Rome were not keeping the place Luther had assigned to them in his model. They had not looked at his texts, and it was clear they just wanted to shut him up, and any method open to them would do. It was a crucial moment. He had counted on the integrity of the Pope and his advisers.

Luther acted immediately, sending Spalatin a message on the day he had the text. He followed it with a letter on the 8th, to Augsburg where Spalatin was with the Elector at the Imperial Diet.

> I now need your help more than ever, or rather, it is the honour of almost our whole University that needs it . . . You should use your influence with the Sovereign and Pfeffinger . . . to obtain for me from the Pope the return of my case, so that it is tried before German judges . . . You can see how subtly and maliciously those murderous Dominicans carry on with a view to my ruin . . . This affair has to be handled in a great hurry. They have given me only a short time as you can see and read in the *Summons*, that Lernaean swamp full of hydras and other monsters . . . let Staupitz know.

But, said Luther, all was well, 'Do not be disturbed or sad on my behalf. The Lord will provide . . .', and ended with a pun to prove it, saying he was replying to the '*Dialogue of Sylvester,* which is exactly like a wild sylvan jungle'. And a final shaft: 'That "sweetest" man is simultaneously my accuser and my judge.'

It was very frustrating. Spalatin was far away in Augsburg.

Luther had to continue with the daily round at Wittenberg, and all the attendant responsibilities of friary, university and town. The days ticked by with the Summons to Rome hanging over his head. If something was not done about it he had the obligation, as an Augustinian friar, to be in Rome by 7 October, two months after receiving the Summons. He would need to start out soon. By 28 August no reply had come from Augsburg, and further rumours had reached Luther of demands being brought to bear on Elector and Emperor to have him arrested. Friends in Wittenberg suggested that the Elector should be asked to refuse Luther a safe conduct for the journey to Rome so that Luther would have a correct excuse for not going; and the refusal should be pre-dated. Luther suggested this in a letter to Spalatin and told him the *Explanations* was at last through Grünenberg's press, though full of mistakes, and he was sending a copy on. His reply to Sylvester together with Sylvester's original piece had gone to Leipzig to be printed – Grünenberg was not up to the current demands for print, either quantitatively or qualitatively. Luther had had to abandon his preference for the local man, for a better equipped firm in the big town. The letter to Spalatin ended: 'All I stand for I have from God . . . If he takes it away, it is taken away; if he preserves it, it is preserved. Hallowed and praised be his name forever. Amen. Thus far I do not see how I can avoid those punishments intended for me unless the Sovereign extends his help . . .'.

A letter came from Spalatin requesting Luther not to publish his sermon on the Ban, the Sermon on *Excommunication*. But Grünenberg had already printed and sold the little pamphlet. Spalatin had also been worrying about a proper reception at Wittenberg for the new Professor of Greek, the first to occupy the chair, a young man of twenty-one, great nephew of the famous Reuchlin. By name Schwarzerd, he used a Grecianised form, Melancthon.* He was a small, dark, elfin-looking man. Luther reassured Spalatin in a letter dated 31 August. The arrival of the young man had clearly brightened the last few days: 'Concerning our Philip Melancthon all has been done . . . Do not doubt it. Four days after he had arrived, he delivered an extremely learned and absolutely faultless address

* Better spelt Melanchthon rather than Melancthon as here, due to a copying error.

. . . We very quickly turned our minds and eyes from his appearance and person to the man himself.' Three days later Luther replied sympathetically to a further worried letter from Spalatin about the difficulties besetting the Elector. The purpose of Luther's letter was to ask that some of the older University courses should be optional. The students had requested this. They were jamming the lecture hall of Melancthon, wanted the Bible and real theology, and not to be obliged to study so much Aristotle.

Luther's case was beginning to attract attention from all over Europe. Fr Wolfgang Capito in Basle, working on the proofs of Froben's edition of Luther's writings, wrote begging Martin to be careful in dealing with the tyranny of the Church. Everyone became anxious as the news filtered out of the Summons to Rome. But then a calmer letter came from Spalatin, hinting that after all things were going to be all right, even a word that Luther might find himself in a specially good position for putting his message across – it must mean a bishopric, if only he would keep quiet at the moment. Luther was bewildered, knowing nothing of the political intrigues connected with the jockeying for the next imperial election. In Augsburg, early in September, Spalatin and the Elector paid a visit to Cajetan. The result was that Cajetan made a suggestion to Rome, and got the Pope's assent to it, for a hearing for Luther in Germany, in which Cajetan would be 'fatherly' rather than threatening. Luther was sent a message to set out for Augsburg. He was not feeling well, but started soon after receiving the message.

Once more accompanied by Leonard Beyer, Fr Luther left Wittenberg again on the long walk south and west towards Erfurt. There were no joyful surprises this time. Indeed, apprehension increased as he journeyed and listened to the worried warnings of friends, some of whom tried to dissuade him from going at all to Augsburg. Anxiety could not be escaped and it had him exhausted and suffering from constipation by the time he arrived. Fifteen years later, what came to his mind as he described the journey was the worry he had had about his parents, what they would think if he was condemned, and worse, what they might suffer – for the property of a heretic's relations could be seized. And he wondered whether he was looking at his beloved Thuringian landscape for the last time.

At Weimar he was surprised to find the Electoral party on their way home. They had left Augsburg the very day the Diet was over. Luther was asked to preach before the Elector, and gave him the usual denunciatory sermon on corruption in the Church. As usual, he did not see or speak to the Elector personally but was able to hear the latest news from Spalatin. Arriving a few days later at Nuremberg, he was supposed to pick up Christoph Scheurl whose legal experience would help him in Augsburg, the Elector believed – but Scheurl was not able to come. However, among those who did join him was Wenceslas Link, eventually to succeed Staupitz as Vicar General. Luther went on and a cart was found for him for the last few miles.

At Augsburg he went straight to the house of the Carmelite Friars – the Superior was another graduate of Wittenberg. The town was still half full of people who were clearing up the final business of the Diet. Johann Eck came to see Luther and they called a truce. Two Saxon lawyers provided by the Elector advised Luther not to go to visit Cajetan at the Fuggerhaus until an official safe conduct through the streets and back again had been obtained from the Emperor's office. Emperor Maximilian had left, but there was a permanent staff in this imperial city. Staupitz arrived to be with Luther. One of Cajetan's Italian courtiers, Serralonga, came round to see Luther, and to warn him that the meeting with Cajetan was not to be an occasion for discussion, but simply for Luther to say *revoco*, I recant. The Cardinal was not inviting him to have an academic disputation. Suave and superior, Luther found in him the same callous and patronising attitude which seemed to have inspired the texts from Rome. Cajetan undoubtedly thought he was being kind in sending an advance guard to warn Luther how he should deport himself. He was in sympathy both with the critics of the Church's corruption and of much of the 95 Theses. But he held to the view that above all the Church's authority must be upheld. He held a high sacramental view of the Church, which in practice often meant simply a dictatorial view.

The courtier outstayed his welcome and exasperated Luther. Eventually, he asked where Luther would go were the Elector to disown him. A slight shrug of the shoulders accompanied the reply 'Oh – *sub coelo*', a typically Lutheran, half-serious, half-amused Saxon ambivalence: 'Under the heavens – God knows where – on the open road – under providence.' The situation felt desperate to Luther, who wrote to Spalatin: 'If I am disposed of by force, the door is open for an attack on Dr Karlstadt and the whole theological faculty – and, as I fear, the sudden ruin of our infant University.'

It has often been asked how it could be that two men of Luther's and Cajetan's intelligence could meet and fail to isolate at least that partial theological agreement which did in fact lie beneath their arguments and positions. To pose the question, however, is to remove the subject from the actual contestants and the historical situation. Cajetan was coming as the personal representative of the head of an organisation, the Church, which laid enormous emphasis precisely on authority. As the courtier had suggested, and as his master did subsequently, there was no way Cajetan could actually discuss with Luther. He had come solely to preside, to judge, to bind or release, albeit in as 'fatherly' a manner as possible. Luther, on the other hand, had released himself from the conventional view or at least practice of the Church as having in its Pope an authority practically equivalent to that of God. Further, his own personal neurosis about authority figures gave him both a strong tendency towards exaggerated obeisance, and in practice a compensating attitude of detachment and freedom. He was not prepared in any way to go along with a view which automatically underwrote the Pope.

The safe conduct came, and Luther, accompanied by Staupitz and the lawyers, went along to the Fuggerhaus. Cajetan was all Italian welcome. Luther prostrated himself. It was not long before it became clear to Luther that Cajetan was only willing to use papal statements, not Scripture, to show that two of Luther's statements in the Theses were in error. Luther must recant. Luther wanted to discuss the truth of the matter, using the Bible as the norm, rather than merely to check the status of papal statements. Cajetan was hard pressed not to engage in debate, and eventually in the course of the three visits tempers were roused and Luther reached the truculent state. At the third meeting Luther tripped Cajetan up on a grammatical point, using the logical weapons he could still wield effectively. By 14 October, Luther was able to write his account of the meetings to Spalatin, in a letter headed 'Personal', but the contents of which he asked him to pass on to the Elector:

The Legate is negotiating with me, or rather I should say, manoeuvring against me . . . He promises to handle everything leniently and in a fatherly way . . . in reality however he is handling everything with nothing but unbending force. He continually repeated one thing: recant, acknowledge that you are wrong; that is the way the Pope wants it and not otherwise whether you like it or not.

After much pleading by the officials who were with Luther, the Legate agreed to look at a written defence Luther wanted to hand him. 'In the end the Legate disdainfully flung back my little sheet of paper and shouted again for me to recant . . . Almost ten times I started to say something and each time he thundered back and took over the conversation. Finally, I started to shout too.' Luther then described the challenge he put out, based on a strictly logical reading of a sentence in a recondite part of Canon Law. The Italians thought Luther had made a mistake: 'O God, how much gesticulation and laughter that caused. Suddenly he grabbed the book and read hastily and feverishly until he came to the passage.' Luther explained the mistake Cajetan had made and continued: 'I was excited and interrupted (I am sure quite irreverently): "Most Reverend Father, you should not believe that we Germans are ignorant even in philology . . ." That crushed his self-confidence, although he still shouted for revocation. When I left he told me, "Go and do not return to me again unless you want to recant."'

It was a bad outcome for Cajetan. He would have to request the arrest of Luther if he could not obtain a recantation, and this would offend Elector Frederick, the one thing he had been told to avoid. So after lunch he called Staupitz round to try to get him to persuade Luther. But Staupitz told him Luther was his superior when it came to scripture and theology. There was no way out. And neither of the topics at the heart of the matter had been objectively considered. Luther had insisted on the necessity of faith, maintaining now, not only that faith alone saved man; but that, as a logical consequence, man 'must' believe if he was to receive grace in the sacrament of penance or any other sacrament. Interpreted mechanically this could mean, as Cajetan observed in a subsequent text, to burden the Christian with a further imperative. But Luther's meaning did not refer to mechanical obligations but to the dynamic of a personal act. However, this substantial question was largely ignored, in favour of concern about what authority had already decided about it. The second question, about the nature of papal authority itself and the relation of the Papacy to Scripture was again taken as decided: the Pope had an absolute and final interpretative right.

It was a stalemate. Luther tried to keep some movement by addressing a letter to the Cardinal from his lodgings, and by making a formal Appeal. The letter is dated 18 October. He emphasised his wish to be obedient, and to be willing to be shown wherein he was wrong. He did not wish to offend. He said he would have to go home now; and the best thing seemed to be to appeal. He asked the Cardinal 'that you interpret in a favourable way my departure and my appeal as being undertaken out of necessity on my part and under the influence of friends'. He said that the Sovereign would prefer him to appeal, rather than to leave matters as they were.

There was no reply. Staupitz and the others feared the worse. The Legate had told them he had the right to throw both Martin and his Superior into prison. The safe conduct might prove to be ineffective. Staupitz was frightened. He decided they had all better leave swiftly. First, he formally released Luther from his vows as an Augustinian friar, in case he needed to take a swift decision, for his own safety, to leave and go into hiding without referring to his superiors. There had been suggestions in the previous few weeks that Luther might do best to go to Paris, if he had to flee. Staupitz gave Luther a valedictory word of assurance that remained deeply rooted in his mind for the rest of his life: 'Remember that you have begun this affair in the name of our Lord Jesus Christ.' In addition to the letter to the Cardinal, Luther decided to make a formal witnessed statement of his position and a formal Appeal from the 'ill-informed' Pope, to the 'better-to-be-informed Pope', a forbidden formula which had in fact been used before and quite recently by such an august body as the University of Paris, when objecting to the recent Concordat of Bologna between the King of France and the Pope about ecclesiastical appointments.

The Appeal, along with Luther's declared ill health, would explain his failure to obey the Summons to go to Rome, which might be thought to be in force now that the interview with Cajetan had come to nothing. The Appeal, which also contained once again a succinct history of the whole affair, was to be sent with the letter to the Fuggerhaus and to be made public after Luther's departure.

A horse was procured and Luther left in a hurry after dark in unsuitable clothes, to travel north to Nuremberg, a frightening and exhausting ride which he was never to forget. At Nuremberg another shock awaited him. There was a package from Spalatin. It contained a copy of the Papal Breve to Cajetan of 23 August, requesting Luther's arrest, which Spalatin thought Luther ought to see. Martin's reaction was to say it must be a forgery – they could not have put out such an inexcusable document. It was never clear whether he half believed his own statement about the forgery. But to refuse to accept the authenticity of a document was always one way to buy time; it was also one way to cushion his own shock at seeing the threatening text. Luther was back in Wittenberg before the end of October, hoping to meet up with Spalatin to discuss the situation, only to find the Electoral party had delayed elsewhere en route for other official business.

A letter to Spalatin dated 31 October began with a sharp statement of Luther's personal dilemma. Any day he might be declared a heretic and the Elector might feel he should flee to another country: 'I do not know how long I shall be able to remain here because my case is such that I both fear and hope.' The suspicions of Luther's advisers had not been wide of the mark. On 25 October, Cajetan sent a letter to the Elector demanding quite sharply that he surrender Luther: 'Take counsel of your conscience and either send Brother Martin to Rome or exile him from your country.' The Elector sent the letter straight on to Wittenberg for comment by Luther himself. Luther handed it on to the University to see, and then sent a full *exposé* of the situation to the Elector. The University asked Luther himself to draft their request to the Elector not to give in to Cajetan. In spite of these promising signs of support, Luther remained in frightening doubt about the outcome. He decided in any case to put the facts on record.

Back at his desk, Luther set about making a detailed report on the Augsburg meetings. He included the text of the document he

had handed Cajetan at the second or third meeting. In it he
claimed that the Pope is not above Scripture, and commented
on the conventional papal interpretation of the reported words
of Jesus to Peter 'I will give you the keys of the kingdom . . .'.
Luther found the interpretation tendentious. 'Many such
things, my reader, you will find in the sacred decretals, and also
others which if you use the nose of the bride overlooking
Damascus [Song of Songs 7.4], that is a nose of flesh and blood,
you will often be offended by the smell.' The reference to the
biblical love poem The Song of Songs, was a sudden gratuitous,
literary conceit – a reflection of the workings of Luther's ironical
and scripture soaked mind. The famous sequence reads:

> How beautiful are your feet in their sandals,
> O prince's daughter!
> The curve of your thighs is like the curve of a necklace,
> work of a masterhand.
> Your navel is a bowl well rounded
> with no lack of wine,
> your belly a heap of wheat
> surrounded with lillies.
> Your two breasts are two fauns,
> twins of a gazelle.
> your neck is an ivory tower.
> Your eyes, the pool of Heshbon,
> by the gate of Bath-rabbim.
> Your nose the tower of Lebanon,
> sentinel facing Damascus.
> Your head is held high like Carmel,
> and its plaits are as dark as purple;
> a king is held captive in its tresses.

It certainly sounds like a fine nose, well able to detect the
smells emitted by tendentious interpretations of Scripture.
Luther included the text of the Papal Breve to Cajetan to arrest
him, together with his own analysis of it indicating his suspicion
that some not too well-educated German had had some part in
drafting it. The text was sent down to Grünenberg, and such was
the public excitement that the printed sheets were taken up by
the public one by one as they came off the press. (The profits
which all printers made out of Luther were phenomenal; he

exacted nothing in return – Erasmus used to get a robe or other gift occasionally from Froben.) When the Elector heard that the *Acta Augustana*, the account of the Ausburg meeting, was being circulated he sent a request to have it stopped, especially as he was in the thick of negotiation with Cajetan. But it was too late, as it usually turned out to be when authority tried to hold up some publication of Luther's. Luther was in any case desperate by now and decided that the Elector was wanting him out of the way. He sent his sovereign a letter saying he would leave Wittenburg – he did not know where he would go. He preached what amounted to a farewell sermon in the parish church.

Frederick managed to deal with most decisions simply by postponing them, asking for more information, handing them back down the line to the questioner, or any of the other numerous ways of coping with governmental decisions. But, in the Luther affair, he was faced with the need to take a specific and definite decision, whether on the one hand to send Dr Luther to Rome or to request him to leave Saxony, or on the other to refuse the request of Cardinal Cajetan. He chose the latter course. He always kept options open if possible. To surrender Luther was something that could not be undone. He told Cajetan he had found Luther's case as expressed by Luther himself and underwritten by the University, convincing. Luther was still waiting to be shown that his interpretation of the New Testament was unacceptable by the norms of the New Testament itself; and he was still maintaining that the Pope had no absolute and final right to tell the Church what the correct interpretation of any part of it was – the Church as a whole must play a part in any such decision.

The German Elector gave the Italian Cardinal the reply direct. No one in his lands had found Dr Luther's teaching heretical, apart from those whose interest it was to do so. He sent along Martin's own rebuttal and said that he waited for proof of Dr Luther's heresy. In Martin's public career this was one of the crucial moments. His sovereign, who seldom altered course, had decided to protect him from the insistent demands of Rome to surrender him in person.

CHAPTER NINE

What is the Church?

From December 1518 there was a lull in the Martin Luther affair. Cardinal Cajetan had failed to deliver either a recantation or Martin Luther in person, and had antagonised the Elector. The Roman Curia put the case into the officious hands of an ambitious young Saxon, papal chamberlain Karl von Miltitz, still in his twenties. The case ceased to occupy a place of much importance by comparison with the future of the Empire. The Emperor was dying, and finally died on 12 January 1519. The lobbying for the election of his successor became intense and remained so until the matter was resolved at Frankfurt in June. Nineteen-year-old French speaking Charles Habsburg, already ruler of most of Spain, the Netherlands and Burgundy was elected in spite of all the attempts by Pope and Curia to prevent it. A full record of the machinations involved with the German Electors, with Francis I of France and Henry VIII of England and his ministers would themselves make a large book. The Luther affair was not resumed by Rome till the turn of the year 1519–20, and it was nine months after that before the resumption began to have any emphatic results as far as the general public were concerned. In the meantime, however, the whole of Germany and much of the rest of northern Europe were becoming flooded with Luther's writings.

The first trickle of writings had begun in 1516 and 1517 with the two German pieces; and Luther was already writing a great number of letters, always in Latin unless he was writing to rulers with whom it was usually wiser to communicate in German. In the second half of 1517 had come the two sets of Latin dialectical theses, the second being taken up very widely to his great suprise and translated into German, becoming 'Martin Luther's 95 Theses'. Then the need to explain these led to the first full-scale

Latin work *The Explanations*, immediately followed by the very
brief German sermon pamphlet, for general consumption, with
similar explanatory but also pastoral purpose. Then began the
experience of having to put out correct versions of texts
published precipitately by both friends and enemies, of spoken
material, in the first case on the Lord's prayer, and in the second
on *The Ban*. And at the end of 1518 came Luther's account of the
Augsberg encounter with Cajetan.

By early 1519, Luther's magnetism as a preacher and lecturer,
his eloquent and imaginative presentation of current concerns,
together with his notoriety, were drawing students, young and
old, to Wittenberg and readers to his writings. The little town
was swarming with them. During 1519 a spate of German
writings began to flow from his pen, non-polemical writings,
designed for the traditional religious purposes of instruction
and comfort, reminding people of that on which they ultimately
depended, designed to nurture their true freedom. People asked
for these things and Luther responded: *A Meditation on Christ's
Passion, The Lord's Prayer, Rogationtide Prayers, On Preparing to Die,
Fourteeen Consolations* (written especially for the Elector who was
very ill in the autumn and likely to die – it was to replace the
Fourteen Saints to whom people commonly turned), and finally
How Confession should be Made. Towards the end of the year
Luther turned to the Sacraments of Penance, Baptism and the
Mass, again in German; these were for general non-academic
consumption, but Luther used them to enable him to move
towards a re-cast understanding of the Sacraments at a serious
intellectual level. Early in 1519, came an important short *Sermon
on Marriage* with a warm confident note to it: 'Married people
can do no better work than bring up their children well' – that
was better than any work of piety. There was also strictly
academic Latin fare; his *Lectures on Galatians* and a volume of his
Psalms Commentary were published for the first time.

Then there were writings connected with the public theological controversy. In February 1519, Luther issued a brief
Latin guide to his position on six controverted matters, Saints,
Purgatory, Indulgences, the Church's commandments, Good
Works, and the Roman Church, in his *Apologia Vernacula*. As far
as concerned the controversial writings, from this time on they
were almost entirely related to a debate with Johann Eck to be

held at the end of June 1519 at Leipzig, leading up to it or flowing from it. Finally, correspondence poured out in a never-ending stream. By 1520, the totality of Luther's writings had come to bewilder the public. Every week there seemed to be some new pamphlet on sale with its wood engraving on the cover. Enemies put around rumours that this or that person was the true author of this or that of Luther's writings. But, in fact, Luther was the author of the whole extraordinary corpus.

Luther's authorship had received something like the seal of respectability. Froben, Erasmus's publisher in Basle, had issued in the autumn of 1518 a collection of his shorter Latin writings. Being in Latin they were available to every educated person in Europe and were soon in sharp demand; 600 copies were sold by Froben at the Frankfurt Spring Book Fair, destined for towns all over Europe from Cambridge to Spain and Italy. Further editions followed. But in no case did the canny Froben, warned by Erasmus, print his name as printer, nor did Wolfgang Capito his assistant put his name to the fervent Introduction he had written: 'Here you have the theological works of the Reverend Martin Luther, whom many consider a Daniel sent at length in mercy by Christ to correct abuses and restore a theology based on the Gospel and Paul . . .'

Luther was drawing every kind of human being to himself from the ordinary layman needing counsel, to civil servants wanting advice, from the Elector himself wanting religious comfort and Spalatin requesting theological explanation, to the scholars and academics trying to keep up with his latest theological speculation, on that which lay at the heart of society's Myth. For a long time there had been crazes for great itinerant preachers. To hear them was both entertainment and inspiration. They were often outspoken about the misdoings of princes and popes, and abuses generally, but they normally kept well within the parameters of the theological party line, and the received structures. As a popular preacher, Luther was exceptional in being also a genuine scholar – a true Renaissance man. But he was unlike the Renaissance man in that his own personal problems lent a bitter urgency, a sense of emotional desperation and intensity and determination to all he said, eyes flashing, calm voice firmly enunciating, occasional smile revealing a man still with roots deep in the Saxon soil from which he continued to draw a stream of homely metaphors and coarse comment. His philological approach to language, encouraged by Erasmus and the whole neo-classical movement, together with his long training in rhetoric and his love of classical literature, all contributed to his success. But, above all, success was due to the personal flair for language, his message, set into the satisfactory and effective sentences of a rough and energetic German, just emerging as a complete expressive medium.

In February 1519, Luther counted four months since he had said a hurried *auf wiedersehen* to Staupitz at Augsburg. Not a word had he heard since then. He was sad about it, even resentful. He longed to be personally close to his spiritual superior and mentor, and to share events with him. But Staupitz stayed safely away from it all in the south, at Salzburg. On 20 February, Luther wrote: 'To the Reverend and excellent Father John Staupitz, vicar of the Eremites of St Augustine, my patron and superior, honoured in Christ. Even though you are so far away and silent, Reverend Father, and do not write to us who are eager to hear from you, I shall nevertheless break the silence. I wish – all of us wish – to see you in this part of the country.'

Luther plunged into an emphatic statement of his own inner emotional and spiritual troubles. It was to Staupitz more than anyone that he could reveal his inner turmoil. 'I believe my *Proceedings* [at Augsburg] have reached you and that you know about Rome's anger and indignation. God is pushing me – he drives me on, rather than leading. I cannot control my own life. I long to be quiet but am driven into the middle of the storm.'

He gave the news of a meeting between himself and Miltitz at Altenburg (where Spalatin held a Canonry): 'He complained that I have pulled the whole world to my side and alienated it from the Pope. He said he had explored all the pubs and found that for every five people, barely two or three favour the Roman party.' Arbitration was suggested by Miltitz, and Luther agreed: 'I nominated the Archbishops of Salzburg, Trier and Freising. He entertained me in the evening, we had a good time at dinner, he kissed me, and so we parted. I pretended not to see through this Italian act and insincerity.' A series of negotiations, which included the Elector, went on all through the next two years, showing a healthy record of activity on Miltitz's work sheet, achieving, however, nothing but the steadily deepening disillusionment both of Luther and of the Electoral Court with Roman ways.

Part of Miltitz's operation, an attempt to mollify Luther, was to make an example of Tetzel the Indulgence preacher, whose financial accounts were not above suspicion. Tetzel was requested to come to meet the young chamberlain at Altenburg, but declared himself unable to travel, being ill, and also without a safe conduct pass. He was frightened to be seen in public, so swiftly and fiercely had public opinion turned against him. Luther told Staupitz: 'Now Tetzel has disappeared and nobody knows where he has gone except perhaps the fathers of his Order.' Later in the year, he wrote Tetzel a letter of kindly commiseration in his serious and eventually fatal illness.

The letter to Staupitz moved on to Johann Eck, who in controversial mood had recently turned to attack Erasmus, much to the astonishment of the latter, as well as Karlstadt and Luther. 'Finally my Eck, that deceitful man, is again dragging me into a new controversy . . . Thus the Lord sees to it that I am not idle; but Christ willing, this debate will end sadly for Roman laws and practices, those reeds on which Eck leans for support.' Then Luther had something to boast about: 'I wish you could see my shorter works, published at Basle, so that you could realise what educated people think of me, and of Eck and of Sylvester and the scholastic theologians.' But Staupitz had seen the Froben volume and knew only too well what 'educated people' were thinking of these matters. Copies of the book were all over Europe. In March, Cardinal Wolsey's agents discovered a copy hidden in a bale of wool imported into England. Luther enjoyed telling Staupitz of his success, and of a deliberate misprint – Magirus (cook) being printed instead of Magister (master): 'The amusing fellows, the printers, by an intentional error call Sylvester *magirus palattii* instead of *Magister Palatii*; they needle him with other remarks which are quite biting. This affair will be quite a blow to the Roman dignitaries.'

Luther continued with his own fears and burdens, and his need of support: 'I beg you to pray for me. I am exposed to and overwhelmed by the world with all its drunkenness, insults, carelessness, and other annoyances, not counting the problems which burden me in my office.'

As he and his cause grew more important, Luther felt it was

time that he was in direct contact with Erasmus. On 28 March, he at last wrote a letter to the great man, attempting an elegant style and a way of speaking not totally congenial to him. In the convoluted embarrassment of his sentences, Luther seems to turn again into the shy young man inviting Fr Braun to his first Mass, self-assertive and self-deprecating at the same time:

> I am foolish that I, with unwashed hands and without a reverential and honorific introduction, address you, such a great man, as it were, in the most familiar tone. But in your kindness, may you attribute this either to my affection or to my lack of skill. Although I have spent my life among academics, yet I have not learned enough to greet a learned man by letter. Were this not so, I would have troubled you a long time ago with I don't know how many letters, and would not have endured that you should always speak to me only in my cell.

It was clearly written by someone who knew his Latin classics. But, equally, it was clearly written by someone who was not fully at home in the Renaissance style, lacking the sophisticated detachment which generally went along with the cult of 'good letters'.

A further section of the letter continued with praise of Erasmus: 'I feel compelled to acknowledge (even if in a most elementary letter) your outstanding spirit . . . My Erasmus, kindly man, if it seems acceptable to you, acknowledge also this little brother in Christ.' Luther said he wanted to remain buried in some little corner (the *angulum* again), but now, to his shame, his lack of knowledge was laid bare for the learned to see. The letter then took on the lineaments of over-familiarity. He told Erasmus that Melancthon overworked and Erasmus might perhaps tell him to be careful. And suddenly: 'Andreas Karlstadt, in great reverence for the Christ dwelling in you, sends greetings. The Lord Jesus himself preserve you into eternal life, excellent Erasmus. Amen. I was verbose; but remember that one ought not always to read only learned letters. Sometimes you have to be weak with the weak. Wittenberg, 28 March 1519.' So a quotation from St Paul on sympathetic weakness brought Luther on to better loved ground, and a suitable ending after a rather artificial apology for the verbosity of a letter which was not in fact very long.

Erasmus was in contact with the Elector at the time (as with so many of the leading figures in Europe), having dedicated a recent new edition of Suetonius' *History* to him. He felt he must do something about Luther, prompted both by Luther's letter and by a visit just then from Fr Justus Jonas, Augustinian, now Rector of Erfurt University. In a letter to Frederick of 14 April 1519, Erasmus expressed his irritation at the cry of 'heretic' which was always being raised, and said he had not studied Luther's writings carefully, but that his character was regarded as above suspicion. The best men in Antwerp read him. The Elector replied, echoing respect for Luther's character, and some official support for his cause generally, without committing himself formally to Luther in person. It would have been most unlike him to make such a commitment in any case in writing to a third party. But in both Frederick's and Erasmus's communications can be sensed a concern about Luther's increasingly strong language and his wayward approach to problems. There was plenty of precedent for Luther's emotive language, not least in the denunciations of evil by the Jewish prophets, and by the greatest prophet of them all, Jesus of Nazareth. But Frederick was a sovereign, with the welfare of his state to think of. And Erasmus was ever intensely concerned above all with the future of scholarship, and was always worrying lest the new learning would be attacked and put into reverse.

The reservations in Erasmus's letter were less important than the sheer fact that the best known literary man in Europe had written a letter essentially in support of Luther to Luther's sovereign. Without scruple, the text of the letter was copied and spread about Europe. Spalatin did a German translation for the purpose. Luther was delighted – and not delighted. He wrote to Spalatin: 'The letter of Erasmus pleases me and our friends very much. However, I would have preferred not only not to be mentioned personally in it, but not to have been praised, especially by such an outstanding man.' Luther continued about various University affairs, and hoped to catch Spalatin before he left with the Elector for the Diet to be held by Frederick, Elector and *Reichsvikar* in Frankfurt for the election of the new emperor.

Erasmus replied directly to Luther late in May, in a supportive
but careful letter, written of course in his usual beautiful style. It
showed up all the temperamental differences between Luther
and Erasmus. Peace rather than violence was the message. The
Pope himself should not be attacked but only those who abuse
papal authority. Erasmus admitted to being concerned that
people thought he had helped Luther with his writings, but
commended Luther for his Psalms commentary. He told Luther
that some of the top people (*maximi*) in England thought highly
of his writings. It was a friendly letter, but one attempting to
turn Luther into a quiet, optimistic, scholarly reformer, rather
than the distraught theologian-poet, the small-town idealist,
the anxious pastor torn with concern for those misled, the
cultured and uncultured alike, by wrong-headed institutional
religion. Erasmus suggested that there was always a danger, as
one became famous, of desire for glory – and anger and hatred
were not good. Luther knew about the anger and its inappropriateness but, as he had said to Staupitz, 'I cannot control
my own life . . . I am driven into the middle of the storm.'
Erasmus, frequently consulted by the highest in Church and
State, continued his efforts to keep the rising storm down, using
his own personal reputation to do so, writing a letter to the Pope
in August and to Albert the Archbishop of Mainz in November.
In the latter, he did not entirely excuse Luther for being too
loud-mouthed but said he was provoked, and blamed
ecclesiastical authority severely for the difficulties with him.
Albert was pleased to be in touch with the great scholar, but continued to keep the low profile he had always cultivated in matters
of theology.

Luther was preparing for the proposed debate at Leipzig. A
letter to Spalatin on 13 March referred to his researches in this
repect. But first on University affairs – Luther resisted the idea
that Melancthon should take over the lectures on Aristotle's
Physics, a suggestion from Frederick's Treasurer intent on
resisting further escalation of salaries. 'Aristotle's Physics is an
entirely useless subject . . . These lectures had better be continued only until they can be abolished.'

After references to his various publications and his evening
parish courses on the Our Father and the Commandments,
Luther went on to the frightening thoughts which were arising

in his mind as he was reading the history of papal decrees. 'I am studying the papal decrees for the debate. Confidentially I do not know whether the Pope is Antichrist himself or whether he is his apostle, so miserably is Christ corrupted and crucified by the Pope . . .'. He was returning to the frightening thought about Antichrist which had first arisen in his mind the previous autumn. *Antichrist* was a word used originally in St John's Letters in the New Testament to indicate those who deny that Jesus is God, and subsequently widely used over the centuries to indicate some final manifestation of the devil before the end of the world – it was resorted to when all ordinary explanations seemed insufficient to explain events, or when the emotions such events aroused needed the greatest possible verbal outlet. Luther was not the first to suggest that the 'Pope', apart from the goodness or badness of the reigning Pope, must be 'Antichrist'. From a belief that he was the Head of God's Church, Christ's 'Vicar on Earth' as a grossly exaggerated theologism sometimes had it, it was not difficult to shift to the extreme opposite. So corrupt, so appalling did events sometimes seem, that perhaps the only explanation of it must be that Evil had crept somehow into the very highest place of all. Following the dangerous reference to Antichrist, Luther said with a deep subjectivism which frightened Spalatin: 'Daily greater and greater help and support wells up in me by virtue of the authority of Holy Scripture.' He thought Luther's arguments well based. But this sense of certainty without reference to anything but Scripture, made him wonder. With a further reference to other letters, books, the administrative work of the President of the University and a farm rent unpaid (by a relation of Staupitz), Luther's letter came to an end.

The question of Church authority, as such, did not really interest Luther greatly. His concern was the heart of the Christian religion itself; the Gospel of Jesus of Nazareth. But Eck had seen Church authority to be his weak point and insisted that it be included on the agenda of topics to be debated at Leipzig. So Luther began his methodical reading of the papal decrees, and a formal consideration of the nature of papal authority. By the following February, he was writing to Spalatin, 'We are all Hussites now', in the same spirit as someone said in the late nineteenth century, 'We are all socialists now'. Truths were becoming self-evident which had not previously engaged people's minds. In the theology school there had been no regular teaching *De Ecclesia*, on the Church.

The Church was all around one, and the need to theorise about it had not arisen. Founded by the followers of Jesus of Nazareth, it was the great 'a priori'. It had hardly been seen objectively for what it was: the most efficient, most successful, most powerful, and oldest polity in Europe. The easy assumption that the Church was just as it should be was never universally accepted, but central and western European society, 'Christendom', had come to be based on a majority consensus that it was. From time to time thinkers and pastors, identified at the time by authority as 'heretics', seen by others as prophets, and by some historians now as social revolutionaries, reached the conclusion that the Christian Gospel spoke of a body of Christians, of an incipient 'Church', of a kind far removed from the type of political and economic structure maintained by Roman Canon Law. But these men and women lacked the printing press; and the theological and political climate did not enable their views to be sympathetically examined. Into this category fell Marsilius of Padua in the fourteenth century with his 'modern' theory of the Church as a spiritual body in an entirely secular society, and Jan Huss (d. 1415), a Bohemian priest and university lecturer in Prague, one of the first to compose a treatise on The Church. His theory reached towards a theology which in some particulars was not so different from that of the Roman Catholic twentieth-century Second Vatican Council, with his statement: 'The Pope is not the head nor are the cardinals the entire body of the holy, Catholic and universal Church. For Christ alone is the head of that Church and all the predestined together form the body . . .' Some of these 'prophets' lacked theological expertise, like many Lollards in England and Waldensians in Southern France; and some, like Huss ended up in flames, though many also did not.

In Wittenberg, in May 1519, a prophet finally found favourable circumstances. In composing one of his preparatory texts for his forthcoming debate in Leipzig (his Resolution on the Thirteenth Proposition), Dr Luther was forced to thrash out what the Church must be if it cannot be defined in terms simply of obedience to Rome, to Canon Law, to Pope and bishops as infallible interpreters of the gospel. 'Where the gospel is preached and believed, there is the true faith, there is the immovable rock, there is the Church', was the sentence which expressed his conclusion. The combined activities of preaching and believing would always enable one to identify the Church – and Luther also held that this real 'Church' would always baptise and would always celebrate the eucharist. Where the Gospel itself was preached and believed, and its central public acts of baptism and the celebration of the Last Supper of Jesus with his disciples were seen to be done, there was the Church founded by him. This went to the heart of the matter but omitted any theory about the inevitable institutional ramifications. 'Seen' by whom? The detail was still to be worked out.

Eck could hardly believe his luck. The man was delivering himself into his hands. Luther was denying the absolute authority over the Church of the Bishop of Rome, both because, as Luther thought, this must be tempered by the authority of Councils, and because of the historical fact that Christians in the east had not in fact been under the authority, either of the Pope or of later Councils.

The prophet does not always know what he does and speaks on several different levels. Luther had been laying his hands for several years on the great Latin texts of scripture, with the grave patina of ages on them. He had been piercing through the noble prose to the Greek behind. And behind the Greek words again he was sensing the Semitic words of the great Prophet himself, Jesus of Nazareth, the Word, with a thousand years and more of Judaic religion wound into everything he said. His superiors had encouraged him. In the self-confidence of centuries, stretching back to secular Rome, they knew that greater elucidation of the text would always be harmonious with their authority. They were the Church, a living tradition, with its vast law book, its obedient priests, and its machinery for dispensing sacramental grace. The scripture said, plain to see, 'Thou art Peter and on this rock I will found my Church'. Peter was the first Pope. Jesus had handed him all authority in religious matters. As for secular matters, there too the Pope had overriding authority. The 'Donation of Constantine' was a text by which the first Christian Emperor had bequeathed imperial authority itself in the west to the Pope.

However, both the religious authority and the secular were based on an objectively insecure base. For several centuries the 'Donation of Constantine' had been suspect. The text was finally proved to be a forgery in the mid fifteenth century by both the philologist Lorenzo Valla and the German theologian, Cardinal Nicholas de Cusa. Nor had the claim to absolute religious authority ever been accepted by all Christians and there remained a majority of theologians who considered that the papacy was of human rather than divine provenance. At the same time the priestly and cultic nature of the Church, as a kind of super-superstition, the epitome of all 'religions', was also under attack by daring thinkers who grasped that Jesus's message was one that was meant to free people from that kind of religion. Their arguments began to assume increasingly convincing proportions, and to be able to be widely disseminated. The light of scholarship, in history and philology, shone threateningly on the papal claims.

In the coming four centuries the steady accumulation of historical fact would work towards a sterilisation of those claims and a dissipation of the tabu surrounding them. But the tabu, 'touch not the Lord's annointed', was strongly resistant. A new romantic ideology grew up round the papacy of the Counter Reformation, once the new Protestant institutions emerged. However, in the mid twentieth century biblical scholarship was welcomed into the Roman Catholic Church. And it had a radical effect on the Protestant Churches as well as on the Roman Catholic Church. Courses of convergence began to appear, clearly based on the fact that they all took the same data as their reference points. If this supposition is correct, Luther would be pleased. Neither in 1519 nor later did he want 'another' Church – he wanted to reform the Church. He left more or less unresolved the matter of the relationship between local Churches, and originally had no wish to exclude the papacy automatically.

By the sixteenth century there was already plenty for a scientific critique of received ecclesiastical positions on the matter of authority to go to work on. And behind it was more than either Luther or Erasmus knew. The twentieth-century reader is able to understand better than anyone in the sixteenth century how

Luther's parents, c. 1526

Georg Spalatin   Luther at 36, in 1520

Luther at 41

Luther in disguise as Junker George
at the Wartburg

Philip Melancthon, in 1523

Erasmus, 1523

Katherine von Bora, 1525

Luther at 44

A group of Reformers, with
Luther in foreground

the contradictory positions arose. It was only in the late fourth century that the biblical text 'Thou art Peter' had begun to be understood as a reference to the papacy. This interpretation arose alongside the taking up of a whole spectrum of legalistic interpretations of the New Testament, directly due to Jerome's translation of the Greek and Hebrew texts into Latin (the Vulgate), a language so well endowed, as a tool of imperial rule, with legal terms. The traditions of the Semitic and Greek world were now transposed into the specific formalism of such words as *ligare, solvere, potestas, imperium, gubernacula, jurisdictio, sententia, justitia*. These terms of the imperial judiciary suddenly became 'biblical' terms. For a thousand years and more only very well-educated theologians, poets and linguists were going to be able to grasp that these words transformed and often betrayed the thought form of the culture from the lands east of Rome, in which Jesus of Nazareth lived. Luther was groping towards this conclusion.

In spite of the threatening nature of the opposition's pre-Leipzig publications, Luther was in an 'up' mood in May, at any rate as far as the University was concerned. In his letter to Spalatin about Erasmus, he had written: 'The number of students is growing tremendously, and they are of good quality . . . Our town can hardly hold them all, due to lack of lodging facilities.' A few days later he was writing to Fr Martin Glaser the Augustinian from whom, without asking, he had borrowed the horse that took him in such an uncomfortable rush from Augsburg the previous autumn. 'You have every right to be . . . annoyed that I have not written a single line to you before this . . . I hope you will be indulgent to a penniless man like me in regard to your horse, bearing in mind the intervention of the Reverend Father Vicar.' Luther wrote to welcome him in Wittenberg:

What a pleasure that we may see you here again . . . I believe you know of my coming Disputation at Leipzig . . . I am lecturing on the Psalms again; the University flourishes and the town is full of students . . . Rome is burning to destroy me, but I coolly laugh at her. I am told that in the Campo di Fiore a dummy of Martin has been publicly burned, cursed and

execrated . . . My commentary on the Epistle to the Galatians
is already being printed . . . Apart from this, we live well and
quietly.

Then a word about the new prior: 'Our Helt is ruling quite well
and also building, but only a kitchen. For thus far he cares only
for the belly; later he will care also for the head . . . The whole
world is wavering and shaking in body as well as soul . . . I
predict massacres and wars. God have mercy upon us. Farewell
in Him, and pray for poor me. 30 May 1519, Friar Martin
Luther.'

The inner tensions expressed themselves now less in the
misery of depressive bouts than in bursts of furious anger and
forecasts of disaster. Earlier, he had sent an uninhibited blast to
a lesser opponent from among the Franciscans who had been attacking his old pupil Frank Gänther, now parish priest at Jütter-
borg. Luther depicted the Franciscans as 'snoring brothers who
perchance have sometime seen a master of arts but have never
known one personally . . . You never read anything, much less
do you understand anything, and yet you claim to judge of doctrines.' Their claims were 'diseased, absurd and foreign to
Catholic doctrine'. It was the same anger as was once directed
against the 'pagan' Aristotle in the private notes on his Erfurt
desk.

The Leipzig debate was preceded by long drawn out attempts
by both the local Bishop and the University to prevent it occurring – neither wanted to risk trouble with high ecclesiastical
authority. But Duke George was determined to have it, and he
was the master. He wrote caustically to the Chancellor of Leipzig
University: 'That our theologians should shun such disputations seems to us contrary to their profession; for to them as
teachers of the Scriptures it ought to be a joy to bring to light
that for which they have eaten many good dinners.' With this
jibe at their privileged position, he made it clear that he was
determined to make them sing for their suppers. And he wanted
to see the notorious young Augustinian from his cousin's
territory and the upstart University of Wittenberg put down by
Johann Eck, who had a reputation for winning debates.

As they rode, walked and drove into Leipzig, the
Wittenbergers who included Amsdorf the Rector of the Univer-

sity, Melancthon, Johann Lang and many others, knew they were entering a town not likely to be too friendly. The arrival began badly. Karlstadt's cart broke its axle and tumbled the Dean on to the ground, his great tomes falling out with him. The party went on with as much dignity as could be mustered to their lodgings, Karlstadt and Luther and the other principal men staying with Melchoir Lotter the printers. Lotter had been taking an increasing volume of Luther's work, as Grünenberg became more and more obviously unequal to the task.

After acrimonious arguments about the judges and about the reporting of the debate; after a tedious procession to church, a new twelve-part Mass, and a long droned out and largely inaudible introduction by a local academic, the debate finally got under way on 27 July between Eck and Karlstadt in the great hall of the Pleissenburg Castle. The next two weeks were reported by numerous eye-witnesses, from all points of view. There were in fact only a few days of debate; 29 June–2 July were a break for Saints' Days. Eck and Karlstadt debated free will and grace. Eck blustered and interrupted. Karlstadt, short-sighted and nervous, kept producing books and papers to quote from. Eck pressured the umpires to rule that Karlstadt must leave his reference books out of the chamber. On paper it looks rather as if Karlstadt had the best of the argument, but in the chamber Eck always dominated the scene, nearly twice the size of his opponent who was almost lost to sight behind his desk. Eck had a memory as good as Luther's and he poured the texts out, loud and confident. Eventually, on 4 July, after the break and various light relief including a magnificent imitation of Eck by the Duke's one-eyed clown, it was Luther's turn, although his participation was in doubt up to the last moment.

The atmosphere changed immediately. All the reporters began to write in electric terms. Luther was at his best, an innate dramatic sense enabling him to appear cool, almost casual; brilliant and genial; sharp yet apparently relaxed; carrying a bunch of pinks – people used flowers as deodorants, but it was unusual to carry them to the podium in a debate. Dr Luther sniffed at them from time to time. But here was no dilettante. The bones of his rather heavy, but still sharply ascetic-looking face, stood out. He glowed, ready to quip, ready to be angry, but confident in his possession of a single master theory which enabled him to arrange all Scripture and all of the traditional understanding of the Gospel, and all devotional life and religious behaviour in an easily understood fashion. He wore his Doctor's silver ring, as always, and a black cowl over a white habit. Some people felt something nearly uncanny about him. Luther projected his inner neurosis and infected his listeners with his extraordinary mixture of nervous excitement, brilliant reasoning and religious commitment. An enemy, Emser, the Dominican theologian from Dresden, described him as 'haughty, bold and presumptuous'.

Eck conceded point after point, as he had done with Karlstadt, at tactical points. On Indulgences, almost every item was agreed. None of that mattered. 'Authority' was the crunch where Eck could make people see that Luther was out of line. The debate went better than he could have hoped. Taunting Luther with being a Hussite heretic, a Bohemian, he had Luther virtually admitting it, saying that not everything that the Council of Constance had condemned was in fact heretical and that Huss was not entirely wrong. Duke George caught his breath. 'Plague take it,' came the exclamation. In Leipzig of all places! Leipzig where the University itself had originated from a group of Germans who seceded from Prague in the early fifteenth century as a protest against the teaching of Huss. The detail of the argument was not at issue – it was enough that Luther was challenging authority, Popes and Councils alike, and defending Huss, a heretic known in the popular mind as one who said the laity should receive the wine at communion (not in fact an heretical claim), and whose followers had set up the still flourishing schismatic Church in Bohemia.

Gradually the debate petered out. Luther grumbled that Eck was like a lute player everlastingly returning to the same old tune. Then it was the turn of Karlstadt again. Luther went home. On the last two days those of Leipzig University who were bound to attend had to be woken for their meals, so one witness reported. Finally, the Duke need the hall for some guests who were coming for a hunting expedition.

Back in Wittenberg, Luther reported at length to Spalatin on 10 July: 'Eck stamped about with much ado as though he were in an arena, holding up the Bohemians before me . . . accusing me of heresy and support of the Bohemian heretics . . . These accusations tickled the Leipzig audience more than the debate itself. In rebuttal I brought up the Greek Christians during the past thousand years' – Luther was right of course that the Greeks did not acknowledge the authority of the papacy – 'and also the ancient fathers who had not been under the authority of the Roman pontiff, although I did not deny the primacy of honour due to the Pope.' When Luther rebutted some decision of the Council of Constance, 'at this point the adder swelled up, exaggerated my crime, and nearly went insane in his adulation of the Leipzig audience'.

The debate had been a draw, though numerous people were convinced that Luther had had the best of the argument throughout. Students and some staff migrated from Leipzig to Wittenberg. But in Leipzig itself it had been a rough time for the Wittenbergers. Luther was angry that Eck had continued to preach in Leipzig churches what he had conceded was wrong in debate. Luther had the opportunity of one sermon to expound his own point of view. Duke George provided massive hospitality for Eck, and the merest minimum of a wine party for Luther and his colleagues.

Luther ended his report to Spalatin: 'Whereas we had hoped for harmony between the people of Wittenberg and Leipzig, they acted so aggressively that I fear it will seem that discord and enmity were actually born here. This is the fruit of human glory. I, who really restrain my impetuosity cannot but vomit out my dislike of them, for I am flesh and blood, and their hatred was very shameless and their injustice was quite shameless – it was thoroughly wrong to be so lacking in fair play in so sacred a matter.' That was it. Luther was unable to adapt himself to the fundamental lack of seriousness on theological issues, the politics and opportunism of the opposition, as he saw it.

In his July letter to Spalatin, Luther welcomed him and the Elector back to Saxony from the imperial election, and wrote a word of prayer for the soul of Treasurer Pfeffinger who had died. It was back to work again now. At the University, the thrust towards reform continued. The appointment to the Chair of Hebrew continued to be a problem. Luther reported to Lang that 'the University is prospering, especially the study of theology. Leipzig is Leipzig as usual.' Friary business was not much different, and there was an increasing new seam of events,

visits and letters from prople who had been impressed by
Luther's reputation and sought advice on government or other
matters. At the end of November came Count Isenburg of the
Teutonic Order for a night; Luther grumbled to Spalatin that
the grand man had had to spend a night in the pub outside the
city gates, because the gatekeeper was already drunk when the
Count arrived and refused to open the gate, which he had closed
for the night at five o'clock. The Count was returning from
Prussia to retire to his family estate on the Rhine, where he eventually introduced Lutheran reforms. Then a request by post for
advice about a disagreement between Regensburg City Council
and the local Bishop on income from a pilgrimage centre was
asked by Thomas Fuchs, the Imperial Agent in the town – he
recognised Luther as the kind of man who had given thought to
problems of this kind and maybe he could help him to sort out
the matter.

The endless letters from Luther to Spalatin included answers
to the latter's theological queries, answers delivered now
without any apologies about Luther's lack of qualification. Into
the new year there was an affair about a local widow who left her
house in a will to the Cathedral Canons and then wished to
change the will. She had already vacated the house and the
Canons were obdurate about allowing her back – Luther did his
best to arbitrate and see that justice was done. In 1520, there was
worry about the town, insufficient supplies and, not surprisingly, insufficient housing. Finally, unrest in the town grew
into a full-blooded 'town' versus 'gown' affair, with the students
and the journeymen of Cranach, the successful painter who had
studios and a shop in the town carrying weapons for serious use.
Luther himself was highly critical of the part played by the
University authorities, much to the annoyance of those
authorities. The Elector had to send in a force to restore order.
Towards the summer of 1520 young Melancthon was thinking,
after two years in Wittenberg, of marrying. Luther was quizzed
about it – he said it was not his job either to advise the young
layman to marry or to choose a wife for him, and that he did not
seem to be in a great hurry anyhow. And there were the continuing references to Karl von Miltitz, still trying to run his
single-handed reconciliation campaign between Luther and

Rome, causing a stream of irritations and misunderstandings to the Elector, Spalatin, Luther and others.

In his cell Luther poured out his writings, and all over Germany printers took them up and sold them profitably. The post-Leipzigian polemics continued, in the bitterest modes on both sides. Luther felt he was simply being used. His opponents were sure of themselves as the defenders of the traditional true faith, defending the Myth in all its purity – just as, in another sense, Luther also saw himself. Supporters of Luther continued to make their appearances. From Augsburg, Oecolampadius (Hausschein) and Adelmann wrote *Canonici Indocti* and from Nuremberg Pirkheimer wrote *Eckius Dedolatus* – 'Doctor Corner polished off'.

Universities were pressed by Duke George and others to place their votes pro or contra Luther. Invited to judge the Leipzig debate, Erfurt entirely declined, and Paris procrastinated for nearly two years. Louvain and Cologne published predictably conservative judgements, the latter in August 1519, the former early in 1520, after consulting Charles V's old tutor, their old member, Adrian of Utrecht, now Bishop of Tortosa in Spain, and destined to become Pope Adrian VI. There was some genuine argument. Bucer wrote to a friend that Cardinal Catejan, on being consulted, considered Luther's statements 'errors' not 'heresies'; he still wanted to minimise the implications in principle. The Franciscans who had so enraged Luther before Leipzig, stuck to their guns, drew in Eck and got Luther's bishop to speak; in a letter to Staupitz, Luther wrote of his bishop, 'He is only a wretched bladder blown up by Eck's wind'. But the bluster gave way to a sad plea: 'You are too neglectful of me. I stretch out to you as a hungry child to its mother's breast.' And then: 'Last night I dreamed of you. It seemed as if you were going away from me and that I was weeping bitterly in great sadness. But you waved your hand and said that I should take courage and that you would return to me' – desperation mingled with commitment and a tragic sense of the inevitable began to grip Luther.

As well as polemics Luther was writing his pastoral theology, his *Fourteen Consolations* for the very ill Elector, and a text on *The Blessed Sacrament of the Holy and True Body of Christ*, compared in its nature as a fellowship event with the degenerate 'religious' fellowship of the craft brotherhoods. The sacrament of communion is 'a ford, a bridge, a door, a ship and a stretcher by which we pass from this world into eternal life'. He believed in the true presence in the bread and wine. 'Through the change wrought by love there is one bread, one drink, one body, one community. This is the true unity of Christian brethren.' The Mass had, by now, ceased to be something he felt he must say every day, a 'good work', a 'sacrifice' – rather it was a communal celebration. Eck had spread the scandalous news that enquiries had revealed that Luther had not said Mass while he was in Leipzig.

This piece on the Blessed Sacrament included a mild recommendation that the laity ought to be allowed to communicate with the wine as well as the bread. When Duke George read this, he was enraged and sent off letters to the Elector and to the Council of Regency demanding Luther's denunciation: he must after all be a Bohemian – perhaps he was one in fact. Spalatin thought he had better be in possession of the precise details of Luther's actual pedigree, and Luther obliged with brief biographical data, but was upset again: 'This does not frighten me at all, but it blows up the sails of my heart with an incredible wind.'

A fortnight later, Luther wrote his usual kind of letter to Johann Lang: 'They are spreading the rumour that I was born in Bohemia . . . They have won Duke George, taken him in tow.' Luther said he was delighted with Erasmus's letter to the Archbishop of Mainz. He ended: 'The Ambassador of the Spaniards is staying with our Sovereign. I and Philip dined with him yesterday. It was a splendid party.' Luther contrived to enjoy himself at Wittenberg, whatever the troubles.

Spalatin tried, towards the end of 1519, to get Luther to write a long series of postils, commentaries on the gospels and epistles for the Sundays, a ruse to get him away from polemical writing. Luther simply found time to do both. So also Spalatin got him to send conciliatory letters to Albrecht, the Cardinal Archbishop of Mainz, and to the Bishop of Merseburg. The worldly Archbishop, prepared now to communicate directly with Luther, dismissed the theological matters as not really important – the right of the Pope and the freedom of the will were trifling matters, he said, *nugamenta*, compared with the demands of the Christian life. But he warned Luther against stirring up the people. Merseburg was more severe. But just at this time came a blast, to wreck Spalatin's plan, from the Bishop of Meissen, who had confiscated copies of Luther's sermon on the Mass, and said it was conducive to eternal damnation. Luther tore off a scorching reply, assuming that the Bishop himself could not of course have written such nonsense: *Answer to the Proclamation of the Stolpen Official*, suggesting the Bishop had better burn Luther's books just as Reuchlin's books had been burnt – fire was the best protection against what one did not like. Miltitz reported obsequiously to the Elector that the language had brought a smile even to the face of Duke George.

It was increasingly a shock to Luther to realise that he was sure Jan Huss was a great and important theologian, and that this 'heretic' had been burnt for his 'heresy'. To Spalatin, in January 1520, he wrote:

> I have taught and held all the teachings of John Huss, but thus far did not know it. Johann Staupitz had taught it in the same unintentional way. In short we are all Hussites and did not know it. Even Paul and Augustine are in reality Hussites . . . I am so shocked that I do not know what to think when I see such terrible judgements of God over mankind, namely that the most evident evangelical truth was burned in public . . . Woe to this earth. Farewell, Martin Luther.

Ten days later, he wrote fatefully to Spalatin after reading Valla's exposure of the Donation of Constantine, that he now had no doubt that the Pope was the real Antichrist, expected by the world. He said 2000 copies of Huss's book on The Church had been printed; and then, suddenly, wanted to see a book Spalatin had 'about the flames and fires that were seen in the sky over Vienna . . . Perhaps my tragedy is contained in them.' The following month, replying to the condemnation of some of his writings by the University of Louvain, Luther referred to Valla in a long list of scholars whose writings were unjustly condemned including Erasmus and Reuchlin – Valla, who was charged, he said, 'with the crime of ignorance by those who are quite unworthy to hand him a piss pot'.

In February, Spalatin sent one of his worried queries about

Luther's doctrine of justification by faith alone. What did he mean? Were people not to do good works? Perhaps, he ventured, Luther's doctrine was one of the causes of the increase in lawlessness and immorality. The question provided Luther with the occasion for his important German text *On Good Works*. He said he meant that good works in their fullness flowed from the man of faith, and that it was no good trying to earn some kind of spiritual reputation or merit by being a 'do-gooder', or worse a mere fulfiller of devotional practices. But of course the behaviour of the justified man, the man of faith would shine like a good deed in a naughty world. And such a man could and would do good works and make good use of spiritual advice – Luther proceeded to run through the Judaic 'Ten Commandments' from the Old Testament and to pour out advice inherited from a long tradition, salted by his own experience, covering most spheres of human activity from insufficient discipline, for instance in sexual matters, to excess of discipline in, for instance, diet. 'Foolish women cling so firmly to their fasting that they would rather run the risk of great danger to the child they carry, as well as to themselves, than not fast with the others.' Otherwise, however, fasting could be useful to keep the body in trim and to combat excesses in food and drink, and sex. There was no question of his championing some kind of subjective righteousness entirely detached from the realities of life.

In this piece Luther's German was coming into its own. The conforming unbelieving multitude were not spared: 'When we are at Mass in our Churches we stand like blockheads. . . . The beads rattle, the pages rustle, and the mouth mumbles. And that is all there is to it.' But he waxed eloquent in expounding his doctrine that God 'justifies' the man who believes. He quoted a catena of Scriptural passages ('If anyone should sin, we have our advocate with the Father, Jesus Christ, who is just; he is the sacrifice that takes our sins away': 1 John 2.1–2) from the New Testament, and five quotations from the Old Testament.

Although begun in March, Luther took time (for him) over this text and it was published in June, with a dedication to Duke John, the Elector's brother, and probable successor: 'Many people think little of me and say that I only write little pamphlets and sermons in German for the uneducated laity . . . Would to God that in my lifetime I had, to my fullest ability, helped one layman to be better', and anyhow 'if I had a mind to write big books . . . I could perhaps, with God's help, do it more readily than they could write my kind of little discourse'. He was in fact already writing the 'big books', in the form of the commentaries on Galatians and Psalms, though they did not seem 'big' to him – and he was right that the little books, were in a way, more difficult, involving genuine communication with the less well educated. In this text on Good Works he put a favourite example of how genuine faith and love work out. A loving husband and wife do not have to be continually doing things to prove their love for each other. They love each other in a deep trust and faith, without demanding proof or earning merit in some arithmetic or calculated love.

It was again a crucial time. Something broke in Luther's mind this spring, as it had done the previous spring. The terrible query about Antichrist had become a certainty. Reports were flowing in about the new examination of Luther's writings going on in Rome; it was known that Eck had gone there to influence the examination. Rumours were rife of plots against Luther's life. It was reassuring, but also a reason for worry, that offers came from two knights to Luther to take refuge in their castles, one from Sylvester von Schaumberg in Franconia, the other from the famous Ulrich von Hutten, to take refuge with his friend Franz von Sickingen in his castle in the hills beside the Moselle. Luther took the offers seriously, and pointed out to Spalatin that if Rome compelled him to flee he had no need to go to Bohemia but could stay in 'the heart of Germany'. And, to his surprise, even Staupitz sent an encouraging letter from Nuremberg, where he was visiting.

In Luther's own mind things were moving fast. He issued a new sermon in April on the Mass: 'Faith is the real priestly office . . . All Christians are priests, man or woman, young or old, lord or servant, wife or maid, scholar or layman.' Mass, he complained had been transfigured into an act of magic. Meanwhile, on the Franciscan front, a Leipzig man called Aveld had issued a piece against Luther and in defence of the papacy. Late in May, Luther issued a twenty-thousand word German piece in reply *On the Papacy in Rome against the most celebrated Romanist in Leipzig*. The words on both sides were more bitter than ever. And the content of Luther's commits him further again against the prin-

ciple of papal authority as neither established by Jesus of
Nazareth nor an authority obligatory for all Christians to obey –
the Russians, the Greeks and the Bohemians do without it.
Aveld had compared the Pope with Aaron in the Old Testament,
continuing the line of the Judaic high priest. Luther asks, 'Must
the Pope let his hair grow then, must the Pope be circumcised?'
Luther had been begged by the Leipzigians not to drag the name
of Leipzig into it, as they had grave doubts about the arguments
employed by Aveld.

> No one should think that when I mentioned Leipzig, I wanted
> to shame this honourable city and its university. I was forced
> to do so by the bravado and arrogance of the imagined title
> 'public reader of all Holy Scripture in Leipzig', a title never
> heard of. This crude miller's beast still cannot sing his hee-
> haw and yet, all on his own, he embarks on a matter which the
> Roman See itself, as well as all the bishops and scholars,
> could not clarify in a thousand years. Moreover, I would have
> thought that Leipzig is too precious in his eyes for him to go
> smearing his drivel and snivel on this honourable and famous
> city.

The substantial pamphlet went through twenty editions in
Germany and Switzerland, so low was the reputation of the
papacy, so willing were people of all classes to listen not just to
abuse, but to solid argument against papal authority, without in
any way supposing this to be an attack on Christianity. The Myth
had been growing a life of its own, independent of its institutions.

Luther had come to the end of the line. The Church
authorities, whatever they were planning about his own
personal case, had shown no interest in the kind of radical, all
over reform which he was now asking for. A hundred reform
programmes had been set on foot in the previous hundred
years, and failed. So Luther followed the logic of his case – he
turned to the Church as a whole, the total membership and particularly to the leaders of society, the most powerful of those
Church members. Over three months, he gradually put together
a great reform programme. It was still ill-stitched in places when
he decided to publish it and began delivering the pages of his
written piece to the printer, heading the piece boldly: *To the*

Christian Nobility of the German Nation concerning the Reform of the Christian Estate.

Here was no proletarian revolution, but an almost medieval turning to the State for action against the Church – only this time it was not a sovereign versus an archbishop, both competing for power. It was a monk asking the ruler and leading men to clean up the Church, which in effect meant to clean up society, so embedded in every way had the ecclesiastical operations become in the life of the country from its fundamental economic and financial resources to the inner motivations of each individual and group. This was an entirely new version of the Church turning to the secular arm to put its judgements into effect.

A torrent of German demands poured forth in this text which shocked even Luther's closest friends, by its fierceness and by, what seemed to them, its sometimes intemperate language. And the programme itself was shocking in the extent of change it demanded. The text was preceded by a letter to his close colleague in the Theology Faculty at Wittenberg, Reverend Nikolaus Amsdorf, also a canon of the castle church: 'Jesus . . . The time for silence is past and the time to speak has come.' He was putting the matter of reform before the nobility 'in the hope that God may help his Church through the laity, since the clergy, to whom this task more properly belongs, have grown quite indifferent'. He excused his impertinence with a current joke about the ever present monk – 'perhaps I owe my God and the world another work of folly. I intend to pay my debt like an honest man. And if I succeed, I shall for the time being be a court jester. And if I fail I still have one advantage – no one need buy me a cap or put scissors on my head. It is a question who will put the bells on whom.' And so he goes on, coming in with his usual thumping doctoral justification: 'I am glad for the opportunity to fulfil my doctor's oath, even in the guise of a fool.'

The text itself was addressed in the first place to the twenty-year-old Emperor, Charles Habsburg, but shortly it moved into a more general tone: 'God has given us a young man of noble birth as head of state, and in him has awakened great hopes of good in many hearts.' Luther then moved into three fundamental matters, three 'walls' by which the 'Romanists' had protected themselves against reform. 1. The temporal power was declared to have no jurisdiction over the spiritual. But, Luther said, all Christians were priests – and quoted a text much beloved of supporters of the Second Vatican Council, 'You are a royal priesthood and a holy people' (1 Peter 2.9). Translated into institutional practice, Luther was suggesting that when a bishop consecrated a priest, he was simply acting on behalf of the community to license a man to use power he already had through his baptism. Luther may well turn out to have backed the right horse in the end, to judge by current Roman Catholic theology, veering as it is towards reformed theology on this point, but what he said was a contradiction of official Roman Catholic theology, and put him outside traditional understanding, teaching and practice. However, his case was that the Church had always intended to be true to Scripture and he, Luther, was pointing to what Scripture actually said, as distinct from interpretations fathered on it.

It was the reform of practice as much as of theory that Luther was advocating in this text. If a priest was murdered, the case should be treated no differently than if a layman had been murdered – the community had not earned an interdict. This kind of attack on Canon Law, with all its privileges over secular law, was 'revolutionary' and was felt as a frightening threat even by some laity, who saw the walls of their conventional world crumbling with its disappearance.

The second wall was the Romanist 'claim that only the Pope may interpret Scripture . . . an outrageous fancied fable', and the third that only a Pope may summon a Council of the Church. In both cases, said Luther, any layman had authority equal to that of the Pope. Karlstadt had in fact said just this about scripture more than two years previously, but no one had bothered because it was said by a rather myopic officious academic whom nobody cared much about, and who never managed to project his message widely. Luther went on to list the things which a Council should look to. It was a long list, including the following.

The Pope should not go about in ostentatious style. Rome should cease to milk the Italians and the Germans in order to provide vast incomes for the cardinals in Rome. This was popular stuff: 'The "drunken Germans" are not supposed to understand what the Romanists are up to . . .' Rome fomented a dispute, then stepped in and confiscated funds. There were all kinds of pluralisms and absenteeism which should end. No dues should be paid to Rome, especially annates, the first year's income from an ecclesiastical benefice, which led to substantial sums leaving every European country (Henry VIII redirected these payments to the crown in England in 1532, and greatly increased them). Luther's anger was now directed obsessively against the Pope and the Roman apparatus. 'Cut down the creeping crawling swarm of vermin at Rome, so that the Pope's household can be supported out of the Pope's own pocket . . . The Pope should have no authority over the Emperor, except the right to anoint and crown him at the altar . . . The Pope should restrain himself, take his fingers out of the pie, and claim no title to the kingdom of Naples and Sicily.' The text went into great detail about the various and very numerous official channels by which money went to Rome. The final scandal of it all was that all this business was itself sold to the great international banker, the Fugger.

With accuracy and well-argued presentation Luther reeled off all the machinery of the ecclesiastical institution, unworthy, as everyone knew so much of it was, unworthy of the spiritual arm of society, claiming to have an authority granted by Jesus of Nazareth. But when Luther turned to the symbol of it all, he became truly enraged. 'What Christian heart can or ought to take pleasure in seeing that when the Pope wishes to receive communion, he sits quietly like a gracious lord and has the sacrament brought to him on a golden rod by a bowing cardinal on bended knee? As though the holy sacrament were not worthy enough for the Pope, a poor, stinking sinner . . . Help us, O God, to get a free, general council which will teach the Pope that he, too, is a man, and not more than God, as he sets himself up to be.'

The desired reforms rolled out. Priests should be allowed to marry. 'The priest should not be compelled to live without a wedded wife . . . many a poor priest is overburdened with wife and child, his conscience troubled.' The priest sometimes needed a woman to keep house and then 'it is like putting straw and fire together and forbidding them to burn . . . The Pope has as little power to command this as he has to forbid eating, drinking, defecating, or growing fat.' The 'Ban' should be banished. Endowed Masses were to be limited, festivals to be abolished, or in the case of the major ones transferred to Sundays; too much work was lost and there was too much drunkenness. Travelling beggars should be banned, and each city should mind its poor.

Luther was quite worried about his request for curtailing the endowed Masses, and abolishing therefore the swarms of priests employed to say them and do little else. He said that theologians were still trying to thrash out the true meaning of the Mass, but meanwhile these Masses should be curtailed because they kept men in idleness. But he made an exception for the great cathedral foundations where important educational work was done. 'My proposal is perhaps too bold, and an unheard-of thing, especially for those who are concerned that they would lose their job and means of livelihood if such Masses were discontinued. I must refrain from saying more about it until we arrive again at a proper understanding of what the Mass is and what it is for . . . I am not speaking of the old Foundations which were established for the children of the nobility . . . I am speaking of the new foundations . . .' There were too many, and as things were at these smaller places their incumbents all got reduced to 'anthem singers, organ wheezers and reciters of decadent, indifferent Masses'. The crowds of Massing priests at Erfurt and Wittenberg were vividly in Luther's mind.

Everything came into this fulminating text. The papal legates and their faculties 'which they sell us for large sums of money' should be driven out of Germany. 'This traffic is nothing but skulduggery.' Luther reminded his readers that Huss was burned at Constance after the Pope and Emperor together had reneged on the safe conduct promised when his theology still stood in need of a careful and honest examination. He defended the taking of bread and wine, the body and the blood, by the laity, which was in no sense a heretical practice. Universities, of course, had to be reformed. Aristotle's 'philosophy' should be removed, though his Logic, Rhetoric and Poetics, at least in abridged form, should be kept. Of the other two major Faculties, he had to leave the Medicine Faculty to medical men. The Legal Faculty simply needed Canon Law removing from it.

Towards the end, Luther turned to social and economic ills, and the clichés of every trimmer of stylish living are heard.

Trade in spices should be curtailed since it carried money out of Germany, and in any case the Germans were able to grow nearly all they needed. Dress, too, was too costly, with silks coming from abroad again. The bankers were taking too much interest. And so on to the common failings of mankind. People were eating and drinking too much. The brothels should be closed. Here he commended marriage at a reasonably early age, and deplored the common picture of young people living wildly, becoming disgusted with themselves and then turning to being a monk or a priest for which 'not one in a hundred' was suited. The motive was simply that they could not see how to support themselves and a family. A vow of celibacy should not be permitted before the age of thirty.

He ended this piece – which was to set the whole of the German-speaking world by the ears – in his usual personal fashion. 'I know full well that I have been very outspoken . . . I have attacked many things too severely. But what else ought I to do? . . . I would rather have the anger of the world on me than the anger of God . . . Well, I know another little song about Rome . . . If their ears are itching to hear it I will sing that one to them too' – he was already pondering the next cannonade. He said he would be worried if his writing was not condemned, since it was the destiny of a just cause to be condemned: 'Therefore just let them go hard at it, pope, bishop, priest, monk or scholar. They are just the ones to persecute the truth, as they have always done. God give us all a Christian mind, and grant to the Christian nobility of the German nation in particular true spiritual courage to do the best they can for the poor church. Amen. Wittenberg, in the year 1520.'

Luther had faced the fact long ago that 'anger' and 'persecution' were main ingredients of real life. It had reached the stage where he positively invited persecution. Only someone willing to embrace it would have been able to bring along a sufficiently large torch flame to get the great bonfire burning, as burn it was certainly bound to do eventually, though damp and green in places. And he had no qualms about allowing anger a major place in his public writing.

When Johann Lang received his copy of the Appeal, he rushed a message to Luther to try to stop publication. But of course it was too late. Luther was in a carefree mood by now. 'Greetings.

Dear Father, is my pamphlet which you call a trumpet blast, really so fierce and cruel as you and all others seem to think? I confess it is free and aggressive . . . Good or bad it is no longer in my power to recall it. Four thousand copies have already been printed and sent away, nor could I cause Lotther, the publisher, the loss he would sustain in recalling these. If I have sinned we must remedy it by prayer . . .'. He gave news that Melancthon was going to marry the Mayor's daughter, Katherine Krapp, and then with a ringing shaft against the Pope, Antichrist, he ended the letter.

The die had been cast. The Church had to be reformed, and it had to be done without Rome. Rome herself had to be recognised as centrally guilty for bringing the Church to the state of corruption it was in. In June a new text of Sylvester Prierias had arrived in Luther's hand, replying to Luther's reply to him. Luther sent back an answer more vehement than ever. Everyone in Rome had become 'mad, foolish, raging, insane, fools, sticks, stones, hell and evil' to allow such an infernal work to go out into the Church. 'Antichrist is enthroned in God's very temple. If Rome believes these things then happy is Greece, happy is Bohemia . . . Farewell, you unhappy, lost and blasphemous Rome; the anger of God has come upon you at last.' The anger of Martin Luther at any rate.

CHAPTER TEN

Towards the Summit

Anti-clericalism, along with demands for Church reform and renewal, further powered by general social unrest, was growing everywhere. Its leaders were coming from the ranks of the priests themselves. In the capital town of the Swiss canton of Zurich, the new young parish priest at the Great Minster, Ulrich Zwingli, was getting into his stride with new-style biblical sermons, denunciations of Indulgences, and a reference or two to Luther as a prophet for the times, a description taken from the Introduction in Froben's volume of Luther's writings.

In London the violent death in prison of Hunne had left tensions unresolved; Londoners felt that same resentment about the numerous members of the privileged class of pensioned Massing priests, and even more about their easy living superiors, which Luther and his contemporaries had felt in Eisenach, Erfurt and Wittenberg. Across England and Scotland were secret groups of Lollards, a network of people who for a century now had nurtured among themselves a tradition of reading translations of the text of the Bible in manuscript excerpts from various popular sections of the Old and New Testaments, and occasionally from the complete edition of Wycliffe's (or Purvey's) fourteenth-century translation, rare though it was, the only English translation in existence. While for the most part conforming to the normal expressions of public ecclesiastical observance, the Lollards privately responded with the special fervour of total commitment to the Gospel, nourished a form of religious egalitarianism which in some respect could be called a proto-Protestantism, and were sharply critical of the established priesthood. The civil and ecclesiastical authorities were continually on the watch for them; church trials and civil burnings occurred regularly for a century and more, in many areas of the two countries. Merchants and shop people as well as peasants were involved, and they were to form a ready seedbed later when Tyndale's New Testament (1526) arrived in the country – in 1520 Tyndale was a mature student at Cambridge, at a time when Luther's works were just coming on sale in the bookshops in the university town. Attempts to keep them out by public burnings of them were not successful.

England was least well served of all European countries in the matter of vernacular translations of the Bible. To possess a copy of the Wycliffe (or Purvey) version, when it was recognised, was taken as evidence of heresy. The version was, however, sometimes in highly orthodox hands and greatly prized without being recognised; this was the case with a copy of it at the Charterhouse in Sheen, which Sir Thomas More thought must be one of the very rare copies of some permitted fifteenth-century translation. Elsewhere in Europe translations were not suspect in the same way, and were now spreading rapidly with the diffusion of printing presses in every town in Europe. While ecclesiastical authority normally held itself aloof from giving its favour to such translations, in some places, particularly Florence, no stigma attached to the practice of reading the Bible in groups in one's own language, and very occasionally as by Bishop Briçonnet in Meaux, twenty miles east of Paris, it was actually encouraged.

Of the various attempts to spread a better understanding of the Bible, much the most ambitious was a Spanish project for a complete text in the original languages of the whole Bible, the work of Cardinal Ximenes de Cisneros at the University of Alcala. It comprised five volumes, and included both the original Hebrew version and the later Greek version of the Old Testament (along with an interlinear Latin crib), an original Greek text of the New Testament, and on every page, for comparison, the standard 'Vulgate' fourth-century Latin translation of Jerome. It was intended as a study volume and on the page was included a variety of Hebrew and Greek grammatical assistance. For the opening five books of the Old Testament (the Pentateuch), across the bottom of the page was printed the Targum, a version in Aramaic (the derivative from Hebrew which Jesus of Nazareth spoke) made in about AD 100. A magnificent work of scholarship this 'Polyglot Bible', or 'Complutensian Bible' can be seen in a number of libraries today. Copies were delivered to the Vatican Library, and eventually registered there in 1520. Not surprisingly, they made no impact on the Luther case. They were part of the world of high scholarship, greatly respected, and used when necessary, but always somewhat suspect. The whole stock of the five volumes had in fact been impounded in Spain for more than three years – the work was completed in 1517 when Ximenes died. This world of theological and biblical study by-passed the Pope, busy with ecclesiastical business, family affairs, and pleasure.

The Luther case was reopened at the Vatican in January 1520. A committee of cardinals, including Cajetan, met at the beginning of the year and put proposals to the Pope in March. He should issue a Bull condemning various theses, some as 'offensive to pious ears', others as actually 'heretical', but not naming Luther. At the same time, further letters were to be sent to Luther's superior, and the Elector. It did not occur to the Vatican authorities to make any attempt to reply directly to Luther's appeal to be shown from Scripture where he had gone wrong; they were apparently unaware of the threateningly critical impact of the new scholarship, and of the revised theology which would inevitably flow from it. However, Cajetan wanted to keep the temperature low, in spite of his own ill-judged threats at the Augsburg meeting. He was more aware than anyone else at the Vatican of the need to improve the practice of theology and the popular understanding of religion.

Cajetan, however, had reckoned without Dr Johann Eck, who arrived in Rome at this moment with the avowed purpose of putting an end to Luther's initiative for good. He quickly obtained an audience with the Pope and got him to reject the somewhat eirenic proposals of Cajetan's committee. He recommended outright condemnation of Luther by name; and his uncomplicated approach convinced the Pope. Here, after all, was an experienced theologian from Germany who really understood the situation. His approach would see an end to the matter which had dragged on for more than two years now, and was threatening to become much more than a local Saxon difficulty. Two recent satires on Cajetan by the knight-poet Hutten, did not help the moderate party which was now overruled. In early May, Eck took fresh proposals, to the Pope's country estate of Magliana, where the Pontifex Maximus was enjoying a hunting expedition in the spring weather. The fun of the chase and the exhilaration of the hilly scenery inspired Eck – or even the Pope himself – to a stirring opening for their text: *Exsurge Domine* . . . 'Arise, Lord! Vindicate your cause against the fierce foxes who are trying to destroy your vineyard, against the wild boar which wreaks havoc there . . . Arise Peter, Paul and all the saints, the Church universal . . .'

Luther was the wild boar who was wrecking the vineyard of the Church and he was said to be guilty, along with accomplices, of all sorts of things which were declared to be heretical. It was another brash Roman text. The text declared that it was heretical to point out that the three parts of the Sacrament of Penance, contrition, confession, and satisfaction are not to be found in the New Testament; it was heretical to say that the laity should communicate in both the consecrated bread and the consecrated wine; it was heretical to say that it was contrary to the will of the Spirit to burn heretics; and so on, along with the more technical doctrinal matters of Indulgences, good works, and free will.

The Pope liked the text which Eck carried triumphantly off to the Consistory of Cardinals. Objections from Cardinals Cajetan and Carvajal that the text was unscholarly and inaccurate in its failure to make distinctions between matters of doctrine, discipline and opinion, were overruled by the majority. Various legal aspects were ironed out, and turned out later to comprise the most efficiently drafted parts of the Bull. Formal assent was obtained on 1 June. Luther would have sixty days from the day on which he received the Bull to recant or be denounced as a heretic and excommunicated. After the usual bureaucratic delays the Bull was sent speeding off by two special emissaries to Germany. One emissary was Eck himself, the other was the highly experienced Jerome Aleander.

Rumours about the new Roman document reached Luther in increasingly emphatic form during the summer round about the time he was penning the remark: 'I know another little song about Rome.' As the final sheets of the *Open Letter to the Nobility* were going down to the printer in the first days of August, Luther was already making notes for this next communication.

It was to be a text in Latin for the Church itself, about itself. It would present his conclusions on the true nature of the community of Christians, the Church, and would cause shock waves throughout Christendom. It was October before author and printer had completed their work. At the same time, throughout August, Luther was composing a formal and personal letter to the young Emperor and a public *Offer and Protest* – these were personal matters and both texts he discussed in detail with Spalatin in sharp distinction from his polemical works about which he seldom consulted anyone once he had settled the truth of the matter in his own mind, and the text began to flow like molten metal. But texts on matters of negotiation about his personal case were quite different. In his letter, Luther asked the Emperor not to 'allow truth or falsehood to be condemned without being heard and defeated' and 'to protect the truth'. He entrusted a copy of it to the Elector, who would be attending the Emperor's coronation and first Diet in the coming months. In fact, the letter only reached the Emperor's hands in January when he finally arrived in Worms. The public *Offer and Protest* was on similar lines and was eventually nailed up on the doors of various churches throughout Germany. Meanwhile, other developments were crowding in.

Very Reverend Father Staupitz, Vicar General of the Reformed Augustinians, was getting weary and felt unable to cope any longer with the threatening developments of the Luther case. Two years previously at Augsburg, the encounter had reduced him to a state of panic when he released Luther from his vows. Now the affair had grown from a merely Saxon affair to one of European-wide concern. Polarisation was proceeding apace, and he found he could not go along with outright opposition to papal authority. The formal excommunication of Luther, immediately in view now, was more than he could face. He decided to retire at the next triennial Chapter. However, this was not due till April 1521, and by July 1520 he could stand the pace no longer. He called the Chapter early, held it at Eisleben at the end of August and duly resigned. Wenceslas Link was elected Vicar General in his stead. Link was a friend and firm but prudent supporter of Luther. They had known each other in the cloister since 1508 and Link was convinced in principle of the rightness of Luther's position, though

like others he had tried a few weeks previously to persuade
Luther not to publish the *Appeal to the Nobility*. The election of
Link indicated the balance of opinion in favour of Luther within
the Order.

Miltitz was present at the Chapter, still worrying away at the
Luther case. He persuaded Link and Staupitz to ask Luther to
write a letter to the Pope in a personal sense, and if possible to
send him some writing as well. Luther was always willing to
listen to reason, and always willing to let his fluent pen flow; and
he had no personal animosity against the Medici Pope himself
but only against the whole system of papal procedures. Miltitz
asked Luther to come and see him at Lichtenberg about the
matter. Luther wrote to Spalatin describing the meeting on 11
October. 'We agreed . . . that I should publish a letter in
German and Latin, addressed to the Pope, as a preface to some
brief writing . . . I am to relate my whole story and show that I
never wanted to attack the Pope personally, and throw all the
blame on Eck.' Twenty-one months previously, Miltitz had
decided to throw Tetzel to the dogs in furtherance of a peace
plan; now it was Eck's turn – but this time it was to be too late.
However, Luther complied with his plan, and with his usual
dispatch composed a remarkable letter and to go with it a fine
piece, *The Freedom of a Christian Man*, often considered the most
successful of all his writings.

It is not known if the Pope ever saw the letter Luther wrote.
He would have been shocked if he did, for it was written as from
one Christian brother to another. It was without rancour,
though not without deliberate irony; and it had all the disarming qualities of Luther at his best – it was factual, honest,
logical, while clothed in the fairly strong language of current
fashion.

> To Leo, Pope at Rome, Martin Luther wishes salvation in
> Christ Jesus our Lord. Amen.
> Living among the monsters of this age with whom I am now
> for the third year waging war, I am compelled occasionally to
> look up to you, Leo, most blessed father . . . Indeed, since
> you are occasionally regarded as the sole cause of my battles I
> cannot help thinking of you . . . Your godless flatterers . . .
> have compelled me to appeal from your See to a future

council, despite the decrees of your predecessors Pius and Julius, who with a foolish tyranny forbade such an appeal. Nevertheless, I have never alienated myself from Your Blessedness to such an extent that I should not with all my heart wish you and Your See every blessing . . . I beg you to give me a hearing after I have vindicated myself by this letter, and believe me when I say that I have never thought ill of you personally . . . I have truly despised your See, the Roman Curia, which however, neither you nor anyone else can deny is more corrupt than any Babylon or Sodom ever was . . . Meanwhile, you, Leo, sit like a lamb in the midst of wolves . . . How can you alone oppose these monsters? Even if you would call to your aid three or four well-learned and thoroughly reliable cardinals, what are these among so many? You would all be poisoned [a sharp reference to an attempt to poison Leo X which had in fact been made three years previously] . . . If Bernard felt sorry for Eugenius [St Bernard wrote a book on the Pope's Duties at the time of Pope Eugenius III, 1145–53] at a time when the Roman See which, although even then corrupt, was ruled with better prospects for improvement, why should not we complain who for three hundred years have had such a great increase of corruption and wickedness?

Luther then related how Cardinal Cajetan failed to make peace with him and how Miltitz, whose previous efforts were defeated by Eck, had now tried again by suggesting to the Augustinians that Luther should write to the Pope himself.

Therefore, my Father Leo, do not listen to those sirens who pretend that you are not mere man but a demigod so that you may command and require whatever your wish. . . . You are a servant of servants [the famous title of the Pope, *servus servorum Dei*, the servant of the servants of God], and more than all other men you are in a most miserable and dangerous position . . . These men are your enemies . . . who exalt you above a council and the church universal . . . who ascribe to you alone the right of interpreting Scripture . . . If men do not see that I am your friend and your most humble subject in this matter, there is One who understands and judges [John 8.50].

Finally, he said he was sending a gift of some writing, small, but 'unless I am mistaken it contains the whole of Christian life in a brief form, provided you grasp its meaning. I am a poor man and have no other gift to offer, and you do not need to be enriched by any but a spiritual gift. May the Lord Jesus preserve you forever. Amen. Wittenberg, 6 September 1520.'

Luther translated the letter into German and had it printed and published in Wittenberg as a separate pamphlet on 4 November. The piece that had gone with it, and of which he himself thought so highly, was also published in German a little later. *The Freedom of a Christian Man* is a kind of epitome of Luther's doctrine. As he told Spalatin in a letter about this time, he was 'feeling so free now'. Having got down on paper all that was on his conscience about the Church and Society, he was able to express the heart of his understanding of Christianity almost entirely without the violence which crept into other texts. It was a moment of special freedom – the trammels had fallen away, new responsibilities had not yet accrued. It was the kind of writing he excelled in, at once practical, spiritual and intellectually authentic. The temptation or need to express his aggression fell away. In the heart of the mystery, in the person of Jesus of Nazareth, understood as the Christ, the Word, in the God of Mercy he found total assuagement for his bitterness and aggression.

Using the traditional dialectical method he took up two statements of St Paul from the New Testament; 1. 'A Christian is a perfectly free lord of all, subject to none.' 2. 'A Christian is a perfectly dutiful servant, subject to all.' From practical, well-judged statements that the liturgy, church services, have their essential place, as symbolic acts, he ran the full gamut through to existential, even mystical, affirmations. 'A Christian lives in Christ through faith, in his neighbour through love. By faith he is caught up beyond himself into God. By love he descends beneath himself into his neighbour. Yet he remains always in God and in his love, as Christ says in John: "Truly, truly I say to you, you will see heaven opened and the angels of God ascending and descending upon the Son of man."'

There was something of Renaissance individualism about the freedom with which Luther penned this piece, but equally of old-fashioned Bernadine, conscientious bluntness about the

letter he wrote to the Pope. The die was cast. His new Latin piece
on the Church was just coming from the presses. If the German
Appeal to the Nobility, written to the propertied, pedigreed,
privileged and powerful in the German lands with their varieties
of inherited responsibilities, created consternation, the new
Latin piece written to the educated of all Europe brought the
realisation that nothing less than a religious revolution was
afoot.

Luther had been lecturing and preaching for eight or nine
years now on the distinctive message of Jesus of Nazareth. But
the body of 'believers' in Jesus, the 'Church', the 'community'
or 'congregation of Christians', sometimes identified as 'the
spiritual arm' of Christendom, the whole Christian world –
about this, he had only adumbrated his ideas, attacking this
anomaly here, or swiping at that obvious corruption there,
albeit with a virulence and sharpness beginning to look unique.
As in the case of Huss in the previous century, and of so many
others in the sixteenth century, the sight of so many activities
which seemed to assort ill with the nature of a 'Church' as it
might be discerned in the text of the New Testament, set him
searching for a description of the Church which would fit the
words of Jesus and his first followers.

But Luther was unable to sit down and write a quiet academic
piece, *De Ecclesia*, on the Church. It had to be polemic. He set it
in a typical late medieval metaphor, taken from the endemic
anti-papalism stretching back to Joachim of Fiore, using the
'Old Testament' metaphor of the 'Babylonian Captivity'. About
the year 600 BC, Jerusalem was attacked and taken by the
Babylonians. The Jews were deported to Babylon, where they
remained for about sixty years. Luther entitled his piece *De Cap-
tivitate Babylonica Ecclesiae Praeludium (Prelude on the Babylonian
Captivity of the Church)*. It was on the captivity of the Church to the
papacy, a veritable deportation of the Christian people to the
papal tyranny. But the thirty thousand words he wrote were only
a kind of overview of it all, so it was a 'Prelude'.

'Farewell, Rome', Luther had written a few months previously, in a kind of desperate apocalyptic, almost ecstatic, half
with terror, half with joy. And this new piece was a spelling out
of that farewell, a farewell indeed to some of the most obvious
characteristics of the Roman Church. Much of it Luther had said

before. But here his ideas were collected together and re-moulded, poured out again within a single scheme. Some of the crucial points were those which are once again being anxiously turned over by the twentieth-century Catholic Church – the nature of the Christian priesthood, the proper understanding of the eucharist, as an act of the Christian Church, the nature of sacraments and the proper place of 'the Word of God'.

In Luther's scheme there was one overriding sacrament, that of the Word, the preaching of the good news of the Word of God found in the Bible, and subsidiary to it two major sacraments of the Church, baptism and eucharist and one minor sacrament, that of confession of sins and forgiveness. The eucharist was emphatically never to be looked on as a 'good work', never a sacrifice or an act of man which would earn him merit. On the contrary, when men celebrated it, it was the self-disclosure of God to man. The Church, Luther thought, had turned it into what amounted to a piece of magic. He was struggling towards an understanding of it which would enable it to be understood, (to use today's quasi-anthropological terms), as an elemental gesture from the heart of humanity, from that divinely oriented spirit which is its soul, and therefore also a self-disclosure of God. One could say that Luther was struggling to free himself from the arid Western conceptualism which could not adequately describe either the gesture as a human rite or the spiritual theology needed to interpret it, let alone the simple Greek text based on the Aramaic words that went with the original gestures.

What really shocked people was the statement that all baptised Christians were 'priests'; they needed a licence from the community to act liturgically, but nothing more. They needed no sacramental 'ordination'. Luther believed that this 'ordination' ceremony, which he had gone through with such enormous anxiety at the cathedral in Erfurt, was wrongly un-derstood, like the Mass itself as a kind of reverse image of the pagan priesthoods and pagan sacrifices. Although not directly connected with it doctrinally, the public symbols of this belief were the demand that the laity share in the consecrated wine as well as the consecrated bread at the eucharist, and that priests should be allowed to marry – the latter a demand which is again being made today.

This demand was now winging its way all over Germany, for Luther's understanding of universal Christian priesthood had been a major basis for his turning to the nobility. All those who could read German were told there by the famous Wittenberg Doctor of Theology:

All Christians possess a truly spiritual status and among them there is no distinction save that of function. This is so because we possess one baptism, one faith, one gospel, and are equal as Christians. Anyone who has emerged from the waters of baptism may pride himself on already being ordained priest, bishop or pope, although not everyone may be suited to exercise such an office. Therefore let every congregation elect a devout citizen to be their priest.

Luther was not the only person to feel utterly dissatisfied with society as it was. Sir Thomas More, Under-Sheriff of London, kicking his heels during a long stay at Antwerp, on behalf of the merchants of the City of London in 1515 had written his Dialogue about Utopia (a pun in Greek which could mean either Nowhere, or Good Place). It was written in such a way that it was in fact impossible to know what More's own opinions were. But, in general, he was speaking up for the option and practical possibilities of a 'true' Catholic Christianity, and against the sinful Christian vices of the (Christian) rulers and citizens of the day by showing the 'natural' virtues of 'good pagans' (who, incidentally, he depicted as practising euthanasia, an option for 'reasonable' men unenlightened by Christian faith) in his imaginary faraway republic.

Another alternative view was given by Erasmus in his *Colloquia*, composed to show how a classically-minded Christian might deport himself in the course of the day's work – sweetness and light pervaded the scene. Both writers wished to purge the Church rather than to reform it in the radical Lutheran way. More ended up dying for the ancient papal traditional Church in defiance of the illegality and hypocrisy of a monarch who, ten years earlier, had got More to help him in a text defending the Pope against Luther. Erasmus remained the detached and increasingly saddened observer, committed, however, to the cause of scholarship which he served to the end with impeccable determination.

But neither More's relatively enlightened Catholicism, nor
Erasmus's quiet following of the gospel, both within the bounds
of the old institution, measured up to the excitement being felt
by so many men and women as they read the New Testament,
brooded on it, compared it with the teaching and life-style of the
monks, nuns and priests they knew. Neither responded
successfully to the practical expectations, economic, political
and religious, which continued to grow among poor and rich
alike. The Gospel spoke to a man individually from the page,
and in worship, and stirred him to join his fellows in being a
'true' Christian. So eventually it was Luther, and Tyndale, and
many other reformers and translators who became the new
leaders. Erasmus and More were remembered as fine men, one a
great humanist scholar, the liberal *par exemple*, the other, the
author of *Utopia*, Lord Chancellor of England, and a martyr of
the Catholic Church, an honest, practical lawyer determined to
stand firm before a power-mad sovereign; both were unable to
harness the complex social energies, at the same time idealistic
and disillusioned, which sought for a radical change.

Resentment and anger, always lying only half dormant, ready
to be roused in many people, found a perfect symbol and
stimulant in the anger and furious resentment which Luther
expressed in his polemical works. These emotions continued to
be expressed by him for another twenty-six years, till the end of
his life, and became a kind of cliché, almost a way of life. But
they reached a special first climax as he responded to the Bull of
Excommunication. It was partly a rage of utter misery – the
misery of a depression due to emotional and intellectual disillusion. He had been misled. The leaders of the most important
group in the world were not, after all, serious. It was a rage of dis-
belief and disillusion – he, Martin Luther, a 'heretic', because
the Pope and his men had not kept faith. 'Did Satan ever speak
so impiously against God from the beginning of the world?',
Luther asked Spalatin, groaning under the horror of seeing the
Bull *Exsurge* which had been delivered to the University on 11
October and shown to him that day: 'The sheer extent of the
blasphemies in the Bull overwhelms me . . . I am convinced . . .
that the last day is almost here. The reign of anti-Christ is beginning.' But he was yet able on that 11 October to go off to
Lichtenberg and deal in notably pragmatic style with Miltitz.

In late September and early October, Eck published the Bull in the episcopal towns of Merseburg, Meissen and Brandenburg. He had added to it, with permission, names of other accomplices, including Karlstadt. Attempts to publish it elsewhere brought strong local resistance. Even in Leipzig the students shouted rude songs after him in the street, and the Bull remained unannounced there and at other places, including conservative Erfurt, where it was thrown in the river. Luther soon published *Against the Accursed Bull of Anti-Christ*, sending it to Spalatin on 4 November, saying: 'This Bull seems to have had its miserable conception at some all-night carousal of a horde of prostitutes; or maybe it was just jumbled together in the raging dog days.' He was not the last theologian to use the Roman summer to explain the poverty of a papal text.

The Bull stated that money and a safe conduct had been offered to Luther at Augsburg, enough to take him to Rome. This, Luther stated, was not true. But if they wanted to send money, let them send enough for him to go to Rome accompanied by twenty thousand foot and five thousand horse. 'In this manner I shall guarantee that faith is kept with me, and this on account of Rome, which devours its inhabitants, never having kept faith nor keeping it now, where the most sacred fathers kill their beloved sons for the love of God, and brothers destroy brothers in obedience to Christ, as is the Roman custom and style.'

Luther's piece against the Bull was in Latin, and included the familiar theological content. But he then made a German version which was a little different. Among other things, Luther told the people that the supporters of the Pope had substituted an infallible Pope for an infallible Christendom. The usual vituperation poured forth. The Bull was defecated by Rome. The booksellers were doing tremendous business. The German *Appeal to the Nobility*, the Latin *Prelude*, and the Latin and German polemical works which followed were in intense demand, and many printers were involved. Luther's case was coming to a final personal climax. Everyone who read, or listened to, writings read out in German was becoming increasingly excited. And now at last the young Emperor was in Europe; the October coronation in Aachen was to be followed by his first Diet, the formal consultation with the Electors and

Estates of the Empire. Luther's case was high on the agenda.

Elected Emperor in the summer of 1519, young Charles Habsburg had delayed coming back to Europe from Spain for nearly a year. Finally, at the end of May 1520, he set sail from Corunna and arrived offshore at Dover on 26 May to make a courtesy call on Henry VIII and to meet for the first time his own aunt, Katherine of Aragon, Henry's Queen.

The next day was Whit Sunday, the great feast of the coming of the Holy Spirit. The King and Emperor rode together in state to Canterbury, where Katherine and the Court were. The whole district was buzzing with thousands of royal retainers, preparing for a crossing of the Channel to Calais, and the meeting of reconciliation between Henry and Francis, King of France, at the Summit Meeting, subsequently called the Field of the Cloth of Gold. Before that, there were two days' dancing, feasting and jousting at which Henry participated with his usual fervour, while Charles, a pious, reserved twenty-year-old, remained a spectator; with his protruding lower jaw, his adenoidal speech, and his reserved and authoritative demeanour he fitted uneasily into Henry's pleasure-filled world. Henry left for Dover and Calais. The Emperor crossed to his lands in the Netherlands by way of Sandwich, but remained in reach of Calais; his advisers had no wish that Henry and Francis should entirely surrender the enmity traditional between the two countries, lest they should combine against the Empire. At Calais, between 10 and 14 July, Henry and Charles met again, in splendour only slightly less than that of the Cloth of Gold. Erasmus was present, being an official councillor for both parties. The interlude was then over, and Charles departed for Antwerp and the business of his territories and the Empire.

It was at Antwerp in late September that the Emperor received Hieronymus Aleander, papal emissary, charged with publication of the papal Bull, and with arranging official burnings of Luther's writings. The two men took to each other. They both spoke French. Charles had the innate conservatism of a scion of an ancient house; for him, heresy was the same kind of creature as secular revolt. Aleander, charged by the Pope with putting down the new heresy, was given cordial support and received an order from the imperial executive to confiscate and burn Luther's books in the Netherlands and Burgundy. But then he found that the local officials were not so co-operative; a legal objection prevented a burning in Antwerp. He went to Louvain, where the conservatives were in power at the University and were delighted to have a burning, with the bonfire lit by the Public Executioner in the market place. But the minority, among whom were the now almost venerable Erasmus and many of the students, was numerous. And they knew Aleander well; he was a humanist of sorts himself, had learnt Greek and had actually been working at the great publishing establishment of the printer Aldus in Venice in 1508 when Erasmus had stayed there. Later graduating to the Rectorship of Paris University, he had turned to diplomacy and the papal service. At Louvain, the students brought works of scholastic theology along to the fire and turned the occasion into something rather different from what was intended. Bitter complaints were made by Erasmus at the irregular procedure which alone had enabled the burning. However, at Liège where Aleander had once been Chancellor to the local Bishop, the burning went without a hitch.

From Antwerp the imperial court moved to Aachen to prepare for the coronation of the Emperor, which was duly held on 23 October. Elector Frederick, along with Spalatin and the Saxon court, had set out in late August on a slow journey to the Rhineland arriving in Cologne in early October. They remained there on account of plague in Aachen. The Emperor came on to Cologne to pay the traditional visit to the shrine of 'The Three Kings' (the magi of St Luke's gospel). Finally, it was on a day late in October in the precincts of a church that the young, French-speaking Emperor met his elderly Saxon *Reichsvikar*. Charles Habsburg had learnt how to behave in such a situation. He deferred a little to the old man, and told him through an interpreter that the first Diet would open at Worms in January, and that his sister would come soon from Spain – a marriage was being arranged between her and the Elector's ultimate successor, his nephew, young Duke John. The language barrier made a quick personal *rapprochement* difficult, but they each played their well-defined roles with genial courtesy.

Aleander found some difficulty in getting access to the Elector in Cologne, but eventually managed to waylay him at Mass. At first he was pleased, since the Elector said he would consider what he had to say about the Luther case. But he soon found

what a mountainous task it was going to be to out-manoeuvre
the wily old Saxon into surrendering either Luther or Luther's
case. The old man insisted on seeing documents, on following
correct procedures, and stood on his rights as senior Elector. He
told Aleander that Luther should go before an independent
tribunal as he had offered to do for so long. That was anathema
to Aleander in the case of a man already judged by Rome. To
accede to it would lose him his job.

During his stay in Cologne, the Elector requested Erasmus,
still at the Imperial Court, for his advice and was told that the
trouble was that Luther had committed two sins: he had
touched the Pope's crown, and the monks' bellies. Erasmus was
persuaded to put his recommendations into print, so he set
down the *Axiomata*, among which were the following: 'Good
Christians . . . are less shocked by Luther's principles than by
the tone of the papal Bull. Luther is right to ask for impartial
judges . . . The Emperor would be ill-advised to begin his reign
over-rigorously . . . Luther has still not been refuted.' The
Elector found a somewhat ambiguous taste left in his mouth. A
decade later, Luther told his friends that the Elector had given
Erasmus a damask coat on this occasion and had said to
Spalatin: 'What sort of a man is he? One does not know where
one is with him.'

Luther's *Appeal and Offer* was on display in the town, with its
appealing tone asking for an honest appraisal of his writings by
the standard of Scripture. Aleander was bewildered and dis-
heartened by the apparent lack of any real, widespread, anxiety
about the Luther case. The official bonfires continued to be
chancy. At Cologne, the fire was held successfully, but only at the
cost of giving it no publicity. At Mainz, Aleander himself barely
escaped a stoning by students. In shops he saw pictures of
Luther with a halo and a dove hovering over his head. In the
street, men recognising an Italian, rested hand on sword and
muttered audible curses. Lodgings were cold and crude. 'Nine-
tenths of the Germans shout "Long Live Luther", and the other
tenth "Death to Rome"', Aleander reported to his masters.

The Electoral party returned to Saxony for a few weeks,
before setting out again for Worms. In Wittenberg, as well as the
ordinary affairs of the University and the ceaseless activities of
writing and publishing, Luther was engaged in meeting people

of great importance and receiving a new batch of promises of support. There were surprising gifts of cash, conscience money from those who in their hearts wanted to support Luther but could not manage to do it openly. A hundred florins came from the Chancellor of the Bishop of Naumburg, who was about to hold a conference with Eck – the latter having requested permission to publish the Bull.

The ultimate heir to the Saxon Electorate, Duke John, seventeen-year-old nephew of Frederick, whom Spalatin had tutored, had written pledging his support to Luther, who replied with a letter which showed his usual deference to authority, expressed his gratitude, and told the young Duke something of what was going on. Luther dedicated a commentary on the Magnificat to him.

Not long after Spalatin's return from Cologne, he received a letter from Luther about another kind of book burning: 'On 10 December 1520, at nine o'clock in the morning, all the following papal books were burned in Wittenberg at the eastern gate near the Church of the Holy Cross: the *Decretum*, the *Decretals*, . . . and the most recent Bull of Leo X; likewise the *Summa Angelica*, Eck's *Chrysopassus* . . . This was done so that the incendiary papists may see that it doesn't take much to burn books they cannot refute. This is the news here . . .' It was the day on which the time limit for Luther to recant ran out, since he had seen the Bull on 10 October. He had now for certain to be declared an excommunicate heretic.

Melancthon had put up a notice the day before and a good crowd had collected for the bonfire. As the day wore on, the students became obstreperous and brought along dummies of the Pope and more books. It was another of those irreversible actions. It was the Canon Law that Luther was burning. Luther's book of books was the great book of the Word, the Bible, not the rule book of the organisation which claimed to have the divine right to control its celebration.

It was an ending both formal and popular to Luther's career within the old institution; it was also a reply to the fires which Aleander had set going. It signalled the beginning of an avalanche of anti-Roman publications. Among numerous polemical texts of the following three months, one that went through ten swift printings was Luther's German language

pamphlet, *Why the Books of the Pope and His Disciples were Burned.*
In it he maintained that Canon Law was in the end supported
solely by the false idea that the Pope is above all human judgement.

The excommunication and the burning of books on both
sides shared in stimulating the flood of pamphlets which now
began to pour out from the presses from many hands. Luther's
were in the lead when it came to quantity and virulence – but in
the latter quality, many were not far behind. Most famous of the
other authors was Hutten, who produced a biting satire on the
Papal Bull, some patriotic German poetry and an open letter
actually calling the Emperor and German princes to arms
against the Romans. More pamphlets also began to appear on
the papal side, now that Luther had declared himself in favour
of revolutionary changes. Many humanists, as well as Erasmus,
began to speak with an uncertain voice, wishing to support
Luther and oppose the Pope but hoping to stop short of
violence and indeed of the rapid change that Luther spoke for.
Wolfgang Capito was one of these. No longer working for
Froben, he had taken service with the Archbishop of Mainz and
sent Luther a long letter in December giving him a gleeful
account of the cynical reception at Court of satires on the
Roman party, and jokes about Aleander and his bonfires. But it
was all written in a context which advised Martin to work for
peace and be patient, in a Latin both silvered and somewhat
rough in spirit. And again Crotus, now Rector of Erfurt University, wrote warning Luther of the physical danger in which he
stood. The Elector of Brandenburg called at Wittenberg on his
way to Worms. More friends sent money.

A network of pragmatism surrounded Luther with the
manoeuvring of those whose actions were all dictated by the 'art
of the possible' and personal interest. Luther felt himself increasingly driven to act on principle. And to drive him on to it
were, on the one hand, his own inner anger and, on the other, in
total contrast, a certainty which had about it the deeply peaceful
assurance of the Word. In his sermons in the parish church he
often made little or no reference to public affairs and his own
battles; in one at this time, he said: 'He who calls on Christ in
faith . . . the Holy Spirit most certainly comes to him. When the
Spirit comes, look, he makes a pure, free, cheerful, glad and

loving heart, a heart which is simply righteous, seeking no reward, fearing no punishment. Such a heart is holy for the sake of holiness and goodness alone, and does everything with joy.' A genuine religious note, authentically Christian was struck.

Luther awaited some kind of final catastrophe.

> Up to now one has only played around in this case; now something serious is at hand . . . All these things are now completely in the hand of Almighty God . . . There is such tremendous turmoil that I think it cannot be quieted except by the arrival of the Last Day.

So wrote Luther to Staupitz, who was trying unsuccessfully to keep out of trouble away in Salzburg. Luther began this letter of 14 January: 'When we were at Augsburg and discussed my case, Most Reverend Father, you said to me among other things, "Remember, Friar, you began this in the name of our Lord Jesus Christ." I have accepted this word not as coming from you but as spoken to me through you, and I have kept it firmly in mind ever since.'

Staupitz had written only ten days before to Link: 'Martin has undertaken a hard task and acts with courage, enlightened by God. I stammer and am a child, needing milk.' Cardinal Lang had been exerting pressure on Staupitz in totalitarian style to stay with the orthodox line, and to sign a legally witnessed document that he agreed that Martin's teachings were heretical. Staupitz gave in. He had never envisaged revolution. His submission was made public. Luther protested in an anguished letter of 9 February: 'If Christ loves you, he will make you revoke that declaration. You should have stood up for Christ . . . You are too yielding, I am too stiff-necked . . . Dear Father, the present crisis is graver than many think . . . The word of Christ is not the word of peace but the word of a sword . . . I fear you will take a middle course between Christ and the Pope . . . Your submission has saddened me not a little.' It was a catalytic time.

From December to March, Luther was in violent controversy with his enemy, the secular priest Jerome Emser of Leipzig, whom he always called 'The Goat' because Emser's coat of arms was adorned with a goat. Emser attacked Luther's *Appeal to the Christian Nobility*, and Luther replied with *To the Goat in Leipzig*. Emser replied with a furious, *To the Bull in Wittenberg*, and Luther came again at the end of January with *Concerning the Answer of the Goat in Leipzig*. This was followed by *Reply to the Raging Bull in Wittenberg*. Luther sent a further blast at the end of March: *Answer to the Hyperchristian, Hyperspiritual, and Hyperlearned Book by Goat Emser in Leipzig* – including some 'Thoughts regarding his Companion the Fool Murner'. It began: 'Dear Goat, don't butt me', and after much badinage it got down to serious matters; but such exchanges were the small change of the public scene, half entertainment.

In early January the Elector was back in the Rhineland at Worms with his court. The Diet was due to open before the end of the month. The Luther case was being fiercely canvassed. The Elector was shown the formal Edict of Excommunication, *Decet Romanum*, which had arrived from Rome. He returned it swiftly to the sender, refusing to receive it on grounds of its inaccuracy, since it named the Elector himself as one of those guilty of inciting Luther to heresy. He insisted that he had never taken any responsibility for the teachings of Friar Martin Luther, though he did believe those teachings had never been properly examined. The document was returned to Rome and rewritten, omitting the Elector's name and also Hutten's, the final and definitive version being issued in May. But of the formal excommunication of Luther there was no doubt. And it immediately affected the young Emperor, made him the more determined not to have Luther examined at the Diet as some were suggesting. He tore up in anger the letter which Luther had written to him in the autumn, which had only just reached his hands. Aleander was present and picked up the bits, for his Roman report.

Aleander began to work very hard along with the Emperor's Confessor, Fr Glapion, to persuade the Electors that the Diet should issue an Edict in support of the excommunication, handing Luther over to the ecclesiastical authorities. Glapion, like Aleander, was a man of some sophistication, a humanist of sorts who admitted the justice of much of Luther's earlier writings, and was under the impression at an earlier stage that Luther might be persuaded to drop some of his provocative statements. The Electors were not well disposed towards Roman inspired demands, and were only too conscious of general unrest and of the widespread support for Luther, who was fast becoming a popular focus and symbol of every public dis-satisfaction. A further difficulty facing Aleander was that the Emperor needed the support of the Electors in raising an army with which to travel down to Italy to claim his coronation by the Pope as Holy Roman Emperor, and to do battle with France in Northern Italy. Numerous sub-plots revolved around the numerous embassies from France, England, Poland, Hungary, etc.

Eventually, the Emperor was faced with such widespread in-sistence that Luther should come to the Diet, that he acceded to it. He had a personal and eirenic letter drawn up, in the form of a safe conduct requesting Luther to come to the Diet. However, he then felt free to make his own imperial will known and issued an Edict on his personal responsibilities, banning all Luther's writings, whether good or bad. Aleander, shocked by the sum-moning of Luther to Worms, was able to write a delighted letter to Rome; wagonloads of Luther's books which had come over from the Frankfurt Spring Book Fair would have to go back. Three weeks later, to Aleander's despair, the Emperor sent the Imperial Herald off to Wittenberg with the Safe Conduct, to fetch Luther. The Herald was a patriotic Rhinelander, one Kaspar Sturm and just the kind of man who would enable Luther's journey to turn into a kind of triumphant progress.

Worms was overcrowded, uncomfortable, swarming with traders and prostitutes, and far from secure. Only a day's march away was a substantial body of fighting men, kept at the castle of von Sickengen, where Hutten also was. If they had been so minded, they could have put the town to massacre. However, Aleander and Glapion went over to the Ehrenburg castle with a substantial bag of gold, and bills for more. They returned with promises from Hutten both of freedom from threat and of service to the Emperor when and as required.

Luther remained in Wittenberg, but he was in constant contact with Spalatin and received the changing and contradic-tory reports of the progress of the three-sided tussle between the Emperor's men, the Pope's men, and the Germans. He assured Spalatin and the Elector himself that he was quite willing to come to Worms, as long as he had a safe conduct and as long as he was not being summoned simply for the purpose of recanta-tion. He had enough work, he said, 'for three of me for six years

and then it would not get done . . . But I am well and have
leisure time.'

Spalatin had the usual practical questions to ask Luther. What
was to be done about confessors who treated the reading of
books by Luther the ex-communicate as a mortal sin? *An
Instruction to Penitents concerning the Forbidden Books of Dr M Luther*
was the result, delivered to the printer on 17 February and
published ten days later. Luther used the traditional advice that
people should follow their conscience and not confess what they
did not consider to be a sin, and priests should not go ferreting
around trying to give someone a false conscience. If a priest
would not grant absolution, one should put up with the
situation; God would not withhold grace. Luther was anxious
that the institution of Confession, which he valued highly, should
not be abused; nevertheless, one did not have to pretend that
authority for it went back to the New Testament: 'For although
private confession is one of the most salutary practices, we know
perfectly well that the authority on which it is based is quite
shaky.'

Three days before Easter there was a flurry at the gates of
Wittenberg, and the rumours were finally confirmed. The
Imperial Herald was there, with a letter for Dr Luther from the
Emperor: 'Honourable, dear and pious Martin, we and the
Estates of the Holy Roman Empire . . . desired to hear you on
the doctrines and books put forth by you over a period of time.
We order you to come here and grant you in our name and the
name of the Empire every security and guarantee as the safe
conduct here enclosed witnesses . . .' Once again, things seemed
to be turning in Luther's favour. The Diet was, at any rate for the
moment, simply ignoring the Roman excommunication.
Luther stayed on in Wittenberg for Easter, to complete his
obligations of preaching and celebrating the Feast Day of the
Raising of Jesus, 'The Resurrection'.

The little party set out on the Tuesday following Easter. The
town rose to the occasion and provided a cart and horses. With
Luther went Fr Amsdorf of the University and Cathedral, Dr
Jerome Schurff the lawyer, a young friar, Johann Petzensteiner,
and a young humanist nobleman from Pomerania, Peter
Suaven. The Herald and his companion led on horses. Luther
was setting out from a Wittenberg solidly behind him; the

solidarity which included the practical men of the Town Council, the University professors and students and many priests was rooted deep in the locality through his blood relations, including his own parents who had recently been present in Wittenberg at Melancthon's wedding.

It was another spring journey through Thuringia. The journey turned out as Aleander had feared, something close to a triumph at times. Yet it was a strange progress, an ex-communicate friar moving across Germany to the first Diet of the young Emperor. Leipzig received Luther honourably with a gift of wine. Luther had been nervous about Erfurt, with the old conservative university men still in power there. He need not have feared. Long before he reached the city, a party of young students met him, having come out to bring him in triumph to the town. He stayed there the Saturday night, 6 April, and preached to a crammed church on Sunday – so much so that the balcony creaked under the weight. Luther told them not to worry, it was only the devil trying to stop him. Four elegies were produced for him by his friend the celebrated German humanist, Helius Eobanus Hessus: *Magna piis pro te Germania stabit in armis* (*Great Germany, piously armed, will stand by you*). He moved on, preaching again to enthusiastic welcomes at Gotha and Eisenach. Luther wrote to Melancthon that the party were 'keeping the Augustinian Rule, and discussing a pious subject, to wit the Book of Joshua as image of the Gospel'. But the journey did him no good. 'Surrounded by men, drinks and chatter' as he put it, each evening, he became ill, and remained so for a week.

Spalatin was worried for Luther's arrival in Worms; he might not be safe there. Luther replied to him from Frankfurt, two days' journey north of Worms: 'I am coming, my Spalatin, although Satan has done everything to hinder me with more than one illness. All the way from Eisenach I have been unwell' – he was getting his usual attack of constipation, but also some further trouble, headaches and exhaustion. He had been bled. He ended the letter: 'So prepare the lodgings.' One more attempt was made, this time by friends, to head him off. At Oppenheim, a small market town a few miles north of Worms, Martin Bucer who had left the Dominicans (with permission) and was now chaplain to von Sickingen, arrived with a plan that Luther should turn off into the hills and go up to the Ehrenberg castle, where the knights von Sickingen and Hutten would protect him and give him a power base from which to negotiate. Luther brushed the offer aside, with thanks.

The entry into Worms on Tuesday, 16 April, was an event witnessed by hundreds, perhaps thousands of people of all classes. Many people on foot and horse had gone out to meet Luther's party. The excitement was intense. Aleander reported that he had heard that some priests tried to reach out and touch, even kiss, Luther's habit. Before he went into the lodgings provided by the knights of Rhodes, he turned, said Aleander, and surveyed the crowds, 'with his demonic eyes'. Luther himself believed that his affair was one of battle for 'the Word' and against Satan.

CHAPTER ELEVEN

Worms and Wartburg

Luther's lodgings immediately became the focus of interest in Worms. To his meal came old friends, including Spalatin; and following them came newer friends and a hundred other people, so that he was 'greeted and visited through the whole night by many counts, barons, gilded knights and nobles, ecclesiastical and lay'. About midday following, came Ulrich von Pappenheim, Master of the Imperial Cavalry, along with the Herald, to warn Luther to be ready to appear before the Emperor at 4 p.m. Returning at that hour, the Herald took Luther out by the garden and through into the next house occupied by the Count Palatine and then by back streets to the audience chamber, to try to avoid the crowds who kept gathering in the hope of catching a glimpse of the famous man, some sitting on the roofs to gain their purpose. With Luther went the Wittenberg lawyer, Jerome Schurf, and his two close priest friends, Nicholas Amsdorf and Justus Jonas, until recently Rector at Erfurt from where he had joined the party.

Luther, in his normal Augustinian habit, tonsure recently shaven, thick-set, a little gaunt for his thirty-seven years, made obeisance to the Emperor and the Emperor's representative, the Archbishop of Trier. The Archbishop's Chancellor, Johann von Eck (another Eck), then addressed Luther, pointed to a pile of books and asked Luther very briefly whether they were his and whether he wished to retract any of them. This blunt approach surprised Luther. His lawyer jumped in immediately and requested that the titles of the books be read out. It was a motley collection of Luther's German and Latin works, but it included both the German *Appeal to the Nobility* and the Latin *Prelude to the Babylonian Captivity*. While they were being read out, Luther and Schurf had a quick word together. Luther then replied, speaking

first in German then in Latin. He asked for time to consider his
answer, 'because this is a question of faith and the salvation of
souls'. It was at first sight an odd reply, apparently unexpected
by the Emperor and his advisers who went into a huddle to
decide what to do about it. But Schurf had given Luther the
obvious advice. Only now had they learnt for certain the mood
of the Emperor – Luther, it was clear, had been summoned
solely to recant. It was best, then, to take time over preparing his
exact reply.

They were told that Luther could have twenty-four hours,
though that should be regarded as a special kindness since he
should have come prepared to answer. He was abjured not to
come with a written statement but be ready, at the same time
tomorrow, to answer verbally.

The next day the hearing was resumed in another, bigger
room, which soon became overcrowded and too hot. The Electors, the Estates, and many others were there as well as the
Emperor and his advisers. It was six o'clock before they started
and by then Luther was feeling ill and was in a great sweat.
However, as soon as proceedings began the adrenalin flowed
and he was able to speak to the brief which he and Schurf had
worked out. It took about a quarter of an hour in German and
nearly the same in Latin, and was recorded in writing by both
friends and enemies; part of Luther's own script has survived.
It was a prepared speech which Luther had more or less learnt
off by heart:

> Most serene Emperor, most illustrious princes, most clement
> lords . . . deign to listen graciously to this my cause – which is,
> as I hope, a cause of justice and of truth. If through my in-
> experience I have either not given the proper titles to some,
> or have offended in some manner against customs and court
> etiquette, I ask you kindly to pardon me, as a man ac-
> customed not to courts but to the cells of monks. I can say
> nothing about myself but that I have taught and written up to
> this time with simplicity of heart, as I had in view only the
> glory of God and the sound instruction of Christ's faithful.

The quiet, persuasive, intellectual voice flowed gently and
deliberately on, emotion held only partially in check, visible in

the changing expressions on his face – 'frivolous' expressions, said one Spanish reporter.

Addressing himself to the two questions, he said that there was not much doubt about the first one. Obviously his books were his books, unless someone had slipped in some of someone else's.

The second question was more difficult, because he had written three kinds of books. 1. Simple gospel works – if he were to renounce these he would 'condemn the very truth upon which friends and enemies equally agree'. 2. Books against the papacy and the concerns of the papists. He asked what was wrong with such works, when everyone knew that the papal tyranny did so much harm to the Christian world and especially to 'this illustrious nation of Germany'. 3. 'I have written a third sort of books against some private and (as they say) distinguished individuals – those, namely, who strive to preserve the Roman tyranny and to destroy the godliness which I teach.'

Against these latter people, he confessed he had been more violent than his religion or his profession demanded – but then he did not set himself up as a saint, nor was he disputing about his life, but about the teaching of Christ. His books against such people could not be renounced without renouncing the battle against the tyranny of anti-Christ. Finally, he repeated that he was always ready to be shown that his doctrines were wrong.

Then, although the substance of the reply was complete, Luther added a more personal kind of comment. They could see, he said, that he had thought long and hard about these things. If disturbance and dissension arose because of his teachings, that was a case for rejoicing, because Christ did indeed say 'I have come to bring not peace but a sword' – Christianity was no easy option. They should not, then, condemn the Word of God, 'lest the reign of this most noble youth, Prince Charles (in whom after God is our great hope) become unhappy and inauspicious'. He ended: 'I do not say these things because there is a need of either my teachings or my warnings for such leaders as you, but because I must not withhold the allegiance which I owe to Germany. With these words I commend myself to your most serene majesty and to your lordships, humbly asking that I should not be allowed to become hateful to you because of the scheming of my enemies. I have finished.' Luther, although sometimes naïve, and exercising poor judgement politically, was never careless of political fact. Man's task always involved attention to immediate responsibilities and loyalties, and the use of appropriate and reasonable policies. So, the effect of his actions was not something which could be left aside, nor 'the allegiance which I owe to Germany'. He was well aware, just as Aleander was (as the Emperor himself could hardly be) of the genuine danger of violent social disruption. It was true that nothing would tend towards the prevention of this more than a movement of genuine reform. Reform was precisely what was required, reform of institutions so deeply involved in the injustices and so deeply implicated as causes of the sheer poverty and misery, the resentment and the envy which were the boiling origins of a likely social revolution.

The Chancellor of Trier then answered Luther in a speech which kept to the high level of debate and rhetoric set by Luther himself. It was an effective reply from the orthodox papal position. The Emperor, he said, would be willing to consider making a distinction between the harmless and the harmful, of Luther's writings, but Luther was only doing what every heretic always did, the Waldensians, the Beghards, the Poor Men of Lyons, etc.; they all turned to Scripture, and they all wished it to be interpreted in their sense. He mocked a little: 'Do not, I entreat you, Martin, do not claim for yourself that you are the one and only man who has knowledge of the Bible, who has true understanding . . . Do not place your judgement ahead of so many distinguished men . . . as wiser than others.' Then he became more confident still, and finally threatening: 'What the doctors have discussed as doctrine the Church has defined as its judgement, the faith in which our fathers and ancestors confidently died and as a legacy have transmitted to us. We are forbidden to argue about this faith by the law of both pontiff and emperor . . . both are going to judge those who with headlong rashness refuse to submit to the decisions of the Church. Punishments have been provided and published.' He then told Martin to answer clearly and simply and not with a 'horned' (*cornutum*) reply.

The two poles were far apart. The Chancellor, as its obedient and humble, believing servant, was defending an organisation which claimed to act from 1500 years of tradition on its own authority as the vicegerent of God. The friar, speaking from his own struggles with the meaning of the Word of the Gospel, listened to in his inner being, worshipped daily in the liturgy in his own local church, himself a product precisely of the same 1500 years, was convinced that the authorities in the organisation had made great errors and that they must be brought back to what he felt he now knew to be the evident Christian faith.

> Since then Your Serene Majesty and Your Lordships seek a simple answer, I will give it in this manner, neither horned nor toothed. Unless I am convinced by the testimony of the Scriptures or by clear reason (for I do not trust either in the Pope or in councils alone, since it is well known that they have often erred and contradicted themselves), I am bound by the Scriptures I have quoted and my conscience is captive to the Word of God. I cannot and I will not retract anything since it is neither safe nor right to go against conscience. Here I stand, may God help me, Amen.

The hour was late, the light poor, the air foul, and the moment of truth occurred in an atmosphere of bathos, which turned speedily to some confusion. The Emperor was rising to leave. The crowd began to chatter and to move to the door – clearly there was no more to be said. The irritated Chancellor wanted the last word. He shouted that Martin must put his conscience aside and that he could never prove Councils had erred. Martin shouted that he could; he and his party began to move to the door, Martin in a state of enormous relief at having given the witness clearly and without hesitation. As he turned to his friends, he raised his two arms in the gesture of a victorious medieval knight. As they left, a clique of Spanish courtiers jeered and gestured. Luther retired, exhausted, to supper and to some malmsey wine, a great crowd of supporters accompanying him noisily through the streets.

Late that evening or early the following morning, young Habsburg took his pen and wrote in French his own response, a famous paragraph, redolent of 'imperial Christianity'. Von Eck and the Emperor were in close consultation about the Luther case, and there were items of similarity between Eck's speech at the hearing of Luther and the Emperor's piece – but the

Emperor's words had the clear stamp of personal conviction, with an authoritarian, slightly impatient note about them. He lost no time. The statement was written out, dated 19 April, signed and addressed to the meeting of the Diet on that day immediately following the day of Luther's hearing:

> You know that I am descended from the most Christian emperors of the German nation, from the Catholic kings of Spain, the Archdukes of Austria and the dukes of Burgundy . . . After death they left us by natural right and heritage these holy Catholic observances, to live according to them and to die according to their example . . . I am determined to support everything that these predecessors and I myself have kept . . . It is certain that a single friar errs in his opinion which is against all of Christendom and according to which all of Christianity will be and will always have been in error both in the past thousand years and even more in the present . . . I am absolutely determined to stake on this cause my kingdoms and seignories, my friends, my body and blood, my life and soul. It would be a great shame to me and to you, the noble and renowned German nation . . . if heresy or decrease of the Christian religion should through our negligence dwell after us in the hearts of men . . . I regret having delayed so long to proceed against this Luther and his false doctrine . . . he is to be taken back, keeping the tenor of his safe-conduct . . . I am determined to proceed against him as a notorious heretic, requesting of you that you conduct yourselves in this matter as good Christians as you have promised it to me, and are held to do it. Given by my hand this nineteenth day of April 1521. Signed *Carolus*.

It was a grand statement, with romance and pride in a great tradition about it, that might captivate in suitable circumstances. It reminds the reader today of the statement Sir Thomas More would be making in circumstances of an opposite kind, in thirteen years' time at his trial, basing his opposition to Henry VIII as Head of the Church, on 'all the Councils of Christendom for over a thousand years'. But noteworthy in the Emperor's statement is the absence of any reference to the Pope or the papacy. For political reasons the Emperor found himself in difficulties with Leo X; there was a danger Leo would make a treaty with the French King. The Emperor's Catholicism was 'traditional', but apparently not necessarily markedly 'papal'. And was it all true? Could the German Electors and Estates be persuaded that it was appropriate, and could it be enforced? Carolus had no idea how fragile the whole great construction of 'Christendom' was in many of its parts, and that only something like the bedrock of the Myth to end all myths remained invulnerable – trust in God through Jesus, prayer, love of neighbour, symbolised in public liturgy.

For two days, Friday and Saturday, the Diet remained locked in debate on the Emperor's statement. Graffiti appeared: 'Unhappy the people whose king is a child', and a great blustering ill-written threat, signed with the revolutionary sign of the *Bundschuh*, the sturdy peasant's clog: 'We are 400 of the nobility. We declare war on the princes of the Diet. I have 8000 men.' The Diet finally requested that a commission of three or four people should be asked to show Luther where his errors lay. The influence of the Elector Frederick was clear – the Diet said that Luther had still not been shown what actually was wrong, by Scripture. The Elector had made the same point over two years previously when replying to Cajetan.

The practical young Emperor was ready to agree to an attempt to persuade Luther to recant. In fact, however, it was an attempt to find some compromise formula. At the heart of the attempt lay the Archbishop of Trier, friend of the Elector. On 24 and 25 April, Wednesday and Thursday, intense private discussions were held with Luther, with varying personnel present. Among those involved was Luther's one-time supporter, and future bitter calumniator, Canon Cochlaeus. An extension of the safe conduct was granted to enable Luther to stay on for these discussions. But they came to nothing. Finally, as a last throw, the Archbishop and Luther met entirely alone, and a bribe was offered to Luther in the form of a good rich priory.

As both parties gradually came to see that there was no way out of the impasse, they became friendlier and more relaxed. They were facing facts. The Archbishop asked Luther what was to be done, and Martin turned to the advice of Rabbi Gamaliel to the Jews, who were wondering what to do about the followers of the recently crucified Jesus of Nazareth, as recorded in the New Testament: 'What I suggest therefore is that you leave these men alone and let them go. If this enterprise, this movement of theirs, is of human origin it will break up of its own accord, but if it does in fact come from God you will not only be unable to destroy them, but you might find yourselves fighting against God.' There was no further way forward. Dismissal documents were issued.

Meanwhile, intense private discussions had gone on between Spalatin and the Elector, who remained publicly impassive; in private he said, 'Dr Martin spoke right well both in Latin and German . . . he is far too bold for me.' The Emperor had presented Frederick with a very serious situation. While the Electors and the Estates seem not to have been universally impressed with the romantic traditionalism of the young French-speaking chevalier, yet they had to avoid a head-on clash with their recently elected Lord. And there was no way of undoing the papal excommunication. The answer, which had already been thought about a number of times, was to put Luther secretly into protective custody.

The idea was that Luther should be kidnapped by unknown robbers and spirited away to some place where he could remain hidden. The plan was to take Luther to the Wartburg, the great empty castle, high up above Eisenach, Luther's boyhood school town where the Castellan would guard him closely for a week or two till his beard and hair had grown, fit him out in suitable gear, and put it about that a landowner, Junker Georg, was staying there for a time. It was a clever idea. If Luther could not be found, he could not be proceeded against. Equally, he himself would be unable to stir things up any further. Meanwhile, perhaps, the whole affair would become less explosive.

Luther agreed to the plan in general, though he did not know his precise destination. The result was a certain relaxation in his mood during the last forty-eight hours at Worms. He spent a convival final Thursday evening, drinking malmsey wine and saying goodbye to all and sundry. On Friday morning after breakfast, the Wittenberg party rode and walked out of the city gate in good heart. They went north to the little village of Oppenheim where the Imperial Herald met them and began his task of accompanying them safely back to Wittenberg. When they reached Frankfurt two days later, Luther wrote to a leading

Wittenberg citizen, and his own friend, to tell him what was happening:

> To the skilled master craftsman . . . Lucas Cranach, painter in Wittenberg and my close friend . . . I am going to allow myself to be 'imprisoned' and hidden, though I don't know yet where it will be. I would have preferred to suffer death at the hands of the tyrants, especially those of the furious Duke George.

Luther was caustic about the appearances before the Emperor: 'I thought his Imperial Majesty would have got together one or fifty scholars and overcome this monk in a straightforward manner. But all that happened was this: Are these your books? Yes. Do you want to renounce them or not? No. Then go away! Oh we blind Germans, how childishly we act and allow the Romanists to mock and fool us in such a pitiful way.' Then he spoke of his impending disappearance. The Easter and post-Easter texts were echoing round his mind from the daily Office and the Mass texts for the Sundays and weekdays after Easter. He quoted the words of Jesus in St John's Gospel: 'For a little while you will not see me, and again in a little while you will see me – so said Christ. I hope it will now be the same with me. But God's will, the very best possible, be done in this . . .' He sent greetings to another friend, a Wittenberg goldsmith, and his wife, who had been responsible for providing the cart which the Town Council had hired from him for Luther's journey, and added, 'Please express my deep appreciation to the Town Council for my ride'. It had meant a lot to him, feeling far from well much of the time, that he did not have to go on horseback.

Later the same day, at a village called Friedberg north of Frankfurt, Luther signed a letter he had drawn up for the Emperor, a very carefully worded epistle totally lacking in his usual rumbustiousness – he was able to exclude it when he had to. The letter was restrained throughout, though intense emotion is implied:

> To the Most Serene and invincible Lord, Charles V, elected emperor of the Romans, Caesar Augustus, King of the Spaniards, of both Sicily and Jerusalem, etc., Archduke of Austria, Duke of Burgundy, etc., my most clement Lord.

Jesus. Grace and peace with all my submission in Christ Jesus our Lord. Most Serene and invincible Emperor, most clement Lord; Your Sacred Majesty had summoned me to Worms, with a public guarantee . . .

There followed a description of his examination at Worms and the subsequent private manoeuvrings, and a description of Luther's unwillingness, as he put it, to allow the Word of God to be bound. He was still hoping that somehow he could get his message across. He explained, critically, that in spite of the Safe Conduct on his way to Worms, he found his books had been burnt and banned: 'These things could have frightened and held back this poor little monk'; nevertheless, he had put his trust in the Emperor's Safe Conduct. Finally, he said, he left Worms without having been refuted.

The letter ended with a sincere and more or less desperate plea 'on behalf of the whole Church; it was my concern for the Church that motivated me to send this letter after having left Worms. With my whole heart I desire, of course, that Your Sacred Majesty, the whole Empire, and the most notable German nation may be served in the best possible way.' The letter was a last rather sad attempt to 'reach' the young man who was now ruling half of Europe, and to save the German lands from disturbances which continued to threaten to increase. Luther requested the Herald to return to Worms with the letters, and was successful in persuading him that he need not accompany the Wittenberg party any further. He was anxious to be rid of him before the planned abduction, to reduce the risk of it miscarrying. Possibly the Herald was even party to the plan.

The party headed north-east towards Thuringia. They received a warm welcome from the famous Benedictine Abbey of Hersfeld. The Chancellor and Bursar came out a mile or so to meet them; then the Abbot himself 'together with many people on horseback, met us at his castle and accompanied us into the small town. The Town Council welcomed us inside the gates.' They had fine food, and Luther slept in the Abbot's own private guest room. Luther also preached, though he warned the Abbot that he was taking a grave risk in allowing it, in that they might lose their privileges. But the truth was that neither Emperor nor Pope had much authority over these powerful ecclesiastical barons. Finally, Luther's party left for Eisenach, accompanied by the Abbot as far as the forest.

Eisenach in its turn sent a deputation out to welcome Luther. And again Luther preached, in his boyhood town, though the parish priest was frightened and insisted on making an official legally witnessed protest against it, so that he could not be held responsible, apologising to Luther for this necessity. Luther said 'preaching the Word of God' could not come within the ban on his speaking in public, which was part of the Safe Conduct. The next day half the party went on to Erfurt and Wittenberg, Jonas, Schurf and a student, so that Luther's own group would be as small as possible for the impending abduction. He, Amsdorf and the student, Petzensteiner, headed south-east to visit relatives at the village of Möhra, where again the local priest welcomed him. The next day they headed north-east to Erfurt.

At a crossing of bridle paths in the forest Luther's little party was attacked. Amsdorf was waiting for it and 'escaped' easily, followed by the student. Both of them returned immediately to Wittenberg. Luther was taken on a circuitous route blindfolded. Finally, long after dark he arrived at a high castle, exhausted. He was given a room, a meal and a bed. The next day he saw where he was, up in the great Wartburg above Eisenach, and closely guarded by a friendly but firm Castellan, Hans von Berlepsch. For a week or more he had to remain inside till, bearded and in lay clothes which were provided, he might not be easily recognised. Respect and kindness were shown; he was comfortable with good food and decent accommodation.

It was not too difficult for a man to keep to himself in the great rambling building on the hilltop, not regularly inhabited except by the Keeper and his family. No one knew where the robbers had taken Luther. Soon he would be hardly distinguishable behind the disguise of Junker Georg. Messengers and stores went up to the castle once or twice a week to von Berlepsch. At first, Luther's presence made little difference.

In spite of conversation with von Berlepsch and the availability of writing materials, Luther was soon lonely and restless. The contrast was fearful, from the crammed daily round at Wittenberg, the intense activities of the journey to Worms and then the fraught days there. He had none of the books he needed. All day long for the first time in his life there was ab-

solutely nothing that he must do – only things he must not do
such as wander out into the air and down the hill. The letters
soon began to flow, one of the first to Melancthon:

> I have had much ado to get this letter off, because of the very
> real fear that my whereabouts may somehow be let out . . .
> Who knows what God plans . . . The monks and priests who
> raged against me while I was free now dread me as a captive
> . . . They cannot stand the worry of the common people's
> threats.

Luther was beginning to sense the growing power which his
person now commanded, as fragments of news were brought to
him by Hans von Berlepsch. He had nothing at all to do but
ponder the situation, standing, perforce, apart from it.
Ecclesiastically excommunicate, his Appeal rejected by the
Emperor, shortly to be put under the interdict of the Empire as
well as the papacy, he had a new sense of alienation – and of
resultant freedom.

On 12 May, Luther had been in the Wartburg for six days, was
used to the regime, but getting very restless, yearning for home,
for community life, for his work, and for some sign from his
friends: 'To Philip Melancthon, evangelist of the congregation
at Wittenberg, my dearest brother in Christ. Jesus. Greetings.
What are you doing these days, my Philip? Are you not praying
for me . . .? I am quite eager to know your reaction to my disappearance. I was afraid it would look as if I had deserted the
battle array . . .' He bewails the state of the Church, and then
speaks in detail of his constipation: 'The Lord has struck me
hard in the hind quarters . . . My stools were so hard that I was
sweating with effort . . . Yesterday on the fourth day I went once,
but I did not sleep all night.' With a biblical greeting to
Melancthon and his wife, 'Farewell to you and your flesh', he
dates it 'in the land of the birds'.

The Wartburg is entirely surrounded by woods and is a
marvellous place for birdsong. It brought out Luther's lyrical
side, while the loneliness encouraged introspection. On 12 May,
he wrote to Amsdorf and told him what had happened after he
fled from the fake attack: '. . . The day I was snatched away from
you, I arrived about eleven o'clock in the dark of the night at my
new lodgings, utterly exhausted as though I had never ridden

before . . . Here I am now a man of leisure, like a free man among captives', and dated it 'in the land of the open skies'. 'Written on the mountain' was the dateline for his letter to Spalatin two days later: 'I am sitting here all day, drunk with leisure. I am reading the Bible in Greek and Hebrew. I shall write a German Tract . . . as soon as I have received the necessary things from Wittenberg.' Other datelines common were: 'From the Isle of Patmos' (the Greek island to which St John is said to have retired in his old age) and 'From my wilderness', which eventually became the norm.

Later in May, he wrote again to Melancthon, dating the letter 'From the land of the birds that sing sweetly in the branches and praise God with all their power night and day', and signed his name 'Martin' in Greek. It was to little, gamin-like, intellectual Melancthon that he felt closest, their temperaments utterly different, complementing one another. This letter has the ring of friendship about it, even more than the letters to Spalatin where there is always the slight restraint involved in writing to one at Court who stood at the Elector's right hand.

Luther was annoyed that Melancthon's own new writing on doctrine had not reached him – this was the *Loci Communes*, 'The Common Places', or 'Agreed Statement', a first version of what would grow into a Protestant doctrinal norm in the Confession of Augsburg (1530). Luther wrote, 'I want to know who stands in my pulpit. Is Amsdorf still snoring and lazy? And what is Dr Karlstadt doing?' – even the tiresome old Dean of the Faculty took on a slightly roseate hue from a distance. Luther said Melancthon should not worry about him and then continued in a way which would not encourage such lack of worry: 'The troubles of my soul have not ceased yet, and my previous weakness of faith still persists . . . I would rather burn in a raging fire than rot here alone half alive.' But it was a test of faith, and he accepted the challenge, turning to the favourite image of Abraham, the great originating Jew-hero who was summoned from his homeland: 'We must go out of our country, away from our kindred and from our father's house, and must be separated from each other for a while.' Luther was looking for a divine healing of his loneliness and the unpredictable future.

He was worried about the state of society – the sturdy peasants would cause an uproar if the Pope went on condemning people. He chided Melancthon and the others for saying they needed him back; the Wittenberg churches had more than enough ministration with Melancthon, Amsdorf and the others there. They had complained that they were without a 'shepherd'. Luther was being identified as their leader in a way much more specific than before. The letter ended: 'I have no more news, since I am a hermit, an anchorite, and truly a monk, though neither shaved nor cowled. You would see a knight and hardly recognise me.'

He wrote a piece on Confession, a follow-up to the piece written for Spalatin, for people bewildered by confessors trying to stop people reading 'Luther', and dedicated it to the Knight Franz von Sickingen to whose castle he might have gone instead of to the Diet. He felt the need to keep some link with him and the group round him, with Ulrich von Hutten and young Martin Bucer, first met at Heidelberg, now out of the Dominicans but acting as chaplain at Sickingen's castle. Luther addressed the letter, 'To my special Lord and Patron'. He was specially conscious that von Sickingen was part of the political power groupings in the country. Power implied responsibility and it was to the powerful lay people, 'the nobles', that he had addressed his *Appeal* a year previously.

Then he also began to think of the members of the congregation he had addressed so many times in the parish church at Wittenberg, and felt he owed them an explanation. 'To the little flock' (a quotation from the New Testament) he wrote explaining his absence, his position which had led to so much criticism from authority, and outlined for their benefit all that had happened, copying at one point a style used by St Paul when rebutting his critics.

In mid June he wrote again to Spalatin, saying that he was both very busy and very idle, studying Greek and Hebrew without interruption, and he sent the manuscripts of his work on Confession and the Magnificat. 'The man in charge of the place treats me far beyond what I deserve. The trouble from which I suffered at Worms has not left me . . . I am more constipated than ever in my life and despair of remedy. The Lord thus afflicts me that I may not be without a relic of his cross.' He signed the letter 'Henry Nescius' in case, on its way to court, it

fell into the wrong hands. Luther did not bother to refer to the
fact that he was in the middle of a 40,000-word Latin text,
entitled 'Against Latomus', replying to an attack on him by an
old opponent at Louvain. When completed he sent it to Justus
Jonas, and at the end of the piece said:

> But to return to you, my Jonas. I have now expelled this
> Latomus from me and sent it to you . . . I have already begun
> to put the Epistles and Gospels into the vernacular: that is
> why it has been so bothersome to read and respond to this
> filth . . . Why doesn't one of you reply to the rest, either you
> or Andreas Karlstadt? And what is stopping Amsdorf? . . .
> Greetings from my Patmos. 20 June 1521.

By July the disorientation seen in the letter to Spalatin was
beginning to bite severely – Luther was restless and tetchy, and
there was a rare sensual or sexual reference in his description of
his troubles. Thirty-three-year-old Luther was ripe for an
emotional crisis. Eleven weeks of loneliness had set his whole
person, physiologically and psychologically into a new slow
rhythm. Sexual tension had begun to be a threat; he had seen it
often enough in other friars, but he had managed to bypass
serious sexual problems in the past three or four years simply
through work. But now his life in a vacuum gave scope to his
inherent disposition towards sadness and depression.

He complained to Melancthon: 'You praise me too much . . .
Your high opinion of me shames and tortures me, since, unfortunately, I sit here like a fool and, hardened in leisure, pray little,
do not sigh for the Church of God, yet burn in a big fire of my
untamed body. In short I should be burning in spirit, but I am
burning in lust, laziness, leisure and sleepiness.' It was the height
of summer in the forest land, and sultry humid days did not
help. Constipation was bad as ever: 'If this thing does not
improve I shall go straight to Erfurt and not incognito either
. . . I shall consult doctors or surgeons.'

He did not know what to think about things 'going so well' at
Wittenberg. Clearly he was not needed. 'You are now well
supplied and you manage well without me . . . the affairs of
Wittenberg progress more favourably in my absence than in my
presence.' He said perhaps a door would open for him in 'Erfurt
or Cologne or anywhere else'. He reprimanded them for

cancelling a disputation at the request of the Elector. They had
to guard academic and spiritual freedom. 'Not one half would
have been accomplished had I obeyed the court's counsel . . .
Farewell. Someone had promised to take along this letter which
I had written some days ago, but he has not kept his word. I ask
all of you to pray for me because I am drowning in sins. From
my wilderness, 13 July 1521, Martin Luther the Hermit.'
Depression and disgust with himself were rolling in again. At
night it all became too much: 'I can tell you, in this idle solitude,
there are a thousand battles with Satan. It is much easier to fight
against the incarnate devil – that is against men – than against
spiritual wickedness in the heavenly places.'

Luther was writing Postils all through the summer, sample
sermons on gospel passages, for parish priests and for more
general consumption, and becoming more familiar with the
Greek and Hebrew texts of the Bible. His mind was turning
again to the serious biblical studies which had started the whole
trouble off. He put the readings for each Sunday Liturgy into
German. He wrote to Amsdorf: 'I would like to be your student
in the course on Hebrew, and Philip's in the course on
Colossians . . . I rejoice so much in your abundance . . . It is not
you who need me, but I who need you.' The depression was
holding off a bit again as the constipation eased: 'I tried the pills
according to the prescription. Soon I had some relief and my
bowels opened without blood or force, but the wound of the
previous rupture isn't healed yet, and I had to suffer a good deal
of pain because some flesh extruded.' Luther was becoming gar-
rulous and hypochondriac under the influence of solitude. He
was in need of something to do which would impinge with some
impact on the outside world. He did not have long to wait.

In Worms the Emperor had had to make the best of a situation which he could not totally control. The Electors, Princes
and representatives of the Estates began to drift home, and
nothing further was done immediately in the Luther case.

Aleander suggested an Edict from the Emperor himself and
presented him with a suitable text. Now that Frederick had gone
home, the remaining Electors might be persuaded to sign; but
the Emperor thought a little further delay might persuade the
Pope not to sign a Treaty of Alliance with the King of France.
Eventually a rump of Electors, which did not include Albrecht of

Mainz, signed and to Aleander's delight Luther was at last declared an outlaw. The Edict of Worms now lay beside the formal Decree of Excommunication, *Decet Romanum*, which had been eventually issued in a form acceptable to all. If the civil and Church authorities had commanded the assent of their subjects there could have been no more place for Friar Martin Luther. Eventually he would have been found, formally arrested and burnt. There was widespread consternation about his disappearance, and to a lesser extent about the Edict. The elderly Albrecht Dürer noted in his diary: 'I don't know whether he is alive or has been murdered . . . Oh God, if Luther is dead, who is going to explain the Gospel to us?'

But, nine weeks after disappearing, Luther was lying up in the Wartburg in regular communication with the Saxon political authorities and with his friends at Wittenberg. It began to seem that much of the established structure of society was a paper construction. Among the first to push open the floodgates and to let a stream of destructive actions loose on to the world were the friars and university men at Wittenberg. Luther's absence made them feel they must vindicate themselves and do something about the challenging blueprints for reform which their colleague and friend had issued a year ago. With Luther away, Karlstadt was able once again to move into the lead with his mixture of unreflected theory and headstrong action. He moved with an obsessive inevitability to the crucial explosive item, celibacy. Only just back from a disastrous few weeks in Copenhagen, where he had been lent to help reformers there but where he was worse than useless, with not a word of Danish in his head, he drew up his usual bunch of theses. They were on the Vows of Celibacy, and on Communion under both kinds.

The minutes of the first discussion of the theses reached Luther towards the end of July. It was not the first time that Karlstadt had taken a step ahead of Luther – he was a man of logic following an idea to its conclusion. Luther was shocked. The theses propounded not just that the compulsory celibacy of Massing priests should be dropped but that all vows of celibacy were wrong. This was to attack the religious orders as such, a central component of society, the monks, the nuns, the friars, the great country abbeys, the little convents, and the city friaries. It was to attack Luther's own status as a vowed religious. Luther had not spoken against the institution of the monastic life in his writings but against the futile lives of so many of those who followed it, or were almost forced into it by one circumstance or another. On 1 August, he wrote to Melancthon:

'You people do not convince me yet that the vows of priests and monks are to be considered as in the same category . . . I am pretty well agreed that those who entered the abyss before or during the age of puberty can leave it with a clear conscience; but about those who have grown old and stayed on in this state, I don't know yet.' There was no reason why a priest had to be celibate. But the very nature of a monk was to take the three traditional vows of poverty, obedience and chastity. Five days later, he wrote to Spalatin: 'Good Lord, will our people at Wittenberg give wives even to the monks? They will not push a wife on me!' He had not begun to digest the idea. In spite of his own sexual difficulties the idea of solving them by marrying was thoroughly repugnant. He was a monk, a community man, with a vocation.

But immediately he found himself arguing and thinking furiously about the matter in the light of Scripture and reason. Yes, of course young people in a monastery or convent against their will should be allowed to leave. In fact, the Roman authorities normally gave permission for such people to leave; Erasmus had been one such, put into a religious order for lack of living parents, and allowed to leave as a young man. But the permission to leave did not include the permission to marry. Luther realised that this was a mere prejudice about sex, and opposed it. But as for the older people, Karlstadt's statement that they should leave if they wished 'in order to avoid the sin of fornication – what is this other than mere quibbling rationalisation?' Luther wanted something more serious than a statement that pressing sexual tension should be a reason for them to leave, and he added sardonically: 'Who knows if he who burns with desire today, will burn with desire tomorrow? . . . I would not dare to act on this principle; so I will not counsel anyone else to do so.' And yet, 'I too would want to help monks and nuns more than anything else, so greatly do I pity these wretched men and boys and girls who are plagued with emission of semen and by sexual desire.' He was determined to treat the arguments objectively on their own merit, but felt that 'if Christ were here . . . he would dissolve these chains and annul these vows'. But Luther was struggling with a tradition centuries old, and his own inhibitions and neuroses: 'I don't know what phantom of pomp and human opinion is plaguing me here.'

In this letter, Luther continued with his theme of finding employment for himself elsewhere, a new ministry: 'I see that you all grow in spiritual matters, so it seems to me that I should decrease.' He was using an expression of St John the Baptist in the New Testament: 'I must decrease. He [Jesus] must increase.'

On the question of communion under both kinds, Luther found himself counselling moderation and gradualism, against Karlstadt's thesis that it was actually sinful not to take the wine as well as the bread. The castle church was pressing ahead faster than if Luther himself had been in residence. However, he was able to tell them of his own determination never again to offer a 'private Mass' – on the principle that the only purpose of such a Mass had to link with the idea that it was a sacrifice one gained merit by offering. 'I will never say another private Mass in all eternity.' The Mass, the eucharist, was essentially a communal exercise.

He ended the letter with a recapitulation of his teaching about grace, including a famous phrase, easily misinterpreted, 'sin boldly'. 'If you are a preacher of grace, then preach a true and not a fictitious sin. God does not save people who are only fictitious sinners.' This was clearly a re-statement of the words of Jesus in the Gospel: 'I came to call not the just but sinners to repentance.' Luther was writing a personal letter to his gentle Melancthon, whom he always suspected of being a little weak-kneed – what he went on to say was a further developed and rubato version of the words already quoted, advice of the kind that Staupitz had also given Luther – 'Do not brood over your sins which are an inevitable part of our human condition; look rather at Jesus the Saviour.' He wrote:

Be a sinner and sin boldly, but believe and rejoice in Christ even more boldly, for he is victorious over sin, death and the world. As long as we are here, we cannot avoid sin. This life is not the dwelling place of the righteous . . . By the riches of God's glory we have come to know the Lamb that takes away the sin of the world. No sin will separate us from the Lamb,

even though we commit fornication and murder a thousand
times a day . . . Pray boldly – you too are a mighty sinner.

The Gospel sometimes identified Jesus as a 'Lamb', the new
sacrifice, god-man offering himself as a redemptive sacrifice, a
life and death which won eternal life for all.

Stirred up by Karlstadt's theses, Luther began to write an
extended piece on the Mass. At the beginning of it, he gave
expression to the agonising questions which must present
themselves to anyone leading a movement to upset long-
standing practice, and venerable tradition: 'I have found it very
difficult to justify my conscience; I, one man alone, have dared
to come forward against the Pope, brand him as the Antichrist,
the bishops as his apostles, and the universities as his brothels.
How much did my heart quail . . . Are you the only wise man?
Can it be that all the others are in error? . . . What if you are
mistaken?' But finally he found the power to resist these worries
– 'as a stony shore resists the waves, and laughs at their threats
and storms'. The piece grew into another major work of forty
thousand words in Latin, on the *Suppression of Private Masses*,
which became in German *The Misuse of the Mass*.

Very swiftly, the Edict of Worms and the Excommunication
were beginning to bite – in a converse sense. The established
authorities could no longer be turned to for the solutions of
problems – in outlawing Luther, they had outlawed themselves.
At Wittenberg the Augustinians, the castle church Chapter, and
the university men turned instead to the man who had set them
all thinking and now acting, the man who had been disowned by
Pope and Emperor. The searchlight turned on Luther and
remained there. He was profoundly disconcerted, in the sense
that he had done nothing to prepare for this moment. In practical terms, nothing was prepared. He was a friar, a teacher, a
doctor of theology, a preacher, and in his own mind certainly to
some extent a 'prophet'. But he had not thought to be the
Leader, the Executive or a politician. In his famous book he had
thrown the task of achieving reform to the nobles, and all those
with social, economic and political power. They had reacted
with praise for his anti-Roman sentiments, and had contributed
their poems and threats to clerics in their guise as opponents of
Rome. But none had shown the slightest inclination to set about

the Reform which Luther had programmed. So back came the programme to Luther, with the specific problems raised by Karlstadt: Celibacy, Monastic Life, Communion under both kinds. Together, these were symbol, and in a sense substance, of key problems in the practice of the Myth which underlay European society.

Luther's Wartburg desk began to resemble his Wittenberg desk. The papers piled up, the written sheets poured out. Unable to go down to the printer, tell him what was coming and supervise the work, Luther was feeling increasingly frustrated. He wrote to Spalatin that the printers were 'sordid money grubbers'; all they thought of was – 'it is enough that I get my money, let the readers worry about what and how they will read it . . . anyhow please take care that those MSS. of mine are guarded carefully'. And the constipation got worse, even 'permanent and must always be relieved by medicine. Only every fourth day, sometimes even fifth day, can I open my bowels. What a vast gut!'

The Castellan suggested a day out with the hunt, just what 'Junker Georg' would think of doing anyhow. It was not a success. Luther described to Spalatin how a baby rabbit came racing up to him and he tried to save it: 'I had rolled it up into the sleeve of my cloak . . . the dogs found the poor rabbit and biting through the cloak broke its hind leg and killed it by choking it.' Luther made an allegory of it – the Pope and Satan raging against souls that had been saved even in spite of Luther; but great people would find themselves with difficulty avoiding hell. He told Spalatin to beware: 'In paradise you courtiers who are lovers of game will also be game which Christ, who is the best hunter, can hardly catch and save in spite of his great efforts. A game is being played with you folks while you play around hunting.'

In October, at Wittenberg, things began to move seriously. Several friars, led by Fr Gabriel Zwilling, began to omit references to 'sacrifice' in their celebration of Mass. At the city church communion was given in both kinds. Trying to keep discipline, Prior Heidt suspended all celebration of Mass in the Friary. In November, thirteen friars simply walked out and left the monastery for good. Karlstadt's Theses, in the main supported by communications from the Wartburg, had broken the tabu. Unspoken thoughts finally broke into action, and men no longer at all committed in their own selves to the way of life they followed, freed themselves.

The Elector was deeply concerned. Spalatin wrote to Luther complaining about the behaviour of his Augustinian brethren. He also objected to a proposal of Luther's to write yet another protest to Cardinal Albrecht who, in desperate straits for cash, had expressed his intention of issuing a further Indulgence, from his favourite residence at Halle (where his mistresses also lived). Luther was incensed with Spalatin's letter, and frustrated by affairs he could not directly influence. He had already responded angrily to one previous attempt by Spalatin to put the brakes on. 'I shall not let myself be restrained from privately and publicly attacking the idol of Mainz with regard to his "brothel" at Halle.' Now, on 11 November, Luther wrote to Spalatin: 'I have hardly ever read a letter that displeased me more than your last one. Not only did I put off my reply, but I had decided not to answer you at all. To begin with, I will not put up with your statement that the Sovereign will not allow anything to be written against Mainz . . . Your idea about not disturbing the public peace is fine, but will you allow the eternal peace of God to be disturbed by the wicked and sacrilegious actions of that son of perdition?' Spalatin had complained also about developments at Wittenberg and a terrible reception which the students had given to the Hospital Brothers of St Anthony on their annual visit begging funds. Luther wanted neither to defend nor condemn them. 'For goodness sake, do you want me to apologise to everyone who is upset by Wittenberg?'

Luther went on to tell Spalatin the latest bit of news that would be troublesome to him: 'I have decided to attack monastic vows and to free young people from the hell of celibacy, totally unclean and condemned as it is through its burning and pollutions. I am writing partly because of my own experience and partly because I am indignant.' But the main purpose of the letter, a further shock to Spalatin, was to send down a long manuscript on the Mass for publication, the one dealing largely with the suppression of private Masses. Its publication would stir things up further. A few weeks later, Luther sent down his MS. on Vows, and Spalatin then had two

MSS. in his possession which he was loathe to pass on to the printers.

The completion of the text on vows was a triumphant moment, emotionally. Luther had full access to copiers; one copy went off to his father and another to Spalatin. In a covering letter to his father, the message was: 'You were right all along to oppose my going into the monastery' – though Luther made the reason why he was right a great deal more complicated than his father would have done. While sweating his way through the problem some weeks earlier, he had written to Melancthon:

> I remember when I made my vow, my earthly father was terribly angry; after he was reconciled to the idea I had to listen to the following: 'Let's hope that this was not a delusion from Satan.' The word took such deep root in my heart that I have never heard anything from his mouth which came back to my mind more persistently. It seemed to me as if God had spoken to me from afar, through my father's mouth – it came late on in the affair, yet it was enough to upset me and reprove me.

Luther's letter to his father doubled as a preface to the work:

> My purpose is to recall, in a short preface, what took place between you and me in order to show the pious reader the argument and the content of the book, together with an example . . . It is now almost sixteen years since I became a monk, taking the vow without your knowledge and against your will. In your fatherly love you were worried about my weakness because I was then a young man, just entering my twenty-second year (that is, to use Augustine's words, I was still 'clothed in hot youth') . . . You were determined, therefore, to tie me down with an honourable and wealthy marriage. This fear of yours, this care, this indignation against me was for a time implacable . . . At last you desisted . . . but your fears for me were never laid aside. For I remember very well, later . . . I told you that I had been called by terrors from heaven and that I did not become a monk of my own free will and desire, still less to gain any human satisfaction, but that I was walled in by the terror and agony of sudden death and forced by necessity to take the vow. Then

you said, 'Let us hope that it was not an illusion and a decep-
tion.' That word penetrated to the depths of my soul and
stayed there as if God had spoken by your lips, though I
hardened my heart against you and your word . . . You said
something else too. When in filial confidence I upbraided you
for your anger, you suddenly retorted with a reply so fitting
and so much to the point that I have hardly ever in all my life
heard any man say anything which struck me so forcibly and
stayed with me so long. 'Have you not also heard?' you said,
'that parents are to be obeyed?'

Luther's complex about authority and his father, all his inner
anxieties, terrors and compulsions, all his sensitive longing to
reach the heart of life, the springs of the dynamo of the world
had been touched in this question of religious vows. The
moment in the thunder storm had triggered off the decision to
fly the world, and fly to God; to bind himself by the canonical
vows. And now he was rejecting that absolute obligation, and
the committing of the self under Canon Law, rejecting it in
favour of a new freedom – a freedom which he believed to be the
heart of the message of the Word, a freedom indeed to be
bound, not by the rules of men, not by Church officials, but
solely by the bonds of grace, which themselves issued in another,
greater freedom.

He had to explain to his father, somewhat tortuously, that
though he rejected the obligation as such, he chose of his own
free will, for the moment at any rate, to remain in the habit, in
the religious community, and his father had to accept this as
God's will. 'Who can doubt that I am in the ministry of the
Word? And it is plain that the authority of parents must yield to
this service . . . Christ . . . himself is my immediate bishop,
abbot, prior, lord, father, teacher . . . I hope that he has taken
from you one son in order that he may begin to help the sons of
many others through me.'

Luther worked out a distinction between the religious life as
such, the life of vows in its essence, and on the other hand its
abuse, as a mere social convenience. Saints had lived a life of
true poverty, celibacy and obedience in a community, notably
his favourite spiritual writer St Bernard. And some men and
women might still live it, he thought. His moderation, in

contrast with much subsequent Protestant opinion, was justified in the event. Monastic tradition continued to flourish, even taking fresh root within the Protestant tradition. But as things were he had to ask whether, in the case of the great majority of religions, the vows were really kept. As for poverty, the 'poor' monks and friars were secure, well fed and clothed, and hardly ever 'poor' in any sense recognisable by the truly poor. The vow of obedience was indifferently kept, and was so often dispensed from that to call it a 'life' vow was a pretence. As for celibacy, each religious pretended that in general it was kept, and that it was only oneself that found it almost impossibly difficult, evading the truth that few seemed truly called to this vocation. Finally, there was the scandal of orphaned boys and girls put into a monastery or convent early in life; they were commonly given dispensations and allowed to leave when they had grown up, but dispensations were not given from vows of celibacy. A vow had to be free, an act of an adult human being. It could not properly be transformed into a legal obligation binding under penalties, enforceable by the Church.

The conclusion was that vows to the life of poverty, celibacy and obedience had always to be in some sort temporary. A man or woman ought not to be compelled to remain in a religious house by force of law. And the religious life ought not to be held up as intrinsically 'better' than any other calling – a view which became acceptable to the Catholic Church only in the present century. 'The true way of salvation is to be subject to God, to yield to him in faith, to stand silent before him, to set aside the offensive presumption of good works . . . Vows are such counterfeit "Good works."' Luther had recently heard of the judgement of Paris University against his teaching on faith and work (though omitting, like the Emperor, any reference to the Pope), and composed a sequence lambasting their purely human judgement and their failure to base their understanding on faith, and so to accept the Gospel fully.

This is exactly what our Parisian street whore, with her brazen effrontery and her virtues long since prostituted has not done. She has recently been bold enough to open her legs and uncover her nakedness before the whole world and say that the law about not returning evil for evil ought now to be

regarded as only a counsel . . . because this makes the
Christian law too difficult . . . What schools! What faculties!
What theologians! What bilge! What new-fangled rubbish!

It seems people were inclined to agree with him when it came
to respecting the Church Law on vows. Many religious houses
had become something like clubs which people inhabited
without any longer believing in their declared purposes. Their
mesmerised inhabitants simply walked out of them, like so
many zombies, once they realised there was no longer any social
bar to doing so. 'Lifelong poverty, obedience, and chastity may
be observed, but cannot be vowed, taught or imposed,'
thundered Luther. And it was so.

Luther was becoming the general of a movement already in
train. Stationed far behind the lines, he was sent reports on the
current situation and had to adjudicate. He was taking possession of himself and of the situation in a new way. Greatness was
being thrust upon him; partly it fitted, partly it did not. He was
moving personally into a new, hyper-active phase. Soon after
sending off the MS. on Vows, following that on the Mass, he
began composing a letter to Albrecht, his third to the Cardinal
Archbishop of Mainz. These letters to 'authority' brought out
the best and worst in Luther, but they were always impressive
documents to relish – the addressee must surely have both
blanched and then perhaps chuckled a little. This one began
abruptly:

> To begin with, Most Reverend and Most Gracious Lord, Your
> Electoral Grace has a clear and vivid recollection of the fact
> that I have twice written to your Electoral Grace . . . Your
> Electoral Grace has now again erected at Halle that idol
> which robs poor simple Christians of their money and their
> souls . . . Perhaps Your Electoral Grace thinks I am now out
> of action and that you are safe from me, and that the monk is
> well under the control of His Imperial Majesty. This may be
> so; but Your Electoral Grace should nevertheless know that I
> shall do what Christian love requires . . . I will not put up with
> nor be silent about . . .

As usual with such texts of Luther's, the letter gathered
momentum as it continued: 'Your Electoral Grace should not

think that Luther is dead . . .' The letter wound up with a
straight ultimatum: 'I beg and expect Your Electoral Grace's
definite and speedy reply to this letter within fourteen days; if
after this appointed fortnight no public answer should appear,
my little book *Against the Idol at Halle* will be released . . . Written
in my wilderness . . . 1 December 1521.' In the event, assurances
reached Luther through Spalatin, and he did not send the book
to a printer.

The hyper-activity culminated in a break-out. Luther
obtained a horse and rode over to Wittenberg, still wearing his
beard, dressed as a knight might be. He wanted to get first-hand
information about the remarkable developments at Wittenberg.
He went straight to Melancthon's house, and the news reached
quickly up and down the street. His friends were soon there.
Amsdorf insisted that Luther sleep the night in his house and
that he must not visit the Friary. Excommunicate, under the
imperial ban, what might not happen to him if he revealed his
presence openly? Cranach came round to the house to paint
him and the picture survives today. The disguise was certainly
effective, though if one looked twice the eyes would surely have
given away the identity of the man to anyone who knew him.

Luther was, on the whole, pleased with what had happened at
Wittenberg. It was something to rejoice about; real progress was
being made with actual reforms in his own town. But now, what
was needed above all was the Word. With Melancthon's encouragement he determined to translate the whole of the New
Testament, the whole of the prime text of the Christian Gospel,
the New Testament, into contemporary German and publish it
in an edition which would be available for anyone who could
read. He reckoned he could do it by Easter. He would return to
the Wartburg until that time and then probably emerge for
good.

But the visit was also shocking to Luther. His friends knew
nothing about Luther's text on Vows, or his text on the Mass, or
about his letter to Albrecht. Spalatin had evidently held them all
up. Luther wrote to him immediately.

'To my George Spalatin, a servant of Christ and a friend.
Jesus.' Perhaps his material had been intercepted, but 'there is
nothing that would disturb me more at this moment than to
know that these manuscripts had reached you and that you were

holding them back . . . For goodness sake, curb that moderation and prudence of which I suspect you, . . . I came to
Wittenberg and amid all the delight of being with my friends
again I found this drop of bitterness . . . Everything else that I
hear and see pleases me very much . . . Commend me to the
most illustrious Sovereign from whom I want to keep my arrival
in Wittenberg and my departure a secret . . . Farewell.
Wittenberg, in Amsdorf's house, in the company of my Philip.'
But the letter also contained a sentence reflecting Luther's worry
about the general social situation; as he travelled across
Thuringia, he had sensed an even greater general disquiet, more
widespread threats of disturbance, and danger of a peasants'
revolution. As soon as he was back in the Wartburg he wrote a
6000-word pamphlet *A Sincere Admonition by Martin Luther to
all Christians to Guard against Insurrection and Rebellion*. The
authorities must have been genuinely pleased to see this text,
with its orthodox start, and its unremitting opposition to any
kind of public violence: 'May God grant grace and peace to all
Christians who read this pamphlet or hear it read . . .' There was
a real danger, he said, that the clerical estate had tried poor
Karsthans, the sturdy peasant, too far. 'He seems to be neither
able nor willing to endure it any longer and to have good reason
to lay about him with flail and cudgel'; the entire clerical estate
'may be murdered or driven into exile'.
   But

no insurrection is ever right, however right the cause it seeks
to promote . . . it generally harms the innocent more than the
guilty . . . I am and always will be on the side of those against
whom insurrection is directed, no matter how unjust their
cause; . . . Those who read and rightly understand my
teaching will not start an insurrection; they have not learned
that from me.

Christ's cause was to be forwarded by word of mouth. 'Have I
not with the mouth alone, without a single stroke of the sword,
done more harm to the Pope, bishops, priests, and monks than
all the emperors, kings and princes. . . ?' And people should
not call themselves 'Lutherans'. 'What is Luther? After all, the
teaching is not mine. Neither was I crucified for anyone . . .

How then should I – poor stinking maggot-fodder that I am – come to have men call the children of Christ by my wretched name?'

Back in the Wartburg, Luther was doing fifteen hundred words a day of his translation of the Greek text of the New Testament into German, and taking a new lease of life. Things were happening. People were listening. Archbishops cowered. The Word was about to be spread abroad in his own beloved Saxon German land and language. But threatening all this was the turmoil of resentment and expectation that still continued to increase throughout society.

CHAPTER TWELVE

In Command

22 February 1522. To my most gracious Lord, Duke Frederick, Elector of Saxony. *Personal.* Jesus. Grace and joy from God the Father on the acquisition of a new relic! I put this greeting in place of my usual assurances of respect. For many years Your Grace has been acquiring relics from every land, but God has now heard Your Grace's request and has sent Your Grace without cost or effort a whole cross, together with nails, spears, and scourges. I say again: grace and joy from God on the acquisition of a new relic!
Your Grace should not be terrified by it; stretch out your arms confidently and let the nails go deep. Be glad and thankful . . .
Do not be depressed for things have not yet come to such a pass as Satan wishes. Your Grace should have a little confidence in me, fool though I am . . .
I hope Your Grace will take this letter in good part. I am in such haste that my pen has had to gallop, and I have no time for more. God willing, I shall soon be there. But Your Grace must not assume responsibility on my behalf.
Your Grace's humble servant, Martin Luther.

The Elector was stunned. Luther coming back to Wittenberg, to add to all the other troubles there, the Friary half empty, a radically altered liturgy celebrated from time to time in the churches, violence in the streets, and other towns affected. A man was sent on horseback immediately with a note to the Elector's Office at Eisenach, to take a message up to the Wartburg, telling Luther to remain hidden, at least for a little longer yet. But the note also asked Luther's advice as to what to do about the disturbances in Wittenberg – disturbances which had escalated greatly and had led Duke George the Elector's cousin at

Leipzig in the neighbouring Albertine Saxony to make an official complaint at the Imperial Offices at Nuremberg about lawlessness at Wittenberg and elsewhere in Ernestine Saxony – a complaint which in its turn brought an official message to the Elector, implying reprimand. The authorities were on edge.

But Luther was not to be put off. The Elector had allowed for that; if Luther insisted on travelling, then he must have an official escort, Michael von Strassen, Head of Tax Collection in the south of the Electorate. By 5 March, Luther was at Borna, at von Strassen's house. He had spent the previous night at the Black Bear pub, at Jena. Two surprised Swiss students asked the landlord who the knight was that sat reading Hebrew in the bar lounge, and were told it was Luther – at first they refused to believe it, and said it must surely be Ulrich von Hutten, the knight poet. At Borna, Luther sat down to write again to the Elector: 'To the Most Serene, Noble Sovereign and Lord, Frederick, Duke of Saxony . . . I take the liberty of supposing, on the basis of Your Electoral Grace's letter that Your Electoral Grace was somewhat offended by that part of my letter in which I wrote that Your Electoral Grace should be wise.' Luther said he was not trying to sneer and that he 'had a thoroughly unaffected love and affection' for the Elector. His attempt at initiating the Elector more deeply into the theology of the cross by encouraging him to identify himself with his crucified Lord, was undoubtedly genuine; but the *brio* in his words stemmed surely from enjoyment of his prophetic office!

The new letter was a long one, trying to explain how Luther saw things and what attitude the Elector should take. As usual it grew apocalyptic and confident, even dictatorial, as it went on. And this could not be construed as mere bluff. Luther's letter to the Archbishop of Mainz about his new Indulgence project, had produced a remarkable surrender in the form of a cringing letter from Cardinal Albrecht, and a mealy-mouthed letter from Capito (until recently of Basle), now Chancellor at his court. Whether genuine or not, Albrecht's surrender indicated clearly the muscle which Luther was now able to exert.

Luther explained to the Elector that the situation was indeed serious and, 'even (Your Electoral Grace will excuse my foolish words) if it should rain Duke Georges for nine days and every Duke were nine times as furious as this one', he, Luther would

still have to come and attend to the situation in Wittenberg.
Luther was now sailing on the winds of practico-spiritual confidence and continued, referring to Duke George: 'He takes my
Lord Christ to be a man of straw. My Lord and I can suffer that
for a while . . . I have more than once prayed and wept for Duke
George. I shall pray and weep once more and then cease
forever.' When Luther said 'wept', he meant it. Emotions of all
kinds were now easily surfacing. The Elector was begged to take
part in the praying. But Luther then went on to the main
purpose of the letter, to tell the Elector that it was not his
responsibility, and he was not to worry if any ill befell Luther. It
was all very well to have an escort, but 'I am going to Wittenberg
under a far higher protection than the Elector's. I have no intention of asking Your Electoral Grace for protection. Indeed, I
think I shall protect Your Electoral Grace more than you
are able to protect me.' The next sentence allowed Luther's
sense of Saxon humour and his own special obstinacy to come
through: 'If I thought Your Electoral Grace could and would
protect me, I should not go.' But it was serious too, because:
'The sword ought not and cannot help a matter of this kind . . .
He who believes the most, can protect the most. And since I have
the impression that Your Electoral Grace is still quite weak in
faith, I can by no means regard Your Electoral Grace as the man
to protect and save me.' Luther remained consciously human,
while emphasising the spiritual reality he believed to be at the
heart of what was happening. It was difficult to win any
argument with such a man. He continued: 'Since Your Electoral
Grace wished to know what to do in this matter and thinks that
you have done too little, I humbly answer that Your Electoral
Grace has already done far too much and should do nothing at
all. God will not and cannot tolerate your worrying and
bustling, or mine . . .' It went on with an explicit statement that
if Luther was arrested by imperial agents, and killed, the Elector
was in no way to blame. The Elector should always obey
imperial authority: 'No one should overthrow or resist
authority.' The letter ended with a word of confidence, and a
note of personal mystical assurance:

> I have written this letter in haste so that Your Electoral Grace
> may not be disturbed at hearing of my arrival in Wittenberg

. . . I must be everyone's consoler and do no harm to anyone. It is someone other than Duke George whom I have to consider. He knows me rather well, and I have some real knowledge of him too . . . Written at Borna, in the house of the official escort, 5 March.

Luther was returning to a strange and certainly changed Wittenberg. To his delight the Town Council had issued a revolutionary Ordinance of the City of Wittenberg (24 January 1522), ordering the surrender of various Church revenues and some plate, including the funds of as many as twenty-one sodalities, much of it spent on social evenings and the like. These monies were now combined to form a 'Common Chest' from which funds were provided for the poor, the aged, the orphaned, and for loans to poor workers and for dowries to poor girls at four per cent. The 'Common Chest' was an actual piece of well-made furniture, and with its prescribed number of locks whose keys were held by specified officials representing various strata of society, it was to become a veritable symbol of the social and economic changes as it was set up in town after town in the coming decades.

The Town Council also formally approved the liturgical changes already made and, prompted by Karlstadt, even required the removal of some of the side altars in the Wittenberg Parish Church, as savouring of idolatry. Luther did not like this. He began to see a spirit of doctrinaire intolerance entering into the way the religious changes were imposed. There seemed to be an authoritarian, not to say legalistic spirit, behind the changes which was giving him furiously to think. Was his envisioned new world of Gospel freedom to be turned into another version of the old canonical world where everything was either obligatory or forbidden? More frightening still, the very 'freedom' itself was being pre-empted. Self-selected visionaries from the town of Zwickau had arrived in Wittenberg, claiming inspiration direct from the Holy Spirit. They had impressed Melancthon, who wrote to the Wartburg asking Luther's advice about them. It was these things, combined with a strong plea in the message from the Wittenbergers, that convinced Luther he should return.

So much had happened in the twelve weeks since he had

visited Wittenberg. Karlstadt had celebrated Mass on Christmas Day omitting references to 'sacrifice' in the liturgical text and given communion in both kinds, he himself wearing lay clothes and no vestments. In his sermon he declared that sacramental confession was unnecessary. The populace were told to take the bread and the wine from the altar themselves with their own hands – and much was made of the breaking of the tabu against this. Further, he had said that learning and priest lore were unnecessary; faith alone gave one the freedom of God's House and access to all the knowledge that one needed. It was the provocative, autocratic and divisive way in which it all seemed to have been done that disturbed Luther so much. The students in holiday mood sang secular songs in the church, and began to harass the older priests in the Wittenberg churches as they said Mass. Luther hated this kind of disorder, just as he expressed his great regret that the friars who had walked out of the Friary, had done it without due order and apparently without even the kind of human exchanges to be expected on a decision virtually to break up the community.

One of the details of Karlstadt's reforms that he was sure was wrong was the wholesale removal and sometimes destruction of visual and aural accompaniments to worship. Paintings and statues, long beloved by many, had been widely defaced, broken or carried off with callous violence, and musical instruments had been submitted to the same fate, on the grounds that the Spirit spoke direct to man, and man should commune direct with God. 'All the pictures on earth put together cannot give you one tiny sigh towards God,' wrote Karlstadt. The sheer insensitivity displayed was an affront to people. The philistine application of a Commandment ('You shall not make images or worship them') from the Jewish writings, the Old Testament, was for Luther a failure to understand the 'Freedom' of the Word, which released one from slavish obedience to the Letter of the Law. The Bible was Good News not a book of precedents.

Karlstadt had often been a thorn in Luther's flesh once he began to support him in 1518 – this was not the first time he had in some sense gone further than Luther. But Karlstadt's commitment was not easily shaken. He had refused to compromise, as others had done, when his name had been added to the first Bull of Excommunication in 1520. He had aggressively refused to have any truck with friends and relations who tried to persuade him to recant and not to continue to share with Luther the liability to capital punishment for heresy. To welcome such martyrdom fitted very well with Karlstadt's special addiction to 'resignation-abandonment' to God's will.

It was all such a mixture of good and bad. Karlstadt had gone out into the country early in January and got engaged to be married to a sixteen-year-old girl, and later in the month held a great celebration of the wedding itself. Luther was partly worried but also expressed himself as pleased with this and said he knew the girl's family, in a letter from the Wartburg – his middle-aged colleague would be delivered from the 'unclean' troubles of the celibate. Luther did not at first join in the sneering when people said the old Archdeacon and Dean had now become a 'Fisher of Women'. Another good thing was that the Prior Wencelas Link, who was also Vicar General, had held a General Chapter of the Augustinians and endorsed the action of those who had left, saying friars need no longer consider themselves bound absolutely by their vows. It was true, in Karlstadt's favour, that in the autumn of 1521 it was actually the layman Melancthon who was all for pressing forward and led the way in taking both bread and wine while Karlstadt was counselling moderation and circumspection. But there was no good burking the fact that Karlstadt had never been a good communicator, and had consistently shown poor practical judgement. Few people found him easy to work with, and early in 1521, in spite of his strongly expressed wish to be appointed to the vacant post of Provost of the Cathedral, he had been passed over in favour of Justus Jonas. Now he was showing himself completely in favour of the three visionaries who visited Wittenberg from Zwickau after Christmas, talking of their divine inspirations.

Of these three men, one was an old pupil of Melancthon's and had read Karlstadt's works, and another was a weaver; all three had been influenced by the religious revolutionary Thomas Müntzer, recently preacher at Zwickau but expelled from the town for fomenting violent unrest – another of the disturbances in the Elector's domains. Luther, unlike his colleagues at Wittenberg, was in little doubt about these men. He had written in reply to amazed queries from Melancthon: 'Do not listen if they speak of the glorified Jesus, unless you have first heard of the crucified Jesus . . .' and much more in the same vein. Luther was already finding that he had to provide exactly that service of distinguishing between authentic and inauthentic interpretation of the Gospel, which he had found so unacceptable in the hands of the Roman authorities. The rub, of course, was how such a service was provided, and what were its norms. For the moment, Luther was simply providing a private service to a colleague and there was nothing to worry about in that. His norms in the present case, while thoroughly orthodox in relation to the general consensus, were also in some ways not far from the same German mysticism which was at work among the visionaries themselves, typical as they were of a chronic spontaneous eruption of apocalyptic and individualistic reaction to the directive legalisms of the official Church. 'You should enquire,' directed Luther, 'whether they have suffered spiritual distress and the divine birth, death and hell.' If they claimed only that their experiences were all pleasant and quiet, then they did not have the sign of the Son of Man. Had they been 'called', he asked, and was there any 'sign' of that calling?

Through January and February the Elector had become seriously worried about the situation. Prolonged discussions had been going on between his officials and the Town Council at Wittenberg since early winter. Finally, the Council offered a moratorium on further change and a request to Karlstadt to cease preaching or at least to leave Luther's pulpit in the parish church. But the Elector continued to insist that none of the changes already made had his assent. They were all *ultra vires*, and while discussions about reform were in order, illegal actions should not be taken. The townspeople, bewildered about how to proceed, sent an earnest plea to Luther asking him to return.

This was the immediate cause of Luther's decision to go back to Wittenberg. He had intended returning at Easter in any case, not least in order to be close to Melancthon for the polishing of the translation of the New Testament. Now the letter from the Town Council beckoned imperiously to his inner spirit. The lead he had given over the last five or six years had elicited action. But something that began to sound like chaos had ensued, and that was the very last thing he wanted.

Luther's letter, written at Borna on his way back, was with the Elector within half a day. Somehow the Elector had to regularise his own position, constitutionally, in regard to the return of Luther, outlaw and excommunicate. So he made a distinction, between approving and merely tolerating, the same distinction, roughly, as he had made over the Town Council's initiatives. Luther had said that the Elector was not to take responsibility for his return. Very well then, let Luther write him a public letter expressing this sentiment in objective terms, giving his reasons for returning, and showing that he knew he was going against the Elector's wishes.

Luther was back in Wittenberg, at the Friary, on Friday, 7 March. The lawyer, Jerome Schurff, was with him immediately, with the Elector's request for a letter. The proposed content fitted exactly with Luther's own views and his own understanding of the situation, so he duly wrote it, giving his reasons for returning and stating specifically: 'I know that my coming to reside in Your Electoral Grace's city is without Your Electoral Grace's knowledge or consent' and saying that he realised the danger for the Elector and for himself 'banned and condemned by papal and Imperial law as I am, and expecting death at any moment'. But the reasons he indicated were for him irrefutable: 1. 'I am called by the whole congregation at Wittenberg in a letter filled with urgent begging and pleading.' 2. There were serious troubles at Wittenberg, which required closer attention than was possible by mail. Luther was the cause of the trouble, so Luther must return. 'I have to deal with them personally via mouth and ear.' 3. 'I am rather afraid that there will be a real rebellion in the German territories.' In this situation, he simply had to come back. The 'gospel is excellently received by the common people, but they receive it in a fleshly sense; that is, they know that it is true but do not want to use it correctly.' With a reference to Karlstadt, he said, 'Those who should calm such rebellion only aid it.' He had to come and set right the ill-judged enthusiasm and superficial destructiveness. 'Therefore I could not take human matters into consideration.' A postscript said the Elector could send Luther back an amended version of the letter for him to sign, if it was not exactly as required. Spalatin did redraft the letter, and before the end of the month the rewritten version had been signed and delivered to the Saxon delegation at Nuremberg, and by them to the Imperial Executive permanently residing there.

As soon as Schurff had gone, Luther's room was filled with people through Friday and Saturday telling him what was happening. The pleasure of seeing Melancthon and Amsdorf again, and of being home, was overriden by the urgency to find out what was really going on and deciding how best to respond to it.

On Sunday morning all Wittenberg pressed into the parish church and Father Luther, once again shaven and clothed in his Augustinian habit, went up into the pulpit. He began quietly, intensely, with a theme very familiar but leading in a quite unexpected direction: 'The summons of death comes to us all, and no one can die for another. Everyone must fight his own battle with death by himself . . .' They were thrilled to hear his voice again and within moments he had them in the palm of his hand. Yes, they could envisage that terrible moment of death very well, with a priest bawling religious texts into the poor dying man's ear. At that moment Luther would be no help to them, he was saying. So they needed to be well prepared. His sermon was becoming a catechism – were they well prepared? He said he thought that they knew not to rely on 'works', and to be sure that God had sent his Son to save them. But there was a third requirement, and here came Luther's analysis of what had gone wrong at Wittenberg. It was the absence of love.

'Without love, faith is nothing, as St Paul says: If I had the tongues of angels and could speak of the highest things on faith and have not love, I am nothing. And here, my dear friends, have you not grievously failed? I see no signs of love among you.' Luther had soon understood what was wrong when he heard Melancthon's and Amsdorf's tales, and the complaints and affirmations of Karlstadt and Zwilling – it was the old trouble, all talk, and no real inner commitment, and none of the Christlike charity which alone enabled man to cope with life. St Paul's great teaching on Faith had simply been transformed into another superficial formula to be mouthed: 'You have a great deal to say of the *doctrine* of love and faith . . . no wonder: a donkey can almost intone the lessons and why should *you* not be able to repeat the doctrines and formulas?' And then Fr Luther was heard to be saying something that looked, superficially, like a complete contradiction of his usual theme – he wanted concrete evidence of their faith: 'Dear friends, the kingdom of God – and we are that kingdom – does not consist in talk or words but in activity, in deeds, in works and exercises . . . a faith without love is not enough – rather it is no faith at all.'

Now he was well launched, and the sermon went on for another twenty minutes or half an hour shaming them. As well as love, patience was needed. They had been moving much too fast on the superficial level because 'there are still brothers and sisters on the other side who belong to us and must be won – I would not have gone so far as you have done, if I had been here. The cause is good but there has been too much haste . . . There are some who can run, others must walk, still others can hardly creep.' Luther asked for public order and inner faith to go hand in hand: 'If you had called upon God . . . and had obtained the aid of the authorities, one could be certain that it had come from God . . . if the unreformed Mass was not such an evil thing, I would introduce it again.'

He was irritated, indeed angry. They should have communicated with him before launching into action, 'whereas not the slightest communication was sent to me'. He said they should watch the difference between 'must' and 'free' and were not to make a 'must' out of 'free', things such as fasting or not fasting. They were not to start telling people they *must* eat meat on a Friday against their conscience, 'It looks to me as if all the misery which we have begun to heap upon the papists will fall upon us. Therefore I could no longer stay away, but was compelled to come and say these things to you.'

Luther came down from the pulpit and people felt they were back on some kind of a known road. Their Pastor was in control again, their revered Doctor of Theology, their Friar, their Father Martin Luther. For the next seven days, Luther went into the pulpit and spoke to those who could find the time from their daily work together with a fair number of students, university men, priests, as well as many women, and, crucially, his colleagues in the Faculty of Theology. Luther himself was finding something like a realisation of a role, that now fitted perfectly. By the end of the second sermon he was well into his stride. He took his own experience as an example of how to achieve things through the Spirit:

> I simply taught, preached and wrote God's Word; otherwise I did nothing. And while I slept or drank Wittenberg beer with my friends Philip and Amsdorf, the Word so greatly weakened the papacy that no prince or emperor ever inflicted such losses upon it. I did nothing; the Word did everything. Had I desired to foment trouble, I could have brought great bloodshed upon Germany . . . But what would it have been? Mere fool's play.

On the Tuesday, Luther turned to the monks and nuns, and again conservatively. They ought not to leave their Orders just because others were leaving. They had the right to marry, and indeed the duty to do so if they could not remain celibate. But if they were to leave their communities it should be done in decent order and after careful thought and prayer. Then he turned to the matter of the statues – they were a matter of indifference, so long of course as they were not worshipped. He would like them to be largely abolished simply because people thought they did a good work when they 'have brought so many silver images into the churches'. But it should not be done by violence, 'and you rush, create an uproar, break down altars, and overthrow statues! Do you really believe you can abolish altars in this way?' Luther was careful not to name Karlstadt, but it was clear that an important aspect of the sermons was what amounted to direct criticism of his academic colleague's activities.

Luther reserved his most scathing remarks for the new attitude to the 'Blessed Sacrament', the eucharistic bread, an attitude which in effect, he said, involved merely an inverse of the old rules and the erection of mere anti-tabus, instead of a genuine conversion. The Roman Canon Law, still in force, had all sorts of superstitious regulations about the consecrated bread, that it was not to be touched by anyone other than a priest, that if one of the breads was dropped various purificatory rules had to be performed; now instead of simply lifting the rules, on the contrary, they almost compel everyone to touch the Sacrament, with a kind of compulsive hysteria, as far removed from the Gospel as the Roman rules themselves, though in the opposite direction. As they heard this, many in the congregation remembered Karlstadt's admonition on Christmas Day in the castle church that everyone should go and take the Sacrament both the bread and the wine with their own hands. The criticism of Karlstadt was quite specific, and Luther became sarcastic.

> If you want to show that you are good Christians by handling the sacrament and boast of it before the world, then Herod and Pilate are the chief and best Christians, since it seems to me that they really handled the body of Christ when they had him nailed to the cross and put to death . . . No, my dear friends, the kingdom of God does not consist in outward things, which can be touched or perceived, but in faith.

They might take the sacrament with their hands or not, it made no difference. Luther was exasperated with the absurdity of the situation: '. . . Even a sow could be a Christian, for she has a big enough snout to receive the sacrament outwardly', if that was the only criterion for being a Christian.

What upset Luther most was to realise that he now seemed to have enemies not only among the followers of the old theology, the papists, but among his own reforming colleagues. He became dictatorial: 'No new practices should be introduced, unless the gospel has first been thoroughly preached and understood.' Then came a strong personal note, revealing how bitterly he felt he had been let down: 'If you are not going to follow me . . . no one need drive me from you – I shall leave unasked . . . you have gone so far that people are saying: "At Wittenberg there are very good Christians, for they take the sacrament in their hands and grasp the cup, and then they go to their booze and swill themselves full" . . . I may say that of all my enemies who have opposed me up to this time none have brought so much grief as you.' 'Grief' was a way of signalling his frustrations and misery. His colleagues, less perceptive and less able than he, were becoming a new 'enemy' and he took refuge in a sarcasm he could handle so brutally. In his hopes for a Christian order, free of corruption, in his vision of a new world he had forgotten perhaps the warning he gave to his fellow friar when he was Vicar General: 'Why then do you imagine that you are among friends? . . . The Rule of Christ is in the midst of his enemies.' Later he recognised the fact only too clearly, and would soon be polarising his colleagues to the left of him as part of the devil's plans for upsetting him and the reforms. He was bewildered and dejected. 'You have the true gospel and the pure Word of God, but no one as yet has given his goods to the poor . . . Nobody extends a helping hand to another, nobody seriously considers the other person, but everyone looks out for himself and his own gain, insists on his own way, and lets everything else go hang.'

In Luther's final sermon on the second Sunday, he spoke about 'Confession'. His unique approach was in evidence again. They might have expected him to brush it aside as part of the Roman bag of tricks. But with his special form of rhetoric he swiped to left and to right and defended the extreme centre:

> I refuse to go to confession simply because the Pope has commanded it and insists upon it. For I wish him to keep his hands off confession and not make of it a compulsion or command, which he has not the power to do. Nevertheless, I will allow no man to take private confession away from me, and I would not give it up for all the treasures in the world, since I know what comfort and strength it has given me. No one knows what it can do for him except one who has struggled often and long with the devil. Yes, the devil would have killed me long ago if confession had not sustained me. For there are many doubtful matters which a man cannot resolve or find the answer to by himself, and so he takes his brother aside and tells him his trouble . . . We must have many absolutions, so that we may strengthen our timid consciences and despairing hearts against the devil and against God . . . I will not let private confession be taken from me. But I will not have anybody forced to it.

It had been an extraordinary week. A Swiss student, Albert Bürer, at Wittenberg wrote home:

> On 6 March, Martin Luther returned to Wittenberg on horseback . . . He came to settle the trouble stirred up by the extremely violent sermons of Karlstadt and Zwilling, for they had no regard for weak consciences which Luther no less than Paul would feed on milk until they grow strong. He preaches daily on the Ten Commandments. As far as one can tell from his face the man is kind, gentle and cheerful. His voice is sweet

and sonorous so that I am struck by the sweet speaking of the man. Everyone, even though not Saxon, who hears him once, desires to hear him again, such tenacious hooks does he fix in the minds of his listeners.

Jerome Schurff wrote to the Elector of 'the great gladness and rejoicing here both among the learned and the unlearned . . . showing us the errors into which we have been led . . . Even Gabriel Zwilling has agreed that he went too far.'

With the second Sunday over, the situation in hand again, students quietened, the congregation reassured, priests and academics also reassured and feeling that Luther knew where he was taking them – it was possible to relax with Philip Melancthon and Amsdorf over some of the Wittenberg beer to which Luther had referred in the second sermon. It was a strange sensation for him, once again of a new freedom. He had experienced a 'new' freedom twice before, once when he understood that he no longer had to try to measure up to God, but that God would do all, then again when he arrived at the Wartburg, free of many things. Now the very Church authority itself seemed almost to have disappeared. Certainly at Wittenberg they were their own masters for the moment.

But the freedom had dimensions to it both welcome and unwelcome. Luther was free to be arrested, at any time. Nothing at all now stood between him and the law officers of both Church and State. But as the days and weeks went by, the situation which had gradually been showing its profile during the last months at the Wartburg began to clarify. The authorities, like Luther himself, were frightened about the general unrest and the danger of an uprising. They were actually afraid to arrest Luther. The arrest itself might miscarry; much worse it might spark off an uprising. Luther's ever present fear of death which accompanied him after leaving the Wartburg, did not go away, but it did lessen. Then there was the freedom also to be attacked by the words and actions of his own colleagues. If he had opportunities now for reforming activity which began to look almost incredible, he was also vulnerable in a new and unlimited way.

He was soon embroiled in a hundred problems and being asked to pronounce on everything from reasonable interest rates for loans to the future of the Teutonic Order of Knights,

from detailed arrangements for the Common Chest in the town
of Leisnig to the order of the Church services, not to speak of
theology, Scripture and the rest. Writings of every kind began to
flow importunately out again to the printers. The return to
apparent normality was partly deceptive. Friars were leaving the
Augustinians almost daily, and within a few months it was impossible to continue with the common recitation of the Office,
the readings at meals, or any semblance of regular community
life – the life which had formed Luther, given him his love of
psalm and plain chant, scripture and prayer, of theology and
preaching. But, meanwhile, the Wittenberg life went on, and the
letters to Spalatin started up again:

> Mr George Spalatin, evangelist at Lochau . . . On my Patmos
> I translated the whole New Testament. Philip and I have now
> begun to polish the whole thing . . . We shall use your service
> sometimes for finding a right word. But give us simple words,
> not those of court or castle, for this book should be famous
> for its simplicity . . . please tell us the names and colours of
> the gems that are mentioned in Revelation 21.
>
> At present I am working on a little tract on gospel-style
> eucharistic communion entitled *On Receiving Both Kinds*. Even
> if this should bring me a lot of trouble, I am not afraid of it.
> Christ lives, and for his sake we not only have to be a strong
> fragrance which will cause death for some and life for others,
> but we may even have to be put to death.
>
> Farewell and greet all at court. From Wittenberg, 30 March
> 1522
>
> Martin Luther

During April a preaching tour was decided on for Luther,
through some of the principal towns of the electorate. On 30
April, Luther left for Eilenberg, Torgau, Borna, Altenberg, and
as far as Zwickau, eighty miles south of Wittenberg. He preached
on Marriage, the Lay Vocation, faith and love, the other current
themes. It was an encouraging experience. People wanted to
listen to him. It was a test of his public viability, both with the
people at large and in respect of the Elector and the bishops.
Although the local Bishop ran a confirmation and a visitation in
the district in competition with Luther – Luther duly denounced

the confirmation, a man-made sacrament – no attempt was made to arrest or hinder him. The Elector was relieved to have someone holding a middle line between the extremism and violence which were now associated with Karlstadt on the one hand, and the purely reactionary papal and imperial stances on the other. Luther preached all the time against extremism, whether civil or ecclesiastical, to right or to left, but above all it was a gospel freshly sited; he emphasised the life of the layman and marriage. What after all, in the end, was the difference between a priest and a layman? – they were both men. This came out in a particularly sarcastic piece on the objection to lay people touching the Blessed Sacrament, an objection which lasted in the Catholic Church until the 1970s. 'The angry papists write . . . that people have received the sacrament with "lay hands". What do you think of that? Isn't that marvellous? Lay hands indeed! . . . Now if I were to ask them with what kinds of mouths they themselves receive the sacrament at Easter, whether they receive it with a lay mouth or with a priestly mouth, perhaps they would say their mouths just then were the mouths of angels or bishops.' Luther was demythologising theology.

After the preaching tour, the balmier days of a festive and welcoming Wittenberg seemed almost to be back. 'Grace and Peace. My Spalatin: Aurogallus asks that, if possible, he be honoured with some venison for his wedding. As you know, he deserves it, and he is far from being the most insignificant member of our University.' Professor Aurogallus, or Goldhann, had been the final satisfactory choice for the chair in Hebrew. And there was a letter to Spalatin begging leniency for a poor man caught poaching in the Elector's waters.

The publications were flowing again. *A Little Prayer Book* was intended for personal use, to take the place of many similar works which, however, were 'puffed up with promises of Indulgences'. These, often with a title such as *The Garden of the Soul* were popular, and Luther's prayer book had some of the same prayers in it, but none of the effusive invocations to Mary and the Saints, and without the spiritual profit motive built in. With the traditional prayers went also some woodcuts showing incidents from the Bible. It romped through many editions.

On the polemical front, Luther had a sharp analysis of the

sexual life and morals of the clergy in *Against the Spiritual Estate of the Pope and the Bishops falsely so-called*. It came out in the summer of 1522.

> Bishops receive the greater part of all their annual interest rates in almost all religious foundations from nothing but the priests' mistresses. Whoever wants to keep a little mistress must give one guilder a year to the bishop. There is a proverb among them: 'Chaste priests are not liked by the Bishop – indeed they are his enemies.' . . . To top it all, if a priest's maid stumbles over a dishpan and breaks in two, so that one part of her must be carried to baptism, the interest rate increases beyond the annual guilder.

He waxed eloquent about the nuns who did not have true vocation to celibacy – and the monks: 'Unless she is in a high and unusual state of grace a young woman can do without a man as little as she can do without eating, drinking, sleeping or other natural requirements. Nor can a man do without a woman . . . Nature does not cease to do its work when there is voluntary chastity . . . To put it bluntly, seed . . . if it does not flow into flesh will flow into the shirt.'

The ex-friars were getting married, and nuns were leaving their convents when they could. There was no sign that Fr Luther thought his praise of marriage might apply to himself. He had no mistress, and had always kept his distance from younger unrelated women. The texts flowed, *The Persons related by Consanguinity and Affinity who are Forbidden to marry by Scripture* (1522), *The Estate of Marriage* (1522), *An Exhortation to the Knights of the Teutonic Order that they lay aside False Chastity and assume True Wedlock* (1523), *That Parents should neither compel nor hinder the Marriage of their Children* and *That Children should not become engaged without their Parents' Consent* (1524). And other texts: *Letter of Consolation to all who Suffer Persecution* (1522), *Temporal Authority: to what extent it should be obeyed* (1523), covering a wide range of the responsibilities of the state, *Ordinance of a Common Chest* (1523), *That Jesus Christ was born a Jew* (1523), a defence of the teaching that Jesus was the promised 'Messiah' of the Jews, *To all Christians in Worms* (1523), *Concerning the Ministry* (1523), *Trade and Usury* (1524), stricter than some earlier medieval theories but not in practice greatly different (and he sent a letter to the Saxon

Chancellor, Gregory Bruck on the same topic), *To the Councillors of all Cities in Germany that they establish and maintain Christian Schools* (1525), *How God rescued an Honourable Nun* (1524), the story of an escape from a convent, *A Christian Letter of Consolation to the People of Miltenberg* (1524).

Just as in the old days, there was a letter to Staupitz. Towards the end of June, Luther was horrified to hear that his old mentor had accepted the offer of the position of Abbot at a wealthy Benedictine abbey, St Peter's, in Salzburg. He wanted to protest, and he wanted also to set the record straight about Wittenberg, since Staupitz had written to a friend deploring what was going on. Luther underlined how a battle was being fought and told Staupitz how an Augustinian prior at Antwerp, a recent graduate of Wittenberg, had been burnt at the stake. He had been lured to Brussels where the Inquisitor General was able to arrest and imprison him, and eventually to have him burnt, following on a repudiation of a recantation obtained by torture. 'They are planning to burn me at the stake too.' It was true that only the Elector and the temper of the common people stood between Luther and the stake. A fundamental uncertainty, an absence of any ultimate legal protection, always lay threateningly over Luther. The letter ended: 'Farewell, my Father, and pray for me. Dr Jerome, Rector Amsdorf, and Philip send their greetings . . . Your son, Martin Luther.' Martin was insisting on the relationship and the mutual loyalty. Staupitz, in his reply months later from his southern hideout, was warm but guarded: 'My love to you is unchanging, passing the love of women, always unbroken . . . But as I do not grasp all your ideas, I keep silence about them . . . It seems to me that you condemn many things which are merely indifferent . . . but we owe much to you, Martin, for having led us back from the husks which the swine did eat to the pastures of life and the words of salvation.' Staupitz asked for a Master's Degree at Wittenburg for the bearer of the letter, and it was granted. Staupitz died later in the year and so ended Luther's most personal link with the papal Church, the Church of his own vital years of development.

The Luther case remained a very large thorn in the flesh of the Establishment. In Ernestine Saxony Church property was being taken over by reformers and local political authority. The case had to be on the agenda again at the next Imperial Diet at

Nuremberg. And once again the papal Legate had to be heard.
But there had been great changes at Rome. While Luther was at
the Wartburg, Pope Leo X died. A growing, reforming party at
Rome found themselves linked with another party which wished
to ensure the best possible links with the new Emperor. A case
was put forward, and triumphed, for the election as Pope of a
Netherlander who had been the tutor of Charles Habsburg
before he was elected Emperor. Adrian of Utrecht was a pious,
devoted man, influenced by the Brothers of the Common Life,
but also strongly orthodox in his theology. Charles had recently
appointed him Bishop of Tortosa and his Viceroy in Spain. It
was August 1522 before this man from the Netherlands, Adrian
VI, arrived in Rome, the last non-Italian Pope until Pope John
Paul II.

Adrian VI came with high ambitions to reform the Church,
and especially to reform the whole Roman administration. But
he lacked any understanding of the art of the possible, and he
lacked the genius which can sometimes turn the impossible into
achievement. Certainly the least likely way to achieve a
successful reform of the financial system of the largest organisation in the world, was by a head-on refusal to perform the
normal tasks of its head. Adrian had decided that he would cease
to issue the normal offices, privileges and the like just as they
were requested in return of cash payments. As a result, it was not
many weeks before the Cardinals in the Curia were coming to
warn him of impending bankruptcy. His reforming tactics had
perforce to be suspended. Then, for the changes in structure and
procedure that he wished to make, they could find no one
suitable to draft the necessary decrees. However, while running
up against a high blank wall at home, the new Pope was able to
do something in the international sphere.

'We know that many disgraceful things have happened in this
Holy See for many years now, such as abuses in spiritual
matters, surfeit of financial demands, and everything used
perversely . . . it is hardly surprising if the disease has gone from
the head to the members, from the chief bishops to the other
lower prelates. We have, all, that is the ecclesiastical prelates,
failed, every one of us, and there was not one who did anything
good for long.' And so to promises of reform. These words were
part of the text which the papal Legate, Francesco Chieregato,

was obliged to read out at the Diet of Nuremberg on 3 January 1523. But this went along with the usual demands for contributions to the defence of Europe against the infidel Turk, and for suppression of heresy, above all of the heretic Luther, who the Pope was surprised to hear was still free and threatening the public peace.

Again a pope had misjudged the situation. The German representatives at the Diet were not impressed by the Roman demands for repression of heresy until the abuses associated with Rome herself had been removed – not just admitted, regretted and deplored. They had heard reform plans a hundred times before and were inclined to jeer at the admission of guilt. The only people they knew to do any actual reforming were Luther and his friends – not that they wished to share in his heresy. Then there were other important things happening in Germany just now. The knights were on the rampage; eventually von Sickingen and his followers were defeated by the troops of the Archbishop of Trier in May, and von Sickingen killed. In any case, the Legate to Nuremberg had a cool reception, at times aggressively cool.

A vast list of complaints, *Centum Gravamina*, with the usual request for a Free Council in German speaking lands was put forward – with full detail, including such things as interference in marriages, in people's diet, limitation of times when marriage may be solemnised, the preaching of Indulgences, financially burdensome interference also in the affairs of local dioceses, and so on, many pages of matters fully itemised. Until these things were put right, until a Council should be held, the Imperial Estates merely ordered the Gospel to continue to be preached in its orthodox understanding, and nothing new to be published unless it had first been approved. That was as far as they would go towards suppressing Luther. Their words, of course, could be variously interpreted. When the Elector drew Luther's attention to the text, Luther said that while he realised that 'my harsh writing has been and still is distasteful to and opposed by many of my friends and enemies, including your Electoral Grace' yet he had never in any way stirred up rebellion or revolution, and indeed had written against them, and had written only to promote the Word. He would gladly refrain from any further harsh writing. But if the Word was attacked, and if Luther was attacked, he must defend them. And since the Mandate of the Diet said only the true Gospel must be preached, he must be allowed to defend it too.

The Roman authorities seemed to be unaware that, with every month, further reforming initiatives were surfacing all over the German speaking lands, not to speak of the rest of northern Europe. They were unable to envisage a situation where the Holy See was not the major power in the land where matters of religion were concerned. And even those few people of great imagination who were well able to imagine such a thing, were not able to see how they should proceed. Too few and too late in the coming two decades, several did try to respond, particularly to Melancthon who had a continuous project of an Agreed Statement, his *Loci Communes*, an attempt at a summary of the central themes of Christianity as understood by the Wittenberg theologians, set out in such a way that papal theologians might be likely to read them sympathetically.

Melancthon always realised that Luther's rumbustious concern with the dynamic of faith, with preaching the Gospel, with a lived and announced theology must arouse opposition, and gladly as he accepted Luther's sincerity and indeed the importance of a Gospel enunciated without compromise, yet he considered it was necessary also to have a conceptual summary of what was believed, which could enable the different viewpoints to come together in what we call today Agreed Statements. But there was little motivation for reconciliation among the majority of leaders on the two sides (and very soon more than two sides, because the reformers began to differ fiercely among themselves), who soon became polarised and set in confrontation.

Later in 1523, Adrian VI died. The cardinals had had enough of reform, turned back to traditional Florentine stock and chose another Medici, a cousin of Pope Leo X. Cardinal Giulio de Medici was elected on 18 November 1523, and took the name Clement VII. To a further German Diet at Nuremberg he sent his most experienced Cardinal, Campeggio – made Bishop of Salisbury that year for diplomatic service in England. But the Nurembergers had moved sharply forward with reforming activities. Communion in both kinds had been demanded by the congregations the previous year, and other changes were afoot. The Legate decided not to enter the town with the usual triumphal progress, due by protocol to a papal legate – it might be considered provocative. He simply rode into the town, though well accompanied by notables, and all on the finest horses and in fine clothes. The new Diet was no more disposed to accede to the Roman demand to have the Edict of the Diet of Worms executed than the previous Diet. There was still indeed a majority of representatives, conservative and more or less unsympathetic to religious change as such, or to any change opposed by Pope and Emperor. But when it came to demands on them from Rome, national feeling and resentment of ecclesiastical privilege, and of Rome, was the overriding sentiment. However, Cardinal Campeggio was a seasoned and persevering diplomat, and was able, subsequent to the Diet, to gain a definite advantage by gathering together the rulers unsympathetic to the reformers and getting them to sign a text forming the League of Ratisbon (7 July 1524), which was to promote reform of the Church within the papal tradition. Religious polarisation was becoming explicitly political.

But something more important was already beginning in Germany. Bands of peasants, armed and on the move, were taking over control of part of the Black Forest in the south-west, by the middle of August. For the next nine months the attention of an increasing number of rulers was to be taken up with the peasant uprisings. At the same time the civil government in an increasing number of towns acquiesced in religious changes. The water was coming to the boil haphazardly in Zurich, in Strassburg, and eastwards across Germany to Saxony and northwards to the Netherlands and Denmark. The ceaseless flood of books and pamphlets from Wittenberg was added to increasingly from authors and presses in other towns. The flood was encouraged by the fact that Luther always disowned any wish to impose a universal style or any norms other than those of Scripture and, while always willing to advise, his advice often included the suggestion that people should work things out themselves as appropriate locally. 'I am not your Pastor . . . turn away from Luther and Karlstadt to Christ.' But one writing of Luther's was everywhere influential, and outshone all others, in the vast numbers sold, perhaps 10,000 a year for several years running. This was the text of the norm itself, the New Testament in Luther's German translation.

The first edition of Luther's New Testament had been published in Wittenberg in September 1522. A translation based for the first time on the Greek (Erasmus's text) rather than on the Latin which Jerome had produced from the original Greek over a thousand years earlier, it was creating a fresh awareness of the Christian Gospel. People read, or heard read, quite different and longer passages than those they were used to hearing in church in the annual liturgical cycle. And they received them in a more or less secular setting, outside the church – or in the church in reformed and less formal services. A fresh awareness of their own German language was being promoted – and the domination, incidentally, of Saxon high German assured. A new vocabulary, a new language, was being provided for people's expectations, hopes, disenchantments, their loves and hates.

After 1522, this work of translation developed into the greatly ambitious task of the translation of the whole vast Hebrew text of the Old Testament, a million and a half words. The translation committee met once a week in Wittenberg for the next decade and worked so hard that they published the opening section (The Pentateuch) in 1523, and much more again in 1524. This work lay at the heart of numerous activities concerned with education and communication. The Wittenberg schools were opened up after being closed during the troubles of the winter 1521–2. Luther plunged into detailed advice here, and eventually published books of guide-lines and encouragement to Town Councils. If they spent one guilder on the defence tax against the Turks, they should spend a hundred on schools. He expressed his own view of the importance of education to his old poet friend Eobanus in March 1523, in a letter which takes us into the Renaissance world of the humanists: 'I do not intend that young people should give up poetry and rhetoric . . . . it is through these studies, as through nothing else, that people are really well prepared for grasping sacred truths, as well as for handling them skilfully and successfully.' He looked back longingly to the time when he read more poetry than he did now, and remembered the time when he bought his own copies of the *Odyssey* and the *Iliad*.

Poetry was ever circling round his mind; the music of the liturgy was in his blood. At Wittenberg, Luther continued to approve of the traditional Latin liturgy, shorn only of the references to sacrifice and other prayers and phrases which implied that to attend Mass was a 'good work', earning spiritual merit. While reformers in other towns were springing up and beginning to experiment with translated texts, Luther himself went very slowly. Requests kept coming to him for new forms, and gradually he started jotting things down, using his own knowledge and love of music to make a German liturgy which was truly German and not just a wooden transposition from the Latin. He kept the old chants, and used the Saxon folk tradition. He published *Concerning Public Worship* and *Order of Mass and Communion for the Church at Wittenberg* in 1523. Meanwhile, he had instituted a weekday service at which Psalms were sung, the Bible read and a sermon preached to replace the weekday Masses which Karlstadt had cancelled, a cancellation he agreed with.

In the same year, Luther wrote words and music for a ballad-type hymn to commemorate two Augustinians, Heinrich Vries and Johann Esch, who had been burnt at the stake for preaching Luther's teaching. Starting with the traditional opening line for a ballad – 'A new song here shall be begun' – it went on:

> The Lord God help our singing
> Of what our God himself hath done
> Praise, honour to him bringing
> At Brussels in the Netherlands
> By two boy matryrs youthful
> He showed the wonders of his hands
> Whom he with favour truthful
> So richly hath adorned.

And continued thus for twelve nine-line verses of rough but singable Saxon, with such sequences as:

> Oh, they sang sweet, and they sang sour
> Oh, they tried every double
> The boys they stood firm as a tower
> And mocked the sophists' trouble.

The next hymn known to us is from Luther's own gruelling
inner life, written to a vigorous tune and starting: 'Dear
Christians let us now rejoice.' It went on with material straight
from Luther's own personal troubles such as 'Forlorn and lost
in death I lay. A captive to the devil . . . My good works were
worthless quite . . . my will hated God's judging light . . . To
hell I fast was sinking . . . Then God was sorry on his throne . . .'
God the Father sends his Son, Jesus, to put things right, and
Jesus says 'Hold thou by me, thy matters I will settle, etc.'

Once started there was no stopping him, and Luther found
yet another identity as poet and composer, and the principal
originator of a whole new tradition of German church liturgy,
rooted in the existing musical culture, and destined to reach its
marvellous climax at Leipzig in the work of Johann Sebastian
Bach. The penitential Psalm, 'Out of the Depths', one of his
favourites, and the hymn to the Holy Spirit, 'Come Holy Ghost',
were among the first he did. Eventually, the demands became so
insistent for a complete chanted Mass in German, that he sent
for the Elector's court musicians, Conrad Rupsch and Johann
Walter, and had them with him for three weeks in the late
summer of 1525. Together they adapted the plain chant
melodies with great care from the Latin to German. Others had
made similar attempts, in Switzerland and not far away in
Allstedt where Müntzer achieved some happy liturgical forms,
which were used until they were suppressed in the 1530s by the
Elector's visitors in favour of Luther's versions.

By the winter of 1523–4, Luther's personal situation had
become anomalous. He was still wearing his Augustinian habit,
but the Priory was empty. It was two years since he had dis-
avowed any canonical alliance, though wishing to remain essentially a 'religious'. But the habit had become an empty symbol,
and one day, recognising the facts, he laid it aside and never
wore it again. He sat down and wrote to the Elector: 'I am now
living in this monastery alone except for the Prior (not counting
some who were exiled by the enemies of the Gospel whom we
lodge here temporarily out of Christian love). The Prior expects
to leave soon, and in any case I cannot endure the daily moaning
of the people whom I must remind to pay their rents', the
income from which originally used to help keep up the
monastery. 'Therefore we are inclined to relinquish and hand

over the monastery, with all its property to Your Electoral Grace.' Luther suggested that perhaps he could live on in the sick bay. As ever, the Elector did not like to act precipitately. He simply let Luther stay where he was and said nothing about the way the monastery was used by ex-monks and ex-nuns, as a staging-post back to the ordinary world. Luther and the Prior stayed on, knowing that the Elector was not likely to ask them to move.

If things were relatively quiet on the right wing, Luther continued to feel threatened from the left, distantly by Zwingli and others in Switzerland and the south-west, but notably by ex-Dean Karlstadt. The latter, thoroughly censored by Luther both as to his sermons and his books which he could not get published, had relinquished his office of Dean of the Faculty of Theology but continued to be a lecturer in receipt of a salary from the University. However, he was seldom seen in Wittenberg, having taken his bride to his parish of Orlamünde, where, calling himself Brother Andrew, he cultivated the Glebe land in peasant's clothes and invited Müntzer to come to join the commune and help with the work. The Vicar originally appointed by Karlstadt to look after the parish had to give way to him. The University missed Karlstadt's lectures.

Luther wrote to Spalatin on 14 January 1524: 'Karlstadt behaves as usual. He has had his material published by a newly founded publishing house in Jena, and so it is rumoured will bring out eighteen more books.' Two months later, complaining about Karlstadt's destruction of statues, vestments, etc., Luther wrote, 'In the name of the University we shall call him back . . . to his office of the Word'. He was to be arraigned before his University colleagues. 'Satan is setting up a sect among us at yet another place and this sect supports neither the papists nor us . . . They boast they are moved by pure spirits.' Enemies to the left, enemies to the right. Only Luther and the Elector were in the middle. Politically and ecclesiastically, that is how it seemed to be working out. Luther warned the Elector in July that Müntzer and his followers were threatening violence against the State. They referred to the Bible as Bible-babble-Babel and relied on direct spiritual inspiration.

In August, Luther made a tour through Thuringia, and went to Orlamünde, almost as on an official visitation. There was a mixed reception from Karlstadt whose writings, not as numerous as Luther's but numerous enough, were now openly opposing both Luther and the traditional Church on sacramental theology; and a mixed reception from some of his congregation. Luther and Karlstadt had a discussion at the famous Black Bear pub at Jena where Luther had been mistaken for Hutten by the Swiss students. It was a sad encounter. Luther was aggressive to his tiresome old colleague. Finally, he challenged Karlstadt to a public debate and threw him the conventional golden coin as a formal sign. At an earlier stage, Karlstadt had promised to return to his duties at Wittenberg. But he never did so. In July he had resigned from being Archdeacon at the castle church. Later, in 1524, he was exiled from Saxony by the Elector who was worried about the general unrest that always seemed to go along with Karlstadt's preaching, as distinct from Luther's – Wittenberg remained quiet and disciplined since Luther's return. Karlstadt took refuge in Strassburg, and from there and elsewhere Luther received queries from people worried by teaching which radically reinterpreted sacramental religion. Finally, Luther took to his pen and wrote a full-scale piece – *Against the Heavenly Prophets in the Matter of Images and Sacraments*, a piece that continually returned to 'Brother Andrew in his felt hat'. Luther's anger and frustration had found a new target: 'There has been a change in the weather. I had almost relaxed and thought the matter was finished; but then it suddenly starts up again, and it is for me as the wise man says: "When man finishes, he must begin again."' So ran the first paragraph of this 45,000-word piece. Among the arguments and invective were some interesting things. Karlstadt had accused Luther of being responsible to some extent for his expulsion from Saxony. Luther wrote:

I have had no dealings with the Elector of Saxony about Karlstadt. For that matter I have in my whole life never spoken one word with this prince, nor heard him speak, nor have I ever seen his face, except in Worms before the Emperor when I was being examined for the second time. It is true that I have often communicated with him in writing through Spalatin and especially insisted that the Allstedtian spirit be suppressed.

But he *had* spoken

> with my young lord, Duke John Frederick – that I admit – and pointed out Dr Karlstadt's wantonness and arrogance. However, since 'the spirit' burns with such blinding intensity, I will here recount the reasons, some of which indeed are not known to the princes of Saxony, why I am happy that Dr Karlstadt is out of the country. And in so far as my entreaties are effectual, he shall not return again, and would again have to leave were he to be found here, unless he became another Andrew [German: *ein ander Andres*], which God grant. God willing, I will fawn before no princes. But much less will I suffer that the rebellious and the disobedient among the masses are to be led to despise temporal authority.

Luther recounted Karlstadt's obstinacy, his failure to return to Wittenberg and the interview at the inn: 'He turned to me, snapped his fingers and said "You are nothing to me."' The long years of seeing Luther usurp his leadership at Wittenberg were too much for Karlstadt, and the quarrel had become bitter and personal. Luther was not going to spare him:

> What do you think now? Is it not a fine new spiritual humility? Wearing a felt hat and a grey garb, not wanting to be called doctor, but Brother Andrew and dear neighbour, as another peasant, subject to the magistrate of Orlamünde and obedient as an ordinary citizen. Thus with self-chosen humility and servility, which God does not command, he wants to be seen and praised as a remarkable Christian, as though Christian behaviour consisted in such external hocus-pocus. At the same time he strives and runs counter to duty, honour, obedience, and . . . the right of the reigning prince . . . which God has instituted.

Then Luther turned to the theology. One main theme was that: 'The Pope commands what is to be done; Dr Karlstadt what is not to be done'; while Luther alone insisted on freedom. Another was an attack on Karlstadt's rejection of the sacraments of baptism and the eucharist as traditionally understood. Karlstadt, said Luther, rejected the true meaning of Scripture on the effectiveness of the sacraments, and instead said: 'The Spirit, the Spirit, the Spirit must do this inwardly . . . Dear Peter, I beg you put your glasses on your nose, or blow your nose a bit, to make your head lighter and the brain clearer.'

These 'heavenly prophets' and all his enemies on the left Luther referred to collectively by the term *Schwärmerei*. It means the 'enthusiasm' or 'fanaticism' of a visionary and is derived from the word 'swarm'. Luther thought of these subjective followers of the Spirit as fluttering about without purpose, 'blown about by every wind of doctrine' as St Paul put it.

Luther published his piece at the turn of the year 1524–5. He was beginning to feel dejected and persecuted again. His enemies on the left were beginning to accuse him of being a conservative, with nicknames like Master Pussyfoot and Mr Easychair. On the right his old papist enemy, Emser (The Goat), called him the Archbishop of Wittenberg. But, worst of all, Erasmus had attacked him. In September 1524 he had come out with a full-scale attack on a central item in Luther's theology, under the title *The Freedom of the Will*.

In April, Luther had heard rumours that Erasmus was finally coming down against him and tried to forestall him with one of his awkward letters, just the kind of thing greatly to irritate the old scholar: 'I have been silent long enough, excellent Erasmus. For although I was expecting you, as the greater and older man, to break the silence, since I have waited so long in vain, I think charity now compels me to take the initiative.' Then Luther immediately attacked him: 'You have behaved most peculiarly towards us, in order that your relationship with my enemies, the papists, should be unimpaired and safe . . . you have not been given the courage . . . that you could openly fight these monsters around us.' But it was only too clear that the real purpose of the letter was to try to pressure Erasmus into not writing against Luther, who defended himself against Erasmus's usual complaint of his violence: 'I myself am easily provoked and have often been prodded into writing sharply', but only against those who were obstinate, he said weakly. Finally came an excruciatingly patronising wish that 'a disposition which is worthy of your fame would be given to you by the Lord', and at last a straight plea: 'Do not give comfort to my enemies and join their ranks . . . do not publish booklets against me.' They should 'bear one another's burdens. Pardon my lack of eloquence . . .'

It was a jumpy letter. Luther did not understand how Erasmus could be in good faith, and was not able to find a wavelength on which to speak to the great scholar whom for eight years now he had believed to be fundamentally mistaken in his theology. How was it possible, Luther asked himself, for Erasmus to compromise with an evidently inadequate theology and not to break with an institution so riddled with corruption as the papacy.

On his side, Erasmus deeply regretted Luther's violent and intemperate language. Encouraged by numerous people, including the Pope and the King of England, to vindicate his own scholarship and his own status, often itself suspect, and to dissociate himself from Luther, he finally discerned an item central to Luther's theology which seemed to him obviously mistaken. It was the matter of common sense to Erasmus that man's will was free. Luther's use of dialectic ('man is totally free . . . man is absolutely bound') to reach the existential affirmation that it was only through grace that man could take the smallest step at all towards anything spiritually good, enunciated with Luther's dogmatism, seemed to be an attack on the whole civilised Christian tradition of good letters: devoted, refined and peaceful. Erasmus never retreated from frequent statements of agreement with Luther's denunciation of the corruption in the Church and especially at Rome. But he believed in reform from within, and through the normal channels.

Erasmus's attack might have left Luther beginning to feel utterly isolated, but the thought did not occur to him. The way of the Word was a way of suffering and persecution, and, like Katlstadt and Erasmus themselves, he drew strength and courage from the idea. However, the strains were beginning to tell again.

There was an emptiness just now at the heart of his life. People saw it and began to fill it with the rumour that he was going to marry. There were ex-nuns living at the Priory, looking for husbands. Luther denied any such intention. He was completely taken up with all the battles which he had to fight. And it looked to him like the end of the world anyhow. Every few weeks came news of more peasant uprisings.

CHAPTER THIRTEEN

The New World

Luther bustled in and out of the Friary, as busy as ever. Meals were eaten swiftly, sometimes alone, sometimes with Prior Brisger, the only other remaining friar. Food for the two priests and any visitors was prepared by Luther's ever present servant, the ex-student Seeberger, and other occasional serving hands. There was an emptiness about the Friary where until three years ago there had been meals in common, chanted Office in church, and a community routine. Now life was haphazard. Luther's bed was not made in a year, he said later, and became foul with sweat. He just fell into it at the end of each day. Occasionally, he would eat with one of his friends in the town, and drink – he boasted of his growing capacity. With it was also growing his own girth. Fatter, he was also less well, increasingly plagued with minor illnesses which threatened to become bigger.

He began to have a ringing in the ears, and the first signs of gall stones. Then there was the malaise of threatening depression, 'attacks' of despair, temptations from the devil as he experienced them. At night, a cloud of terrible sadness often enveloped him – then he would see only the bad things, the increasing violence in the countryside, the warring of the political authorities, the failure to get people to live by the Word, enemies to the left, enemies to the right, and his own unfaithfulness. He would turn and shout at the devil, and speak a verse of the Psalms. 'Lord you are my stronghold and my only God.' Then as he recounted, he broke wind, farted at the devil – take that you swine, you can't stand up to my God, to the Word, to Christ. Or, in worse agony, he would express his feeling of despair directly to God. The last 'freedom' he now had was terrifying. He was fighting phantoms. Every battle had been won. He was left with himself, God – and the idiotic chaos of 'Satan'.

On 5 February 1525 he preached in the parish church, and spoke from his own anguished heart:

> Christ makes a special point of saying that he is gentle. It is as though he were saying: 'I know how to deal with sinners. I myself have experienced what it is to have a timid, terrified conscience.' As the letter to the Hebrews says, he 'in every respect has been tempted as we are, yet without sinning' . . . He says 'My yoke is easy and my burden light' . . . It is called gentle, sweet and easy because he himself helps us carry it and when it grows too heavy for us he shoulders the burden along with us . . . then one has a good companion and, as the saying goes: 'With a good companion the singing is good.' When one person alone cannot carry a load at all well, two can carry it easily.

People were beginning to say something like that, in another sense, about Luther's household. They were asking why he did not marry. Luther had to admit himself that it was an odd business. Two years previously he had received in Wittenberg nine nuns who had managed to escape from a convent near Grimma. Since then he had been operating what amounted to a marriage bureau, matching them up with husbands in Wittenberg and district. The escape had been effected by means of a herring merchant, who always brought his barrels of fish into the convent in a covered wagon. 'A cart load of vestal virgins has just arrived in the town,' wrote a student. Some were lodged with families, others in the empty rooms at the Friary. What more eligible bachelor was there than Luther himself? A noble lady had pointed this out to Spalatin in November 1524, and the latter passed the comment on to Luther, who replied:

> I am not surprised about such gossip . . . give her my thanks and tell her I am in God's hand as a creature whose heart God may change and change again, kill and revive again at any moment. Nevertheless, the way I feel now . . . I shall not marry. It is not that I do not feel my flesh or my masculine sexuality, since I am neither wood nor stone, but my mind is far removed from marriage, since I daily expect death and the

punishment due to a heretic, so I shall not limit God's work in me, nor shall I rely on my own heart. Yet I hope God does not let me live alone.

In the turmoil of public affairs it was still likely enough that the turn of events would enable the law officers to arrive at Wittenberg and carry him off, and it would be welcome enough, for it would be the end of problems too big for solution. It was no time to think of marrying. In any case he felt no spirit for the married life. He had lived by the Rule and kept his distance from women. Sexual tension was sometimes a problem, but he did not think to solve it in married life. In any case, perhaps the world would end soon. The Turks were ever threatening and he might die himself.

But a seed had been sown, and began to live – a barely expressed movement towards filling the emptiness. Once it started to grow, it went quickly – and took root in his mind, doubtless emotionally and sexually, but less so than apocalyptically and polemically: very well, he would show them. He realised that his closest friends might well be shocked – he was by now on a pedestal, someone special, the leader who should not marry. So he said little about his thoughts. If he did do it, he would present them with a *fait accompli*. In mid April, he teased Spalatin in a letter encouraging him to marry, saying of himself it was strange that 'a famous lover like me does not get married' and referring to the ex-nuns who had been of material help in the Friary: 'I have had three wives simultaneously . . . but you are a sluggish lover who does not dare to become a husband of even one woman. Watch out that I, who have no thought of marriage at all, do not one day overtake you . . . just as God usually does what is least expected.'

As the spring lengthened, the violence in the country worsened rapidly, the Elector became more ill, and all things seemed to be moving to some terrible crisis. Then the Count of Mansfeld, near his old home, invited Luther and Melancthon to go and organise a school in Eisleben. While any journey was now dangerous, it would be an opportunity to preach to the peasants en route through Thuringia. Luther decided to go, and took Melancthon in his party. They found unrest everywhere, and Luther wrote *Admonition to Peace*, which eventually appeared too late to influence those peasants who were already committed to massive violence by extremist leaders. In Nördlingen, where Karlstadt had been for a time, Luther's sermon was heckled. However, they reached their destination and Melancthon provided guide-lines for a school there, which was duly established.

On the way home they visited Luther's parents and other relations. And suddenly the decision was made. His father was still longing to see grandchildren from Martin's loins. There was one nun left unmarried at Wittenberg, living with the Cranachs, and she had set her cap at Luther herself. Having declined two successive suggestions for husbands after a previous abortive engagement, she had said she would consider Amsdorf – or Luther. Katherine von Bora seemed to have some spirit about her. She was twenty-six, rather old for marrying at that time.

On his return, Luther spoke to her and they agreed. The projected wedding then became part of a terrible threefold crisis in Luther's life: the Elector was dying, and a full-scale civil war was now in progress. The 'peasants', who included numbers of underprivileged from the towns, were plundering the countryside massively and taking control of castles, religious houses, food supplies and some towns. The rulers were uniting their military forces to oppose and defeat them. Luther saw both sides to be in the wrong: the peasants suffered widely from injustice, but in the end they did not have the right to resort to violent revolt against the established rulers. He then issued his blistering advice to the princes to suppress the peasants ruthlessly in his *Against the Robbing and Murdering Mobs of Peasants* – this again appeared too late, when the princes were already victorious and indulging in brutal vengeance.

On 4 May, when the military issue was still in the balance, Luther wrote to John Rühel, a councillor to the Count of Mansfeld and married to a relative of Luther, about the need to resist the peasants with all necessary force, speaking also in reckless mood about something he had not confided to closer friends: 'I would rather lose my neck a hundred times than approve . . . the peasants' action . . . If I can manage it, before I die I shall marry my Kate to spite the devil, even though the peasants are still fighting. I trust they will not steal my courage and joy . . . Give my greetings to your dear Rib.' Rühel and his wife to whom Luther had mentioned Katie von Bora on his recent visit, wondered what kind of a marriage this was going to be. A marriage 'to spite the devil'? To enable Luther to show his freedom?

Luther's projected marriage began to look like a function of public affairs. It fitted nicely into the total crisis. The Elector died on 5 May. On 15 May, a series of encounters between the armies of the peasants and of four rulers who had united to defeat them, was capped by a final and total victory for the latter at Frankenhausen. The wedding itself had to wait a few weeks while things got sorted out subsequent to the death of the Elector, and the terrible massacres of the peasants.

Luther wrote of his deceased sovereign that he 'departed this life in the enjoyment of his full reason, taking the sacrament in both kinds and without the Last Anointing. We buried him without Masses or vigils, but yet in a fine and noble manner . . . He died of the stone . . . The signs of his death were a rainbow which Melancthon and I saw one evening last winter over Lochau [a residence of the Elector], and a child born here at Wittenberg without a head, and another with feet turned round.' Luther's 'signs' lay in the world of superstition, but his comments on the Elector were not unjust: 'When the genius of a financier, a statesman and a hero concur in the same prince, it is a gift of God. Such a one was Frederick. He was indeed very wise. He took care of the administration himself and did not leave everything to a pack of fools.' The 'wisdom' had often irritated Luther; two years previously he had written: 'His way of acting does not please me, for it savours of I don't know what unbelief and courtly infirmity of soul, preferring temporal to spiritual things.'

Frederick was succeeded by his brother Duke John, whose first task was to make sure that the campaign against the peasants was satisfactorily concluded, and to meet up with his allies, young Landgrave Philip of Hesse, Duke George, and Duke Henry of Brunswick. Luther was well acquainted with the new Elector and felt sufficient confidence to send him, on 15 May, a memorandum about the urgent financial and other needs of the University, a memorandum originally intended for Elector Frederick, who in the last twelve months of his life had slowed down his normally very deliberate procedures almost to stopping point. On 8 June, Spalatin was in Wittenberg with the reply, which was reassuring and thoroughly favourable – the 'praiseworthy University' would not be neglected, but they must be a little patient while the problems of the civil war were settled. Meanwhile, there was a substantial rise in salary for Luther and other professors; and two new courses in Law were instituted.

In spite of his letter to Rühel about it, Luther had kept his counsel for the most part about his proposed marriage, especially from his close friends. He wanted no advice, practical or spiritual. Melancthon in particular was not consulted. Then, in the second week in June, Luther alerted his colleagues Johann Bugenhagen and Justus Jonas, Herr and Frau Cranach, and a professor of Law, Dr Apel, but not Melancthon. They foregathered with Luther and Katie von Bora in the Friary on the evening of 13 June, and the legally binding ceremony of marriage was gone through before the witnesses. Luther had ceased to believe in marriage as a true Church sacrament, and no ceremony in church was necessary as far as he was concerned. However, he and Katie immediately set about organising a grand party, to include a service of rejoicing in church, for a fortnight later, to celebrate the *fait accompli*, when Katie would move in to the Friary.

'Indeed the rumour is true. I was married all of a sudden, to silence the mouths which are so used to complaining about me,' he wrote to Amsdorf, by now the local pastor in Magdeburg. Luther spoke of the great wish of his father for grandchildren, and then in his open German way averred: 'I feel neither passionate love nor strong sexual desire for my wife, but I cherish her. To give a public witness to my marriage, I shall give a party next Tuesday and my parents will be there. I definitely want you to be there too . . . if you can possibly do so.' The letter went straight on to political matters concerning the Peasants' War. The massive totals of peasants killed were terrifying. But, meanwhile, he had taken a decisive step in his own life:

> Mr George Spalatin, a servant of Christ, my dearest brother in the Lord. Grace and peace in the Lord! The wedding banquet for me and my Catherine will be held this coming Tuesday, that is after the festival of St John the Baptist. I am inviting

you, my Spalatin, to it so that I may see myself that you really rejoice in my marriage. Please do not miss it. I have also written to the Marshall for some venison.

At the same time Luther dropped a note to the good citizen of Torgau who had effected the original abduction of the nuns from the convent, and asked him if he would contribute a barrel of beer.

The celebration went off well, in spite of the difficult times. All Wittenberg was there, together with many of Luther's relations. Above all, his gnarled old father and his mother with the eyes of Luther and an air of well-earned suffering, were there. The Cranach portraits date from shortly after this time. It was a day-long affair, with a procession through the town to church, dancing and feasts. Luther aged forty-two and the bride in her mid-twenties were jolly and confident. Towards the end of the evening there was a rumpus outside, and the voice of someone Luther knew but had not seen for a year, and the last person he expected to see calling on him without notice. The old ex-Dean was standing there, Karlstadt, bedraggled and begging a night's lodging. He had escaped at the last minute from Frankenhausen when the peasants were making their last stand. Let down over the city walls of Rothenburg in a basket, he had fled to Frankfurt-am-Main. He then decided to try to return and reside in Wittenberg under the new Elector, and wrote a letter to Luther begging forgiveness. Katie and Martin put him up for a month or two before he went off again, on a journey which took him and his wife widely over German speaking lands during the next fifteen years, and left her a crippled old woman in her late thirties when he died. 'That unhappy man took refuge in my house. The world is not big enough for him now – he is under such pressure that he had to look for protection from his enemy,' Luther wrote in August.

Luther's new married status was soon accepted – though more easily by some of his cynically minded enemies than by his friends. Cardinal Albrecht of Mainz, promoter of Indulgences, pluralist, who at one time thought of publicly marrying one of his mistresses, and at other times bitterly persecuted married priests in his diocese, sent Luther and Katie a wedding present of twenty guilders. Luther wanted to refuse it. Katie had it handed to a trustee. Melancthon, however, had grave reservations about the whole thing, only barely managing in public to accept the marriage with something like good grace. In late July, still unable to bring himself emotionally to terms with it, he wrote in Greek to an academic friend, Camerarius, a letter which he later regretted:

> On 13 June Luther unexpectedly and without informing any of his friends in advance . . . married Bora . . . You might be amazed that at this unfortunate time . . . he turns to self-indulgence and diminishes his reputation, just when Germany has special need of his judgement and authority.
>
> . . . The man is certainly pliable; and the nuns have used their arts . . . society with the nuns has softened or even titillated this honourable, high-spirited man . . . the rumour that he had previously dishonoured her is clearly a lie . . . Now that the deed is done, we must not take it too hard, or reproach him; for I think, indeed, that he was compelled by nature to marry. When I see Luther in low spirits and disturbed by his change of life, I really try to comfort him, since he has done nothing that seems to me worthy of censure or incapable of defence . . . I have hopes that this state of life may sober him down, so that he will discard the cheap buffoonery that we have so often criticised.

There was further moralising and practical comment as Melancthon came to terms with something which he was still seeing essentially as a 'failure' on the part of his leader. It had been a severe experience. Melancthon had written a few years before: 'If there is anything on earth that I love it is the studies of Martin and his pious writings, but above all else I love Martin himself.' They were soon reconciled, however, and the two families were frequently in each other's houses.

Before it took place, the marriage had begun to look like a mere function of Luther's public life, or his spiritual witness. And Melancthon implied in the letter just quoted that Luther was already regretting the matter in July. But the truth was otherwise. The language of public affairs and spiritual crisis had been doing duty for a language and an experience as yet unknown. Luther knew nothing of courtship, or of emotional and sexual fascination. But he very swiftly began to enjoy Katie's presence in both bed and house, as something a good deal more than merely an adjunct to his public career. Even before the month of June was out, he began to refer to her as 'My Lord Katie', half mocking and half pleased as she began to take over the household with the traditional efficiency and bonhomie of the German housewife. In no time, Luther's letters took on the joyous lineaments of the family household, and less was heard about imminent death. For a few months, his change in status was a shock to himself, and he wondered what he had done. His 'Table Talk' a few years later has: 'In the first year of marriage one has strange thoughts. At table he thinks: "Previously I was alone, now I am with someone." In bed when he wakes he sees beside him a pair of pigtails which he did not see before.' But the first phase was over swiftly. He soon felt at home with Katie, whom he nicknamed 'The Morning Star' because she was up so early in the morning.

Luther's marriage had given Spalatin the courage to take the matrimonial plunge, too, shortly after Luther's own wedding. In December, Luther wrote to him: 'I wish you grace and peace in the Lord, and also joy with your sweetest little wife. Greet your wife kindly from me. When you have your Katherine in bed, sweetly embracing and kissing her, think: Look, this being, the best little creation of God has given me by Christ, to whom be glory and honour. I will guess the day on which you will receive this letter and that night I will make love with my wife in the same way in your memory and think specially of you. My rib and I send greetings to you and your rib.'

The letters began to be full of all sorts of domestic matters. To the erstwhile tiresome friar, Gabriel Zwilling, he wrote in January 1526, 'My Gabriel, I am sending the measurements for the length and width of the mattress as I would like to have it made.' Zwilling, however, was still tiresome. The letter went on: 'Recently you returned some money by placing it in my Psalter. But since the little book was thrown into the wagon, most of the coins were lost . . . It would have been better if you had left the coins for the household servants than that I should have lost them in this way . . . Goodbye, and pray for me.'

As the first months of marriage went by, Luther had a new anxiety: perhaps they would have no children. He waited and worried. But not for long, though afterwards it remained a bad memory. Eventually, all was well. By May 1526, Katie's condition became part of a little domestic drama. Luther wanted to give a pewter dish to his old student Agricola. Katie did not want to part with it and hid it. In a letter to Agricola, Luther said: 'Just wait until Katie is confined to childbed; then I will steal it and carry it off.'

On 8 June, he wrote to Rühel: 'Please tell Mr Eisleben that yesterday at two o'clock my dear Katie by God's great grace gave to me a Hänschen Luther. Tell him not to be surprised . . . for he should remember what it is to have a sun at this time of year.' Luther could never resist a pun. 'Please greet *your* dear sun-bearer and Eisleben's Else . . . Just as I write, my tired Katie is calling for me.' Two months later he was in the young husband's seventh heaven still – wondering how he could have deserved such happiness: 'God has blessed me . . . with a healthy and vigorous son, Johann, a little Luther. Katie, my rib, sends her greetings . . . She is well and by God's grace compliant and in every way obedient and obliging to me, more than I had ever dared to hope (thank God), so that I would not want to exchange my poverty for the riches of Croesus.'

In some sort Luther's life was transformed, and he began himself to live the very thing he had been preaching, family life lit by the faith of the Gospel. Katie turned out to be very able. She did some gardening which gradually blossomed into smallholding; and she encouraged Martin to turn his hands to practical matters he had almost forgotten about – letters went off asking for a quadrant and for melon seed. She enjoyed company, as Luther did. From the beginning she kept the doors open for the inevitable stream of students, who tended to linger longer and longer; and some she began to board in the Friary which the new Elector handed over to Martin and Kate. So began twenty-one years of a newly energised patriarchal household, which became famous both for the perpetual flow of wisdom and buffoonery (to quote Melancthon in a bad mood) from its head, leading eventually to the published 'Table Talk', famous too for its rowdiness – older people thought twice before accepting an invitation to stay.

Without Katie, one is tempted to think Luther would hardly have survived the two and half years from midsummer 1525. His reputation was severely damaged by the Peasants' War itself, and by the defeat of the rebel armies. Erasmus's book against Luther had finally polarised almost all opinion either pro or contra Luther, and Luther's reply to it would confirm this. The civil war with its massive death toll (conceivably as many as 100,000), had pulled down the whole of society. Wittenberg was thought of, in a general way, both as guilty and as the losers, by those who were not entirely committed to serious reform, and that was the majority of people. Public opinion had it that Luther and his friends had suffered a serious knock. The intake into the University sank low in 1525, and in 1526 to sixty or so (Erfurt was down to a mere fifty). Strict traditional Christians would no longer send their children to Wittenberg. There was no sense yet of 'Catholics' versus 'Reformers'; a separate structure for religion was not thought of by Luther or anyone else. But Luther's own theology was now clearly committed to the importance of the local church, the relative unimportance of any centralising religious agency, and a conviction of the positive evil of the papacy as it was.

The conservative mass of people, recovering from the shock of civil war, acknowledged that Luther might be in the right on many matters, but were waiting to see whether, after the war, an excommunicate and an outlaw still had might on his side. Undoubtedly a minority of rulers were on Luther's side, the Elector of Saxony, and Philip of Hesse, and many towns. But many had a waiting policy. The burghers of Erfurt discouraged papists from preaching and did not encourage the reformers, either. They excused themselves to Duke George by saying they had to preserve the civil peace. In Saxony, Luther had become a leader, without whom nothing of real importance could be done. But there was also a sense in which Luther was now distanced from many groups of people.

To himself, the situation was dispiriting. Men seemed to be deserting the Word on all sides, and God to be turning away from them. Reformers, with what looked like erroneous views, were springing up everywhere. It was no longer just the swarm of spiritists in Saxony; news kept coming of new reformers giving new teaching in Switzerland and the Rhinelands; Zwingli, Oecolampadius – and, among them, his old acquaintance Bucer. He did not wish to get involved with them, any more than he wished to get involved in government at home. But his situation could not be made into something other than it was.

Luther was caught in a political bind commonly unavoidable for any man who emerges as a religious leader of a large number of people. But, furthermore, Luther's solution to the problem of how to reform the Church was that the rulers of society, itself God-given like everything else, should take on the task of reform if the Church authorities themselves would not do it. But then the rebelling peasants had identified their cause with that of religious reform. In spite of a long record of disowning reform from below, disorderly and unplanned, Luther was thought of as implicated, especially as he had often denounced the rulers for their injustice towards the under-privileged, and as the peasants had referred to him in their pamphlets. Public opinion selects, usually arbitrarily, to give a particular identity to public figures. Luther's texts of April and May 1525 enabled this to happen in a notable way.

In March 1525, moderate peasant leaders had put out The Twelve Articles, which listed the usual and reasonable complaints: that peasants were sometimes held as property, that wild venison and fish were appropriated by the wealthy, that too much work was demanded for rent, that fields and meadows were misappropriated. But at the head were religious demands: 'Each community should choose and appoint a pastor . . . to teach us the Gospel pure and simple . . .' and this was preceded by a statement that the demands were not intended as 'revolt and disorder' and that they only asked that 'the Gospel be taught them as a guide in life'. Also they wanted to control the tithe money collected to support the pastor whom they should choose.

Luther replied to it in his *Admonition to Peace*. He agreed that many of the demands were reasonable, but insisted that the secular matters were concerns of justice and injustice, and not immediately relevant to the heart of the Gospel message. As for their demands concerning their pastors and the tithes, these demands should only be looked at in the context of existing rights, structures and laws. As it stood, he told them, their demand to control tithe money was simply an attempt at 'theft and highway robbery'.

Both rulers and peasants came under Luther's lash as he urged the peasants to be peaceful and the princes to come to terms with them. The text also reflected something of his desperation in the face of past failure to get his message across to either party:

> The peasants who have now banded together in Swabia have formulated their intolerable grievances against the rulers in twelve articles, and have undertaken to support them with certain passages of Scripture . . . the thing that pleases me most . . . is that they offer to accept instructions . . . Since I have a reputation for being one of those who deal with the Holy Scriptures here on earth, and especially as one whom they mention and call upon by name in the second document, I have all the more courage and confidence in openly publishing my instruction. I do this . . . as a duty of brotherly love, so that if any misfortune or disaster comes out of this matter, it may not be attributed to me, nor will I be blamed before God and men because of my silence . . . We have no one on earth to thank for this disastrous rebellion except you princes and lords, and especially you blind bishops and mad priests and monks whose hearts are hardened . . . The murder-prophets [a reference to Karlstadt, Müntzer and all the *Schwärmerei*] who hate me as they hate you, have come among these people . . . for more than three years, and no one has resisted and fought against them except me . . . I beseech you not to make light of this rebellion . . . The peasants have just published twelve articles some of which are so fair and just as to take away your reputation in the eyes of God . . . Because you made light of my *To The German Nobility* you must now listen to and put up with these selfish articles.

To the peasants he preached almost undiluted non-violence and resignation: 'Even a child can understand that the Christian law tells us not to strive against injustice, not to grasp the sword, not to protect ourselves, not to avenge ourselves, but to give up life and property, and let whoever takes it have it . . .' The punishing of wickedness 'is not the responsibility of everyone but of the worldly rulers who bear the sword'. He begged them: 'Can you not think it through, dear friends? If your enterprise were right, then any man might become the judge of another.' Society ought to respect the legal sovereign and established authority.

Luther was truly at his wits' end – faced with the chaos of civil war and the breakdown of society:

> It is not my intention to justify or defend the rulers in the intolerable injustices which you suffer from them. They are unjust and commit heinous wrongs against you; that I admit. If, however, neither side accepts instruction and you start to fight with each other – may God prevent it – I hope that neither side will be called Christian . . . Your declaration that you teach and live according to the Gospel is not true . . . You want power and wealth so that you will not suffer injustice . . . The Gospel however . . . speaks of suffering, injustice, the cross, patience, and contempt for this life and temporal wealth . . . You are only trying to give your unevangelical and unChristian enterprise an evangelical appearance.

'Take a hold of these matters properly, with justice and not with force or violence, and do not start endless bloodshed in Germany,' he wrote in a final combined appeal to both sides.

Luther composed this text on his trip to Eisleben in April, his mind full of a rising conviction that some fearful final crisis might be brewing, and that part of it would be his own marriage. By the time it was in the hands of the public, he was beginning to hear of the fall of the cities of Erfurt and Salzungen to the peasants' army, and the occupation of many castles, monasteries and convents. At Eisleben, or on the journey to his parents, he realised that the whole situation was out of control, not least because his own ruler, the dying Elector had refrained from using military force, hoping for a negotiated settlement. After all, it was now too late to talk about peace and negotiation. Violence had to be put down, violently. On his way home he threw all his anger into a very brief pamphlet *Against the Robbing and Murdering Mobs of Peasants*, the content of which was echoed in his letter to the Mansfeld Councillor Rühel – already quoted – in which he also said: 'If there were thousands more of the peasants, they would still be altogether robbers and murders, who take the sword simply because of their own insolence and wickedness, and who want to expel sovereigns and lords and to destroy everything and to establish a new order in this world . . . The peasants are committing perjury to their lords.' It seemed possible the peasants would win: 'If I get home

I shall prepare for death with God's help, and await my new lords, the murderers and robbers.' It was the apocalyptic mood of the pre-marital month.

On 23 May, Luther wrote to Rühel after hearing of the fall of Frankenhausen to the rulers, horrified and fascinated: 'I am specially pleased at the fall of Thomas Müntzer. Please let me have further details of his capture and of how he acted, for it is important to know how that proud spirit bore itself . . . It is pitiful that we have to be so cruel to the poor people, but what can we do? . . . Do not be troubled by the severity of their suppression, for it will profit many souls.' It was only towards the end of May that Luther's *Against the Robbing and Murdering Mobs of Peasants* came into the hands of readers, when the rulers were already victorious and were indulging in revenge and unnecessary violence. The effect was brutal. The little sentence which was repeated and repeated for the next four and a half centuries ran: 'Let whoever can, stab, strike, kill.' Its immediate context, with its unwelcome feeling of a holy war ran:

> Therefore, dear Lords, here is a place where you can release, rescue, help. Have mercy on these poor people [the prisoners which the peasants had taken]. Let whoever can, stab, strike, kill. If you die in doing it, good for you! A more blessed death can never be yours, for you die while obeying the divine word and commandment in Romans 13 and in loving service of your neighbour, whom you are rescuing from the bonds of hell and of the devil.

Public reaction, already aghast at the massive slaughter of the peasants, was immediate. Criticism reached Luther swiftly. At the end of May, he wrote to Amsdorf: 'You inform me of a new honour, . . . that I am called a toady to the sovereigns', and there followed much talk of Satan, and a quotation from the Psalm used at Compline in the last Office of the day: 'He who has thus far so often beaten Satan . . . will not allow the basilisk to tread on me . . . It is better that all of the peasants should be killed rather than that the sovereigns and magistrates should be destroyed.'

The day after the legal marriage ceremony, Luther was smarting still and wrote to Rühel: 'What an anguished outcry has been caused by my pamphlet against the peasants. All is now forgotten of what God has done through me. Now lords, priests, and peasants are all against me and threaten my death.' In his letter inviting Amsdorf to the wedding party, he described some of the military detail he had heard about: 'In Franconia eleven thousand peasants were killed in three different places . . . sixty-one intact cannon were captured . . . In the Duchy of Würtemberg, six thousand peasants were killed . . . Thus the poor peasants are being killed everywhere.'

In July, Luther wrote a pamphlet defending himself, *An Open Letter on the Harsh Pamphlet*, spelling out with clarity and aggressive emphasis that there was no way of avoiding one's obligation to obey established civil authority. He outlined his doctrine of the two kingdoms, the Kingdom of the world where all is law and severity, intended to restrain evil doers on earth, and the Kingdom of God where all is peace and goodness. The same man may be involved in both at the same time, acting appropriately according to the role he fulfils. It was Luther's solution to the problem of the Church and politics. It had a certain realism about it, and echoed his theology of man, always a sinner, always redeemed.

The pamphlet had something of the air of the 'explanation' in which inevitably *qui s'excuse s'accuse*. But, on the whole, Luther took the argument into the enemy country and deliberately repeated the words to which exception had been taken, reinforcing them: 'Therefore, as I wrote then so I write now: Let no one have mercy on the obstinate, hardened, blinded peasants who refuse to listen to reason; but let everyone, as he is able, strike, hew, stab, and kill, as though among mad dogs, so that by so doing he may show mercy to those who are ruined, put to flight and led astray by these peasants, so that peace and safety may be maintained.'

For some, Luther became a synonym for a man who might turn angrily on his supporters. Ex-friar and professor, the preacher became *Führer*, he knew little or nothing of the art of politics, the art of the possible, of compromise, of government – at least he was commonly unable to exercise it. His pronouncements on public policy began sometimes to sound as dogmatic in their way, and as vulgarly insulting as pronouncements from Rome had done. Melancthon bitterly disapproved of this rough side of Luther. Yet he and Luther's many other friends continued also to retain deep affection for him, knowing that this uncontrolled anger and aggression came from a too sensitive Luther, a man otherwise gentle and generous, of intellectual and moral integrity. The price of leadership in public life is liable to be misunderstanding and type-casting, and the deepening of wounds in one already delicately balanced emotionally. Luther never trimmed. He tended rather to accept the identity handed out to him and to wear the cap he was fitted with.

Polarisation meant more enemies. It also meant firmer friends – and political security, even though it was some years before the new Elector was able to assure one of a safe journey so well as his 'Wise' brother had succeeded in doing. However, by the autumn of 1525, in spite of the new enemies, Luther had in his own immediate world new opportunities, and in many ways was living in what was substantially a new world.

CHAPTER FOURTEEN

Into Battle Again

Luther was still university professor and local preacher, and more than ever virtually the master of Wittenberg. In many ways, however, it was a new world. The old Elector had died and in his place was a man, not young but at least able to attend to business expeditiously. He was already showing active signs of coping with requests about the University administration, though he had been irritated by Luther's impatience. The civil war had ended and rebellion been put down. The general sense of threatening unrest had, for the moment, abated. Karlstadt had gone off on his travels; the reformers on the left, in Saxony and Thuringia, Luther's '*Schwärmerei*', were lying low. Luther was a respectable married man with a stable household, settled in the old Friary. There were regular meals and someone to rely on; Seeberger had stayed on to assist the new household. There was talk of Katie's aunt, also an ex-nun, joining the household. Eventually she did, adding to the feeling of familial stability. Luther quickly adapted to marriage. At the personal level almost everything was better. Luther had a new lease of life.

Wittenberg itself had settled down. The reformed Mass, in German rather than Latin, Luther's own text using adapted plain chant and folk modes and melodies, was inaugurated in Wittenberg in the autumn of 1525. And in spite of frequent news of fresh 'wrong headed' reforms arising in the west, some of the international news was good. Luther heard that the Grand Master of the Teutonic Knights, Albert of Hohenzollern, had declared himself Duke of Prussia and put through Lutheran reforms.

Society at large was in a low state and gave cause for concern both because of the results of war and plague and because of the loosening of the old religious bonds. It had become urgent to give people and priest some detailed idea of how to carry on. The Elector came to see Luther in Wittenberg about it; they worked out a detailed plan which the Elector took away with him. With this personal contact Luther had a greater sense of security than under his predecessor, the so-reticent 'Wise' elder brother of the Elector. He turned again to his desk and to Erasmus's *Discourse on Free Choice*, which had lain unwontedly unanswered for more than a year.

> That I have taken so long to reply to your Discourse, venerable Erasmus, has been contrary to everyone's expectation and to my own custom; for hitherto I have seemed not only willing to accept, but eager to seek out opportunities of this kind for writing. There will perhaps be some surprise at this new and unwonted forbearance – or fear! – in Luther, who has not been roused even by all the speeches and letters his enemies have flung about, congratulating Erasmus on his victory . . . I yield you a palm such as I have never yielded to anyone before; for I confess not only that you are far superior to me in powers of eloquence and native genius (which we must all admit, all the more as I am an uncultivated fellow who has always moved in uncultivated circles – *barbarus in barbarie versatus*) but you have quite damped my spirit and eagerness, and left me exhausted before I could strike a blow.

However, within a few sentences Luther was settling down to abuse. It had hardly seemed worth replying since what Erasmus had said had been refuted so often, and

> has been beaten down and completely pulverised by Melancthon's *Commonplaces* – an unanswerable little book . . . Compared with it, your book struck me as so cheap and paltry that I felt profoundly sorry for you, defiling, as you did, your very elegant and ingenious style with such trash, and quite disgusted at the utterly unworthy matter that was being conveyed in such rich ornaments of eloquence, like refuse or dung being carried in gold and silver vases.

Luther was well launched on the reply. For nine years he had been privately expressing his strong distaste for Erasmus's theology. Now he was saying it publicly. How could the great scholar, whose Greek text of the New Testament had opened up the original words of the Word, be so superficial when it came to theology, indeed to a true understanding of the text?

The answer was not far to seek. For Erasmus, 'theology' was a byword for hypocrisy and irrelevance and word spinning. In *In Praise of Folly* he had written, amongst other such sharp words: 'I myself once heard a great fool (a great scholar I would have said) undertaking in a laborious discourse to explain the mystery of the Holy Trinity. In unfolding it, in order to show his own cleverness and reading, and satisfy itching ears, he proceeded with a new method, expounding letters, syllables and proposition, the harmony of noun and verb, and that of noun substantive, and noun adjective . . . At last he . . . demonstrated the whole Trinity to be represented by these first rudiments of grammar, as clearly and plainly as it was possible for a mathematician to draw a triangle in the sand.' Luther agreed with something of this caricature but wanted to put a right theology in its place. Erasmus wanted simply to get rid of theoretical theology as far as possible.

The original texts, first of the New Testament, then of the thinkers and leaders of the early Church, were what Erasmus wanted to present to the World. And he wanted the text of the Gospel to be put into the language of ordinary people. His was a world of sweet reasonableness. He envisaged the Church continuing much as it was in essentials, albeit thoroughly purged of all kinds of superstition and corruption, which he tried to outlaw with laughter. Christians should have the text of the New Testament and should try to live by it, with the help of the Church, its pastoral guidance and its sacraments. Theology could be left to the professionals – though from time to time others might need to keep an eye on them. Just such an occasion arose when a reformer began to talk of man's entire lack of freedom of choice. Then Erasmus thought it was time to throw some common sense on the scene. The absurd doctrine seemed part and parcel of Luther's extremism, and deserved to be exposed. He considered it was a clear theological and philosophical mistake, which would enable him to accede to the frequent requests of Luther's enemies in high places, to controvert the extremist. He could do it without compromising over superstitions and corruption.

Luther was never very good at seeing the other man's point of

view when it came to matters of theology. With a man like
Erasmus, the gap was unbridgeable. He could not stomach the
quiet scholar's qualifications nor his obeisance to Church
authority. How typical of Erasmus it was, he suggested, to object
to Luther making assertions: 'You censure me for obstinate
assertions . . . But it is not the mark of the Christian to take no
delight in assertions . . . By assertion I mean a constant
adhering, affirming, confessing, maintaining, and invincible
persevering.' Erasmus was prepared, with measured tolerance,
to accept the Church's doctrinal decisions, preferring not to
argue about them. Here Luther got on to a central matter which
lay between them: 'Is it not enough to have submitted your
personal feelings to the Scriptures? Do you submit them to the
Church as well? What can she decree that is not decreed in the
Scriptures?' The use and style of authority in the Church, in the
interpretation of the Gospel and management of its followers,
were at issue. Erasmus wanted to keep both interpretation and
management in a low key. Luther wanted the theology to be
played loud. He was a medieval theologian. Theology should
have a universal range if the discipline was to be meaningful at
all. Theology was still the queen of the sciences. For Luther it
had become almost synonymous in its style with interpretation
of Scripture and preaching. It was concerned with the truth of
the Word, of Christ to whom man owed total commitment. He
still dreamed of a Church in which the authority of the Word
would be self-operative and would not need anything like the
kind of detailed organisation which had grown up in the Roman
and papal Church in Europe. For Erasmus, theology was a
rather tiresome professional necessity, tending towards blurring
of fact, and often a threat to genuine scholarship, simple piety
and good morals.

The quarrel was tragic in that Luther and Erasmus had a
central goal in common. Erasmus said he wanted to hear the
farmer singing the words of the New Testament in his own
language as he worked. Luther said he wanted the Bible to speak
good German, the real German of the housewife and the lad in
the street. This drive to communicate what they both understood to be some kind of ultimate truth in the person and
teaching of Jesus of Nazareth, the man who showed forth God in
his own person, was central to both their lives. They had in

common the wish to see all members of the Church having free access in their own language to the great source document. But, from that point on, they differed nearly as widely as it was possible to do.

Erasmus understood that Luther was obsessed with the need for a true understanding of the Gospel and equally with the terrible corruption, functionalism and cynicism of so much of the personnel of the Church. Even after Luther's scourging of him in this text, he continued to say that people should have listened to Luther and that while Luther had indulged in unacceptable violence, Rome deserved all it got. On the other hand, Luther was quite unable to understand the authenticity of the quiet though often acid scholar dedicated to a policy of neutrality, of attempting as far as possible to stand outside polarising polemic – Erasmus came eventually to wonder whether it might have been better not to have written *In Praise of Folly*, because it had led to just such polarisation.

Their subject was freedom and the quality of human acts, looked at *sub specie aeternitatis*; could a man take any step towards his own salvation by his own action? Or did he always need God's grace, even to make that first gesture towards faith? The truth is, they were often speaking at different levels, Erasmus thinking of the mechanics in the mind, Luther looking at the nature of God as free, necessarily the ultimate author of good and at man's ultimate dependence on God:

> I confess that even if it were possible I should not wish to have free choice given me, . . . by which I might strive toward salvation . . . I should be unable to stand firm . . . Even if I lived and worked to eternity, my conscience would never be assured . . . There would always remain an anxious doubt whether it pleased God. But now since God has taken my salvation out of my hands into his, making it depend on his choice and not mine, and has promised to save me, not by my own work or exertion, but by his grace and mercy, I am assured and certain that he is faithful and will not lie to me . . . if we do less than we should or do it badly, he does not hold it against us. Hence the glorying of all the saints in their God.

The publication at the end of 1525 of his *On the Bound Will* gave Luther yet another batch of 'enemies', and pushed him, in a sense, one step further away from being able to see some kind of general cleansing of the Church, in the way that he thought it must occur. To enemies on the left and enemies on the right he had now added enemies in the centre. His pathological obsession with enemies increased, and from now on Erasmus was sometimes referred to in terms that were absurdly inappropriate. 'A slippery eel' he may well have been. But to say of him, as Luther is reported to have done in the 'Table Talk', 'in all his writings there is no statement anywhere about faith in Christ, about victory over sin' was a calumny. In Erasmus's most famous book the *Enchiridion*, precisely a book of advice about coping with temptation, he had written, 'Treat each battle as though it were your last, and you will finish in the end, victorious. It is possible that God might in the end reward you for your virtue by freeing you from your temptation.'

Erasmus eventually wrote a lengthy reply. In April 1526, he sent a letter, very pained at Luther's violent and aggressive sneers: 'How do your scurrilous charges that I am an atheist, and Epicurean and a sceptic, help the argument? . . . It terribly pains me as it must all good men, that your arrogant, insolent, rebellious nature has set the world in arms.' Luther let it go. It was a final rupture, and revealed the glaring weakness of Luther, when he gave himself up to his anger and to attitudes which to others seemed self-righteous, dogmatic and self-indulgent. But Luther found himself at the head of a vast movement, while Erasmus found himself shunting uncomfortably from town to town, from Louvain to Basel, to Freiburg to Basel, in search of tolerance for his quiet Catholic life style, not too welcome either to papists or reformers.

New editions of many of the major Fathers of the first centuries of the Church poured from Erasmus in his last twenty years (1516–36): Jerome, Athanasius, Basil, Cyprian, Irenaeus, Ambrose, Augustine, Hilary, Chrysostom, Origen, Gregory, Nazianzus. He remained faithful to the ideals he had spelt out in his Introduction (the Paracelsus) to his Greek New Testament:

> To me he is truly a theologian who teaches not by skill with intricate syllogisms but by a disposition of mind, by his very expression and his eyes, by his very life, . . . these writings

bring you the living image of His [Christ's] holy mind and the speaking, healing, dying, rising Christ, and thus they render Him so fully present that you would see less if you gazed upon Him with your very eyes.

It was not far from what Luther sometimes said.

Odium Theologicum, genuine disagreement, resulting in enmity and even hatred, was liable to become as intense in theology as in any discipline; understandably, in that theology was concerned precisely with the definition of human life, the relation of man to the Divine. Theological models still provided the normal medium for most serious discussion of man and his destiny. Today a common model is economic or social – the quality of life as measured by social and political norms is what is most likely to lead to expressions of violent disagreement between people and groups. In the sixteenth century the Renaissance was beginning to provide an alternative model, but theology still predominated: 'I am sending you, my Michael, my rebuttal of Erasmus, which I completed in a short time and in a hurry. I like your idea that the ruler of this word (Satan) is so powerful in obstructing any fruit of the World and in sowing sects of the ungodly' (to Michael Stiffel, 31 December 1525). The world was a battlefield and the man of faith had no choice but to align himself. And Luther was able to praise Erasmus for one thing: 'Unlike all the rest, you alone have attacked the real issues and have not wearied me with irrelevancies about the papacy, purgatory, indulgences and such trifles.'

The letters and memoranda poured out from Luther to the Elector about the University and about the parishes: 'Your Electoral Grace should have all the parishes in the whole territory inspected.' Ernestine Saxony should be divided into four or five districts; money should be raised locally to support the pastors. But the Elector did not feel so free to go ahead as Luther assumed. Although secular governments sometimes made supervisory visits to parishes, yet such a formal visitation would be in direct contravention of Canon Law, usurping the rights of the local Bishop. And the Elector was still deeply concerned with the problems of the external relations of his government.

Immediately after the end of the Peasants' War he was approached by Duke George to line up with an anti-Reformist

front. The absolute defeat of the peasants and the general idea of
the discomfiture of Luther, led the Duke to suggest to the
Elector and to young Philip of Hesse, who had married Duke
George's daughter, that they should stay in alliance with him
and cap their victory over the peasants with a victory over the
ecclesiastical revolutionaries. His blandishments had the
opposite effect. The pro-Reform rulers, encouraged notably by
the politically ambitious Philip banded together in the League
of Torgau to present a united front at the Imperial Diet, which
was to open in Speyer on 25 June 1526.

The international background to the new Diet was turgid. The
previous year the Emperor had finally collected an army
together, defeated the French at Pavia and taken the French
King, Francis II, prisoner to Madrid where he was held until the
Treaty of Madrid was signed. But the Treaty soon fell apart.
Instead of supporting the Emperor against the Turks, Francis II
began to intrigue with the Turks, with the political and military
arm of Pope Clement VII, and finally also with reformist rulers
in the German speaking lands. The Turks were to attack Spain
by sea and go through Hungary into the Spanish territories in
Italy. The Pope was keeping strange company. The result of this
international circus was a very uncertain voice at the Diet in
Germany, presided over by the Emperor's brother Ferdinand,
who attempted once again to get agreement to the formal execution of the decisions of the Diet of Worms. The Emperor and the
Pope, who both wanted this, were in fact almost at war. And in
any case the pragmatic, somewhat cynical and politically independent attitude of the majority of the members of the Diet
remained unchanged. They were not in favour of formally supporting the reforms, but neither did they wish to suppress them.

The two extreme parties both kept some initiative; and the
result was a compromise. The Reformers were there in force
with their preachers, and labelled their doorways VDMIE
(*Verbum Domini manet in eternum* – the Word of the Lord shall
remain for ever). A famous compromise was agreed: 'The Electors, Princes, Estates of the Empire and the ambassadors of the
same . . . while awaiting the sitting of a Council or a national
assembly, agreed . . . each one to live, govern, and carry himself
as he hopes and trusts to answer for it to God and his Imperial
Majesty.' In other words there was to be no change.

News of a Turkish advance had hastened the decision which was agreed on 27 August 1526. Two days later the Turks won the battle of Mohacs, and on 10 September they swarmed into Budapest. The neutral decision of the Diet was regarded by the Emperor (occupied in Spain) as a mere stopgap while he saw to his other concerns, the Turks, his European political rivals (including the papacy as a political power), and his Spanish kingdom. He and his advisers looked to a future Council where the Church troubles would be sorted out. In fact, however, Speyer was the first step towards the 'territorial church', to a *de facto* arrangement by which each political unit settled its management of religion according to the decisions of its own rulers. Effectively, this was the first formal act of major political authority leading to the dismemberment of the univocal structure for the Church throughout Europe, other than the East. Luther woke at night to agonise over the terrifyingly large changes which were flowing from his actions. But the Diet itself he thought little of, seeing it largely as an occasion for the sovereigns to go carousing.

During the spring and summer months of 1526 Luther was much taken up with the affairs of his own household. He was ill from kidney stone. Katie was having their first baby. But the writing still flowed – a stirring criticism of a right wing anti-Reformist *Ratschlag* or Brief, issued by Cardinal Albrecht to the clergy of Mainz; and the usual lectures and sermons. The Bible translation continued. Luther kept worrying about the state of the parishes. Eventually, things began to move. The Diet of Speyer gave Elector John some kind of a legal basis for proceeding with the plans for the visitation of the parishes which Luther had recommended to him and for more formal claims on so much Church property. In the winter of 1526–7, they began to be put into effect. So the recommendations of Luther's *Prelude on the Babylonian Captivity of the Church* were being realised; if the officials of the Myth, the Christian bishops and priests, would not themselves reform the Church then secular officials would do it, as Christians with the responsibility to act in society. Luther was concerned solely with the here and now. He would have been surprised to be told that he was founding an alternative Church, a state Church, with consequences for centuries to come. He would have been equally surprised to know that Henry VIII of England, with whom he was having an angry exchange of letters, was laying the foundations of another non-papal state church. There was much writing and re-writing of the Instructions for the visitations, and Luther had to mediate when theological argument broke out between Agricola and Melancthon as to whether repentance came before faith, or vice versa. Reports from the parishes began to show an abysmal state of ignorance, in priest and people.

Luther had been in Wittenberg off and on for nineteen years now and knew its people, its paving stones and problems too well. When he was weary, he was very weary. When he thought about the decline in numbers at the University (Duke George had forbidden students living in Albertine Saxony to attend Wittenberg University), the rise of many reformers opposed to him, and so many other problems, it all seemed overwhelming. Illness threw him into new acute attacks of depression. He had fantasies of leaving Wittenberg. He had threatened to depart in his sermons on return from the Wartburg. Now he built a picture of himself earning a living at some practical work, somewhere else. Katie encouraged him to take an interest in gardening and joinery. He wrote in January 1527 to his old friend, the ex-friar Wenceslas Link, now a Reformed pastor in Nuremberg:

'I wrote a suppliant and humble letter to the King of England . . . He has answered me with such hostility that he sounds just like Duke George . . . These tyrants have such weak, unmanly, and totally sordid characters that they deserve to be servants of the rabble . . . I appreciate that you promised to send seeds in the spring. Send as many as you can . . . I will turn my attention to the gardens, that is, to the blessings of the Creator, and enjoy them to his praise.' He continued, a little apologetic and embarrassed by this turning to handwork (shades of Karlstadt on his farm): 'Since among us barbarians there is neither art nor style of life, I and my servant Wolfgang [Seeberger] have taken up the art of operating a lathe. We are enclosing a gold guilder . . . be so kind as to send us some tools for boring and turnings, and what lathe operators call a clamp – any lathe operator can easily tell you what this is . . . If the world should indeed not want to feed us on account of the Word that we preach, then we

shall learn how to get our bread through the work of our hands.'
His friends smiled.

Luther found Seeberger not the best of assistants and ironically suggested to Link that he might find them some lathes which would work by themselves so that Seeberger could remain devoted to his beer. Luther had bought Seeberger a plot of his own, and wrote an amusing piece about his activities there, to give expression to his irritation with the man: '*Complaint of the Birds to Luther against Wolfgang*: We thrushes, blackbirds, finches, linnets, goldfinches and other pious birds . . . are credibly informed that one Wolfgang Seeberger, your servant, has conceived a great wicked plot against us . . . has bought, very dear, some old rotten nets to make a trap . . . pray restrain your servant or . . . at least make him spread corn . . . in the evening and not get up in the morning before eight . . . If not . . . we will pray God to plague him . . . and send frogs, grasshoppers, locusts and snails into the trap by day and to give him mice, fleas, lice and bugs . . . Written in our high home in the trees with our usual quill and seal.'

A few days after asking for the tools, a letter from Luther to Nicholas Hausmann provides another part of the current picture. 'I have no other news except that the Sovereign has replied to the University that he wishes to speed the visitation of the parishes . . . Zechariah is now on the press, ready for publication.' The Bible translation progressed. 'At the same time I am attacking the Sacramentarians [those who thought that Sacraments depended for their validity on the faith of those who received them, and denied the Real Presence]. Please pray that Christ may guide my pen successfully and advantageously against Satan . . . I believe you have heard that the cause of the Emperor in Italy has developed successfully. The Pope is afflicted from all sides, so that he will be ruined. His end and his hour have come. But persecution rages everywhere and many are being burned at the stake.'

Again to Link, he wrote in May: 'Zwingli has sent me a letter along with his most foolish booklet.' The arguments with the left wing continued and Zwingli considered himself a moderate: 'He raged, foamed, threatened and roared with such "moderation" that he seems to be incurable . . . May Christ grant that a healthy child has been born to you. Amen. My Katie has nausea again from a second pregnancy . . . All the seeds you sent us have sprung up; only the melons and gourds have not, although such plants *are* also sprouting – but only in other people's gardens!' The saga continued with a letter to Link on 5 July: 'I congratulate you on the birth of your daughter Margaret . . . I looked forward to this with great eagerness so that you too might experience "the natural" affection of parents for their children . . . We received the tools for the lathe, together with quadrant and clock . . . Tell Nicholas Endrisch that he should feel free to ask me for copies of my books . . . Since I take nothing for my various works, I occasionally take a copy of a book if I want . . . The melons or pumpkins are growing and want to take up an immense amount of space; so do the gourds and water melons. So don't think you sent the seeds in vain!'

One more letter to Hausmann in July rounds off the sequence. It starts with Luther making the decisive judgements in particular cases for which people no longer turned to the Church officials. Luther was becoming a substitute guardian and bishop: 'If that man's case is as he described it, my Nicholas, then I think he may lawfully keep his wife, since the former husband deserted her such a long time ago . . . The visitation has begun. Eight days ago, Dr Hero and Master Philip set out upon this work . . . Rome and the Pope have been terribly laid waste. Christ reigns in such a way that the Emperor who persecutes Luther for the Pope is forced to destroy the Pope for Luther . . . My Katie and little John send greetings. Farewell in Christ. I have had a severe fainting spell, so that even now my head prevents me from reading and writing.'

On 6 May, the Emperor's army had got out of control, and submitted the city of Rome to an appalling sack, destroying, plundering, raping. The Pope took refuge in the St Angelo Castle by the Tiber, which remained impregnable. Luther sat back and watched his enemies apparently destroying each other – though it was not to be so for long. In any case, it was a time of deepening mental and physical depression for Luther. At the Frankfurt Spring Book Fair, his printers had sent along his full-length reply to numerous works of the other Reformers, Zwingli, Oecolampadius, Pirkheimer, Bucer, Capito and others,

on the meaning of those words of Jesus at his Last Supper with
his disciples which formed the heart of the Mass, or eucharist:
'That these Words of Christ "This is my Body", etc., still stand
firm against the Fanatics.' But at the same Fair were further
works of Zwingli, propounding his radically different view.
Luther felt weighed down by it all. Bugenhagen calling one day
found him laid up in bed 'praying aloud to God the Father, then
to Christ the Lord, now in Latin, now in German'. Then in later
summer, still ill and liable to fainting fits, came something
further for his depression to latch on to, but at the same time
a strong physical challenge. The plague struck again at
Wittenberg.

The Elector ordered the University to be evacuated to another
town; it left for Jena on 15 August, and subsequently to
Schlieben. As on the previous occasion of a major outbreak,
Luther remained at Wittenberg. Motivation is not too difficult
to disentangle. He always believed in meeting trouble head on.
He had in some sort a 'heroic' nature and lived up to it and to his
own reputation. He also had a vastly compassionate nature and
loved to give rein to it. At times of plague he nursed and
consoled people to the limit of his energy. Bugenhagen, now the
parish priest, also remained in Wittenberg. When his sister, who
was married to fellow pastor, Deacon Rörer, died, Bugenhagen
and his wife moved into the Friary with the Luthers, to get away
from the contaminated house. Rörer moved into the Jonas's
empty house – Jonas being in exile with the University. The
Mayor's wife died, Luther with her till the last. Luther's little son
Hans nearly succumbed, and Kate, pregnant with their second
child was ill.

The old Friary was more like a hospital. 'There are battles
without and terrors within, and really grim ones; Christ is
punishing us . . . pray for us that we may survive bravely under
the hand of the Lord and defeat the power and cunning of Satan,
be it through living or dying. Amen.' Luther was asked about
the morality of fleeing the plague and in a pamphlet published
in Wittenberg said pastors should stay with the dying, and that
indeed many others would really do best to stay, officials and
those who had responsibilities to neighbours. But, he said,
otherwise naturally it was better to go away.

He gave advice on improving hygiene. The cemeteries could be

much improved and indeed made into places where there was
more reverence. And he had some things to say about pastoral
practice which make him sound like the good Catholic parish
priest that in some ways he continued to be: 'Everyone should
prepare in time and get ready for death by going to confession
and taking the sacrament once every week or fortnight. He
should become reconciled with his neighbour and make his will
so that if the Lord knocks and he departs before a pastor or
chaplain can arrive, he has provided for his world, has left
nothing undone and has committed himself to God.'

A letter to Jonas now at the University's place of exile
expressed the extreme anguish of some moments during the
plague:

> I have not yet read Erasmus [the reply to Luther] or the
> Sacramentarians . . . These people are right in despising me,
> miserable one that I am, to follow the example set by Judas
> . . . I am suffering God's anger because I have sinned against
> him. Pope and Emperor, sovereigns and bishops, and the
> whole world hate and attack me; and even this is not enough,
> even my brothers torment me . . . What could save and
> console me if Christ too should abandon me? . . . Oh that
> God would grant – and again I say, oh that God would grant –
> that Erasmus and the Sacramentarians could experience the
> anguish of my heart for only a quarter of an hour . . . Now my
> enemies are strong and alive they even add grief upon grief
> and persecute him whom God has smitten. But this is enough
> – lest I be one who complains about and is impatient with
> God's rod, for he smites and heals, kills and makes alive and is
> blessed in his holy and perfect will . . . I am concerned about
> the delivery of my wife, so greatly has the example of the
> Deacon's wife frightened me. But He who is mighty has done
> great things for me . . . My little Johann cannot now send his
> greetings to you because of his illness, but he desires your
> prayers for him. Today is the twelfth day that he has eaten
> nothing; he has been somehow sustained only by liquids. It is
> wonderful to see how this infant wants to be happy and strong
> as usual, but he cannot because he is too weak. Yesterday the
> abscess of Margaret von Mochau [a sister-in-law of Karlstadt
> whom the Luthers took in] was operated on . . . I have put her

in our usual winter room, while we are living in the big front hall. Hanschen is in my bedroom, while the wife of Augustine [Schurff] is staying in his. . . . Thus the wickedness of Satan and men!

'Thus we Wittenbergers are the object of hate, disgust and fear . . . Martin Luther, dirt for Christ's sake' – *Lutum Christi*. Luther was punning, even now, with a quotation from St Paul, keeping up a front, behind which lay despair and anger at the thought of what he had done, what he was failing to do, and of his sufferings.

During these bad months Luther lectured to a rump of students who had stayed behind. He turned to the thing that kept him going, the doctrine of Christ, expounded by St John in his First Letter. From now on his lectures tended to progress from concentrating primarily on faith to concentrating primarily on the object of faith. For the rest of his life he preached and lectured on St John, the Gospel and the Letters more than on any text. The first letter of St John in the New Testament opens:

Something which has existed since the beginning,
That we have heard,
and we have seen with our eyes;
that we have watched
and touched with our hands:
the Word, who is life –
this is our subject.
That life was made visible:
we saw it and we are giving our testimony.
Telling you of the eternal life
which was with the Father and has been made visible to us.
What we have seen and heard
we are telling you
so that you too may be in union with us.
as we are in union
with the Father
and with his Son Jesus Christ.
We are writing this to you to make our own joy complete.

Luther pondered on this text, rooted in the writer's convic-

tion that he had met the incarnate God, which ended in a tough
doctrine of love:

> Let us love one another
> since love comes from God . . .
> We are to love, then,
> because he loved us first.
> Anyone who says, 'I love God',
> and hates his brother,
> is a liar.

'God,' said Luther, 'is a glowing oven full of love.' The love
from this oven's heat filled heaven and earth. The warmth of
Katie's oven as she prepared to bake the bread provided Luther
with his metaphor as he scribbled notes for his lectures. The heat
radiated.

He spoke to his little group in glowing terms of what he called
the 'first article and cardinal point' of Christian faith, that
'Christ is in the Father', quoting from another part of the New
Testament: 'In his body lies the fullness of divinity, and in him
you too find your own fulfilment, in the one who is head of every
sovereignty and power.' The lecture became a sermon, and then
a lecture again as Bible and theological tradition jostled each
other in his exposition of what, formally, was called 'the incarnation', 'the enfleshing of the Word of God': 'God places Christ
in himself, so that he is utterly and completely made human and
we are utterly and completely made divine . . . So now God
together with his beloved Son is utterly and completely in you,
and you are utterly and completely in him, and all together is
one entity – God, Christ and you.'

A further booklet from Zwingli arrived, a reply to Luther's
text on the words 'This is my body'. Zwingli called it 'Friendly
Rejoinder and Rebuttal to the Sermon of the Eminent Martin
Luther against the Fanatics'; he saw himself as an Erasmian and
peace-loving, reasonable and humanist, indeed Christian. But
his text was laced with sharp criticism of Luther, answering
Luther's violent language with snappish reprimands and
demonstrations of the absurdity of Luther's arguments.

Eventually came the worst days of Luther's life. 'For more
than a week I was close to the gates of death and hell . . . All my
limbs shook. Christ was wholly lost. I was convulsed with

despair and blasphemy against God.' It was a very severe depression, a night of the spirit, utterly unrelieved.

From these desperate days as he emerged from them, came Luther's most famous hymn: 'A strong city is our God' – *Ein Feste Burg*, 'a mighty fortress' in the old translation. Luther was thinking of the old walled cities he knew so well, where a man could be safe behind the high walls with the gates shut. He was thinking of Jerusalem, the heavenly city, he was thinking of Christ – 'God has established another temple for his dwelling place: the precious manhood of our Lord Jesus Christ. Here and nowhere else God wants to be found.' Guilt and horror of a practically psychotic intensity had combined with physical illness, and ordinary disappointments, to effect a spiritual desolation which was eventually assuaged by prayer to Christ, by meditation on the person of Jesus Christ, on his Words in the New Testament and his sacramental presence.

The depression lifted and the plague retreated. He wrote his hymn, setting it to his own fine Germanic tune, and sat down to pour out a reply to Zwingli, which became his famous 'Confession concerning Christ's Supper'. At the end of it he set out the detailed content of his own Christian faith, including his understanding of many of the central doctrines of Christianity. When it came to the Church, he said:

> There is one holy Christian Church on earth, that is the community or number or assembly of all the Christians in all the world, the one bride of Christ, and his spiritual body of which he is the only head. The bishops or priests are not her heads or lords or bridegrooms, but servants, friends . . . stewards.
>
> This Christian Church exists not only in the realm of the Roman Church or Pope, but in all the world, . . . dispersed among Pope, Turks, Persians, Tartars, but spiritually gathered in one gospel and faith, under one head, i.e. Jesus Christ.

Christianity was more than a conventional Myth religion. It was a universal community. Its members could be everywhere.

The Visitation started up again in greater earnest. The Instructions were developed into a formal text for the most part drawn up by Melancthon, but with an Introduction by Luther which harped on the State backing. Luther was aware of the historical significance, referring to Constantine, the Emperor who made Christianity semi-official in AD 330. 'His Electoral Grace is not bound to teach and rule in spiritual affairs . . . he is bound as temporal sovereign to order things so that strife, rioting and rebellion do not arise among his subjects; even as the Emperor Constantine summoned the bishops to Nicaea since he did not wish to tolerate that dissension which Arius had stirred up.' The Instruction was strong once again on obedience to secular authority and against 'those who shout out against the law of the land'. It was beginning to look as if the State was Luther's only really important ally.

The heart of the Instruction had much in it of the official Catholic norms, but the sacraments were cut to two, there were no references to sacrifice, Indulgences or merit; special devotion and saint days were omitted. With regard to public services there was a good deal of flexibility: 'Holy days such as Sunday shall be observed and as many others as the respective pastors have been accustomed to observe . . . Some sing Mass in German, some in Latin, either of which is permissible.' Sometimes there was great detail: 'At vespers it would be excellent to sing three evening hymns in Latin, not German, on account of the school youth, to accustom them to Latin . . . a lesson in German . . . a German Hymn . . . During the week there should be preaching on Wednesdays and Fridays.' All sorts of things had to be sorted out: 'Many pastors quarrel with their people over unnecessary and childish things like pealing of bells . . . Although in some places the custom of ringing the bells against bad weather is retained, undoubtedly the custom had its origin in a good intention, probably of arousing the people to pray to God that he would protect the fruits of the earth.' And on to items which set a whole future structure for religious observance and organisation: 'The Pastor [*Pfarrherr*] shall be superintendent of all the other priests who have their parish or benefice in the region, whether they live in monasteries or foundations of nobles or of others.' Schools should educate children for a practical future; and education should not be abused as a way to a soft living as a Massing priest.

Luther wrote ten sermons to go with the Large Catechism. Once a quarter on four days in each of two successive weeks, sermons were to be given on the essentials, the Creed, the Sacraments, the Lord's Prayer. Luther preached the first set. He appears in these as a new kind of authority figure. No longer was it a bishop, or a pope, nor indeed 'The Word', but the pastor and the father of the family who was obliged to take the lead: 'Assemble with your families at the designated times . . . Do not allow yourself to be kept away by your work or trade and do not complain that you will suffer loss if for once you interrupt your work for an hour. Remember how much freedom the Gospel has given you, so that now you are not obliged to observe innumerable holy days and can pursue your work. And, besides, how much time do you spend drinking and swilling!' Heads of families must compel their children and their servants to come; and they were not to say '"How can I compel them? I dare not do it." You have been appointed their bishop and pastor. Take heed that you do not neglect your office!' It was a big development from ten years ago when he was trying to get across to them his idea of the real nature of free salvation in Christ – which needed no running across the frontier to pick up Tetzel's Indulgences!

Luther and Melancthon and the others occasionally allowed such thoughts to cross their minds as they relaxed over the Wittenberg beer. There was a certain feeling of satisfactory confidence as they ended the Instruction: 'We have given these instructions to the pastors and explained . . . these most important matters of the Christian life . . . namely repentance, faith and good works.'

Instead of the dialogue of choir and counter choir, Luther's life was woven through with the comedies and tragedies of domestic life. His desk, as of old, groaned with texts for letters, lectures, sermons, state business – for he was often consulted now, not only by Spalatin but more directly by the Elector. To Jonas still exiled, with the University, he wrote again on 10 December 1527: 'At this hour, ten o'clock, when I returned home from a lecture, I received your letter. I had read only ten lines of it when at that moment I was told that my Katie was delivered of a little daughter. Glory and praise be to the Father in heaven. Amen. The mother in childbed is well but weak. And our little son Johann is also well and happy again; the wife of Augustine Schurf is well too; and finally Margaret von Mochau, against all expectations, escaped death. Instead of these people we have lost five pigs. My own condition is just what it has been, namely, as the Apostle says: "As dead and behold I live". . . . Deacon John intends to move out of your house and return to the parsonage. Pomer [Bugenhagen – the Pomeranian] will await his wife's confinement at my place. The students gradually return. Dr Jerome expects to arrive around Christmas, if the situation with the plague remains the way it is now. May Christ gather us together again at one place. Amen. Even weddings are becoming more frequent . . . In the outlying Fishermen's quarters nothing has been heard of the plague or of death for almost two months.' The students trickled back; the University formally returned in April. The full official lecturing programme was resumed and the regular meetings of the Bible translation Committee. They had reached the most difficult part. 'We are sweating over the work of putting the Prophets into German. God, how much of it there is, and how hard it is to make these Hebrew writers talk German! . . . It is like making a nightingale leave her own sweet song and imitate the monotonous voice of a cuckoo.' That was in June 1528 to Wenceslas Link, now a Pastor at reformed Nuremberg. Luther loved the semitic language, while Erasmus was scornful of Hebrew and loved only Greek.

5 August 1528 to Nicholas Hausmann: 'My little Johann thanks you, excellent Nicholas for the rattle. He is very proud of it, and delighted with it. I have decided to write something on the Turkish war [Luther felt strongly that Christendom must be defended], and I hope it will be useful. My baby daughter, little Elizabeth, has died. It is amazing what a sick, almost woman-like heart she has given me, so much has grief for her overwhelmed me. Never before would I have believed that a father's heart could have such tender feelings for his child. Pray to the Lord for me.' The little girl, born just after the end of the plague, had been weak from the start.

But the family with its sorrows and happiness was faced with threats, once again, to its very survival in Wittenberg. The fantasy of leaving the town returned. In May 1528, Luther wrote a long letter to 'The Most Serene, Most Noble Sovereign and Lord, Sir John, Duke in Saxony, Elector . . . landgrave in Thuringia, margrave in Meissenberg; to our Most Gracious

Lord: *Personal* . . .' The heart of the letter was a threat which Luther had felt he and Melancthon must utter, though with the utmost diffidence: 'Even though we should regret the need to do so, we would be compelled to speak out to testify against your Electoral Grace, our most beloved Lord, by whom to this day we have been graciously fed, protected, and overwhelmed . . . we would have to emigrate . . . for the sake of the Gospel in order to avoid having all this disgrace appear to fall justifiably on the innocent Word of God. What could grieve our hearts more than that we and perhaps many fine people should have to be separated from such a father and prince?'

The dire event which threatened to make Luther take himself, Melancthon and others away from Saxony was nothing less than armed confrontation between the forces, on the one hand of the Elector, Philip of Hesse, and the Margrave of Brandenburg-Ansbach, defenders of the Reformers, and on the other forces deployed by supporters of the imperial and papal cause, Bishops of Bamberg and Würzburg and the Archbishop of Mainz, Luther's old enemy, Cardinal Albrecht, and others. Philip of Hesse had continued his drive to give political unity to the states which were supporting the Reformers, and to enable them to defend themselves against possible imperial military intervention. He had the idea of a pre-emptive strike. There were rumours of an elaborate plot to justify it. He and the Elector consulted Luther about the morality of military action against the Emperor a number of times in 1528, 1529 and 1530, soliciting his support for it. Luther expressed himself as utterly opposed to this on all the numerous occasions he was consulted by the two of them.

There was a possible case in law for saying that the Emperor was 'only' one's feudal superior and in some circumstances might be disowned. But Luther saw him as the real secular authority in German-speaking lands, and felt a strong, somewhat romantic loyalty to the imperial office and its young occupant. Unless the Emperor was shown by due process to have betrayed and abandoned his task and had been unanimously removed from office, then he must be obeyed. To take up arms against him was unthinkable. He refused to countenance war against the Emperor's supporters, and made it clear that he greatly disliked the alliance based on religious differences.

Philip was disappointed. In the summer of 1528, Hesse and
Saxony had actually mobilised their forces, but then parleyed
with the bishops, and for the moment abandoned the idea of
defence by attack.

   Immediately after the Diet of Speyer, Philip had drawn up a
Church Ordinance intended to enforce reforms on the Church
in his territory, and began to take over Church property.
However, on asking Luther's advice, he had been advised in the
strongest terms that such things could not be done satisfactorily
by legislation alone. There should first be some consensus;
legalisation could only succeed with a secure basis in public
opinion. In 1528, Philip used Luther's own less strict Saxon Or-
dinances. But Luther was not done with Philip, whose military
initiatives were deeply resented by the conservative forces. With
the encouragement of the Emperor's brother, Ferdinand
(though actually beyond the Emperor's own wishes not yet
known), a Second Diet of Speyer (April 1529) passed a resolution
which reversed the decision of the first Diet of Speyer, opposed
reforms, and demanded the return of Church property. But this
was in turn followed by a further reaction from the militant
minority at the Diet, a 'Protest' drawn up by the reforming
group. Their text, labelled 'Appeal and Protest', became the
origin of the title 'Protestant'. Polarisation was continuing. But
the Reformers continued to disagree violently among
themselves, especially about the reformed Mass and the correct
understanding of the words of Jesus at the Last Supper. This was
a poor basis on which to build a unified political alliance of
reforming states. Philip, therefore, began to badger Luther and
Melancthon to come to a general meeting of reformers.

   Melancthon at least saw something useful coming out of
Landgrave Philip's usually disastrous initiatives; an Agreed
Statement was exactly what his Common Places had been
aiming at for the last eight years. Luther disliked and distrusted
the idea of a meeting. In any case, he had written his own last
word on the matter in his two long treatises in 1526 and 1527.
He wrote to the Landgrave: 'I certainly know that I am unable to
give way just as I know that they [other reformers] are wrong. If
we should meet and then part from one another in disagreement, then not only Your Sovereign Grace's expenses and
troubles would be lost . . . but our opponents would continue

their boasting.' But the two Philips, Melancthon and Hesse, persevered, and a Colloquy was set up. Luther and Melancthon departed for the Landgrave's castle in Marburg in September 1529, being joined also by Justus Jonas and Osiander.

> 4 October 1529. To my kind, dear lord, Katherine Luther, a doctor and preacher in Wittenberg. Grace and peace in Christ. Dear Sir Katie! You should know that our amiable colloquy at Marburg has finished and we are in agreement on almost all points, except that the opposition insists on affirming that there is only simple bread in the Lord's Supper, and on confessing that Jesus Christ is spiritually present there.

The Landgrave had been astute in organising the meeting, referring only to Oecolampadius and not to Zwingli in his invitations to Luther. At the meeting itself he worked hard at a compromise, on the matter of the nature of Christ's presence in the Eucharist, looking for an agreement to disagree, asking all to consider themselves 'brothers and members of Christ', even though there was no agreement on this particular matter. Luther commented to Katie: 'The Landgrave works hard on this item. But we do not want this Brother-and-member business though we do want peace and goodwill.'

Luther had been partly amused at the whole occasion with its magnificent banquet and politics. Years later, he commented: 'At Marburg Philip went around like a stable boy, concealing his deep thoughts with small talk as great men do.' Philip seems to have been successful in keeping the well-fed horse-contestants close to the mark in spite of Luther's determination to look for an encounter. At the start they had all been paired off in separate groups, Luther being allotted to Oecolampadius, the usually mild though pernickety scholar who had taken to a convent in 1521 in search of peace for his writing, had found it unsatisfactory and had joined Bucer at the von Sickingen castle and, liking it less, went to Basel where he stayed for the rest of his life. But eventually there had to be a plenary session, and then Luther found himself greatly irritated by Zwingli, just as he expected. The latter insisted at times on speaking Greek or Hebrew. This drove Luther to play, disingenuously, the man of common sense. He chalked on the table *Hoc est corpus meum*, Jerome's Latin translation of the Greek in the New Testament for 'This is my Body', the implication being that there was really nothing to argue about, the meaning was clear. But Luther knew quite well that the Gospel writers wrote in Greek, and were Semites – they did not express their meaning in Latin. Though rejecting, like the other reformers, the definition of the presence of Jesus in the Eucharist as due to 'transubstantiation' of the bread and wine into body and blood, Luther insisted on the objective presence of Christ in the food and drink. His opponents spoke of the words 'body' and 'blood' as being 'only symbolical', or of the sacrament as dependent on the faith of the recipient. All the Reformers were of one mind in wanting to abandon the implications of the sometimes hysterical piety of the faithful towards the 'Blessed Sacrament', marvelling at a kind of almost horrific miracle in the 'transubstantiation' which occurred, as it were automatically, when the correct words and gestures proceeded from a properly ordained priest. But they could not agree on the words to express the true meaning. One product of the meeting was a reconciliation between Luther and his old admirer Bucer, who for a time had been violently opposing Luther in the belief that he believed in some kind of literal 'localisation' of Christ's physical body in the bread, as in a butcher's shop, to quote their common scathing rejection of the idea.

But fourteen other points were unanimously agreed. Fourteen out of fifteen was a substantial achievement for the Landgrave, especially as it included a long list of central doctrines: the Creator, the Trinity, the Son of God, Jesus, Original Sin, Redemption, Faith, Holy Spirit, Baptism, good works, confession, the State, optional traditions – a formidable list. Luther and Melancthon were rushed by the Elector on to a further meeting at Schwabach, where the Marburg Articles sharpened up by Luther were made the subject of a further declaration and further political alliance, between the Elector and the Hohenzollern Margrave of Brandenburg-Ansbach. Philip of Hesse failed to persuade the towns of Ulm and Strassburg to join the alliance. But an alliance with Ernestine Saxony, Marburg and Schwabach was a step forward in his plan for a well-based alliance of reformed German states.

News came that the Emperor was on the move from Spain, would go to meet the Pope in Italy and then come to Germany, his first visit since the Diet of Worms. Would he call the General Council which continued to be bruited, or would it be just another Diet? The Emperor had seemed to be reacting more strongly recently. In Spain, on receiving news of the 'Protest', he had issued a Mandate demanding its withdrawal, and this he followed up by imprisoning the official Delegation from Nuremberg which had come to present the 'Appeal and Protest' formally. It was an action he was perhaps more likely to take in Spain, where due process of law was not held so high as in Germany. But it was a little alarming. Meanwhile, Luther had sad personal news to which he could respond only by letter, because his friends did not like the idea of him moving about the country alone, what with continuing military threats, and the general uncertainties.

'To my dear Father, Hans Luther, a citizen at Mansfeld in the valley; Grace and Peace in Christ Jesus, our Lord and Saviour. Amen. Dear Father: James, my brother, has written me that you are seriously ill. As the weather is bad now, and as there is danger everywhere, and because of the season, I am worried about you. For even though God has thus far given to and pre-served for you a strong tough body, yet your age gives me anxious thoughts . . . I would have liked to come to you per-sonally' but 'friends have talked me out of it'. However, he and Katie had a suggestion: 'It would be a great joy for me, however, if it were possible for you and Mother to be brought here to us; this my Katie, too, desires with tears, and we all join her.' Meanwhile,

> I pray from the bottom of my heart that the Father, who has made you my Father and given you to me, will strengthen you according to his immeasurable kindness . . . Let your heart be courageous . . . we have there, in the life beyond, a true and faithful helper at God's side, Jesus Christ . . . This cursed life is nothing but a real vale of tears, . . . And there is no respite until someone finally battens us down with a shovel. Then of course it has to stop and let us sleep contentedly in Christ's peace, until he comes again to wake us with joy. Amen . . . My Katie, Hänschen, Lenchen, Aunt Lena, and all my household send you greetings and pray for you faithfully. Greet my dear mother and all my relatives. God's grace and strength be and

abide with you for ever. Amen. Your loving son, Martin
Luther. Wittenberg, 15 February 1530.

The letter was despatched by the hand of Cyriac Kaufmann, a
nephew, who was to report back.

The international situation now began once again to dictate
Luther's movements. Nine days after he wrote to his father, the
Emperor was crowned Holy Roman Emperor in Bologna by the
Pope. 24 February was his thirtieth birthday. Charles V looked
back to the great crowning of Charlemagne in 800. But this was
to be the last crowning of an Emperor by a Pope. It was a symbol
of aspirations based on nostalgia and theory not well adapted to
the facts of the situation, but it did serve to increase Charles V's
own personal morale and boost his conviction that he had a
duty and a right to preside over both the religious and the
political future of northern Europe. An Imperial Diet would be
held in Augsburg in the summer, he announced. Urgent matters
on the agenda were two well-tried topics; 1. The Defence of
Christendom against the Turks, now extremely urgent since
Vienna was threatened. 2. The Reforms. On the latter matter,
the Emperor apparently took a surprisingly paternal but
realistic stance, intending 'to give a charitable hearing to every
man's opinions, thoughts, and notions, to understand them, to
weigh them, to bring and reconcile men to a unity in Christian
truth'.

Luther, Melancthon, Jonas and others were bidden to
prepare texts and to meet the Elector at Torgau, and to be
prepared to accompany him to Augsburg. They set out from
Wittenberg, along with a postgraduate student, Veit Dietrich,
on 3 April – another springtime journey towards the south-west,
which took them quickly on in the Elector's entourage to
Coburg, where they stopped. It was the last city in the southern-
most tip of the Elector's territory. To go safely beyond it they
needed safe-conduct passes, and beyond it Luther could only be
safe with special precautions. In any case there seemed to be
doubt as to when the Emperor was going to set out from Italy.

Luther reported to Nicholas Hausmann, Pastor at Zwickau,
on the news at Coburg:

Yesterday a letter and a messenger arrived telling us that the
Emperor is still at Mantua and will celebrate Easter there . . .

The Papists are trying extremely hard to stop the Diet, since they are afraid something might be decided against them . . . The Pope is angry with the Emperor, since the latter intends to interfere with ecclesiastical matters, and to listen to the parties . . . The Turk has promised, or rather threatened, to return to Germany next year with very great forces, even leading large numbers of Tartars against us.

Then, on 22 April, came a letter from Imperial Headquarters in Mantua that the Emperor expected to be in Augsburg before the end of April. The Elector had therefore immediately to continue his journey, and to make arrangements about Luther. At Coburg was a castle where Luther would be safe. He was to stay there for the duration of the Diet, and be as available as fast messengers could make him, for consultation. The Elector had hoped to take Luther on with them, as far as Nuremberg and lodge him safely inside that town, with its church reforms now well established, and backed by the Town Council. But the latter had not been prepared to condone what would be a direct challenge to Imperial Law. So Luther had to remain in Coburg. The Elector did not want attention to be drawn to Luther's stay there. It was still dark in the early morning of 24 April when Luther, Cyriac Kaufman and Veit Dietrich moved into the castle. A few hours later, the rest of the Elector's party along with Melancthon and Jonas set out on the journey to Bavaria, to the imperial city of Augsburg.

For Luther it was the Wartburg all over again, though not nearly so bad. By the afternoon of the first day he was very bored, and still waiting for his baggage and papers – however, he carried a pen and some scrip with him and sat down to write to his close friend, to whom he had said goodbye only a few hours before:

To my dearest brother, Master Philip, a faithful and skilled servant of Christ . . . This place is certainly extremely pleasant and most suited for studying except that your absence makes it a sad place . . . I am asking Christ to grant you sound sleep, and to free your heart from worries . . . I am writing this as I have nothing to do . . . Nothing interferes with our solitude . . . we have been given the keys of all the rooms . . . Twelve night watchmen and two look-out guards with bugles are

stationed in different towers. But what am I going on about?
As you see I have nothing else to write . . . .

He sent greetings by name to the rest of the party, and signed
off 'From the Kingdom of the Birds at the third hour, 1530,
Martin Luther.'
As at the Wartburg, the birds once again took his fancy. In a
further letter to Spalatin he indulged in an Aesopian-type
allegory about the jackdaws holding a Diet:

> They live under the open sky, so that the sky itself serves them
> as panelled ceiling, the green trees as a floor of limitless
> variety, and their walls are the ends of the earth. They also
> show contempt for the foolish luxury of gold and silk . . . All
> are equally black, all have dark blue eyes, all make the same
> music in unison . . . I have not seen nor heard their emperor
> . . . As far as I could understand from the interpreter of their
> resolutions, they have unanimously decided to make war
> throughout this whole year on the barley, raw as well as
> malted, and then on the summer and winter wheat, and
> whatever else are the best fruits . . . From the kingdom of the
> wicked jackdaws, the fifth hour, 1530. Your Martin Luther.

CHAPTER FIFTEEN

The German Prophet

'To my dearest Katherine Luther, mistress of the house, . . ., Wittenberg: Personal. Grace and peace in Christ! Dear Katie . . . I have received all your letters . . . I got the picture of Lenchen (Magdalen). At first I didn't recognise the little minx, she looked so dark. I think it would be all right if you stopped breast feeding, gradually, so that at first you leave out one feed a day, then two, until finally it stops completely.' Luther said he got this advice from a friend who called recently, and went on: 'Tell Mr Christian that in all my life I haven't seen worse glasses than those which arrived with his letter. I couldn't see a thing through them . . . The Emperor still delays at Innsbruck, the priests are conspiring and there is foul play . . . The messenger won't wait longer. Greetings, kisses, hugs and regards to all and everyone as fits. 5 June in the morning, 1530, Martin Luther.'

The letters poured forth from Luther, once again the frustrated 'General' at the Castle – frustrated by his distance from events. He commonly added a letter to Katie to each batch of his other letters, while the messenger waited. The Emperor finally arrived at Augsburg in the fourth week in June. Letters and memoranda flew to and fro between Luther and the Elector, Melancthon, Spalatin and Justus Jonas. It was a time of jockeying for position. The Emperor's previous official visit to Germany nine years earlier had ended in the outlawing of Luther; now he seemed to be inviting Luther's associates to present their case.

Melancthon was busy with negotiations, re-casting his ever newly polished commonplaces, turning them now into an 'Apology' and finally into a 'Confession' to be presented to the Emperor. On 15 May, Luther received a copy from the Elector for his comment. He sent it back the same day by return

messenger as requested: 'I have read through Master Philip's
Apologia which pleases me very much; I know of nothing which
needs to be corrected or changed, nor would this be appropriate
since I cannot step so softly and gently.' Melancthon's style he
knew well, and he had seen the great majority of the sentences
themselves in one form or another, in previous documents. But
was it really feasible to do business with the papists? That was
what worried Luther. He had already prepared his own text for
Augsburg and it was even now printing at Wittenberg.

As soon as he had settled in at the Coburg he began to write a
piece for the clerics and theologians assembling for the Imperial
Diet. In letters to friends he told of a literary programme he had
set himself for the duration of his stay: he would work on the
Prophets, stemming from the still continuing work of
translating the whole Old Testament, he would do commentaries on some of his favourite Psalms, and he would work on
Aesop – this would fulfil a long cherished ambition to bring out
an edition of Aesop's fables, which he eventually did. The
jackdaws in the trees outside had set his mind off again in that
direction. He spun tales to his correspondents about their bird
Diet, and their war on the crops. But the first ten days were very
largely occupied with his *Exhortation to all Clergy assembled at
Augsburg*. He had soon completed twenty thousand words and
sent it off to Wittenberg for printing.

It was a rumbustious farrago, mixing his usual bombast with
sharp insights and practical proposals. In the opening sections
he laughed at the way in which the theme of faith and works had
now been taken up so widely by all preachers – 'they slyly leave
their sermon book under the bench and whatever else the shouting in the pulpit used to be about, and they begin to preach to
us again on faith and good works, about which one never used
to hear or know anything'. Yet, he complained, nothing much
else seemed to have changed – if they did not learn their lesson,
another Müntzer would arise, and more violence supervene.
Then he turned to the accustomed list of items in the Catholic
tradition which he had been denouncing in the last ten years,
that remained largely unreformed: Indulgences and special
confessional arrangements, the 'sale of Masses', private Masses,
and the teaching that Mass was a sacrifice and a good work, the
Ban, the faithful confined to one kind at Communion, celibate

priests – on the latter he was his usual eloquent self and included a reference to the fact that the Pope, Clement VII, had been born out of wedlock, and another reference to the mistresses of Cardinal Albrecht.

Then he came to a series of 'Offers' to the Church authorities: 1. 'Allow us to teach the Gospel freely . . . Do not persecute and resist that which you cannot do and are all the same supposed to do and which others want to do for you . . .' 2. Luther and his followers would continue to work without any expectation of payment from the established Church authorities. 3. Bishops and priests should be allowed to remain in possession of their property and to be recognised as 'princes and lords'. He summed up as a fourth point: 'You could restore the episcopal jurisdiction again, as long as you left us free to preach the Gospel. For my part, I will readily give help and counsel so that you may have something of the episcopal office after all.' Luther was granting favours, not soliciting them.

This was as far as he was ever to go in compromise, and he was reluctant and worried at the prospect of agreement. Melancthon was busy all his life trying to patch a detailed doctrinal agreement together. But Luther felt he could never really trust the ecclesiastical authorities. And he was concerned about the practicalities of what was being talked about. The Christian faith was expressed in human terms, earthen vessels, in public worship, in gestures, words and music, and these were important. Luther claimed with some justification that the reformers celebrated the liturgy with greater reverence than the papal Church; Mass at Wittenberg still looked Catholic in many ways. The 'Host', the consecrated bread was still 'elevated', lifted up for all to see – other reformers had omitted this for some years. Luther was always trying to stretch beyond mere rites, to the liturgical expression of the Gospel, to an occasion for the recognition of Christ and his message. In his youth he felt irretrievably hampered by the Church's insistence that to offer Mass was to do something 'meritorious'. But eucharistic worship remained central to his theology. He wanted it to be a free act of worship and thanksgiving.

In his text for Augsburg, Luther went on to a great list of actions, gestures and symbols, which he found either unacceptable, or only acceptable as a kind of cultural decoration, or

possibly welcome but not to be imposed – the Freedom of the
Word was the great thing. And yet he was increasingly aware of
what he considered abuse of that freedom by preachers who
ignored all tradition and relied on a purely personal spiritual
understanding of the New Testament. In all his writing at this
time there was a reaching out to distinguish acceptable norms in
the received tradition, and a wish not to discard what had
assisted faith. While at the Coburg he wrote a long 'pastoral' text
on the Eucharist, encouraging Christians to go frequently to
communion. First in his Augsburg list comes a list of thirty-
seven unacceptable things: 1. Indulgences . . . 10. Masses at
Four Weeks. 11. Soul baths. 12. Venerations of Saints some of
whom were never born . . . 14. Mary made a common idol with
countless services. 15. Butter letters. 16. Countless relics, with
fraud . . . 29. Sacrament of Marriage. 30. Sacrament of
priesthood. 31. Sacrament of Confirmation.

Then comes a list of lesser things 'beyond necessity, purely as
a special service to God, which is contrary to faith . . . Tonsures,
chasubles, albs . . . altar cloths, lights . . . bells, holy water, holy
salt, incense', and a further list of ambivalent things: 'veiling of
statues, keeping fasts (except for the clergy), Litany of the Saints,
Hymns to Mary of an evening, Confession torture, Palm
swallowing, Passion sermons eight hours long, Consecrating the
fire, . . . St Martin's Goose . . . three Christmas Masses, Oats on
St Stephen's Day, St John's draught'. These were by no means all
bad in themselves, but should not be imposed.

> Some of these have declined which I did not want to see
> decline, but which can easily come back again. Among them
> the very best to remain are the fine Latin songs, for particular
> seasons, although they have been almost drowned out by the
> new saint-songs . . . If these things had been left as child's
> play for youth . . . as one must give children dolls, puppets,
> hobbyhorses, then they would confuse no conscience. But
> that we old fools march around in bishops' hats and with
> clerical pageantry and take it not only seriously but as an
> article of faith, so that it must be a sin and must torment the
> conscience of anyone who does not venerate such child's play
> – that is the devil himself.

Working long hours on the translation of the Old Testament

and suffering from severe headache, exhaustion and depression, he could not summon up much comment for the messenger waiting to return to the Elector with Melancthon's *Apologia*. He had written to Philip on 12 May: 'I am suffering from a ringing, or rather thundering in my head – I nearly passed out.' In spite of it, he punned: 'My head (Caput) has become a Chapter (Capitulum) and will soon be a paragraph, and then a bare sentence . . . Satan so crushed me that I had to get out of my room and look for company.' He was fortunate to have Veit Dietrich with him, and his nephew Cyriac Kaufman. Dietrich was a major help with preparing his texts. He was also beginning to collect a file of Luther's passing comments, which would become the first of the famous series of 'Table Talk'; and he wrote letters to Katie, telling her how her husband was.

Luther wrote to his son's tutor, Jerome Weller, now living with the family, and suffering like Luther from depression.

> Whenever this temptation comes to you, don't argue with the devil and don't dwell on the lethal thoughts . . . Don't be alone . . . Joke and play some game with my wife and others . . . go into company or drink more . . . We are soon defeated if we try too hard not to sin. So when the devil says 'Do not drink' answer him: 'I shall drink, and right freely, just because you tell me not to!'

And Luther laughed at advisers, medical and spiritual: 'Whatever one does in the world is wrong . . . One physician advises me to bathe my feet at bedtime, another before dinner, a third in the morning, a fourth at noon . . . So it is in other things: if I speak I am thought turbulent, if I keep silence I am thought to spit on the cross. Then Mr Wiseacre comes along and hits the poor beast on the rump.'

The Elector was the first sovereign to arrive at Augsburg. He and his advisers waited for news of the Emperor, who had reached Innsbruck early in May and delayed there for lengthy consultation with advisers from Church and state. Campeggio was there, his mind still abuzz with the troubles of the Emperor's aunt, Queen of England, now dismissed by Henry VIII who was threatening fearful things if the Pope did not give him a divorce. Delay was the best answer, play for time, when no solution could be seen. Campeggio advised the Emperor to delay the Diet. He

was worried that Charles was going to temporise with the
Reformers, or to strengthen his political position and weaken
the papacy again. Luther's old debating partner was also there,
Johann Eck, with a list of 404 reasons why the Reformers were
heretics. Eck had been working hard at pastoral work in several
parishes around Ingolstadt, and had become a devoted
Reformer within the established Church – he had always
granted Luther's thesis against Indulgences, but reform should
keep within the bounds of established canonical and papal
norms. He had written numerous Latin works and had engaged
with Zwingli in a disputation in Switzerland.

To encourage Elector John and his theologians Luther sent
encouraging letters to Augsburg, including one strongly supportive to the Elector, assuring him that time was not heavy on
his hands as the Elector had feared it might be (what might not
happen if Luther were bored?), and that they were comfortable
and well fed at the Coburg. He recalled the solid achievements
which were now to be seen in Ernestine Saxony, the results of the
Visitation, of the preaching of a theology of faith and the cir-
culation of the Little Catechism, and the German New
Testament: 'The young people, both boys and girls, grow up so
well instructed in the Catechism and the Scriptures that I am
deeply moved when I see that young boys and girls can pray,
believe, and speak more of God and Christ than they ever could
in the monasteries, foundations, and schools of bygone days, or
even of our day. Truly your Elector Grace's territory is a
beautiful paradise . . .' On the same day that he wrote to the
Elector, he wrote a second German letter to Landgrave Philip to
keep him on the correct doctrinal lines in the coming Diet – the
letter ended with Luther's byline 'From the Wilderness'.

At the end of May, copies of his Exhortation to the Clergy at
Augsburg arrived at the Coburg; by 2 June they were selling fast
at Augsburg itself. On 5 June, after the messenger had left for
Wittenberg with his letter, including the one for Katie, another
messenger arrived with sad news. His father had died. Luther
had been writing a letter to Melancthon and now added: 'We die
many times before we die once for all. I succeed now in the
legacy of the name, and I am almost the oldest Luther in my
family . . . Since I am now too sad, I am writing no more; for it is
right and God-pleasing for me, as a son, to mourn such a father

. . .' For twenty-four hours, all his emotions were turned to this personal grief. It was the end of an epoch for Luther. Standing apart from affairs at the Coburg, he digested it easily. A long day and night's sorrow and he was through with it. Death had always been a central theme; now it became more familiar still. Two weeks later, Veit Dietrich wrote to Katie to describe how he took it. The news had come in a letter from Hans Reinecke (Luther's boyhood friend with whom he travelled to his first boarding school at Magdeburg):

> Looking at Reinecke's letter he says to me: 'So my father is dead!' Then he hurriedly took his Psalter, went into his room, and wept so much that the next day he had a headache. Since that time he has not betrayed any further emotion . . . You did something very good when you sent the picture of Magdalen to Doctor Luther, for the picture helps him to forget many troubling thoughts. He has pinned it up on a wall opposite the table in the room where we eat.

That was a letter dated 19 June. On the same date, Luther wrote again to Jerome Weller, and he wrote also to four-year-old Hans himself: 'I am pleased to hear that you are doing well in your lessons, and that you are praying well. Go on like this, my son, and when I return home I shall bring you a nice present from the fair.' It was a relief to turn aside from an argument he was having with Melancthon and Spalatin, who seemed to be keeping him short of information and made him fear the worst. He sent Hans a story of a garden full of things gold and silver, little coats, ponies, saddles, reins, apples, pears, cherries, yellow and blue plums, with many children playing in it. He had asked the owner if his own child might join in and 'eat such fine apples and pears, and ride on these pretty ponies and play with these children', and the reply was yes, 'if he too likes to pray, study and be good, he too may enter the garden, and also Lippius [Melancthon] and Jost [Jonas]'. They would get 'whistles, drums, lutes and would dance and shoot with little crossbows; and Aunt Lena could go too'. Luther's fantasies were not all horror, anger and despair. 'Works' and rewards were also apparently acceptable for four-year-olds.

At Augsburg the atmosphere grew more tense and the jockeying more active as the Emperor arrived at Munich and then started out on the final leg for Augsburg. Rulers and representatives from five states and two towns, also two princes had been persuaded by Elector John to sign the now very long text of Melancthon's Confession. It was in two distinct parts. In the first part, the essentials of the Christian religion were set down in a way which it was hoped all at the Diet would agree to; the second part referred to matters in dispute. Justification by faith was treated moderately in the first part; Melancthon presented it in a way that did not necessarily contradict traditional Catholic teaching – even though it put sacramental practice into a less 'legal' and obligatory context. The headings of the matters in dispute were: on both kinds in communion; the marriage of priests; the Mass; Confession (both these last two were also listed under matters in agreement); Fasts and pious Conventions; monastic vows; the authority of the Church. It was a text that had been long in the making, well thought out and carefully constructed: so much so that it became the confessional document of the subsequent 'Lutheran Church', and was still being discussed in detail on its recent 450th anniversary.

Meanwhile, Luther was ill and in an increasing state of emotional turmoil. What was going on at Augsburg? Nobody sent him any news; there must be dirty work. He wrote angrily like a sulky child and said he would not write to them if they did not write to him.

Eventually a packet of letters arrived, together with the latest text of the Confession. The Emperor had entered Augsburg on the eve of Corpus Christi, 15 June, and had immediately summoned those rulers who had signed the Protest at Speyer, and ordered their preachers to cease public preaching in the imperial town. But this was not acceptable to the 'Protestants'. Eventually, it was agreed that neither reformed preachers nor papal preachers should give sermons; the Emperor would appoint the preachers at his own public worship. It was a bad start. The Elector was annoyed, but there was some sympathy for the withdrawn and still youthful looking Emperor. 'The Emperor greets Elector John in quite a friendly way and I wish our party would be more courteous,' wrote the sensitive Philip Melancthon to Luther. The letters began to flow again from the Coburg, with extended explanations about the rights and wrongs of the long 'silence', together with emphatic abjurations from Luther that there was to be no retreat by the Reformers: 'For me more than enough has been conceded in this *Apologia* [now the Confession] . . . Day and night I am occupied with this matter, considering it, turning it round, debating it and searching the whole Scripture.' His desperation of mind and body were poured out: 'It seems that that demon, which till now has beaten me with fists, has given up (as if broken by your prayers) . . . instead another one has followed which will wear down my body . . . I would rather tolerate this torture of the flesh than that executioner of the spirit.' And the devil 'will have no peace until he has gobbled me up. All right, if he eats me, he shall eat a laxative (God willing) which will make his bowels and his anus too tight for him.'

Melancthon spoke in a letter to Luther of how he followed Luther's originating authority. But Luther objected, in a per-nickety and prickly, academic way, that if his name was going to be used he would handle the matter by himself. Melancthon was trying to give credit where due. The opportunity with which he was now presented could hardly have been greater. Luther was gripped with frustration at the lack of verve and the absence of imaginative criticism in Melancthon's text. He could not leave Philip alone. 'The outcome of this case tortures you because you cannot comprehend it. But if you could comprehend it, then I would not wish to be a partner in this cause, much less its originator. God has placed this case into a certain paragraph which you don't have in your rhetoric, nor in your philosophy. This is entitled "Faith" . . .' and on Luther went, line after line of rhetoric to teach Melancthon once again about faith and the incomprehensible nature of God. 'I wish an opportunity would present itself to me to come to you . . . God's grace be with you and with you all. Amen.' And then a PS – he had not replied properly about the details of what they should be willing to concede: 'I am willing to concede all things if only the Gospel alone is permitted to remain free with us. What is contrary to the Gospel, however, I cannot concede. What else should I answer?'

Then news came that the Confession had been read to the Emperor in an official assembly of the Diet, not exactly a plenary assembly, but two hundred were present in the Emperor's chapel. Campeggio was beside himself at this outrage. For the Reformers it was a milestone. A formal reading of their credal statement at an Imperial Diet. On hearing about it, Luther relented. To Conrad Cordatus and Nicholas Hausmann he wrote triumphant letters on 6 July: 'I am tremendously pleased to have lived to this moment when Christ has been publicly proclaimed by his staunch confessors in such a great assembly by means of this really most beautiful confession', and 'Our confession (which our Philip prepared) has been publicly read by Dr Christian [Beyer, Saxon Chancellor], right in the palace of the Emperor . . . There is no one in this whole Diet whom our friends praise more highly for his peacefulness than the Emperor himself . . . all are filled with affection and applause . . .' He had heard from Jonas that he had studied the Emperor's face during the reading of the Confession and there was a certain *humanitas* in it. To Melancthon himself, two days earlier before he had heard the great news, although grumbling about some of it, Luther had written: 'Yesterday I re-read your whole Apologia, and I am tremendously pleased with it.'

But what was to be the result of the reading? Luther continued to worry that no good would come of it, and his own desk was littered with texts of further pamphlets criticising the unreformed Church. He was anxious about the absence in the Confession of sufficient criticism, and he was worried that unacceptable concessions would be made to the papal representatives, impressed by Melancthon's text and wishing to end disunity. Cardinal Cajetan, still a power in Rome, had always assented, like Eck, to much of the criticism of Indulgences and of corruption. He was not alone in the Roman Curia, or among churchmen generally, in this stance.

Some of the bishops and papal representatives at the Diet were impressed by Melancthon's piece, and assented to the reasonableness of the demands for Communion under both kinds and for the abandonment of clerical celibacy. But they were few and were unable to force discussion of the real issues, as distinct from negotiations on a political basis. In the end they had to choose between the Freedom of the new movements and the canonical Tradition embodied in Rome. The theological and disciplinary matters at issue were never argued out. The momentum, ideological, political and economic of the papal Church, and increasingly now of the new Protestant movements dominated the scene. The result was polarisation of the two positions and the rapid institutionalisation of 'Protestantism'. In the twentieth century the two positions, roughly of the 'Gospel' and of the 'Church', have been partially reconciled within the Church of England and other reformed Churches. At the extremes the papal Church itself has still not entirely shed the mantle of imperial Rome; and the Gospel fundamentalists and evangelicals still sometimes lack ascertainable norms, and appropriate symbolic and sacramental channels of communication. Both extremes find spiritual authority difficult to handle, tending to lapse either into authoritarianism or indifference. Until 1530 these contradictions and difficulties had been kept either out of sight or under repression for a very long time. They now broke out uncontrollably. The will to reconciliation was lacking in the majority on both sides, in spite of a minority which worked hard for it.

'Let your Majesty be well advised . . . not to promise or concede to them anything whatever, because you would then enter a labyrinth from which you could never emerge any more, and so they would have gained their will. But . . . extirpate these heresies, proceeding against them with order and system, . . . using, you your temporal arms and I the spiritual, and thus zealously punish them as is right . . . and show yourself the true and undoubted successor of Charlemagne amongst whose other greatest undertakings there still resounds the fame of the conquest he made of the Saxons . . .' Campeggio replied in this way before the Emperor at the session following that at which Melancthon's text had been read. Although he did request a theological examination of Melancthon's text, it was perfectly clear that Campeggio intended a mere formal refutation of it. No genuine examination was intended of the Reformer's careful survey of theology and Church conventions. Campeggio was sure it was essentially 'heretical'. The substantive theological issues were in fact treated as a function of the great ecclesiastical structure – or to put to it as its defenders essentially understood it: the papal Church had an absolute right and duty to suppress all fundamental criticism of its own divinely instituted authority. Any radical questioning of current theological and disciplinary norms clearly implied such criticism.

The Emperor agreed. But, at least, he argued with the Pope and his representatives, they should call a Council to settle these matters formally. They should call one, also because the German nation had for so long been demanding such a 'Free Council' to right all the grievances under which it laboured. In any case, it was the only possible way to solve the disagreements. He was unable to impose a solution because, he said, in a letter to the Pope: 'The Protestants are more unyielding and more obstinate than ever – while the Catholics are generally lukewarm and but little inclined to lend a hand in the forcible conversion of those who have fallen away . . . the welfare of Christendom absolutely requires a Council.' The Emperor requested a designated place and date for it, concluding that he 'submitted in advance to the decision of the Vicar of Christ'. It was to be fifteen years before the Council was to open at Trent under Pope Clement VII's successor. Clement himself was terrified at the prospect and always intended to avoid calling a Council. It might undermine the authority of the Pope.

The meetings at Augsberg multiplied over the following two and a half months. The Electors, their deputies, the theologians, the Emperor's men, the Roman Curia's men, the ambassadors and assistants from all over Europe met in small groups and big groups. The Reformers had their own sub-plot. Neither the Swiss reformers inspired by Zwingli, nor Strassburg (together with Constance, Memmingen and Lindau) agreed with all of Melancthon's text. The latter four cities sent in their own version (*Confessio Tetrapolitana*) of the true understanding of the Gospel. To the horror of the curialists the Emperor allowed even this to be read out half officially in a committee though he had previously declined the statement of Zwingli's group. Negotiations took place. Melancthon gave a little. The papal group appeared, after all, to be willing to talk. But the Emperor always intended the 'conversion' of the Protestants, if necessary by force. And the papal party always wanted their bishops, and it was never likely that they could be conscientiously obeyed by the Reformers. But for six or seven weeks the discussions flowed. To Luther's intense concern substantial ground was conceded at one stage by both sides. On 15 July, Luther wrote a joint letter to Jonas, Spalatin, Melancthon and Agricola: 'You will have to hear "fathers, fathers, fathers, church, church, church, usage, custom". Moreover you will hear nothing taken from Scripture. Based on these norms the Emperor will pronounce a verdict against you . . . Our case has been made and beyond this you will not accomplish anything better. To Campeggio's boasts that he has the power to grant dispensations I reply with Amsdorf's words: "I shit on the legate and his lord's dispensations" . . . Home, home! Gruboc [Coburg – backwards]. 15 July. Martin Luther. D.'

The Emperor eventually gave his official assent to the official Confutation of Melancthon's text, refusing to accept replies to it. On 22 September he issued an imperial Edict at a plenary meeting. It demanded that the Reforming sovereigns (the 'Protestants' as the Emperor called them elsewhere – the 'protesters' at Speyer) conform with traditional norms (reference was made to *sancta fide et religione Christiana – Ecclesia Christiana*) giving a deadline of six months. The implication was that thereafter the Reforming sovereigns would be legally out of order and might be proceeded against if they had not conformed. An attempt to take the sting out of this was made by referring to the summoning of a Council which the Emperor would request from the Pope to remove abuses and other burdens. The Reforming sovereigns were also to assist the Emperor in 'coercing' and 'punishing' the Anabaptists, which seemed to mean roughly all the Reformers to the left of Luther.

The Edict was clearly unacceptable to the Reformers. The Elector obtained dismissal papers and left abruptly the following day. His son (and designated successor) young Duke John Frederick had left ten days previously without a final audience with the Emperor. There was now a kind of stalemate, but a dangerous one. The Turks were no longer threatening in the east. The Emperor had made a political treaty with the Pope. He was free then to raise an army in Europe should he decide to try to impose his will. Some of the pro-papal German sovereigns at Augsburg immediately formed an alliance with the Emperor to defend the Empire and the faith. Discussion of this serious international situation by the Elector and his advisers began immediately and culminated in a conference at the electoral court at Torgau, as soon as they arrived back.

The flow of letters to and from the Coburg had continued unabated. Messengers going north were given notes to Katie – 'My dear Katie: This messenger called here in haste . . . I have not had any throbbing in my head since St Lawrence day' (10

August). Again: 'To my dear lord, Frau Katherine Luther at Wittenberg *Personal* . . . Greet Aunt Lehne . . . Here we are eating bunches of ripe grapes even though outside it has been very wet this month. God be with you all. Amen. From the wilderness, 15 August 1530 Martin Luther.'

Luther was also writing a commentary on Psalm 118 and his mind kept turning to the plain chant as it had gone from side to side of the choir in the old days. The music went on round his mind, and he chalked up the Psalm with its melody on the walls. Then he found another theme from the evening office, using Psalm 4, 'In peace I will lie down and sleep', and it spoke to him of a welcome end to life, which might perhaps come sooner rather than later. Disillusion, ill-health and great weariness beckoned to death. Luther's fantasy was no longer of a death at the hands of the State, instructed by the Church, but of a natural death. Instead of the ideas about life being better in his own little corner in the Friary, now it was a looking forward to release from all the public palaver and problems. And the music kept running in his head. From the Coburg he wrote to Louis Senfl, chief conductor and composer at the Bavarian court, to send him

a copy of that musical text: 'In peace I will lie down and sleep . . .' For this tenor melody has delighted me from youth on, and does so even more now that I 'understand' the words. I have never seen the antiphon arranged for more voices. I do not wish, however, to impose on you the work of arranging; rather I assume that you may have available an arrangement from some other source. Indeed I hope that the end of my life is at hand; the world hates me and cannot bear me, and I, in turn, loathe and detest the world; therefore may the best and most faithful shepherd take my soul to him. Forgive my temerity and verbosity. Extend respectful greetings to your whole choir on my behalf.

On 24 September, Luther wrote to his wife that he hoped to be home in fourteen days' time. It took longer. The Electoral party arrived from Augsburg in no great hurry, on 1 October. They all reached Torgau and the Electoral court by the last week in October. There they held a brief conference on international affairs. Should the Emperor bring military force to bear on the

Reforming States, the lawyers had thought up arguments to persuade Luther to sanction military defence. The political bind turned tighter still. It was put to him that armed resistance to the Emperor would be right if the Emperor were to disregard his own imperial laws. Luther put down his distressing conclusions in his long post-Augsberg piece, 'Warning to his Dear German People by Martin Luther'. By the end of the month during the Conference at Torgau, he was able to reply succinctly to the hypothesis put to him. Theoretically his position was unchanged – one should always obey the secular law. Practically, however, his position was transformed. Ex-Chancellor Brück had persuaded him that it was part of the secular law that one might resist the imperial authority in some circumstances.

> A piece of paper has been presented to us from which we see what the Doctors of Law are concluding with regard to the question: In what situations may one resist governing authority? If then this issue has been settled by these Doctors of Law or experts in this way, and we certainly are in those situations in which one may resist the governing authority . . . we are unable to oppose . . . if in this instance it is necessary to fight back, even if the Emperor himself attacks, or whoever else may do so in his name . . . That until now we have taught absolutely not to resist the governing authority was due to the fact that we did not know that the governing authority's law itself grants the right to do so; we have of course always diligently taught that this law must be obeyed.

It was a kind of surrender for Luther. No longer could he commend the idealistic and Christ-like non-violence which he had preached to the peasants, and to everyone who wanted to oppose the Emperor. The theory had not changed – one should obey the laws, in the kingdom of this world one had to submit to its ways. But practically it was a volte-face. The text of his 'Warning' to the German people mirrored the anguish. Justus Jonas in a letter to him from Augsburg had referred to Luther as 'the German prophet'. The ascription pleased Luther, and made this text easier to do. But its inner contradictions were clear on the surface. The situation had become unthinkable. Loyalty to the young Emperor had been part of an almost romantic idealisation of him:

'One of two things will happen: either a war or a rebellion . . .
we are speaking now as in a dream' – a dream, because never had
Luther thought of himself as an enabler, even less a promoter of
rebellion. It was a new identity and the dream more like a night-
mare. But his prophetic task could not be evaded, and what he
had to say was honest enough: 'They [the Emperor's supporters]
cannot take it for granted that no one will attack them just
because we [Luther] wrote and taught so emphatically not to
resort to rebellion . . .' He began to speak with a radical ambivalence, and what he said could be interpreted variously: 'If
now the masses should reject our teaching against rebellion, especially if they were provoked by such a godless outrage and
wanton war . . .' then his message was that he could not hold
them back, that his teaching against rebellion would not be so
emphatically promulgated as before, and that people should
not accept any order to join the Emperor's army since such an
army would be fighting directly against the things of God. He
remembered the Peasants' War: 'I will surely hold my pen in
check and keep silent and not intervene as I did in the last uprising. I will let matters take their course even though not a
bishop, priest or monk survives and I myself also die.' But this
writing itself was a kind of 'intervention' before it all happened,
an intervention in the other direction: 'I will not reprove those
who defend themselves . . . I will accept their action and let it
pass as self-defence . . . Not that I wish to incite anyone on to
such self-defence, or to justify it'. Ambivalence hung over the
text.

Then he went on to outline the outrageous happenings at
Augsburg, and to indulge in the kind of language the delicate
Melancthon so detested: 'They thought that when they brought
the Emperor in person to Germany, all would be frightened and
say "Gracious Lords, what is your wish?" When they proved
mistaken and the Elector of Saxony was the very first to make his
appearance, my heavens, they dirtied their breeches in their
terror.' Then his text turned to his old opponent Johann Eck:
'Dr Eck . . . declared openly within the hearing of our people
that if the Emperor had followed the resolution arrived at in
Bologna and attacked the Lutherans with the sword . . . then the
problem would have been solved. Many of our opponents were
astonished when our Confession was read and admitted that it

was the simple truth and could not be refuted by Scripture. On the other hand, when their confutation was read, they hung their heads and admitted with their expressions that it was a flimsy and empty thing compared with our confession.' But, in fact, said Luther, it was not a confutation – 'Their well-grounded confutation has not yet been brought to light. It is perhaps still slumbering with old Tannhauser in the Venusberg', the legendary mountain of sensual delight. Later in the piece, Luther let fly about the debauchery in Rome and set down some of the more unsavoury pieces of gossip. If people took up arms for the Emperor, they would be defending this kind of thing: 'You would burden yourselves with the chastity of pope and cardinals . . . a special type of chastity transcending the common spiritual kind . . . about which they jested as though it were a game of cards . . . I am not lying. Whoever has been in Rome knows that conditions are unfortunately worse than anyone can say or believe . . . by means of a Bull . . . they decided that a cardinal should not keep as many boys in the future. However, Pope Leo commanded that this be deleted; otherwise it would have been spread through the whole world how openly and shamelessly the Pope and the cardinals in Rome practise sodomy.'

As well as listing their vices, including murdering and betraying each other, Luther turned once again to describing the well-known examples of their doctrinal errors: 'They put that noble child Mary right into the place of Christ. They fashioned Christ into a judge and thus devised a tyrant for anguished consciences, so that all comfort and confidence was transferred from Christ to Mary, and then everyone turned from Christ to his particular Saint. Can anyone deny this? Are not books extant – specially those of the shabby Barefoot Friars and of the Preaching Friars – which teem with idolatries, such as the Marialia, Stelleria, Rosaria, Coronaria.' These books of special devotions were indeed still in use, and remained so in many parts of the Roman Catholic Church until the present day.

He described how much better things were now. People 'know how to believe, to live, to pray, to suffer, and to die'. If the Emperor's troops came and turned things round again: 'You will have to help burn all the German books, New Testaments, psalters, prayer books, hymnals, and to keep everyone ignorant about the Ten Commandments, the Lord's Prayer, and the Creed . . . baptism, the sacrament, faith, government, matrimony, or the Gospel. You will have to help keep everyone from knowing Christian Liberty . . . from placing their trust in Christ and deriving comfort from him. For all of that was non-existent.' Luther spoilt his case here by exaggeration.

He wound up: 'I swear again that I do not wish to incite or spur anyone to war or rebellion or even self-defence, but solely to peace . . . if the papists . . . insist on war . . . May their blood be on their heads!'

The Saxon prophet summed it up in a piece called *The Keys* (1530): 'We know pretty well that the Romans do not consider us Germans to be human beings, but empty shells and shadows . . . they think that when a cardinal lets wind, the Germans believe a new article of faith is born.' The official text of the Imperial Edict at Augsburg only reached Luther in the spring of 1531. He tore off a further blistering text which came out shortly after the 'Warning'. It was entitled *Commentary on the Alleged Imperial Edict*. Near the end, he looked back to the Bohemian founder of the schismatic Church in the Czech lands, in an acceptance of a popular idea of Luther as the fulfilment of a prophecy: 'St John Huss prophesied of me when he wrote from his prison in Bohemia "They will roast a goose now (because 'Huss' means goose) but after a hundred years they will hear a swan sing and him they will endure." And that is the way it will be, if God wills.'

CHAPTER SIXTEEN

The Shining of the Sun

The Saxon Elector lost no time. By February 1531, he was ready at Schmalkalden in western Saxony to sign a document of wide-ranging alliance. It set up a League with the Landgrave of Hesse, the Dukes of Brunswick and Luneberg, the Prince of Anhalt, the Counts of Mansfeld, and the representatives of eleven 'cities of Upper Germany, Saxony and the Sea', Strassburg, Ulm, Constance, Reutlingen, Memmingen, Lindau, Bibrach, Isny, Lübeck, Magdeburg and Bremen. This Schmalkaldic league was an alliance for their mutual defence if attacked 'on account of the Word of God and the doctrine of the Gospel'. Nuremberg was not in the alliance. Rich, commercial, cultured, the home of Albert Dürer and Hans Sachs, both of them 'Lutherans', Nuremberg had been one of the first cities to implement Church reforms. But it liked to keep its independence at all times, whether in pioneering liturgical reforms in the 1520s, or in declining now to join in a possibly dangerous alliance against the Emperor. The Town Council's Chancellor, Lazarus Spengler, sent a message to Wittenberg enquiring whether Luther (an old acquaintance) had changed his mind on the matter of resistance to a possible attack from imperial forces. Put on the spot, Luther replied that he had not changed his mind about the correct way to approach such a matter, but that the lawyers had changed theirs about the legal facts! He was much more guarded than in his 'Warning to his Dear German People'. But the practical outcome did not escape the Nuremberg Council. It was a turnabout.

The Schmalkaldic League was founded on 27 February 1531. For fourteen months thereafter, its members worked at building up a network of organisational procedures; these were confirmed at Schweinfurt in April 1532. The deadline for com-

pliance with the Augsburg Diet was now a year past. No action
had come from the Emperor, who was taken up with renewed
threats from the Turks in Eastern Europe. Something like the
political birth of modern Germany was in process. The Emperor
requested the pro-imperial and pro-papal Electors to come to
an arrangement with the Schmalkaldic League. The latter was
growing. The recent death of Zwingli in a local Swiss canton
battle of Protestant versus Catholic had reduced the level of
worry about maintaining some kind of credible doctrinal unity.
The League was willing to negotiate with the Emperor, who had
one demand – he wished to retain the Imperial office for the
Habsburg family. A formal agreement with the League would
depend on acceptance of his brother Ferdinand, as Emperor
elect. The Saxon Elector, not surprisingly, was bitterly opposed
and consulted Luther, who advised that the condition was not
intolerable. It would be best to negotiate:

'I am of the opinion that the negotiations proposed by the
Cardinal of Mainz should not be rejected – "Gain a night, gain a
year,"' Luther wrote to Altkanzeler Brück on 16 June 1531,
when negotiations had already begun. By the following
summer, Nuremberg itself was involved in the setting up of an
entirely new kind of 'Peace' between the Emperor and those
political entities which favoured the Reforms but were part of
the Empire. Again Luther backed it and disapproved of delays:
'If we want cleverly to arrange matters exactly as we wish them to
be . . . it will be for us as Solomon says: "He who blows his nose
too hard forces blood from it."' The Peace of Nuremberg was
signed on 23 July 1532 between the Emperor, nine princes and
twenty-four cities, which now included Hamburg. Essentially, it
was a temporary abrogation of some of the imperial powers.
The Emperor had again to forgo the solution of the religious
issue which was thrown forward to a 'Council' – and the council
was again foreseen not as a normal Church Council but a 'free',
and 'Christian' Council in Germany. Local religious independence and political independence on a national basis,
were again being actively intertwined and this progress, laced
with the duplicity and corruption common to such affairs, was at
the heart of local and international politics during the coming
twelve years.

A definitive stage was being reached for the political future of

Germany and for the organisational future of Christianity everywhere. In Nuremberg and the surrounding Margraviate of Brandenburg-Ansbach, documents, emerged to regularise Christian liturgy and discipline. On 1 August 1532, the four Wittenberg leaders, Luther, Melancthon, Jonas and Bugenhagen, sent their comments on an Ordinance submitted to them, approving it in principle. It concerned the use of excommunication by the new Christian authorities, and other difficult matters like the celebration of Mass when there was no congregation (not approved) and the reservation of the Sacrament – also not approved because Communion should not be separated from the Word. Luther had earlier been in correspondence with Link, still the Pastor at Nuremberg, on the regulation of baptism. (Link had also sent him some oranges, a wash basin and a candelabrum, with no note – Luther asked whether they were a gift, or what.) In April 1533, Luther was again in contact with Nuremberg about Confession, insisting, with Melancthon, that both public and voluntary private confession should be retained. In the letter of 1532 the Wittenbergers had expressed concern about being thrust into the position of assessors of new norms. But the logic of the situation demanded it 'in order to maintain pure teaching, and also external Christian discipline and behaviour . . . until the Almighty grants more peace and unity both in ecclesiastical and political governments'.

The Peace of Nuremberg had included an item obliging the signatories to assist the Emperor in the defence of Europe against the Turks. Swiftly came a request, in August 1532, to Luther from Duke Joachim of Brandenburg, who was to lead a contingent of the Saxon army against the Turks. He wanted prayers for his undertaking and spiritual advice. In the old days he would have had a blessing from the local bishop and an Indulgence. In his response, serious and detailed, almost paternal, if not quite episcopal or pontifical, Luther said he wished to 'move out to war spiritually with our earnest prayers, to join with the dear Emperor Charles and his soldiers' – he still thought Charles V ill-advised rather than perverse. He spoke of the dangers of useless self-congratulation: they were

not to place reliance in the Turks being altogether wrong and

God's enemy while we are innocent and righteous . . . rather
fight in the fear of God and in reliance on his grace alone . . . I
pray that in such a war our people by no means seek honour,
glory, land, booty, etc., but only the glory of God and . . .
defence of poor Christians and subjects . . . May Your
Sovereign Grace now go forth in God's name, . . . Our *Pater
Noster* shall follow you.

In the summer of 1532, the Emperor left Germany and was
not forcefully present again for nearly a decade. He could not
move far between November and March each year on account of
weather and transport difficulties; and his pressing concerns
were in areas widely separated geographically; the Turks in
eastern Europe, his Spanish territories in Italy, the attempt to
insist with the Pope on the calling of a Council, Spain itself, a
new war with France (in conspiracy with the German
Protestants), a revolt in the Netherlands, and the Turks again, in
Northern Africa. In the Emperor's long absence the Church
reforms in Germany spread more widely and pushed their roots
more deeply down. They went hand in hand with reforms in
Switzerland and Scandinavia and to a lesser extent in some parts
of France, and in England. Luther was free again to follow all
the normal demands on his time, university lectures (*Galatians,
Psalms, Genesis*), sermons in the town, Bible translation and activities in the whole field of strengthening the new or reformed
Church institutions. In spite of increasing illness, vigorous initiatives began to flow from him again. Sometimes he felt a
decline in energy and output; in 1534 he wrote to a friend
Schlaginhaufen: 'I do not know how the days pass without me
achieving what I would like and want to do. I live such a useless
life that I cannot stand myself.' However, inner desperation was
held at bay. Domestic life enlivened him.

On his return from the Coburg the family had welcomed him
home, his wife Katherine, four-year-old Hans, baby Lenchen,
Seeberger the handyman, Jerome Weller the tutor, and Aunt
Lena. Family life burgeoned. They took in a number of orphan
children. Students boarded. Relations and friends visited. The
garden did well and increased in size. Pig-keeping was undertaken. Katie brewed beer where lay brothers had brewed it in
days gone by. Eventually, in 1540, with a view to her

widowhood, Luther bought for her from her brother a little farm at Zölsdorf, south of Leipzig, and she spent a few weeks there in the year. The door into the old Priory, now the 'Lutherhaus', was ever open. In and out went young students, and old students, fellow lecturers and their families, preachers and pastors and their families, men from the Elector, men from the local Council, local residents, men and women with their various problems. And occasionally came representatives from afar, from England, even from the papacy, implicitly recognising Luther's new status.

The German prophet became a patriarch, and the living room was dominated by his presence. He enjoyed his beer and had a great mug with three rings on it, one 'the Ten Commandments', the next 'the Creed' and third 'the Lord's Prayer'. He boasted that he could encompass all three with ease. Once in 1535 away from home he wrote to his wife about some bad beer he had drunk 'which did not agree with me, so that I had to sing . . . I said to myself what good wine and beer I have at home, and also what a pretty lady, or lord.' On another occasion, he told Katie how well he was sleeping because of the beer but that he was 'sober as in Wittenberg'.

They sat down to meals sometimes a dozen and a half, or more. Luther would grow irritated as everyone came to hang on his word. Sometimes he was silent and all were silent. He was ill with ringing in the ear, violent headaches, stone. He was not often contradicted. Melancthon came in and would dissent, so quietly that no one heard. But Katie spoke up, and there was usually some young man jotting down the table talk – openly, and with the approval of the master who sometimes gave a specific direction about what to write. Graduate Johann Schlaginhaufen recorded in April 1532 that Luther came out with the remark:

'The time will come when a man will take more than one wife.' The doctor's wife responded, 'Let the devil believe that!' The Doctor said: 'The reason, Katie, is that a woman can bear a child only once a year while a husband can beget many.' Katie responded: 'Paul said that each man should have his own wife.' To this the doctor replied: 'Yes, "his own wife" and not "only one wife", – the latter is not what Paul wrote.' The doctor joked in this way for a considerable time, and finally the doctor's wife said: 'Before I put up with that, I'd rather go back to the convent and leave you and all our children.'

Luther enjoyed getting a spirited response out of his wife. She managed him and tolerated his wayward reactions, his sometimes coarse but not obscene conversation and his increasingly frequent illness in a way which some thought he hardly deserved. He would suddenly erupt with: 'The world is a gigantic anus, and I am a ripe stool, ready to drop from it.' Then in a moment he was back on the religious tack. When he was depressed and despairing he said that a word from 'Pomeranus or Philip or indeed my Katie' would bring him round: 'I was comforted as I realised that God was saying this through a brother who was speaking it from duty or from love.' The marriage was happy. They were real companions and friends to each other. 'There is no sweeter union than that of a good marriage. Nor is there any death more bitter than that which separates a married couple. Only the death of children comes close to this; how much this hurts I know from experience.'

In November 1531, Martin Luther the second was born. A month later, when Katie was finding the trials of the children too much, Luther passed the remark: 'God must be friendlier to me and speak to me in friendlier fashion than my Katie to little Martin.' Seven months later Katie was pregnant again, and Luther repeated a phrase which had been made before on the difficulties of a mother swiftly pregnant again while still nursing a previous infant: 'It is difficult to feed two guests, one in the house and the other at the door.'

In November 1532, Luther wrote to Amsdorf, now Pastor in Magdeburg: 'My Katie is ill from lack of sleep and close to her delivery.' In January 1533, he wrote to a friend in the Electoral service, Johann Loser, asking him to be godfather to his son 'whom God has given me this night by my dear Katie, so that he may come out of the old Adam's nature to the rebirth in Christ through the holy sacrament of baptism, and may become a member of sacred Christendom. Perhaps the Lord God may wish to raise a new enemy of the Pope or the Turk. I would very much like to have him baptised around the hour of vespers and then he will be a heathen no more.' He ended the letter 'at

1 a.m. in the night of 29 January 1533'. The new child was named Paul. The sixth and last child, Margaret, was born on 17 December 1534.

Marriage and its problems, including the trauma of marital breakdown, occupied Luther's mind much at this time: 'Marriage consists of these things: the natural desire of sex, the bringing to life of children, and life together with mutual fidelity. Yet the devil can so rupture marriage that hate is never more bitter.' Luther's solution was to start off in the right way. The breakdown 'comes from our beginning everything without prayer, and with presumption. A God-fearing young man who is about to be married should pray "Dear God, add thy blessing."' Veit Dietrich recorded this in the early spring of 1532 when he was soon to be married. 'So, dear Master Veit, do as I did. When I wished to take my Katie I prayed to God earnestly. You ought to do this too.'

The domestic scene was conjured up in many of Dietrich's entries. Luther's dog Tölpel 'watched with open mouth and motionless eyes, and Luther said "Oh if I could only pray the way this dog watches the food! All his thoughts are concentrated on the chunk of meat."' Another time, when Luther was 'writing or doing something else, my Hans may sing a little tune to me. If he becomes too noisy I tell him off a bit, and he continues to sing but does it more to himself and with a certain concern and uneasiness. This is what God wishes; that we be always cheerful, but reverently.'

There were the ordinary disagreements between husband and wife. '"Anger in the home is God's plaything; it's only like a slap or a cuff from him. Political fury, on the other hand, carries away wife and child through massacre and war . . . If I can put up with battles with the devil, sin and a bad conscience, then I can also put up with the irritations of Katie von Bora." This he said when he happened to get involved in a quarrel with his wife about some trifling thing.' But conscience still made a coward of him: 'Without the forgiveness of sins I can't stand a bad conscience at all; the devil hounds me about a single sin until the world becomes too small for me, and afterwards I feel like spitting on myself for having been afraid of such a small thing.'

Luther was aware of his own tiresome nature, and of his anger, yet often defended it. 'When asked by the younger

Margrave why he wrote with such vehemence he said, "Our
Lord God must precede a heavy shower with thunder and then
let it rain in a very gentle fashion so that the ground becomes
soaked through. To put it differently, I can cut through a willow
branch with a knife, but to cut through oak requires an axe and
wedge, and even with these one can hardly split it."' Again,
'Philip stabs, too, but only with pins and needles. The pricks are
hard to heal and they hurt. But when I stab I do it with a heavy
pike of the sort used for hunting boars.' Philip must have found
the pike stabs quite painful, too, presumably, but somehow they
expected such things from Luther and it was not intolerable.
They listened with some resignation as he held forth: 'I am free
from avarice, my age and bodily weakness protect me from
sensual desire, and I am not afflicted with hate or envy towards
anybody. Up to now only anger remains in me, and for the most
part this is necessary and just. But I have other sins that are
greater.'

   The other 'sins' were still grouped around lack of faith, and
the tendency to despair. In 1533 the Table Talk has 'My temptation is this, that I think I don't have a gracious God – Beware of
melancholy.' Life was unacceptably burdensome and he felt he
only kept on through a continually repeated act of turning to
God, and by spontaneity of action. 'No good work is undertaken with prudent reflection. It must all happen in a half-sleep.
This is how I was forced to take up the office of teaching. If I had
known what I know now, ten horses would not have driven me
to it.' But once he had been called to be a Professor, and notably
a Doctor, there must be no turning back. And now, in his fifties,
he was irreversibly involved in the shaping of new forms of
Church and State. They were not wholly new, since there had
always been local independence. But now this independence was
being given doctrines and institutions. And, although previously there had been translations of the Bible, the wide and
entirely new availability of the New Testament and later of the
whole Bible was central to them, and also entirely without
precedent.

   The translation of the Old Testament had taken a leap
forward during the five and a half months at the Coburg. Luther
pondered on the principles involved, and on the strictures of his
critics. In the 1520s, Duke George of Albertine Saxony had com-

missioned Luther's old enemy, 'the Goat' Emser, to produce a
competing translation of the New Testament, acceptable to
Catholics. Emser produced a translation which looked very like
Luther's, at first sight, with some of the same woodcuts by
Cranach; but also very like at second sight. Although Emser said
he had translated from the 'orthodox' Latin of Jerome's
Vulgate, in fact it soon became clear that he had lifted long
sequences straight from Luther's own translation. 'Just take the
two Testaments, Luther's and the scribblers, compare them;
you will see who is the translator in both of them. He has patched
and altered it in a few places . . . I had to laugh at the great
wisdom which so terribly slandered, condemned and forbade
my New Testament when it was published under my name, but
made it required reading when it was published under the name
of another,' wrote Luther in a piece about translating the Bible,
written at the Coburg. He enjoyed his running battles with Duke
George. An illustration to the first edition of his New Testament
had shown 'the whore of Babylon' (featured in the last book of
the New Testament), wearing a triple crown – clearly it was the
papal tiara. Old Frederick the Wise had received such a blast of
complaint from Duke George that in the next edition the head-
piece had to be cut down to a single crown. But later again,
Luther had the triple tiara reinstated.

In the text on translation Luther defended his addition of the
word 'alone' to St Paul's famous definition of justification by
faith. Luther said he was only bringing out the real sense of the
original Greek. Previous interpreters, including Aquinas, had
made the point before. St Paul did clearly mean 'by faith alone'.
Luther also defended his translation of the famous words in St
Luke's Gospel of the angel telling Mary that she would have a
child. Instead of 'Hail Mary full of grace', he had translated:
'Dear Mary, thou most gracious one.' In reply to critics, Luther
attacked the old literal translation: 'Tell me . . . when does a
German speak like that, "You are full of grace"? . . . He would
have to think of a keg "full of" beer, or a purse "full of" money.
So I have translated it "Thou gracious one" and then a German
can at least think his way through to what the angel means by
this greeting.'

Why should I talk so much about translating? . . . well, I

would need a year to say everything . . . I have never taken nor
looked for a single penny for it, nor made one. Neither have I
looked for any honour from it. God my Lord knows that.
Rather have I done it as a service to the dear Christians . . . I
have not just gone ahead any old how and disregarded the
exact wording of the original. Rather with my assistants I have
been very careful to see that where everything depends on a
single passage, I have kept to the original quite literally.

For a while in early 1531 the Bible Translation Committee
reassembled in a number of sessions to give a final revision to
the translation of the Psalms. Matthew Aurogallus, still the
Hebrew professor, was always there, and of course Philip
Melancthon, the Greek expert. The fourth member was the
Professor of Theology, Caspar Cruciger; and finally the Master
Secretary, Georg Rörer. In his Introduction to the subsequent
definitive draft of the Psalms in German, Luther expounded
their method again and threw out a challenge: 'We praised the
principle of at times retaining the words quite literally, and at
other times rendering only the meaning . . . if my critics are so
tremendously learned and want to display their skill, I wish they
would take that single and very common little Hebrew word,
chen, and give me a good translation of it. I will give fifty gulden
to him who translates this word appropriately and accurately
throughout the entire Scriptures.' Luther's translation of the
Bible survived in active use into the present century, praised by
Catholic and Protestant alike, and formative of the framework,
style and idiom of the German language.

Luther's mind continually came back to that which had been
central to his life for so long, the principal liturgical action of the
Christian Myth, the Mass. He wished to celebrate it only in the
context of the 'Word', the message of Jesus of Nazareth, Christ,
speaking through the Bible. But he did still wish to keep the
reformed Mass central. At the Coburg he wrote: 'Admonition
concerning the Sacrament of the Body and Blood of our Lord.'
It was a pastor's text, expounding the reasons why people
should go to Mass and take communion. While not a 'sacrifice'
as a good work, Mass was a 'sacrifice of thanksgiving'. He
pointed out that Christians of the first centuries called it
eucharist, thanksgiving, and the sacrament of thanksgiving. By it

Christians were reminded of grace; faith and love were stimulated. One should take part often. It was easy to put it off and say 'I will go next week', and then faith grew cold until one 'becomes completely bored of thinking about "his dear Saviour."' He had experienced this himself, putting it off from week to week: 'I broke out of the vicious circle and took part in the Sacrament, even without making confession' – he assured the reader that he had not been guilty of any gross sins. His approach here is indistinguishable from that of the most conventional Catholic. 'Where such faith is thus continually refreshed and renewed, there the heart is also at the same time refreshed anew in its love of neighbour and is made strong and equipped to do all good works and to resist sin and all temptations of the devil . . .' He repeated a facetious approach, also part of the traditional armoury of Catholic spiritual advisers. Someone who thought he did not need to take the sacrament had to be a saint already: 'Bells should be rung wherever you go on the street to tell of the saint coming.'

The subject of the eucharist was never far from his mind. He was still fighting to retain what he saw to be the true tradition and meaning as against other Reformers who wished to 'spiritualise' it, and against the practice of the papal authorities who had not modified their functional and canonical position. Bucer was the principal go-between with the other Reformers and found himself closer to Luther's view than he had at one time thought he was. Eventually, a new statement of reformed doctrine on the eucharist was agreed in the Concord of Wittenberg (1536). It preserved above all the idea of divine initiative in an objectively significant sacramental act; it was signed by a wide range of representatives except for the Anabaptists. The latter remained apart, retaining something like the position of many 'heretics' of the previous several hundred years; they continued to attract many converts and martyrs. They rejected infant baptism and declined to respect the authority of the local minister and Christian community, whether papal or Lutheran, trusting to a 'spiritual' and unstructured approach.

In his fundamental acceptance of a single visible Church with appointed ministers and a sacramental structure, the position of Luther was closer to that of Rome than to that of the Anabaptists. But little or no progress was being made towards an understanding with the papal authorities, and Luther was continually stung by the absence of any practical response to his criticism of received Church practices, criticism which had been admitted quite widely as justified. The Mass still seemed in effect to be bought, particularly in the case of money left in a will to pay for priests to say Masses for one's soul, sometimes hundreds or even thousands of Masses. The associated scandal of Indulgences remained untouched. The whole solid structure of the ordained priesthood and of the Mass as a propitiatory sacrifice remained unreformed along with its financial basis. Luther started off on another attempt to explain what was wrong and to denounce it in 'The Private Mass and the Ordination of Priests'.

He went once again into the basis of the celebration of Mass. One of the old names for Mass was *communion*, a direct contradiction of a *privatam missam*, the private Mass. Then he remembered incidents from his early life. The text became an angry tirade. He recalled how his fellow priests had in many cases become very casual, and how in Rome 'I heard, among other clever and coarse anecdotes at mealtimes, members of the papal curia laugh and boast about how some said Mass and with reference to the bread and wine spoke these words:

'"*Panis es, panis manebis; vinum es, vinum manebis*" – "Bread you are and bread you shall remain; wine you are, and wine you shall remain" – and with these words they elevated the host and the wine in the usual way. Now I was a young and particularly earnest devout religious . . . What was I to think of such words? . . . It also disgusted me very much that they could say Mass with such assurance and expertise and in such haste as if they were engaged in juggling. For before I had reached the Gospel reading [less than half way through the text], the priest next to me had concluded his Mass, and they called aloud to me: "*Passa, passa* – hurry up, hurry up."'

It was this 'juggling', this seemingly magical element that still offended Luther so deeply, and he criticised theological theories, enshrined in such a phrase as *ex opere operato*, referring in various ways to the automatic realisation of a sacrament when performed correctly by a properly ordained priest, with little or nothing said about the recipient and the faith he should have.

He also ridiculed the use of chrism (olive oil scented with balsam) in anointing, which was an obligatory part of the sacraments of baptism, confirmation and ordination. In place of the doctrine that only an ordained priest could perform a sacrament and in particular effect the 'miracle' of transubstantiation, Luther said that every baptised Christian was a true priest.

Sitting in the barber's chair at Wittenberg, one day, Luther was talking to his old friend Peter Beksendorf, who had been cutting hair and beards there for many years. The barber said he did not know how to pray. This was a challenge. In a few hours Luther had sketched out what amounted to a new version of the Little Catechism, presented more personally and biographically. His text on how to pray went through twenty editions. 'I will tell you as best I can what I do personally when I pray . . .' He was still using the well-tried texts of the old tradition, and his childhood, the Our Father, the Ten Commandments, the Creed. His recommendations differed little from what had been taught for centuries, only they were shorn of the incentives provided by Indulgences and the earning of merit, and of the fulsome prayers to and reliance on Mary the Mother of Jesus, and the Saints, which had often almost submerged the biblical texts and Creed. 'I take my prayer book and hurry to my room, or if it be the day and hour . . . to the church.' He recited to himself slowly, meaning the words, and seeing how they might apply in his day, the Our Father, the Ten Commandments and the Creed. 'Watch out for those deluding ideas: "Wait a little. I will pray in an hour; first I must attend to this."' Work could be prayer. But actual prayer still needed to be done, and the only way was not to put it off. Mornings and evenings were the times. Luther said people should make their own applications, and they were not to treat the actual words as essential – if they found personal prayers welling up of their own accord. The texts were not incantations. But 'a good and attentive barber keeps his thoughts, attention and eyes on the razor and hair and does not forget how far he has got with his shaving or cutting. If he wants to engage in too much conversation or let his mind wander or look somewhere else, he is likely to cut his customer's mouth, nose or even his throat . . . How much more does prayer call for concentration.'

At this time, Luther was preaching on St John's Gospel at the parish church. Though he was the reformed practical pastor, the incarnational theology which he preached still had about it something of the divine glow of the thirteenth- and fourteenth-century Rhineland movements, as he preached on Jesus of Nazareth, son of God, and man's nourishment: 'God has set his seal on the Son, who is man. He is the food, but also the grain merchant, the baker, the waiter, and the storehouse.' Christ 'tears all our hearts and eyes away from all bakeries and granaries, from all cellars, shops, fields, and purses, yes, from labour at all, and points them to Himself'. He was 'the bread, the dish and the plate that gives us imperishable food'. And he made 'one cake', *ein Kuchen* of us all. Divinity and humanity were 'one cake' in Christ.

Although Luther was not the Wittenberg parish priest, often it was the pastor talking, drawing on twenty-five years' experience of death beds, marriages, baptisms, and the giving of counsel in every kind of trouble. The counsel he gave was strongly rooted in a Saxon religion, five centuries old or more, itself stemming from a religious tradition of a millennium in the Mediterranean basin, the Roman and the Celtic lands. There was a traditional piety about it. But he was putting a renewed biblical stamp on it, practical, personal and with a mark of violent antithesis to some of the standard conventions. However, in situations of need his human sympathy was still expressed in tones of late medieval piety:

> That sickness of yours is God's fatherly, gracious chastise-
> ment . . . you should accept it with thankfulness as being sent
> by God's grace . . . how slight a suffering it is, even if it be
> sickness into death, compared with the sufferings of his own
> dear Son, our Lord Jesus Christ . . . You also know the true
> centre and foundation of your salvation from whom you are
> to seek comfort in this and all troubles, namely Jesus Christ,
> the cornerstone. He will not waver or fail us . . . He says 'Be of
> good cheer; I have overcome the world . . .' Let us therefore
> now rejoice with all assurance and gladness, and should any
> thought of sin or death frighten us, let us oppose it and lift up
> our hearts and say: 'Look, dear soul, what are you doing:
> Dear death, dear sin, how is it that you are alive and terrify

me? Do you not know that you have been overcome? Do you, death, not know that you are quite dead?'

These words came from a letter which began: 'My dearest mother, I have had a letter from my brother James about your illness.' It continued after the excerpt above: '"Be of good cheer" by such words and none other, let your heart be moved, dear mother', and she was to be thankful that she lived in a time when they no longer had to see Jesus as a Judge. He continually repeated the words 'Be of good cheer', and drew fresh comfort from them. And finally: 'All our children and my Katie pray for you; some weep, others say at dinner: "Grandma is very ill." God's grace be with us all. Amen. 20 May 1531. Your loving son. Martin Luther.'

The streets of Wittenberg were different. There were no friars and many fewer Massing priests as the castle church gradually transformed its liturgical life. Tensions were still there, some just as before, some new. The ideals and demands of religion were still there. There was still fear of death and judgement, heaven or hell. Obedience was still required to the great negatives, not to murder, slander, steal or take another man's wife; and God should still alone be worshipped, and parents should be honoured. The two last commandments were emphasised more than before. And here was both a new tension and a new opening. The preachers spoke more directly and practically of spiritual things and with less fantastic metaphors. And those who could read or could listen to someone reading aloud, began to know more of the foundation document of Christianity. Jesus of Nazareth became more 'available'; a wider vocabulary both of humanity and of divinity reached them. The Church services themselves, the prayers and the hymns and psalms were in their own language. Though still the stock-in-trade of professional priests, the rites were less distant, people went to communion more often, receiving the consecrated wine as well as the consecrated bread, both together being the sacrament of the Saviour, bringing his real presence.

There was some loss. The houses of vowed religious, though often so worldly and often denaturing the message of Jesus of Nazareth, had still in spite of everything spoken of the selfless

and encouraging commitment of their founders, and had
enabled some men and women to live out lives of inspiring
charity and holiness. The perpetual round of prayers of praise,
thanksgiving and petition in the churches had still spoken of
God's all-comprehending presence. The absence was not all
good. Some negative, primitive and cruel aspects of society
remained largely unchanged. Witches were still burnt. 'Heretics'
were still burnt, though the exact process by which they came to
be judged to be in heresy was different. In some towns torture
and judicial murder still thrived. Strange signs in the sky, the
birth of deformed children, the mentally handicapped, vivid
dreams all still roused inarticulate fear. But the beginning of a
new atmosphere was apparent. The mentally handicapped and
indigent old people who now inhabited the old Cistercian
monastery of Haine in Hesse was a symbol of a society taking a
new control over itself. It was not a simple process. In
Nuremberg the burghers had, already prior to the Reform
movement, taken over many aspects of life previously controlled
by the Church. Reform in that town led to more not less supervi-
sion of life by the Church in the form of the new Lutheran pastors.

The transformation of society that was just beginning, was
one still inside the old medieval unity. Religion continued to
dominate all. Indeed, a new religious authoritarianism was
already apparent, though more local, more 'moral' and more
Saxon. It was some generations before the first emphatic notes
of an alternative, agnostic, sometimes atheist ideology were to
be heard regularly, and two more centuries before it began to
burgeon to produce a quite new, secularised world. In that
world the Myth would have to find a new place, supported by its
followers, sometimes by states and wealthy institutions and
persons, for reasons ambiguous, not wholly welcome or at least
somewhat disharmonious with the message at the heart of the
Myth. Christianity spoke of a Founder who had been property-
less and had died as a criminal. The gospel message always
tended to be contradicted by its medium. But something like a
purification of Christianity, the beginning of its removal from
any final dependence on other social institutions, had now been
set on foot.

The Saxon streets of the 1530s witnessed the first bemused
blinkings of Christianity reborn, re-identifying itself from its

sources and wondering what its forms should be. There were still churches, the local community still met in them, there was still a local and apparently universal Church community. How to define it properly continued to worry Melancthon, and he continued to try to see the reformed local churches in Germany as bodies that should really be in communion with the rest of the western Church, centred in Rome. About this latter 'worldly' matter, Luther worried little. Preaching, administering the sacraments, praying, and doing one's job in life, here and now, was the task of a Christian – it was God's rather than Man's concern to see how the world aggregate of such activities hung together. He believed in the Church as a local, 'face-to-face' community of believers such as he had understood the early Christians to have formed. But a sense of need for conformity and consistency over a large geographical area did not go away. As the reformed Churches grew up, their leaders, independent of Rome, had regularly to take crucial decisions which were destined to serve as precedents and formers of fresh traditions in the future Protestant and Anglican Churches. And Luther's own theology of the Church did itself encourage the formation of new visible structures substituted for the Roman papal structure. His thoughts on the Church were 'high'. The Church was the bride of Christ, and although it was composed of a people scattered abroad throughout the world, the Church was 'one body with Christ through faith'; and this unity he loved to illustrate: 'The husband confides all his secrets to his wife; she has become part of his body, and she bears the keys at her side. In just this way Christ is the bridegroom and flesh of our flesh.'

The most notable and the most ironical aspect of the new Churches was that, in order to make themselves independent of the great units of Empire and Papacy, they fell, almost inevitably it seems, into the arms of the lesser local political units, the newly maturing nation states. The bonds of political authority bound ever tighter. And the doctrine of the 'Godly prince' led to conclusions far from welcome to Luther, notably the persecution of the Anabaptists. Essentially, he wanted to let these 'heretics' believe what they wished – faith could not be forced: 'It is not right that the poor people are so pitifully executed, burnt, . . . Let everyone believe what he likes . . . one should oppose them with Scripture and God's word. Fire achieves nothing.' But, exactly as with the medieval papacy, he found himself agreeing with the state that their heterodox beliefs were in effect 'seditious'.

In a Memorandum of 1536, he and Melancthon advised Philip of Hesse that Anabaptists by their rejection of government, private property and other social structures were in effect guilty of deliberate sedition, and this in spite of the hesitations of Philip of Hesse himself. Luther worried about it, and added to the Memorandum a recommendation to mercy. But the logic of his position was difficult to evade and behind his texts on 'The Infiltrating and Clandestine Preachers' (1532) lurked the same appeal to charges of sedition as had lurked behind his denunciations of Müntzer in the early 1520s. In the 1532 text he wrote: 'I have been told how these infiltrators worm their way to harvesters and preach to them in the field during their work, as well as to the solitary workers at charcoal kilns or in the woods.' Luther deprecated their going to work secretly. If they thought they had a call from God let them go about it publicly and go first to their local pastor. 'If God wants to accomplish something over and beyond this order of office and calling and to raise up someone who is above the prophets, he will demonstrate this with signs . . . When God does not do so we are to remain obedient to the office and authority already ordained.' The place of true spiritual authority was in practice difficult to identify with certainty when there were competing candidates. Special signs from God were needed if the, as it were, failed candidate was yet to be recognised.

The year before Luther and Melancthon wrote their Memorandum, there occurred the violent take-over of the town of Münster by Anabaptists, declaring they had guidance and revelation to unseat the government. There followed a year of cruel tyranny and chaos which looked like a justification of what had been written about the dangers of Anabaptists to the State. The majority Protestant position increasingly came to be identified with that of local political authority. Luther himself sometimes saw nothing to worry about and was happy with the situation. History was unknowingly adapted: 'Orders in the Church are civil positions which were taken over and made into spiritual offices', was recorded in the 'Table Talk'.

The irresistible drive towards local political sovereignty was present in England as elsewhere. Henry VIII found a minister of great efficiency, Thomas Cromwell, driven by a twofold wish to rationalise and then close down or transform the religious houses, or to produce a useful adjunct of property and wealth to his sovereign, all things which he could see being done in the German lands. But it was not that which precipitated a formal quarrel with the papacy itself. Henry needed to have a blessing and judicial seal from the Lords of the Myth, from the Pope and bishops, on his persecution of his ex-Queen and wife, Katherine of Aragon, aunt of the Emperor, to have a formal divorce from her and a recognition of his marriage to Anne Boleyn, on which he pinned his hopes for a male heir. Sexual gratification as such was not in question. The optional taking of numerous mistresses was conventional in every court from that of the Pope and Emperor downwards – Charles V was notorious for the number of his illegitimate children. A slight complication had indeed arisen in that Anne had held out for the position of Queen as long as she dare before admitting Henry to her bed. However, in any case, Henry needed his first marriage of twenty years standing to be nullified. His case was that since Katherine had previously been married to his brother Arthur who died aged fifteen, the Pope should never have given him permission to marry his deceased brother's wife. The Archbishop of Canterbury, William Warham, died in 1532. It was the King's opportunity. He had been granting swift promotion in diplomatic service abroad to a Cambridge don, who had suggested that the universities of Europe might be persuaded to give an opinion supporting the nullifying of his first marriage. Thomas Cranmer's name was sent to Rome as the best (and only) choice for the vacant See. He was duly appointed and as soon as possible held a Church Court hearing to annul the first marriage, and then officiated at the coronation of the greatly pregnant Anne.

In the course of the enquiries to the universities about Henry VIII's marriage problems, the query reached Wittenberg. In a letter to the Englishman, Robert Barnes, Luther wrote out an exposition of the problem. Unabashed that he found himself on the same side as the papacy (which had declined to grant a divorce) and of the conservative University of Louvain, which he commonly castigated, and out of step with most of the other

European universities which had all been bribed, he came down resoundingly with a judgement of authentic common sense and morality. A man might not thus easily disown his wife. 'Under no circumstances will the King be free to divorce the Queen to whom he is married, the wife of his deceased brother, and thus make the mother as well as the daughter into incestous women . . . Before I would approve of such a divorce I would rather permit the King to marry a second woman and to have, according to the examples of the patriarchs and kings, two wives or queens at the same time.' The possibility of bigamy or polygamy, following Old Testament example, had often been canvassed and Luther's suggestion was nothing unusual. 'At the risk of losing his salvation and under the threat of eternal damnation, the King is to be held responsible for retaining the Queen to whom he is married.' The marriage of a deceased wife's brother was forbidden in the Old Testament. But so was it to remain uncircumcised. 'The legislator Moses is dead and invalid for us. Matrimony is a matter of divine and natural law. In cases where the divine and the positive laws contradict each other, the positive law must yield to the divine law.' Luther's grasp of the legality and the morality of the situation was integrated and convincing. He shone a largely unwelcome light on the matter.

In spite of this rebuff, Henry and his ministers from time to time made overtures in the direction of the Schmalkaldic League, seeking for a satisfactory alignment in relation to the Emperor or to ecclesiastical developments. An attempt was made to get Melancthon to go to England, and a similar attempt was made by the French government to get him to go to France. He was a scholar of prestige who wanted to keep things together and could be relied on not to make trouble. Luther was consulted on both occasions and tried to persuade the Elector to let Melancthon go, but the Elector had no special reason for sending hostages to either country, and Melancthon had to remain in Saxony. Henry wanted to be invited to join the Schmalkaldic League; and he wanted to deign to join it, without any doctrinal strings attached. Protracted negotiations finally led to a nil result in 1536, when the Elector and the League as a whole continued to insist on formal assent to the Confession of

Augsburg, but also now to the new Articles agreed at the Concord of Wittenberg in that same year.

Still trying to agree on a definition of the Eucharist, theologians over a wide range of background had finally agreed in the Wittenberg Concord that 'with the consecrated bread and wine, the body and blood of Christ are truly and substantially present, shown forth and received', also that 'the sacrament has its authentic value in the Church and does not depend on the status of either the minister or the recipient'. Soon after the English delegates had declined to agree to the doctrinal demands, the horrific news arrived of Anne Boleyn's execution. The Elector was glad the English had left the Continent empty-handed, and that he had not agreed to Melancthon's trip. Luther himself had been mystified by the varying attitudes of Robert Barnes, at one moment apparently a crypto-ambassador of Henry VIII and the next moment in terror for his life. In a letter to Thomas Cromwell he showed he was as good as the next man at saying little in the nicest possible way. However, as a reformer Cromwell could be encouraged: 'You are capable of accomplishing very many things throughout the whole kingdom, and with the Most Serene Lord King you can do much good. I do pray and shall pray to the Lord to strengthen abundantly his work . . . Through Doctor Barnes, Your Lordship, whom I commend to the Father's mercy, will become thoroughly acquainted with the situation here. Wittenberg, 9 April 1536. Your Lordship's dedicated Martin Luther, Doctor.' More to the point for Luther had been William Tyndale's achievements. But now in this year came the news of his violent death in Brussels, having been arrested for heresy by agents of the local Council in the Imperial city.

Tyndale had come to Wittenberg for a short time in 1525, going on to Cologne and then to Worms where he completed the printing of his translation into English of the New Testament. He finally settled in Antwerp in a house belonging to the association of English merchants who had been his patrons in London and enabled him to start on the translation work. In Antwerp he remained translating the Old Testament and reissuing the New, for which he provided Introductions inspired by Luther until 1536 when he was lured out of the protection of the merchants' house. Tyndale's work and martyrdom was one of similar events throughout northern Europe, news of which kept reaching Luther. Reforms progressed in Iceland, Scotland, Scandinavia and Denmark.

In 1536 Luther heard of things in Switzerland which he liked more than the Zwinglianism of previous years. Young Jean Calvin had arrived in Geneva, and published the work which he had been writing to justify and reorientate himself after his conversion to the reforming camp. A Renaissance humanist of formidable ability, he proceeded to provide a detailed *Summa* – something much more substantial than Melancthon's Commonplaces. He called it *Institutio Religionis Christiani*, and had it published in Geneva. Later, in 1539, Luther read with delight Calvin's reply to Jacopo Sadoleto, a Catholic Reformer who was trying to persuade the Church in Geneva to return to papal obedience. Calvin's reply, from Strassburg, was a sign of a new generation of intellectually well-based reformers.

The University continued to be at the heart of Luther's daily life and if the plague kept returning so did good reasons for celebrations and feasts. For most of the decade he was regularly reappointed as Dean of the Theology Faculty. In that capacity he wrote in 1535 to Melancthon, at that time living away from Wittenberg with other members of the University on account of the plague. There was to be a disputation, graduation ceremony and a feast in honour of Jerome Weller:

'Here are the disputation papers, excellent Philip, which we would kindly ask you to distribute to the theological candidates . . . I have been suffering from diarrhoea.' He was weak, could not sleep, and there was no beer in the town. 'In the last two days I have had fifteen bowel movements.' To Jonas, Luther wrote: 'The chief cook, our Lord Katie, asks you to accept this coin and to buy for us poultry or other birds, or whatever in the airy kingdom of our feathered friends is subject to the dominion of man (and may be eaten) – but for God's sake no ravens . . . bring rabbit or similar meaty delicacies . . . My Katie has brewed seven Quartalia . . . into which she has mixed thirty-two Scheffel of malt . . . She hopes it will turn out to be good beer. Whatever it is, you and others will be tasting it!' Then came some blustery comment on the international news of the Emperor, about Africa and Constantinople, sharp remarks on their mixing the old religious styles with their fighting, and some classical references to Terence, and finally: 'My Katie cordially and reverently greets you and all your family. But hold a minute, if my wife greets you, I, in turn greet your wife. What is sauce for the goose is sauce for the gander. Farewell in the Lord! 4 September 1535. Yours, Martin Luther.'

In the daytime he could rejoice. At night-time the horrors came. But the next day he could share them with his family and house guests. Dietrich noted down in the spring of 1533, with Luther's own approval, as a source of comfort to others who suffer such terrors:

> I have heard no argument from men that persuaded me, but the bouts I have engaged in during the night have become much more bitter than those in the daytime . . . External temptations only make me proud and arrogant – as you see in my books that I despise my enemies. I take them for fools. But when the devil comes he is the lord of the world and confronts me with strong objections . . . I will defy Duke George and all the lawyers and theologians, but when these knaves, the spirits of evil come, the Church must join in the fight . . . Whether God wishes to take me hence now or tomorrow, I want to leave this bequest, that I desire to acknowledge Christ as my Lord. This I have not only from the Scriptures but also from Experience, for the name of Christ often helped me when nobody else could . . .

It was at this time that he recollected how Staupitz had said he did not understand him and reminisced about the old days.

> When I was sad and downcast, Staupitz started to talk to me at table and asked: 'Why are you so sad?' I replied, 'Well, what on earth can I do?' Then he said, 'You don't know how necessary this is for you; otherwise nothing good will come of you.' He himself didn't understand what he said, for he thought I was too learned and that I would become haughty if I remained free from spiritual trials. But I took his words to be like Paul's, 'A thorn was given me in the flesh to keep me from being too elated . . . the Lord said to me "My power is made perfect in weakness" '.

Luther was often still obsessed with thoughts of what had flowed from his actions – was it really all right? He comforted himself with having sincerely answered a 'Call', words from his superiors and his brothers in the monastic community. He made this an example for all life: 'One should be glad to have a brother who says "Brother, do this, for it is the call of your superior or of God (which is a call of faith) or of an equal (which is a call of love)". Nobody realised how great and necessary a place was occupied by the calling, by saying to someone "Do this".'

These were traditional Christian precepts, redeployed to show that at their heart was not a threatening God but an all loving, all understanding God. It still seemed like thin ice, sometimes. It was still strange to sit in the living room, to live with his wife and children in the old Friary buildings. So much to be done always, so much still wrong, but so much about it also seemed right. News from England came that reformers there were still accepting the idea of the unattended private Mass. He wrote to Jonas (October 1535): 'I am thinking about putting theses together against the private Mass . . . My lord Katie sends greetings; she drives the wagon, takes care of the fields, buys and puts cattle out to pasture, brews, etc. In between she starts to read the Bible, and I have promised her fifty guilden if she finishes before Easter.' Then a sentence in German: 'she is very serious'; then back to the Latin used in all letters except to those who might not understand it, officials of State and Church, his wife and, in the past, his father and mother.

The depression syndrome led to bouts of exaggerated pleasure or displeasure. At the Coburg, Luther had written: 'The world hates me and I hate the world.' Feelings of hopelessness and despair continued to invade him, and bursts of great anger. The mood became particularly unnerving, to himself and to others, when he was expected to act as an Authority. In 1536, when the theologians gathered for the meeting at Wittenberg, having had to come from Eisenach and Torgau because Luther was not well enough to go there, he lectured them like schoolchildren, himself almost intolerably overcome with irritation. Then, suddenly, the 'Concord' was worked out and accepted, and he was transfigured with joy, and a feast was laid on.

But if it was still possible to think of trying to work out an agreement with other reformers, towards Rome his mind had become totally closed and what seems like compulsive abuse was directed at them. And any mention of Erasmus was liable to lead to a string of expletives. Yet if the abuse was compulsive, he would still think through the arguments again, as he did on 1 April in 1533 when, so Conrad Cordatus told in his 'Table Talk', Luther spent most of the day re-reading Erasmus's prefaces to the New Testament. Luther found them pernicious: 'He obscures the authority of Paul and John.' But he went on puzzling about it. In 1537, Lauterbach said:

He sat at the table after breakfast and after some reflection he wrote on the table with chalk: 'Substance and words – Philip. Words without substance – Erasmus. Substance without words – Luther. Neither substance nor words – Karlstadt.' Philip Melancthon came in later and said that too much was attributed to him, and that 'words' must also be attributed to Luther.

Elector John died in 1533 and was succeeded by his son John Frederick, educated by Spalatin, deeply devoted since adolescence to Luther. The Pope died the following year. The choice fell again on a man from one of the wealthy Italian families, the Farnese this time, and an old man too. But Paul III immediately applied himself seriously to the task of calling a Council, which Clement VII had continually postponed. He summoned it to Mantua, failing to grasp the extent to which this choice of a city in Italian speaking lands could not be acceptable to the Germans. He sent off an ambassador, Vergerio, round Europe to prepare the way. Luther wrote to Jonas on 10 November 1535:

Suddenly out of the blue the Legate of the Roman Pope visited this town as well. Now he is with the Margrave. This man seems to fly rather than ride. How I wished you had been here! The legate invited me and Pomer for breakfast, since I had declined an evening meal on account of having a bath. I went and ate with him up at the castle. But I am not allowed to write to anyone about what I said. During the whole meal I played the proper Luther.

Vergerio was surprised to see Luther, looking so young at
fifty-two, and remarks were made on both sides about pre-
parations made at the barber's to present himself as still lively.
Luther went the short distance up the street to the castle by
coach with Bugenhagen, and dressed not in academicals but in
his best Renaissance hose, short coat and fur. The Legate had to
listen to Luther telling him that a Council was indeed necessary
for the papists, but that the evangelicals did not need one as they
were already reformed. Vergerio was, on the whole, agreeably
surprised by Luther, with the quiet timbre of his voice, though
he found the eyes trying. Years later he became a Protestant
himself.

Luther was increasingly often ill. He had phlebitis in the leg,
and a vein had been opened, so that he could bleed himself at
will. He felt ill most mornings, and suffered increasingly from
the vertigo which had begun ten years previously. The fantasy
of death began to take on more credible and personal
characteristics. Luther grew more philosophical about it, joking
more gently and less melodramatically about himself as too old.
To Caspar Muller in January 1536, he wrote: 'I too am sick with
cough and catarrh. But my worst affliction is that the sun has
shone on me for a long time, a vexation which, as you well know,
is common, and certainly many people die of it!' He apologised
for not taking a particular student in to the household as
boarder, there was no room left. Then he spoke of the lately
dead Katherine of Aragon: 'We poor beggars, the theologians in
Wittenberg, are the only exceptions who would like to maintain
her in royal honour . . . Tell my brother that my cough and his
silence kept me from answering him! Give my greetings to his
black hen . . .' After a further reference to the tiresome shining
of the sun, he continued: 'I am quite rough and coarse, large,
grey, green, overburdened . . . sometimes in order to survive I
have to force myself to make a joke . . . Greet all good
gentlemen and friends. 19 January 1536. Doctor Martin
Luther.'

The Schmalkaldic League determined to meet at Schmalkalden
in a full session to work out its response to Pope Paul III's sum-
moning of a Council. Although ill with heart trouble, stones and
frequent dizziness, Luther worked out a first draft of Articles for
the Conference. On the way there, early in 1537, it was Jonas not

Luther who was taken ill and had to be left behind at Torgau. When he reached Altenberg, Luther wrote him a cheering letter with the latest information and hopes for his recovery, and a request that Jonas, who was to return to Wittenberg, should greet his family 'and also the Pomeranian Rome and his little Quirites', the little Bugenhagens. Luther and all of them were being very well entertained; they were playing a game of verses, and Luther sent his attempt with his letter: 'Master Philip, that is Homer, sends his too . . . 1 February, at Altenberg, at 8.00 p.m. Yours, Martin Luther, Doctor.'

But then, at Schmalkalden, it was Luther's turn. He had trouble passing water. By the end of February he was in great trouble, but finally he had relief and wrote to his wife the next day: 'Not one little drop of water passed from me; I had no rest nor did I sleep, and I was unable to retain any food or drink. In summary I was dead; I commended you, together with the little ones, to God and to my gracious Lord, since I thought I would never again see you in this mortal life . . . But soon several litres passed from me, and I feel as if I were born again.' He gave her directions about renting some horses. Then there was a further relapse. Luther made a confession of his sins to Bugenhagen, received absolution and prepared himself for death. However, eventually he passed six stones. He then began to get better but the convalescence was lengthy.

Back at home on 21 March, Luther wrote to Spalatin: 'By God's grace I gradually recuperate and learn to eat and drink again. Yet my thighs, knees and bones are still shaky and are unable so far to carry my body . . . My Katie is sorry she brought nothing in the line of a present for your daughters . . . She raves about your thoughtfulness and your great kindness.'

From now on, Luther was an old man. In the seven years since Augsburg, he had become an institution. The river of reform was in full flood, destroying as it went and providing water for new growth. Luther could not control it, and he was no longer by any means the only reformer of stature. Men of the hour burgeoned in every country. Tyndale's English Bible and Calvin's great systematic theology were the new wonders. But Luther was revered everywhere as the principal and original begetter. His own complete Bible translation had finally been published in 1534. But the great thing was that he had done what had been thought to be impossible. He had survived as a heretic and had provided a re-presentation of Christianity which more and more people began to see to be right. He was a nuisance to himself, and to his friends, and sometimes made his own insights difficult to grasp, making them seem, with his bombast, less convincing than they truly were. But, briefly, who could really believe in a God whose love was full of threats and sly reckoning? Man was made for better things. He was made for faith in the incomprehensible but all loving God, seen and embraced in his Word.

CHAPTER SEVENTEEN

The Old Man

'I am a veteran who has served his time and would prefer to spend his time in the garden, enjoying the geriatric pleasures of watching God's wonders in the blooming of the trees, flowers and grass, and in the mating of the birds!' wrote Luther to Justus Jonas on 8 April 1538. The note of weariness and longing for death was becoming more frequent. He was seldom in good health and became impatient for the end: 'I am more dead than alive. I am overwhelmed with writing letters and books; theological lectures and the stone, and much else weigh me down.' But there was content, too. Later in the same letter to Link of 20 June 1543, he wrote: 'I desire a good hour for passing on to God. I am content, I am tired and nothing more is in me. Yet see to it that you pray earnestly for me, that the Lord take my soul in peace. I do not leave our congregations in poor shape; they flourish in pure and sound preaching, and they grow day by day through many excellent and most sincere pastors.'

Still alive at the end of the following year in a letter to James Propst, he was back again to a certain despair of the world: 'Yes, I am sluggish, tired, cold – that is I am an old and useless man. I have finished my race. It remains only that the Lord call me to my fathers, and that my body be handed over to decomposition and the worms. I have lived enough, if one may call it living. Please pray for me that the hour of my passing will be pleasing to God, and a blessing for me . . . It looks as if the whole world, too, has come to its passing.'

But these final years were to last nearly a decade and were again crammed with activity, even though undertaken in the face of great weariness and ill-health.

Before midsummer 1537, Luther had recovered sufficiently from the attack of stone to be able to return to work. The

University lectures on Genesis were resumed. Then it also fell to him to start regular preaching in the parish church on a Saturday. Bugenhagen, the parish priest, had been asked for by King Christian III of Denmark to assist the reforms there. The Elector agreed that he should go, on condition that his parish duties were properly covered. The Saturday preaching originated in a suggestion of Luther's in *The German Mass* (1526), for a preaching service on that day based on St John's Gospel. So at the beginning of July 1537, Luther started on St John, chapter 1, in Wittenberg parish church. Bugenhagen was supposed to be back by the autumn, but it was two years before he returned. From time to time Luther was too ill or too tired, but apart from that he preached every Saturday on this his favourite text. It was the incarnation which held him. He got into his stride and was only on chapter 4 when Bugenhagen returned, even then continuing for a few weeks in order to reach the end of the chapter. It was Christ, 'the God-den man', whom he was never tired of propounding. In his opening sermons he took John's chosen title of Christ, 'the Word', and spoke of the tumultuous feelings of man's heart to provide some analogy of God's own internal 'conversation' in the Trinity. Luther drew again on his early studies of Augustine in developing such ideas:

> Suppose it were possible to peer into each other's heart, I into yours and you into mine . . . We could either impart the whole content of our heart to each other out of love, or, to use a current expression, we would devour and choke each other out of anger. Now if it is true that I cannot fully express the thoughts of my heart, how many thousand times less will it be possible for me to understand or to express the Word or conversation in which God engages within his divine being . . . God, too, in his majesty, is pregnant with a Word or a conversation in which he engages with himself in his divine essence and which reflects the thoughts of his heart . . . It is an invisible and incomprehensible conversation.

Luther also published at this time his *Three Symbols or Creeds of the Christian Faith* to develop the assertion of traditional Christian doctrine in the Schmalkaldic Articles. Luther calls on the early Fathers to expound the Trinity, comparing the Father to the sun, the Son to its brilliance and the Holy Spirit to its heat.

By the end of the preaching stint, Luther was drawing on a less speculative seam of traditional teaching, personal and practical, commenting on the incident of the Woman at the Well:

> When God wants to speak and deal with us, he does not avail himself of an angel but of parents, of the pastor, or of my neighbour. This puzzles and blinds me so that I fail to recognise God, who is conversing with me through the person of the pastor or father. This prompts the Lord Christ to say in the text: 'If you knew the gift of God, who it was that is saying to you "Give me a drink" then I would not be obliged to run after you and beg for a drink.'

He seemed unable to leave the incarnation alone. At the University on 11 June 1539, he presided over a Disputation on 'The Word was made Flesh', the purpose of which was to show the inadequacy of elementary logic in theological matters. Again, he was harping back to his thought of thirty years ago.

The pulpit, the lecture podium, and above all the home continued to be Luther's theatre of operation. At home he still found time for numerous interests. Music was increasingly a delight and a refuge. He wrote and published a Latin piece in Praise of Music: 'Music has often stirred me . . . so that I wanted to preach . . . Nothing on earth has greater power to make the sad joyful, the joyful sad, the despondent courageous, to incline the arrogant to humility and to lessen envy and hatred'. An ability to sing was an essential qualification for a schoolmaster, 'otherwise I would not look at him'.

Luther's favourite composer was that now newly famous late medieval musician Josquin des Prés: 'A very special master . . . the notes have to do what he wants them to do; the other musicians have to do what the notes want.' Josquin was not well known in Germany and it was Luther's particular musical perception to pick him out. Some thought the new polyphonic style more for the court than the church. But Luther delighted in the new developments. 'One single voice continues to sing the tenor, while at the same time many other voices play around it, exulting and decorating it in exuberant strains, and as it were leading it forth in a divine roundelay,' wrote Luther in the Preface to Georg Rhau's *Symphoniae Jucundae*, 1538. Rhau was at St Thomas's church, Leipzig, where Bach would be and it was he who had composed the Mass for the opening of Luther's Leipzig debate with Eck. In the last years of his life Luther tried his own hand at a motet, using for the melody a *cantus firmus* of the Gregorian plainchant which he loved so much. The Latin words were *Non moriar sed vivam'* – 'I shall not die but live and declare the works of the Lord'. It was this text of hope which Senfl had sent back to him, set to music, as a word of encouragement when Luther had written him in melancholy mood from the Coburg asking him to set 'In peace I will lay me down and sleep'.

Complicated Latin motets were suitable for the well educated. But in the ordinary church services Luther had continued to follow the pattern he set in the twenties, providing German words and music which were simple to sing and hear. A stream of words and musical compositions had continued to flow from him to the printer. He wrote a Christmas carol for his children in 1534. He did a setting of the Our Father in 1539. In general it can be said that Luther, using the rich musical culture that he inherited, set the words of the Bible to music and originated the church chorale.

Music and grammar were bracketed together as the two disciplines in which Luther wished his son to progress further, when sending sixteen-year-old Hans up the river to Torgau (26 August 1542) to the flourishing school there run by a graduate of Wittenberg, one Marcus Crodel. Luther had become by now the traditional German parent, and mirrored his own father's mixed jocularity and severity. A nephew, Florian von Bora, was sent up along with Johann Luther. Crodel was told 'be very strict with this one'. Then, two days later, there was an angry letter from Luther demanding a thrashing for Florian for his misdeed in stealing a knife from Johann and then denying it. Luther had had the story from an indignant Paul Luther on his return from accompanying the two older boys.

Two days later there was another emotional letter from Luther to Crodel:

> . . . Keep quiet to my son about what I am writing . . . my daughter Magdalen is ill and almost in her last hour; in a short while she might depart to her true Father in heaven . . . She longs so much to see her brother . . . They loved each other so much; perhaps his arrival could bring her some

relief. I am doing what I can so that later the knowledge of having left something undone does not torture me . . . Without giving Johann any reason, tell him to fly back in this carriage. He will return to you soon, when Magdalen either has fallen asleep in the Lord or has recovered.

Thirteen-year-old Magdalen died a few days after Johann's return. Her parents were distraught, although also comforted by the way their daughter had accepted the foreseen death. Luther wrote to Jonas: 'Magdalen had, as you know, a mild and lovely disposition and was loved by all. Praised be the Lord Jesus Christ who has called, elected and made her glorious.' Still upset a few weeks later, he wrote to Papst: 'She died having total faith in Christ . . . I loved her so very much.' He still could not tame his emotions and confessed to 'a certain threatening murmur against death'. In between the usual sagas of the family – Katie complained in 1539 that Luther had patched his trousers with a piece out of his son's – there was still, never far below the surface, the fantasy of leaving it all and departing from Wittenberg. It was to come out fiercely again before the end.

There was plenty on Luther's desk. He had still to be studying the nature of the Church and the style of authority. His text 'On the Councils and the Churches' written in German was published in 1539. He concentrated on the first four centuries, and deprecated the need for and importance of later councils: 'A council has no power to establish new articles of faith, even though the Holy Spirit is present. Even the apostolic council in Jerusalem introduced nothing new in matters of faith but rather held that which St Peter concludes in Acts 16 . . . the article that one is saved without the laws, solely through the grace of Christ.' However, he thought there might be a place for a council when something like the Pope's tyranny had to be abolished. So there might be a need for a council now, even though there was a risk it would just be an occasion for arguing about the order of speaking and for debauchery. A Free Christian Council in Germany might be a good thing 'if we did our part in it and sincerely sought God's honour and the salvation of souls', and so it might have an echo in other countries. But the local Church was what really mattered. They could have little councils, 'small and young councils, that is parishes and schools, and propagate

St Peter's article in every possible way'. He elaborated at length on what he had been saying for the previous fifteen years: 'The holy Christian people are recognised by their possession of the holy word of God . . . the holy sacrament of baptism . . . the holy sacrament of the altar . . . by the holy possession of the sacred cross. They must endure every misfortune.' Its publication showed that Luther was still in full possession of all his intellectual abilities. Other writings gave rise to the query whether the extreme anger and spleen manifested in them indicated a genuine failing of his personality, and whether he was not seriously ill. But the two things seemed to go side by side, both a continuing marked intellectual penetration and an almost desperate fury. Undoubtedly he was in pain much of the time, with head pains, heart trouble, aches in his limbs, and stone. There seems no doubt that his mind remained essentially clear, but that his inborn sensitivity was often having to digest more than it could really cope with, and that the habit of anger led to ever more violent outbursts.

Suspicion continued to be an ingredient of Luther's relationship with other reformers, though he often tried hard to be fair to them and to be at one with them. The Wittenberg Concord which, at the time and since, had a somewhat ambiguous air about it, was a challenge. On returning to Strassburg in 1536, Capito and Bucer hatched a plan to publish Luther's collected works, which was also a plan to bring in some much needed cash. But Luther was not enthusiastic. On 9 July 1537 he wrote to Capito: 'I am quite cool about it . . . For I acknowledge none of them to be really a book of mine, except perhaps *On the Bound Will* and the *Catechism*.' Capito had sent the Luthers a gold ring, and Katie had been delighted but now was furious that it had been stolen. Martin and Katie had been convinced that the ring was 'a good omen and token of the fact that your church really is one with ours. And so the woman is crushed'. All the same 'we have total and sincere hope regarding unity'.

More than two years later, Luther had failed to answer a number of letters from Capito and Bucer at Strassburg, and Luther implied to the latter that he simply could not manage to write: 'So assume that you have been promptly answered each time you write to me. For I hope there is real unity of heart between us . . . Greet reverently Herr Johann Sturm and Jean Calvin, I have read their books with special pleasure.' The address was to 'the illustrious man, Herr Martin Bucer, Bishop of the Church at Strassburg, a true servant of the Lord, my dearest brother in Christ'. Nearer home there was less peace.

Karlstadt was no longer a trouble. Professor of the Old Testament in Basel in the thirties and giving Henry Bullinger the same troubles that Luther had suffered in Wittenberg, he finally died of the plague in 1541. But an old pupil of Luther's took his place at Wittenberg of local, least loved ally. Agricola began to preach and write a variation of the teaching about the Law of the Old Testament, virtually rejecting it, instead of giving it the essential place it had in Paul's and Luther's dialectic of Law and Grace. The resultant disagreement and quarrel was violent and led to Agricola's leaving Wittenberg. It brought out the worst in Luther. He could not bear to see God's revelation being torn apart, but it looked also as if he could not bear being crossed. Other members of the Theology Faculty felt he was being too brutal to Agricola, and a movement arose to elect Agricola Dean of the Faculty. However, it failed, and the field was held by a short piece of Luther's *Against the Antinomians* (1539), drawn up by him as a form of retraction by Agricola but containing also Luther's complaint: 'Good heavens, I should at least be left in peace by my own people. It is enough to be harassed by the papists. One is tempted to say with Job and Jeremiah, "I wish I had never been born."' In the end Agricola did finally recant and was reinstated in the good graces of the political and University authorities, though he was no longer in Wittenberg.

Not all the writing in 1539 was negative. Luther had been unable to stop the drive to collect and publish his German works, and eventually wrote an Introduction to a collection published in Wittenberg under the guidance of Kaspar Cruciger and Georg Rörer. In his Introduction he wrote ironically: 'My consolation is that in time my books will lie forgotten in the dust anyhow', and the Scripture which he had translated would be read. But he took the opportunity to tell people the correct way to study theology, which was not so far from the advice he had given Spalatin in regard to reading Scripture more than twenty years before. Prayer came first:

> Despair of your reason and understanding . . . kneel down in
> your little room and pray to God with real humility and
> earnestness that he through his dear Son may give you his
> Holy Spirit, who will enlighten you, lead you and give you un-
> derstanding.

Then:

> Meditate, that is not only in your heart but also externally by
> actually repeating and comparing oral speech and literal
> words of the book . . . so that you may see what the Holy
> Spirit means . . . do not grow weary or think you have done
> enough when you have read, heard and spoken them once or
> twice and that you then have complete understanding. You
> will never be a particularly good theologian if you do that, for
> you will be like untimely fruit which falls to the ground before
> it is half ripe.

> Thirdly, there is the real touchstone, temptation, attack,
> *Anfechtung.* These 'teach you . . . to experience how right, how
> true, how sweet, how lovely, how mighty, how comforting
> God's Word is wisdom beyond all wisdom . . . As soon as God's
> Word takes root and grows in you, the devil will hurry you, and
> will make a real doctor of you and by his attacks will teach you to
> seek and love God's Word. I myself (if you will permit me, mere
> mousedirt, to be mingled with pepper) am deeply indebted to
> my papists that through the devil's raging they have beaten, op-
> pressed, and distressed me so much . . . They have made a fairly
> good theologian of me.' Six years later, Spalatin and Rörer got
> the publication of Luther's Latin works under way and per-
> suaded Luther to write the Introduction which provided confir-
> mation for and remains an important witness of various events
> in Luther's life.
> Although stormy rather than peaceful, the heart of Luther's
> theology remained something personal, inward and spiritual.
> Luther was still the man who had responded in his early thirties
> to the Rhineland mystic Tauler. And there is a real sense in
> which he can be seen as part of a vast movement which was
> always starting up again in the Church to seek out the heart of
> Christianity, what the Germans called its *Innerlichkeit*, its in-
> wardness. Inevitably, the protagonists of such movements

compared the spiritual teaching and ideals which they un-
covered with the daily practice of the functionaries. The
movement then became one of practical reform, as well as of
inner experience. Italy had seen many such movements. During
the 1520s and 30s there was a new outcrop. They were mixed
movements of priests and lay people, often including women,
devoted to following a strict rule of life in society. In Rome,
Cardinal Cajetan was a member of a group called the Oratory of
Divine Love. Many other groups grew up, and new Orders were
started, included a new reformed version, the Capuchins, of St
Francis's famous Order of Brothers. The new theology, that of
Luther and of others began to be read. A lay theologian, Contarini was convinced that much of Luther's theology was
authentic, having himself had an experience which linked with
Luther's. 1530–40 was the time of the pre-history of what came
to be known as the Counter Reformation, a reformation within
the papal Church itself. In 1540, the Spaniard Ignatius of Loyola
and his companions visited the Pope and official recognition
was granted to their Society of Jesus.

Part of this genuine movement of reform was Pope Paul III's
determination to call a Council and to undertake a serious consideration of all the ills in the Church. To this end he set up a
commission to report to him. The result was the secret Report
Consilium de Emendenda Ecclesia. It was a step forward from all
previous reform documents. For the first time reform was not
bracketed with extirpation of heresy and the defeat of the Turks,
but was unashamedly itself. The authors felt themselves to be
greatly daring in setting at the head of their analysis of the
troubles a 'false theory', that the Pope owns every benefice in the
Church and may sell them without doing wrong. A flurry of
apology and justification surrounded this daring statement.
Then the text moved on to a formidable list of reformanda: inadequate procedures for selection and training of priests,
pastoral responsibilities allotted to those living elsewhere
(Campeggio as Bishop of Salisbury would be an example – but
Rome was full of such men who used a part of their salary to pay
a vicar to look after their diocese while they did other more congenial work in Rome); the bequeathing of benefices in wills especially to the children of priests, pluralism, failure to correct
those who make money by hearing confessions. Higher educa-

tion was to be looked to. The Orders had to be reformed. Occasionally, the voice became uncertain with the realisation that the Roman bureaucracy would need to find an income from somewhere. The text ended with a sequence on the public scandal of the Massing priests, ill-tempered, wearing tattered vestments as they officiated in St Peter's. Finally, the spectacle, often referred to, of Roman hostesses who 'walk about like honourable matrons or ride on mules and following them even in high noonday, come the most prominent of cardinals and priests'. There were seven signatories, four of them cardinals, Contarini, Carafa, Sadoleto and the Englishman Reginald Pole. It was a secret report, but within weeks copies were circulating.

Luther received a German translation of it in 1538. It seemed to him only another way of delaying the Council which had been promised so often. There was little about doctrine in it, and it seemed to be a mere tampering with the structures. He wrote to Nicholas Hausmann: 'Those monstrosities of the Roman cardinals will be published both in Latin and German. But the malice of the matter and the wickedness of those people are beyond indignation and words . . . I am sending the papal coat of arms which I have drawn or caused to be drawn, [a cardinal's hat over a Judas bag]. The report seemed a mere piece of hypocrisy to Luther, who published it in full with a brief introduction by himself and sharp remarks in the margin. 'The Pope is trailing his poor council round like a cat with kittens.' Originally destined for Mantua, then Vicenza, a number of other places had been mentioned for the Council and Trent was beginning to be thought of, up on the Brenner pass between Italian and German speaking lands. 'If I thought they valued my advice at all I would advise these holy people simply to spare themselves the trouble of a council. After all, the only kind of council which they will tolerate . . . is one in which they can do what they please . . . Well, who then is being reformed? That great scoundrel, Nobody?' The text was totally vitiated in Luther's eyes by lack of attention to 'God's Word and correct doctrine . . . Nothing regarding this has to be reformed, or even considered' were his final words in the margin.

Two months after his letter to Hausmann, Luther's old enemy Duke George of Albertine Saxony died, and was succeeded by Duke Henry who immediately introduced reforms and

Lutheran theology into his domains. It was a gain for the reformers, but the results were not all easily welcomed. The Leipzig printers had to turn over from anti-Lutheran material to the opposite. And they wanted to print Luther's Bible. Luther wrote angrily to the Elector that he should stop them, as it would take bread out of the mouths of the Wittenbergers – 'for it can easily be reckoned that the printers in Leipzig can sell a thousand copies more easily because all the markets are in Leipzig, than our printers can sell a hundred copies'.

In the turmoil of politics, Luther, Melancthon and others were drawn towards the end of 1539 into the marital affairs of Philip of Hesse. He had always been sexually promiscuous, but now he conceived a plan to make a high-born mistress into his wife, even though he was already married. The reformers were finally manipulated into giving permission for the old gambit of permitted bigamy actually to be practised on the example of the Patriarchs of the Old Testament. The second marriage was to be kept secret. In March 1540, Philip was secretly married in the presence of Melancthon, Bucer and others to his mistress Margaret von der Saale. The secret was soon out. Duke Henry, uncle of Philip's first wife, the true Landgravine, was furious. A storm broke loose. Philip received such a volume of abuse that he feared for the safety of himself and his land, and began to woo the Emperor. The political leader of the reforming states was suddenly absent, and intriguing with the Emperor's representatives. It was a loss which more than balanced out the accession of Albertine Saxony; the loss was one not only of politics but also of credibility. The reformers were widely condemned for hypocrisy or naïveté.

It proved too much for Melancthon, who was taken seriously ill on his way to yet another round of negotiations on the future of the reforms that the Elector and the Emperor's representatives were holding in Hagenau. Luther was summoned to take his place, and wrote to Katie from Weimar, at the Elector's court, where Melancthon lay seriously ill, an euphoric letter. Doubtless he was glad to be able to see that no agreements were come to with the papists: 'To my dearly beloved Katie, Mrs Doctor Luther, etc., to the lady at the new pig market: Personal. Grace and peace. Dear Maid Katie, Gracious Lady of Zölsdorf (and whatever other names Your Grace has). I wish humbly to

inform Your Grace that I am doing well here. I eat like a
Bohemian and drink like a German; thanks be to God for this.
Amen.' Philip Melancthon was already better. Then a sheaf of
orders, domestic and pastoral, were fired out ending with a
command to Seeberger referred to as Lyacon 'not to neglect the
mulberries by oversleeping . . . also he should tap the wine at
the right time . . . Weimar, 2 July 1540, Martin Luther who loves
you from his heart.'

Three more letters continued to Katie from Eisenach, in the
same vein. Nothing was achieved at Hagenau, and Luther was
clearly pleased with his efforts to make sure of that result.

However, Melancthon was soon well again and able to go a
few months later to further talks at Worms, and then to a Diet at
Ratisbon at which both the Pope and the Emperor seemed to
be making one more effort to respond to Melancthon's eirenic
gestures. Cajetan had roughed out a proposal even more liberal
than before, agreeing to married clergy, communion under
both kinds, no doctrinal recantation and a liberal policy on the
sacraments which were no longer to be operated under the same
kind of canonical system. The Pope encouraged the optimists.
The lay Cardinal Contarini was the leader of the peaceful party,
but his fellow Cardinal, the priest Carafa (later to become Pope
Paul IV) was determined to oppose him. In a similar way,
Melancthon was largely alone among the reformers in looking
for a compromise. Eck was there once again for the Catholics.
Melancthon finally took a firmer line than expected, influenced
perhaps by Jean Calvin who was present. There was agreement
about justification, always possible. But when it came to the
Church, the eucharist, the nature of the Mass, the invocation of
Saints, negotiations broke down. Carafa won the day and per-
suaded the Pope to set up the Roman Inquisition.

Meanwhile, Luther had written a piece generally thought of as
one of his most scurrilous, though it was not noticeably more so
than many previous pieces, if equally rumbustious. *Against Hans
Worst*, attacked and ridiculed Duke Henry of Braunschweig, a
man of notorious private life, who had enraged Luther by attacking the Elector. 'Hans Wurst' was a German carnival clown
with a leather sausage hung round his neck. The piece was
largely concerned with showing, once again, that the Gospel did
not need the papacy, and giving an affirmation of the

Reformers' idea of the Church. Some of Luther's own personal history was included in the piece. In the opening pages Luther set the pace, speaking of the Duke rubbing 'his scabby and scurvy head' against the Elector, saying that the Duke 'curses, blasphemes, shrieks, struggles, bellows, and spits', and says that such books as the Duke's 'make me tingle with pleasure from head to toe when I see that through me, poor wretched man that I am, God the Lord maddens and exasperates the hellish and worldly princes . . . while I sit under the shade of faith and the Lord's Prayer, laughing at the devils and their crew as they blubber and struggle in their great fury'. The Psalms, the old Jewish poems and hymns which were and are a staple prayer diet of many Christians often have expressions not much less expressive of common human emotions.

But much worse was to come. In 1543 Luther launched into a full-length tirade *On the Jews and their Lies*, of about 60,000 words. It was an answer to a Jewish apologetic pamphlet. It displayed Luther in a mood of extreme combativeness, aggression, bitterness and cruelty. He inherited the medieval Christian feeling that the Jews were the villians of the Christian story, as indeed passages in the New Testament make them out to be. Without the benefit of modern psychology he was unable to see how the Jews simply became a scapegoat on to whom were projected every bitter emotion of misery and revenge. If the papists and the left wing reforms had frustrated God's purposes then the Jews had done so even more. In the twenties, Luther's enthusiasm for his Christian faith had sometimes led him to think a time for converting Jews could be coming. The failure of this to happen added to his desperate bitterness towards the Jews. In the final section came the scandalous and brutal recommendations that synagogues should be burnt, houses razed, prayer books seized and the Jews reduced to a condition of agragrian servitude. It was almost as if Luther was determined to show, by his own example, how appallingly evil man could be.

In the following year, Luther's fury was turned once again against his colleagues to the left in his *Brief Confession*, 1544. At Wittenberg he had continued to have the consecrated bread 'elevated', lifted up by the minister for all to see, as in the old papist days, right up till 1542 when he felt the point had been

sufficiently made. It had been a gesture against the watered
down theology of 'Jack Absurdity', Karlstadt. Luther said he
preferred not to have the elevation but he did not wish to be
thought to be one of those who did not believe in the true presence. Now that they had ceased to use the elevation at
Wittenberg he must explain that their theology had not
changed. Schwenkfeld was Luther's current *bête noir*, and in this
piece he is regularly called Stinkfield, *Stenkfeld*, lumped along
with the other 'loathsome fanatics'. In this piece all the old
arguments about the precise definition of the 'presence' of
Christ in the consecrated bread are gone over, because Luther
felt that the agreement in the Wittenberg Concord had been
betrayed by the Swiss reformers. While he did not believe in a
'local' presence of Christ's body (the cannibalistic concept) yet
Christ is 'definitely' and truly present. Here the anti-Catholic
abuse reached fresh depths. The Pope 'has made himself the
head of Christendom, yes the anus, as the place of excrement for
the devil, through which so great an abomination of Masses,
monkery and unchastity has been passed into the world'.

The words were Rabelaisian, yet never verging on the
obscenity of Rabelais. And through the barrage of thorough-
going dungheap language, there was always something being
said, some clear content. And commonly it was a reply to
someone else's attack on him. But many fellow reformers did
not like the language and were now able to stand up to Luther in
a new way. The leader of those who did so was Henry Bullinger
in Switzerland, who presented an upright moral and moderate
Swiss front to Luther. He objected to Luther's attacks on the
Zurichers and was not going to wait till Luther's death to reply.
'He boasts of being the German prophet and apostle who need
learn from no one, but from whom all others must learn.' They
agreed that he had shown the way but objected to his arrogance:
'If someone does not say what he says or if someone wishes to
say more than he says then he is banished and condemned as
a heretic.' He thought Luther should not have attacked Duke
Henry in such an undignified way as he did in *Against Hans
Worst*. The Confession was answered courteously point by
point.

Twenty-five years had gone by since Luther had been
denounced and excommunicated by Rome, shortly followed by

the Imperial outlawing. He had got used to expecting the failure of both papal and imperial policies in respect of himself. Total disillusion about their commitment either to reform in a general way or to serious examination of the doctrines of the reformers, had become a habit. But some disillusion with the results of the reforms he had achieved himself had also become a habit. Although objectively he could stand back and count up the changes which had been made and which he believed to be good, yet, he would ask himself, had anything really changed? At the heart of things? It was the same disillusion which he experienced on returning from the Wartburg in 1522, when he was horrified to find people not living by the Word. But at that time he was able to take control. After his week of sermons he was in charge. The opportunities opened up before him and his colleagues. And he found a response that enabled him to forget his threat of leaving Wittenberg for good. But now, in 1545, he looked out with increasing sadness on the standard of behaviour in Wittenberg. The shorter skirts behind, and the lower blouses in front seemed to be a signal that people were simply abusing the freedom he had brought them. The brothel was still there. Alcohol was still taken grossly in excess. In spite of all the reforms, God's word was still ignored.

For him personally there were marvellous compensations. Katie always stood by him. She was a good wife and mother and his close companion for life. Melancthon was always there with his reverence for Luther and his subtle mind. Bugenhagen managed the pastoral scene as it should be. The University was famous, and flourished. And so the count could continue. But Luther's depression would strike again as he turned to the deviations, the failures, his own and others. It was a world which still hardly seemed to recognise the message of the Word, still seemed to live in the world of Law. The Jews, the papacy, other reformers, obstinate old worldly Wittenbergers, they were all ripe targets for his anger compounded now with the frustration of illness and old age. At the beginning of the year, fresh news came from Rome.

On 26 January 1545, Luther wrote to Jonas: 'A letter of the Pope is circulating which the brethren have sent to Veit Dietrich from Venice . . . written in an absolutely arrogant and violent tone . . . to the Emperor . . . the Pope with much and great and openly Italian arrogance demands . . . why the Emperor dares to permit and promise colloquies about religion since it is not the Emperor's place to teach but rather to listen.' Luther wondered whether the Emperor really would start behaving like an Emperor in the days of the fourth century and call a Council: 'What a lively reformation that will be! If it is true, then the Pope's goose is really cooked.' But Luther thought the idea was just a trap to coax the Protestant rulers to a political agreement.

At the Diet of Speyer in 1544 the Emperor had needed once again to gain the political support of the Protestants, or at least to assure their neutrality during his war against both Francis I of France and the Turks. On 10 June, a Recess was agreed which took the big step of agreeing to the legal rights of Protestant holders of benefices and revenues now in their hands. The Emperor was growing increasingly sceptical about whether the Pope would ever call a Council, due to duplicity or inefficiency or sheer lack of will. So the Recess spoke of a further German Diet at which a 'Christian reformation by devout and peace loving men' would be discussed. The Roman reaction was emphatic. The Emperor was severely put in his place in the papal text. His initiative had had a strongly stimulating effect on the Pope and Curia which made further efforts to bring a Council into being. It was now firmly called for 25 March 1545 at Trent.

Luther felt he must reply to the Roman reprimand of the Emperor, and produced the most virulent of all his anti-papal texts, *Against the Roman Papacy, an Institution of the Devil*. It was published on Lady Day, the date the Council was due to open. Again it was primarily a statement of the authenticity of the Church as understood by the Reformers, and the invalidity, indeed positively anti-Christian nature, of the papal church. But its invective is what remained in the minds of most people. On its cover was a woodcut by Cranach showing the Pope in the jaws of hell. It opened: 'The Most Hellish Father, St Paul III, in his supposed capacity as the bishop of the Roman Church, has written two briefs to Charles V, our Lord Emperor, wherein he appears furious, growling and boasting, according to the example of his predecessors that neither an Emperor nor anyone else has the right to convoke a council, even a national one except solely a pope.'

In May 1545, the political merry-go-round produced a

sudden reversal of priorities. The Emperor's military fortunes rallied, and he began seriously to think about military action against the Schmalkaldic League. He began to retreat from the idea of a Christian Council called by himself and to think seriously about the Pope as an ally rather than a competitor. Pope and Emperor, with faltering steps, and ever alert mutual suspicion, moved together towards enabling a traditional Council of the Church to open at Trent.

When news reached Luther that the Council was still being expected to open in Trent, he could only dismiss it with increasing irritation and anger, beginning to glimpse that the Catholic forces, theological, political and military were in fact beginning to come together. To the Elector he wrote on 7 May: 'The news about the council at Trent and those who supposedly are present there, I consider to be gossip and nonsense spread by the men of Rome and Mainz . . . God does not want them and they do not want him either.' After so many false starts, and considering the great scepticism still abroad even in Trent itself about the possibility of a council actually starting, Luther's attitude was well justified. But he was beginning to sense that he was wrong.

On 3 June he wrote to Amsdorf: 'I do not care about diets and councils, I do not believe in anything about them, I do not expect anything from them, I do not worry about them. Vanity of vanities.' On 9 July in a letter to Amsdorf, he was able to draw comfort from a contradiction between the Pope and the Emperor but it was a contradiction which, however it was resolved, threatened the reforms: 'The Pope shouts that we are heretics and that we must not have a place in the council; the Emperor wants us to consent to the council and its decrees. Perhaps God is making fools out of them; indeed Satan reigns, all of them are so totally mad that they condemn us and at the same time ask for our consent.' In fact, no 'consent' was now being asked for, but rather the assent of subjects. Luther was beginning to take the matter of the council at Trent seriously, and felt he must make his own position about the relation between Pope and Council clear: 'Let the Pope first acknowledge that the council is superior to him and let him listen to the council . . . Farewell in the Lord, my Reverend Father! Both of us are old; perhaps in a short while we will have to be buried. My torturer, the stone, would have killed me on St John's day [The Nativity of St John the Baptist, 24 June] had God not decided differently. I prefer death to such a tyrant.'

On 16 July in a letter to Jonas, Luther retailed further evidence of the progress of the Council of Trent, and of its futility: 'The man of Mainz [Cardinal Albrecht] has sent some ridiculous delegates to the council but that monster laughs at the same time about us and the Pope. The council is really Tridentum [the Latin for Trent], that is, in German, torn apart, split up, and dissolved . . . I absolutely believe they do not know what they are doing.' On 17 July the anxiety about the Council is mounting, as he writes to Amsdorf: 'From Trent comes news that twenty-three bishops and three cardinals are present . . . May they have a bad time, as the wrath of God moves them.'

Later in the month, on a journey to help settle a controversy at Zeit, near Naumburg, and to ordain a bishop in Merseburg, all the burdens suddenly became more than Luther could tolerate, and the simple decision not to return to Wittenberg took hold of him. A scandalous story of seduction in Wittenberg was the trigger. He sent blunt and practical instructions home to Katie in a letter (28 July), written in his normal matter-of-fact vein as though nothing very special was really being said. Katie must have known very well the anguish and misery that lay behind the words, understood how her husband was making the greatest gesture he could of protest against a life which had become finally too burdensome: 'To my kind and dear mistress of the house, Luther's Katherine von Bora, a preacher, a brewer, a gardener, and whatever also she is capable of doing. Grace and peace! Dear Katie, Johann will tell you everything . . .' The oldest son had accompanied Luther. 'I would like to arrange matters in such a way that I do not have to return to Wittenberg. My heart has become cold, so that I do not like to be there any longer. I wish you would sell the garden and field; house and all. Also I would like to return the big house [the old Friary] to my Most Gracious Lord. It would be best for you to move to Zölsdorf as long as I am still living and able to help you to improve the little property with my salary.' He says she will never be able to stay in Wittenberg after his death, they will hound her out one way or another. 'They have started to bare women and maidens in front and back, and there is no one who punishes or objects . . .' And then a reference to the scandal: 'While in the country I have heard more than I find out while in Wittenberg. Consequently I am tired of this city . . . I shall keep on the move and would rather eat the bread of a beggar than torture and upset my old age and final days with the filth at Wittenberg which destroys my hard and faithful work. You might inform Dr Pomer and Master Philip of this (if you wish) and if Doctor Pomer would wish to say goodbye to Wittenberg on my behalf. For I am unable any longer to endure my anger and dislike.'

It was the dangerous acting out of fantasy. Two days previously, Luther had preached at Leipzig and had been the guest of honour at the house of one of its wealthiest citizens, Heintz Scherle. The letter was a great sigh of the spirit, 'My heart has grown cold', a protest and a shout of pain. It put Melancthon into a great state. He worried that arguments which had been going on between Luther and the Law Faculty, and with himself, were the real cause. He had been pegging out once again his understanding of the eucharist, with some sympathy with Swiss ideas, and using words noticeably different from those Luther used. He feared greatly that these things were the real cause of the trouble. Doubtless they had contributed to the psychological pressure which had finally triggered the only action tolerable to Luther, to rid himself of the whole terrible burden of his daily life. But they were not at the heart of the pressure, which was not essentially different from what it had always been. Only now it became intolerable to the weary, prematurely aged revolutionary.

The practical men saw what to do. The Elector and High Chancellor Brück, along with Rätzeberger, Luther's medical doctor, took the matter in hand. Luther was told it could be quite complicated getting the property on to the market. Measures for the reform of morals in Wittenberg were promised, doubtless in good faith. Kind, practical men provided medical attention, hospitality and genuine sympathy, and Luther was talked round. The miseries did not go away but he came back to Wittenberg and life went on as before. And somehow, in the eyes of his friends and his family, he was not diminished. They were glad to do him a service, to see him needing help, and glad to be able to give it. He came back and resumed his lectures on the final pages of Genesis, lectures which he had begun ten years before.

Luther's family, including a wide range of distant relatives, were always part of his life. His childhood home was only forty miles away, and it was there to Mansfeld that he was asked to go in October along with Melancthon and Jonas, to help untangle an argument about property and privileges and jurisdiction among the ruling family. But nothing was achieved. They had to depart. Back in Wittenberg, Luther reached the last verse of Genesis with its symbolical ending, and its atmosphere of promise and faith which were so much part of Luther's faith: 'At length Joseph said to his brothers, I am about to die; but God will be sure to remember you kindly and take you back from this country to the land that he promised on oath to Abraham, Isaac and Jacob. And Joseph made Israel's sons swear an oath, "When God remembers you with kindness be sure to take my bones from here." Joseph died at the age of a hundred and ten; they embalmed him and laid him in his coffin in Egypt.' Luther closed his book and said: 'May our Lord God grant to somebody else to make a better job of it. I can no more, I am too weak – pray to God for me that he will give me a good, blessed end' – a *Stündlein*, a little hour, a word he often used for his last hour. He was ever more and more waiting and hoping for it.

In January, Luther set out once again to solve the quarrels of the Counts of Mansfeld, with his sons in attendance. At Halle on his way to Eisleben, he was held up by floods which he personified in a letter to Katie of 25 January as a 'huge she-Anabaptist' which 'met us with waves of water and great floating pieces of ice; she threatened to baptise us again and has covered the countryside'. They had left Halle but had to turn back. 'I am sure that, if you were here, you too would have advised us to proceed in this way; you see, at least once we are following your advice.'

On 1 February, Luther wrote again to Katie now in the thick of the attempts to solve the family quarrel. It was addressed in the usual way to the lady of Zölsdorf and the pig market, discussed the possibility that a local community of Jews were responsible for the blast of cold wind which had attacked him as he travelled, recorded the excellent local and laxative beer ('three bowel movements in three hours'), and told Katie, 'The day before yesterday your little sons drove to Mansfeld'. John, Martin and Paul took the opportunity to visit uncles and aunts and cousins. To Melancthon he revealed in a letter of the same date that he was not well, suffering from heart trouble, that he was upset by the arguments he was having to umpire and wanted to be shot of the whole thing as soon as possible. It was all 'totally incompatible with my disposition, and quite bothersome to my old age'.

Two days later he wrote again to Melancthon that he was 'playing the role of a sick goat', unable to solve the difficulties, said that the chimney in his room had caught fire, and ended, 'Pray for me that the Lord may bring me back before I am killed by these battles of the wills.'

On 6 February, he wrote again both to his wife and Melancthon, asking the latter to get the Elector to send him a letter ordering him home, in an attempt to shock the Counts and the rest of the family into agreement. He was finding the lawyers as tiresome as ever: 'You may say this is a word-war or a word-insanity, a pleasure one owes to jurists . . . so many ambiguities, sophistries and chicaneries . . . their jargon is more confusing than all the tongues of Babylon.' To Katie he reported that he still could not get away and that the children were still at Mansfeld.

On 7 February, a letter to Katie told her to stop worrying: 'You prefer to worry about me instead of letting God worry, as if he were not almighty . . . Free me from your worries. I have a caretaker who is better than you and all the angels; he lies in the cradle and rests on a virgin's bosom, and yet, nevertheless, he sits at the right hand of God, the almighty Father.' But the quarrel went on, and he told Katie and the rest of them to 'pray, pray, pray' so that it could be finished. Meanwhile, however, 'we are living well; for each meal the city council gives me one half *Stübig* of Italian wine'. Three days later, he is again saying he is healthy and she must stop worrying and the quarrel is still tiresome. Then at last, on 14 February, he was able to write that the quarrel had been resolved. 'We hope to return home again this week . . . The young lords are happy and ride around together in sleighs decorated with fools' bells as do the young

ladies . . . I am sending you the trout.' The children remained at
Mansfeld. There were rumours again of political troubles, of
mercenaries being hired.

Luther had to stay on another two days to get documents
signed and the whole matter sealed. But the effort of it all had
proved too much for him. He had a heart attack and became
seriously ill on 17 February. He sank rapidly. Friends gathered.
He reaffirmed his faith. In the early morning of 18 February he
died, in pain but mentally alert. He was always writing and no
one can be sure what were the last words he wrote. But among
the last was a note on his desk, which ended 'The truth is, we are
beggars'. A funeral service was held in Eisleben and an attempt
was made by the Counts of Mansfeld to have him buried there.
But the Elector insisted that the body be brought back to
Wittenberg.

Epilogue

When the news of Luther's death arrived in Wittenberg, Melancthon announced it dramatically to his class: 'Alas, gone is the horseman and the chariots of Israel.' They were the words spoken in the Old Testament story by Elisha when Elijah was taken from him. Melancthon was conscious that a great Prophet had gone, and that he had been left perhaps with the burden of the Wittenberg movement on his shoulders. It was Melancthon who spoke in the castle church, along with Bugenhagen, when the funeral service was held there on 22 February. The procession up the long Wittenberg street was led by the coffin, followed by a carriage in which Katie and others were. Following them came the children and relations on foot, and then the University and town authorities. Finally there were thousands of mourners, many of whom had come specially and crowded the town. Melancthon turned again to the great names in Christian history, as others did elsewhere, to find some measuring rod. He said God had raised Luther up as he had raised up Isaiah, John the Baptist, Paul, Augustine. He faced up to the matter of Luther's language and said he would 'not deny or excuse or praise, but reply as Erasmus often did: "God gave the world in these later times when severe and acute disease and failures prevail, a harsh and severe doctor."' Dr Martin had indeed written too violently but he, Melancthon, had never known him to be anything but gentle and loving in person. Now, he said, they were 'entirely poor, wretched, forsaken, orphans, who had lost a dear noble man as our father'. The great historic figure and the deeply loved friend were both saluted.

Luther had died just in time. Two months before he died the Council of Trent had finally opened officially. While it would be years before notable results were to flow, it was clear that a serious reforming Council of the (Roman Catholic) Church had opened. Only a few months later the Emperor held a Diet, and suddenly without legal order declared the Electors John Frederick and Philip of Hesse outlawed. He had seen at last that he had the French beaten for the moment, that the Turks were contained, that he could make common cause with the Pope and could now at last use military force to bring the Protestant states to order. Luther's death had made it easier, but he would have done it anyway. Luther would have seen the end of the world come even nearer.

But no military action could reverse Luther's achievements, and meanwhile there was the great legacy of memories, of writings, of institutions and ways of carrying on in church and out of it, of music, and song. And, for a time, a special legacy of personal memories. Two months after his death, Katie wrote to her sister:

> Who would not be sorrowful and mourn for so noble a man as was my dear Lord? Truly I am so distressed I cannot tell the deep sorrow of my heart to anybody and I hardly know what to think or how to feel. I cannot eat or drink nor can I sleep. If I had a principality and an empire it would never have cost me so much pain to lose them as I have now that our Lord God has taken from me this dear and precious man. God knows that for sorrow and weeping I can neither speak nor dictate this letter.

Luther had put the life of the great European 'Myth' into a new gear. The hordes of pensioned functionaries had gone from the streets and churches. A new sense of authority and responsibility was seen in the local communities. Doctrinally and institutionally, what Luther had put in the place of the papal Church was not, in one sense, so different. Christians were still required to live by a range of received doctrines and morals. And these were still underwritten by the civil authority. But the norm had changed. It was now the Bible, and not a Law Book. In practice both needed interpretation, so in a sense Christians were still back with Church authorities which had to be obeyed. And the Reformers' Church could be narrower and more legalistic, in the end, than the papal Church; everything had to conform to the style of a single overarching doctrine, instead of being allowed to be deployed over a wide range of options. Puritanism was soon born.

But the changes were qualitative and substantial. The 'Myth' began again to look less like a myth and more like the Gospel of the New Testament. Jesus of Nazareth began to look less like a god, and more like the Word of God, suffering for and with his people. The ministers began to look more like disciples with a Christian message and less like purveyors of a marketed 'grace'. It was possible to understand the Church as a community and a mystery, not just an institution with a set of rules. But polarisation hindered both the old Church and the new. Both turned away from the 'almost everything' which in fact they had in common. The new Church was powered by norms which the old Church had protected and conveyed to it. The Bible had appeared, though largely dishonoured, in its best modern edition (the Spanish Polyglot edition) under the auspices of the old Church, from one of its oldest homes in the Mediterranean basin. The Reformed and Roman Catholic Churches tended to become reverse images of each other, both institutionalised. As Rome finally produced its own reforms during the following twenty years, it became more law bound than ever. Luther never loved institutions, and a central factor in his disillusion was the continuing absence of the autonomous Word leading people to a life of faith, love and good works.

Of Luther himself it is impossible to speak summarily. The complex and remarkable story of his life, the tally of his works, and the witness of a great number of friends, acquaintances and enemies are there. Many loved him, many revered him, some were frightened of him, a few resentful. No one accused him, with any semblance of justification, of double dealing, or of cowardice. My principal image is of a man driven, driven by a passion for the Divine, driven, too, by a horror of evil; convinced of its eventual futility, he was ever conscious of its threat, and his life was one of prayer. His friends remembered him standing by the window of his room praying, often aloud. Under the rumbustious lover of life lay sensitivity, intelligence and imagination, and a failure to come to terms with a world which was never good enough, a failure he found confirmed in the crucifix, but glorified in what followed. At the Wartburg he wrote: 'They threaten us with death. They would do better to threaten us with life'.

Indulgences

This is an attempt to provide a brief account of the theory and practice of indulgences in relation to Luther's criticism, in language as far as possible non-
technical without losing any theological nuance. It is impossible to make a
really simple explanation. Twnetieth-century Roman Catholic preachers find
it hard to explain indulgences to congregations. For a more complete *exposé*,
together with extracts from many of the most important historical documents,
see *Sacraments and Forgiveness*, Paul F. Palmer, SJ (Volume II, *Sources of Christian
Theology*, pp. 321–69). Among these texts is a masterly theoretical *rationale*
provided for indulgences by Aquinas. Nothing short of Luther's 'dynamic'
theology would suffice to contradict the answers provided by Aquinas to the
obvious objections. But his *rationale* ends with an economically worded
warning whose implications are exceedingly far-reaching and implicity add a
very strong rider to any conclusion that might be drawn from his doctrinal
exposé, such as that indulgences should be widely granted and the people
strongly encouraged to use them: '. . . yet other works of satisfaction are more
meritorious with respect to our essential reward, which is infinitely better than
the remission of temporal punishment'. There are two points in that brief
sentence, and the failure of the medieval Church to observe them or to reform
its practice in conformity with them, is highly typical of the general failure to
reform itself, with which Luther was so radically concerned.

Indulgences existed and still exist in the following Catholic framework. A
Christian does not live a perfect life; he sins. He sins, offending against the
Gospel, against a moral principle or breaking a commandmeht of the Church.
Subsequently he is sorry for this lapse, turns to God inwardly and is forgiven.
His sin was not only an act against his own nature destined for glory with God,
it was an act against God's Church. It was an injury to every member of the
Church, for all depend upon one another, the health of one works for the
health of another, the sickness of one for the sickness of another. So, as when a
Christian first joins God's Church, he does so through the formal Church rite
of the sacrament of baptism, and as when his life further progresses it is
marked and strengthened by other sacraments of the Church, so when he had
damaged his relationship with God and his Church, and, by doing so,
threatened or injured that of others, a sacrament of the Church makes provi-
sion for formal statements of sorrow by the sinner, of God's forgiveness by his
Church, and for a means of spiritual help, grace, to help the sinner to carry out
his intention to amend. The questions then arise whether the sinner needs to

make reparation or satisfaction, and whether he must receive some punishment for sin. The Church seems to have given an affirmative answer in principle to all three questions from very early times. This does not affect the forgiveness always and immediately forthcoming from God to a repentant sinner who turns inwardly to God; reparation, satisfaction and punishment were linked with the Church's formal sacramental ratification of repentance and forgiveness. In the early Church the sinner was only formally reconciled after doing penance, sometimes public penance in which the parish might join with him on his behalf, for a certain number of days. The sinner was excluded from the Eucharistic liturgy (a form of excommunication) until the penance was complete. Clearly the early Church only bothered itself with what Staupitz called 'real sins'; shortness of temper cannot have been a cause for confession unless it led to murder or grave slander or some other such definite abrogation of the law. But people soon felt a need, apparently, to express their sorrow for the lesser things. In time they confessed more frequently; smaller penance was done, and this was subsequent not prior to the sacramental reconciliation. The sin hardly deserved excommunication.

When penances became small the possibility occurred to men that at the time of his death a Christian might not have done all the penance which his sins deserved in the sight of God. He might still be due to receive some of what the theologians later came to call the 'temporal punishment due to sin'. It was assumed that this remaining debt must be paid after death. The sinner had been completely forgiven, but he might still in justice have some reparation or satisfaction to make, or punishment to bear. To state it in another way, perhaps more in tune with the Gospel, the forgiven sinner might still need a further time of preparation or purging before he was fit for the marriage feast of heaven.

The Church then said that a Christian who had received the sacrament of penance, could by various good works, the saying of particular prayers or doing such pious works as assisting in the building of churches (by a cash payment) achieve release from some part of, sometimes all of, whatever 'temporal punishment' he might still be due to undergo after death. An indulgence was a statement to this effect – the Church promised release to the repentant sinner, duly shrived, on the condition specified, of undertaking such good works. And if the release was not plenary (a 'plenary indulgence') it was measured, and the amount specified. How measure punishment in purgatory? Only by some equivalent. The standard used was that of the old traditional penance, which was measured simply by days of visible penance and exclusion from the liturgy. So indulgences were issued as releases from so many 'days of exclusion', and they were intended to release the sinner from the equivalent in purgatory, whatever it might be, of so many days' penance in the early Church.

All this was in harmony with the general doctrine of the authority which the Church understood that Christ had given her: 'Whatever you loose on earth, it shall be loosed in heaven. Whatever you retain on earth, it shall be retained in heaven.' Salvation itself is not at issue. It is only a question of relationship to the Church on earth, and in so far as it was linked to it, of punishment in purgatory.

Meanwhile, the medieval theologians had propounded an explanatory, mechanical theory of 'merits' which further rationalised the use of sacraments, and of indulgences. The saints and Christ had been good, and gained 'merit', far above what was necessary to avoid damnation and achieve heaven. The principle of solidarity, of the health of one working for the health of another, was transformed into an accounting system by which the merit of each member was theoretically measured in heaven, and all of it beyond what that member required put in a bank for the help of others. 'The treasury of merits', a typically medieval gambit, was not really necessary for a theological justification of the granting of indulgences, but it helped to explain the solidarity principle for the canonically-minded theologians of the time, who also found it easier to encourage people to gain indulgences with this ingenious and readily intelligible theory. In practice this theory was translated so widely that it tended to overshadow the simple theology of the redemption of all men by Christ once for all. The scale of indulgences became a principal source of income for ecclesiastical authorities.

Indulgences left plenty of room for abuse, both in a basic doctrinal sense, and in their being granted for cash payments. When more emphasis was given by preachers to the gaining of indulgences – for instance, by the good work of making a cash contribution to the building of a church – than to the sacraments, the liturgy and ordinary acts of charity, then it was made to appear as though the values of the Gospel were being abandoned. Ordinary Christians were appealed to as though their first concern should be to obtain release from sufferings in purgatory by a cash payment. If the sermons were frequent enough, and enough publicity and external pomp accompanied the offer of an indulgence, it could very well be that the matter of salvation itself could become confused in the popular mind with what could be obtained by an indulgence. Then it was commonly supposed, and the Church seems specifically to have encouraged such a supposition, even though theology could not and did not finally support it, that a cash payment could in appropriate circumstances buy an immediate release from purgatory for the souls suffering there. The Church had always encouraged Christians to pray for those who had died; when indulgences began to be issued with the idea that they might be transferred to the souls in purgatory this was seen, not without reason, as a praiseworthy raising of the motive for gaining an indulgence, from something selfish to an act of charity towards others. It was commonly supposed and preached that a transferred indulgence certainly guaranteed a soul's immediate release. But this cannot be maintained, in traditional Catholic theology, and the Church has not maintained it on the few occasions when the matter has been directly and authoritatively treated. This became one of Luther's more bitter points of protest* on a matter which was controversial

*Palmer makes it clear that though there must have been some doubt, dogmatically, about this in Luther's time, and in the nineteenth century, the conclusion must be drawn that the Church has definitely declined to believe that a plenary indulgence transferred by prayer to a soul in purgatory can guarantee its release, though the Church hopes, as it were, that Christ will respect her wishes in the matter (note, p. 357). It seems to be true that in this respect an abuse against which Luther fought still exists, since many Catholics seem still to believe that when they gain a plenary indulgence it can be applied at will so as to obtain the automatic release of a soul from purgatory. And the dogmatic im-

and in fact remained in some doubt, dogmatically, for several centuries. Abuses in connection with indulgences were recognised and combated from an early time. The Fourth Lateran Council of 1215 was an early case of a formal attempt by the Church to prevent abuse.* The doctrine itself was regarded by the more scrupulous as one to which not too much emphasis should be given. The conclusion of Aquinas makes this clear.†

It is not difficult to see that the whole theological atmosphere in which indulgences thrive is inimical to the dynamic theology of justification which Luther had been working out. This juggling with 'days' to be got for so much monetary contribution, or so many prayers, the very idea that something one did oneself could produce a change, could cause God to act – all this would seem unworthy of one who owed a complete surrender to God, who could never be of himself worthy of the sovereign creator, but who had in fact been saved and justified by the Word of God, made one with the saints by the free act of Jesus. From a more abstract point of view, as we have seen, Aquinas puts out a very stringent criticism, sober and terse, though it is in the final sentence on the subject.

But the incompatibility was not absolute. Luther did not at first contradict indulgences in principle. He knew the value of simple explanations for the people. He never turned away from the broadly sacramental – in the sense of a visible formal rite – attitude to religion, nor from the Church doctrine of solidarity in Christ which provided the theological background essential for indulgences. Luther's theses include a proposal (thesis 38) for a 'correct' interpretation of them: 'The Pope's remission and distribution are in no way to be despised since, as I have said, they are a declaration of divine forgiveness.' But on the other hand they are to be given only a minor place, less than that of acts of kindness: 'Christians must be taught that it is not the Pope's intention that the purchase of indulgences is in any way comparable with the works of mercy.'

Luther's primary concern was that the palaver accompanying the offer of indulgences, their mechanical side, and the emphasis laid on them had radically covered over that first essential – sorrow for sin, turning to God, use of the sacrament of confession. The tremendous publicity given in 1517 to the preaching of the most recent indulgence by Tetzel and his preachers confirmed him in the feeling that the people were being encouraged to forget the essential inner realities and to substitute a commercial transaction for it. In the first place, then, it is a matter of emphasis. Instead of the Word of God the preachers are preaching a commercial and almost magical recipe.

But Luther was also concerned specifically with that part of the doctrine which involved a claim by the Church to release souls, whether on earth or in purgatory, from the punishment which they might need to undergo before they would have fully expiated their sins, or would be fit for heaven. The theses were of course at first a controversial technical matter, intended for debate, and intended no doubt to focus public attention on the undoubted abuses,

---

plications are important, for they concern the matter of the claim of the Church to exercise a certain direct executive role in purgatory.

*See Palmer, *op. cit.*, p. 336.

† See n. 1, p. 279.

theological and practical, involved in the preaching of the indulgences. It does not seem to be certain that Luther believed them all, explicitly, at the time when he drew them up. Quite probably his mind was open, he was prepared for some of the theses to be contradicted, proven wrong in public debate. In the course of such a debate, the theological bases of the granting of indulgences might be more clearly expounded, perhaps modified, and the abuses perhaps exposed, and those responsible for them reprimanded. This would seem to be Luther's position from his *Appeal to Leo X* in 1518* in which he states clearly, even at this later date, his entire willingness to abide by the authority of Rome: 'I shall acknowledge your voice as the voice of Christ who is enthroned in you, and who speaks through you.'

*See Palmer, *op. cit.* p. 359.

On Sources and Further Reading

My primary source has been the American edition of *Luther's Works*, published in fifty-four volumes (plus one Introductory Volume) jointly by Fortress Press and Concordia Publishing House. The translation is of a high standard, generally using contemporary English, only lapsing occasionally into antique language. Each volume has a general introduction, often with many further introductions to the particular texts it contains. These introductions together with numerous notes, cross referencing and indexes provide a superb structure of information and comment. The volumes contain frequent reference to the standard complete edition of Luther's Works in the original Latin and German, the one hundred or so volumes in the *Weimar Ausgabe*. As a result, it is easy to find one's way back to the original texts, whether or not included in the American edition. Apart from the Weimar edition itself, undoubtedly the American translation must be the main recommendation for further reading.

For elucidation of background, and of Luther's life and thought, there is a very large library of books available. Everyone will have his favourites. I provide a small, select list here. Several of these books themselves contain lengthy bibliographies valuable for further wide reading. But first I single out five specially valuable books of which three on the life and background are by A. G. Dickens:

A. G. Dickens, *Martin Luther and the Reformation*, English Universities Press, London, 1967.

A. G. Dickens, *Reformation and Society*, Thames & Hudson, London, 1968.

A. G. Dickens, *The German Nation and Martin Luther*, Edward Arnold, London, 1974.

It is difficult to single out further reading for Luther's theology. Often he used biblical language, also that of the early Church and of the medieval schools. Then he will suddenly transform it all into urgent contemporary sixteenth-century phrases, Latin or German. Twentieth-century books on Luther's theology are coloured, inevitably, by the thought of the four subsequent centuries and often impart meanings and nuances quite absent from the original. With this caveat I single out two books from a great multitude. Gordon Rupp's book is a classic, written thirty years ago, but still with much more to tell us of Luther than most other books on his theology. Its quotations from Luther are more numerous and range more widely than those in any other comparable book. Something similar can be said of the book by J. D. K.

Siggins. And both contain helpful detailed references to the Weimar edition:

Gordon Rupp, *The Righteousness of God*, Hodder & Stoughton, London, 1953.
J. D. K. Siggins, *Martin Luther's Doctrine of Christ*, Yale University Press, 1970.

For Luther's early years (my Chapters 1 and 2) there is no substitute for the 726 pages of R. H. Fife's *The Revolt of Martin Luther*, Columbia University Press, New York, 1957. Further useful detail can be found for background and life in E. G. Schwiebert's *Luther and his Times*, Concordia Press, Missouri, 1950. For Luther's early years a few statements in my text are surmises, but always based on well-attested fact. The relevant pages in Fyfe have copious references to original German and Latin texts.

From Chapter 3 onwards the selection of Luther's Letters translated in volumes 48, 49 and 50 of the American edition of the *Works*, are the source for the majority of the quotations from his letters. Volumes 51 and 52 provide a useful selection from Luther's sermons. Volume 53 is an exceptionally interesting volume, devoted to Liturgy and Hymns; Volume 54, the Table Talk, comes into its own at a later stage. Fife continues to be an invaluable source from Chapter 3 to Chapter 12 inclusive. *The German Theology* of 1515, with Luther's Introduction is available from SPCK in London and Paulist Press, New York (1980). Of a number of books which deal with the thought of the early Luther, very valuable is Jared Wicks's *Man Yearning for Grace*, Corpus Books, Cleveland, 1968.

The following is a select list of books under three headings to provide a variety of further reading, but again there are many others.

1. Background

Roland H. Bainton, *Erasmus of Christendom*, Collins, London, 1970.
Christian Humanism and the Reformation, Selected Writings of Erasmus, ed. and transl. by John C. Olin, Harper & Row, New York.
The Collected Works of Erasmus, Toronto University Press, a growing edition.
Hans J. Hillerbrand, *The World of the Reformation*, Dent, London, 1975.
Hubert Jedin, *A History of the Council of Trent*, Vol. I, Nelson, London, 1957.
Joseph Lortz, *The Reformation in Germany*, D.L.T., London and Seabury, New York, 1968.
Documents Illustrative of the Continental Reformation, ed. by B. J. Kidd, Oxford, 1911.
Gordon Rupp, *Patterns of Reformation*, Epworth Press, London, 1969.
John M. Todd, *Reformation*, Darton, Longman & Todd, London; Doubleday, New York, 1972.

2. Luther's Life

Ronald H. Bainton, *Here I Stand*, Abingdon Press, 1950; Mentor Books, New York.
Erik H. Erikson, *Young Man Luther*, Faber & Faber, London, 1958.
V. H. H. Green, *Luther and the Reformation*, Batsford, London, 1964.
H. G. Haile, *Luther*, Sheldon Press, London; Doubleday, New York.

Erwin Iserloh, *The Theses were not Posted*, Geoffrey Chapman, London, 1968.
Daniel Olivier, *The Trial of Luther*, Mowbrays, London, 1978.
Preserved Smith, *The Life and Letters of Martin Luther*, Boston, 1911.
John M. Todd, *Martin Luther*, Burns and Oates, London; Newman Press, subsequently Paulist Press, New York, 1964.

3. Luther's Thought

Mark U. Edwards, *Luther and the False Brethren*, Stanford University Press, 1975.
Gerhard Ebeling, *Luther*, Collins, London, 1970.
Luther, ed. by H. G. Koenigsberger, London & New York, 1973.
Harry J. McSorley, *Luther, Right or Wrong?*, Newman & Augsburg, New York, 1969.
Jaroslav, Pelikan, *Spirit versus Structure*, Collins, London, 1968.

Index